The Middle East and Islamic World Reader

The Middle East and Islamic World Reader

by
Marvin Gettleman
and Stuart Schaar

Grove Press
New York

Published simultaneously in Canada
Printed in the United States of America

The copyright acknowledgments on pages 379–380 constitute an extension of this copyright page.

FIRST EDITION

Library of Congress Cataloging-in-Publication Data

The Middle East and Islamic world reader / [edited] by Marvin Gettleman and Stuart Schaar.
    p. cm.
  Includes bibliographical references (p.).
  ISBN 0-8021-3936-1
  1. Middle East. 2. Islamic countries—Civilization. I. Gettleman, Marvin E.
II. Schaar, Stuart.

DS44.M523 2003
956—dc21   2002044682

Grove Press
841 Broadway
New York, NY 10003

03 04 05 06 07 10 9 8 7 6 5 4 3 2 1

Dedicated to the memory of
Saundra Shepherd and Nora Sayre

Contents

Map List

General Introduction

W e conceived this *Reader* after September 11, 2001, as a comprehensive source book for understanding the history and current situation in the Middle East and the Islamic world. We quickly realized, however, that no one volume could possibly examine each and every country or explore all facets of the realities of the region's history, society, politics, and culture. Our solution has led us to selective concentration on the most important regions and topics, including the core areas of the Middle East, the rise and fall of the Muslim empires, Islam in Central Asia and Afghanistan, oil, U.S. policy, Arab and Palestinian nationalism, Zionism, Islamic radicalism, and the implications of September 11, 2001.

We chose documents and essays that represent each major era since the establishment of the first Islamic community by Muhammad in seventh-century Arabia. They graphically reveal the Muslim world's great diversity. Our selections show the differences among *Shiite* and *Sunni* Muslims; Crusaders and those who fought against them; nomads and agriculturalists; nationalists and imperialists; leftists, moderates, and conservatives; Islamic radicals and secularists. We devote an entire chapter to the conflicts between Zionists and Palestinians in the mandate period and after Israeli statehood. The book includes the voices of women and men, political activists and mystics, *Al Qaeda* terrorists and Bush administration hard-liners, orientalists who believe the Islamic world hopeless and those who see it as a more multifaceted, complex reality and contemplate eventual peaceful solutions of current problems.

Our historical tapestry begins fourteen centuries ago and it contains many strands, tendencies, and designs. Still, we see no direct line of simple progression from the Prophet Muhammad's experience of the majesty of a single God to the crimes committed at the dawn of the twenty-first century in New York and elsewhere by daring terrorist groups. Instead, we see turning points, opportunities taken and missed, and much contingency.

We hope that the historical texts in this book—often the words of actual participants in key events and movements past and present—will enable readers to make up their own minds about present issues and their antecedents. The scholarly articles and analyses that amplify the part Introductions and notes to readings supply needed context. The glossary at the end of this *Reader* will help nonspecialists with important concepts and terms. We hope that this book will stimulate further study of the Middle East and the Islamic world, and to encourage this we offer a select bibliography of some of the most useful works in English.

English-language writers on the Islamic world often despair at the difficulties in devising consistent transliteration and spelling of Arabic, Turkish, and

Persian words. In our own contributions to this book (headnotes and Introductions) we use such non-English words sparingly, omitting the Arabic *'ayan* (')
and *hamza* ('). We avoid most Arab plurals by adding an "s" to each singular. In
the readings we adopt the spellings found in standard English dictionaries and
often add our own parenthetical translations at the first appearance of each
non-English term and repeat these in the glossary for easy reference. We have
adopted American rather than British spellings of words where possible. We
make no attempt to impose consistency in the spelling of transliterated words
in the book's readings. These may appear as *Al Qaeda* in one piece and *Al Qaida*
in another, *Taliban* in one place and *Taleban* in another, Usama or Osama and
Hussein or Husayn for the same person.

In preparing this book we have benefited from the assistance of many people,
among them our editor at Grove/Atlantic, Brando Skyhorse, our literary agent,
Ronald Goldfarb, and our indefatigable research assistant, Hamid Irbouh. We
owe special thanks to the City University of New York and its chancellor, Matthew Goldstein, for a timely research grant. Sandi Cooper's encouragement
greatly aided our project. Also rendering valued advice and assistance were
Ervand Abrahamian, Michael Adas, Kemal Boulatta, Ahmad Dallal, Tom
DeGeorge, Bernard Horowitz, Nubar Hovsepian, Greg Keuker, Rashid Khalidi,
David Partington, Jim Paul, Barnett Rubin, Sheila Ryan, Ariel Salzmann, Dan
Schrecker, Ellen Schrecker, and Joe Stork. Finally we want to convey special
thanks to Carol Stock, who helped with editing and preparing the final drafts
of our manuscript.

—M.G., S. S.
New York, 2003

Chapter I

Islamic Beginnings: Revelation, State Building, and Culture

Introduction

The Prophet Muhammad (c. 570–632), finding the inhabitants of the thriving mercantile city of Mecca hostile to his religious beliefs, led a group of Muslims on the *hijra,* the migration to a northern agricultural settlement, Yathrib. There he founded an Islamic state, which, after his death, developed into a mighty empire. A member of one of the minor branches of the Quraysh tribe, Muhammad worked as a trader and business manager for a wealthy widow, Khadija (d. 619), whom he later married. Troubled by the feuds among the competing Arabian tribes and selfishness of clan members, Muhammad experienced revelations of the monotheistic faith he called Islam. This faith brought all believers under the single, majestic God, *Allah,* and into a unified Muslim community, the *umma.* Transmitted orally in the Arabic language, and later written down, these revelations became the *Quran,* Islam's scripture, selections from which we present, along with other early Islamic texts, in Reading 1.

Islam (meaning submission to *Allah*) requires Muslims to acknowledge and follow God's will, and live according to the model of public and private righteousness set forth in the *Quran* and in the *hadith,* records of the Prophet's actions and pronouncements, some of which are also in Reading 1. Muslims also must carry out specified ritual observances: praying five times daily, participating in congregational prayer on Fridays, paying religious taxes to benefit the *umma,* and fasting from sunrise to sunset during the lunar month of *Ramadan.* All Muslims able to do so should make at least one pilgrimage (*hajj*) in their lifetimes to the *kaaba* shrine in Mecca, a pilgrimage destination even before the rise of Islam. Muslims also believe that the all-knowing, omnipotent God who created the universe will preside over a final Day of Judgment and will send the immortal souls of the righteous to heaven and the wicked to hell.

Some of the beliefs and practices of Islam continued and modified long-standing Arabian customs and those of the preexisting faiths of Judaism and Christianity. The *Quran* recognized the Old and New Testaments of the Bible as God's earlier revelations and referred respectfully to the Hebrew prophets, including Abraham and Moses, and acknowledged them as early prophets of Islam. Jesus was also a Prophet, a righteous man and teacher of truths, but not considered by Muslims a son of God, or part of any holy trinity, which they view as an impermissible departure from monotheism. Muhammad received God's final revelations, and became His final Prophet. Muhammad's prophetic status means that Muslims view him as an exemplary human being, eminently worthy of emulation, transmitter of God's word, but not himself a god.

The *Quran* portrays women as the spiritual equals of men, allowing them a share of family wealth and prohibiting female infanticide. But Islam, continuing customs then prevalent in Arabia, also upheld such patriarchal social values as male domination of family and public life. Muslims also adopted some of the practices of societies they had conquered, such as cloistering upper-class urban women in the *harem* (literally, a sacred place), a custom already widespread in pre-Islamic Middle Eastern empires. Some modern feminists claim that the early years of Islam, in which Arabian women played important public roles, constituted an historical precedent for women's freedom and equality.

An Islamic State in Madina

Khadija, Muhammad's first wife, accepted his teaching before all other Arabs. Some of Muhammad's relatives and friends, and a number of young men disillusioned with tribal values in the city of Mecca, also joined the *umma*. The merchants who dominated Muhammad's own Quraysh lineage became increasingly hostile, fearing that Muslims, committed to a community that transcended tribal ties, would pose a threat to Arabia's traditional social order. In 622 the Muslims migrated from Mecca to Yathrib, later called Madina, where Muhammad and his followers constructed the first Islamic social order. Converts responded to the appeal and advantages of a divinely inspired, unified community that protected its members. Even at a distance, however, the new *umma* came into direct conflict with the Quraysh merchants. Dispatching an army against the outnumbered Muslims, the Meccans ended up losing to their adversaries. Before his death in 632, Muhammad had converted most of the Arabian tribes to Islam, and Mecca became the new Islamic state's capital.

Strife Within the *Umma*

Controversy exists over whether the Prophet had indicated how the Muslims should choose new leaders. On his death his companions selected a caliph (*khalifa*) from among their own ranks to lead the *umma*. At first they passed over his close male kinsman and one of the first converts to Islam, Ali ibn Abi Talib (d. 661), husband of Muhammad's daughter, Fatima (d. 633). As Muslim armies won major victories beyond Arabia, disputes over Islamic succession flared into open warfare. When an assassin killed the third caliph, Uthman, in 656, the previously overlooked Ali became the new caliph. But not all Muslims accepted Ali, and civil war ensued. Ali, too, was murdered and Uthman's kinsman Muawiya ibn Abi Sufyan (605–680) became the fifth caliph, the first of the Umayyad dynasty.

Ruling from their capital Damascus for almost a century, the Umayyads conquered a vast empire, but they remained a largely Arabian ruling class, living in garrison towns apart from their non-Arab subjects. The *Shiites,* or partisans of the dead Ali, began to press the competing claims of Ali's son, Husayn (b. 626), who led his supporters against a far larger Umayyad army in 680 and died on the battlefield. *Shiites* continued to believe in the legitimate succession only of those who descended from Ali's lineage. The Twelver *Shiites* (who later became dominant in Persia) believed that descendants of Ali constituted a series of twelve legitimate *imams* (leaders of the *umma*), who lived under the rule of *Sunni* caliphs deemed by the *Shiites* as illegitimate. The twelfth *imam* disappeared in 878 but would, these Twelvers believed, some day reappear and usher in a reign of justice. Other Muslims accepted the precedent set by the Prophet's companions, which eventually evolved into the majority (*Sunni*) position—dynastic succession, upheld by military force and ratified by prominent religious scholars (the *ulema*) along with other important figures. Reading 2 discusses the divergent views on how to choose a legitimate Muslim ruler developed by the Middle Ages. The inability to settle disputes over what constituted legitimate succession reappeared periodically in the Islamic world, sometimes flaring into conflict but most of the time lying dormant. Even among *Sunni* Muslims, diverse positions emerged over legal matters, allowing for the multiple readings of the law we later discuss.

Expansion of Muslim Domains

Having expanded rapidly into Syria, including Palestine, the triumphant Umayyads then extended their conquests to Persia, northern Africa, and Spain by 711. They erected the shrine in Jerusalem known as the Dome of the Rock over a sacred boulder at the site of the Jewish Temple destroyed centuries earlier by the Romans. Earlier still, according to tradition, the patriarch Abraham nearly sacrificed his son Isaac at the same spot. Yet the site has additional significance for Muslims, who also believe that the Archangel Gabriel led Muhammad there years before his death on a miraculous night journey, ascending from that rock to heaven. (See the Night Journey section in Reading 1.)

Unified and inspired by their Islamic faith, the seemingly unbeatable Muslim armies quickly imposed peace on a vast, now integrated empire. The spread of Muslim power beyond Arabia did not mean forcible conversion of the conquered populations; Christians of many denominations and Jews, collectively known as the *dhimmi*, found toleration in the Umayyad and later empires. The *Quran* distinguished between these non-Muslim monotheistic "people of the book" and polytheistic, nature-worshiping faiths, whose adherents were expected to convert.

Although Umayyad conquests had succeeded in ushering in a century of prosperity for the Middle East, problems arose. The dynasty found it difficult to supply the material needs of its far-flung populations. In addition, recent converts resented the favoritism toward Arab elites shown by Umayyad rulers. By the middle of the eighth century a rival faction claiming descent from the Prophet's uncle Abbas (d. 653) mustered support from *Shiites* and other discontented subjects throughout the weakened empire, successfully challenged the Umayyads in battle, and established a new dynasty in Baghdad. Once in power, however, these new Abbasid caliphs (750–1258) ruled as *Sunnis* and initiated an epoch known as the Golden Age of Islam.

The Abbasid Dynasty

The Abbasids inherited from the Umayyad dynasty a vast empire, which they further expanded and ruled by reaching out beyond the Arabian elites to embrace recent Muslim converts and grant them equality with Arabs. The Abbasids also continued the earlier practice of giving adherents of other monotheistic religions protected status within imperial domains. Residents of *dhimmi* communities had to pay higher taxes than Muslims, but in return they maintained local autonomy under the leadership of their clergy, and later (when Muslims extended their conquests to India) Hindu princes. Abbasid caliphs incorporated much of the elaborate courtly style and pomp of former Persian rulers. Their power and inclusiveness also diffused for a time much of the potential for conflict between *Sunni* and *Shiite* subjects, until the rise of the competing Fatimid dynasty in tenth-century Egypt (which we discuss in the introduction to Chapter 2).

Without the empire's economic prosperity, none of this tolerance (rare at the time anywhere in the world) would have developed. Imperial territory stretched from Spain along the North African coast, through the eastern Mediterranean basin, the Middle East, Central Asia, and northwest India (see Map p. 9). This vast area formed a flourishing commercial system protected by Abbasid military and naval power. Much of the empire's wealth derived from trade. Spices, jewels, textiles, and porcelain came westward from Indonesia, China, and India along the ancient Silk Road to the Middle East. Merchants purchased this precious cargo in Abbasid domains or shipped goods via the Red Sea and then transported them up to Mediterranean ports. Gold from West Africa arrived via North Africa. Textiles, metals, and olive oil moved eastward to reach markets in Damascus, Baghdad, and Cairo. Abbasid manufactured goods, metalwork and armaments, paper, and fine textiles also found their way into the region's trade networks. Farmers in Abbasid domains produced a variety of food crops, including citrus fruits, melons, sugar, rice, and cotton, for the export trade.

This expanded, prosperous Islamic empire no longer resembled the austere simple community in Arabia, but by the tenth century it also no longer wielded its earlier military might. Abbasid caliphs and officials relied increasingly on warriors from frontier tribes and slaves captured in battle to defend border regions, and within the imperial heartlands they had to cede power to local military chieftains who became, independent rulers. Even as Abbasid power weakened, however, the empire's vibrant Islamic culture remained intact and flourished.

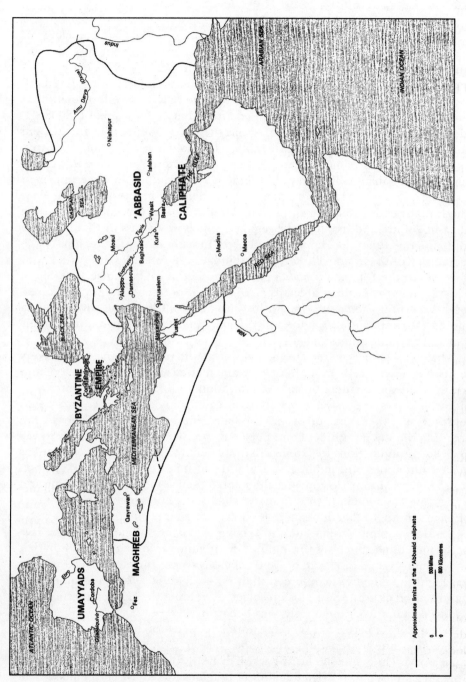

The Abbasid Empire in the Ninth Century

Islamic Law, or *Sharia*, and the *Ulema*

The Muslim *ulema* (playing a very different role than the Christian clergy of Europe) lent stability to the far-flung empire in many ways, none more important than the devising of legal codes, a component of *sharia*. This body of law, derived from the *Quran* and *hadith*, regulated Muslim behavior. During the eighth and ninth centuries there emerged four separate schools of interpretation in Muslim law. The Hanbali school, named after Ahmad ibn Hanbal (780–855), adhering closely to the religious texts, has the fewest followers in the Muslim world and now prevails in Saudi Arabia. The Malikis follow Malik ibn Anas (c. 715–795) and predominate in northern and western Africa and in parts of the Persian/Arabian Gulf. They allow judges some latitude to voice informed opinions on points of law, and permit use of analogies in interpreting the law. The Hanafi school, deriving from Abu Hanifa (700–c. 767), took hold in the Abbasid empire and its successor regimes, which we discuss in Chapter 2. In contemporary times the Hanafi school predominates in Muslim regions of the Indian subcontinent and Turkey. Hanafi judges use reason to interpret law in cases where the *Quran* and *hadith* provide no definitive guidance. The Shafii school, named after jurist al-Shafii (767–820), also permits judges to use reason to interpret *hadith*, but only within strict limits. It functions in Indonesia and East Africa. *Shiite ulema* developed legal schools as well, based upon their own sect's codification of *hadith*.

Whatever school it emerged from, *sharia* deals with personal behavior, property rights, business agreements, inheritance, and marital and family obligations and hardly at all with matters of state organization and policy. To minimize conflict with rulers, the *ulema* conceded that caliphs and their successors could substitute for the *sharia* provisions of state-generated law, especially in the areas of criminal punishment and personal law. *Sharia* enjoins Muslims to follow *Quranic* injunctions to extend charitable aid to the needy, and prescribes strict prohibitions on gambling, usury, and consumption of pork and alcohol. It also obliges Muslims to convince their coreligionists to avoid wrongdoing and to struggle to maintain their own piety, which constitutes one of the meanings of *jihad* (another related meaning is "holy war" [see Reading 1]).

Besides shaping Muslim law and serving as judges, religious scholars have performed other functions throughout the Islamic world as teachers, notaries, and administrators of charitable and religious trusts. During Abbasid times a few highly qualified women joined their ranks. Eminent *ulema* and other holy figures acted as arbiters of Muslim societies, at times daring to criticize rulers and to demand from them righteous behavior.

When caliphs began to lose their worldly power to military dynasties in the mid-tenth century, a separation developed between state and religion in the Islamic world. The Seljuk sultans, a Turkish dynasty, ruled alongside the enfeebled Abbasid caliphs, now restricted mainly to religious functions. The Seljuks, eventually usurping Abbasid rule, exercised power over most of the Middle East during the eleventh and twelfth centuries. These Turkish dynasts, unable to claim descent from the Prophet's lineage and lacking traditional legitimacy, enhanced their authority by turning to the *ulema* for assistance in garnering and retaining popular support. The Seljuks also built and endowed scores of *madrasas* (Islamic schools) where the *ulema* spread *Sunni* orthodoxy. By supporting the religious establishment from an invincible military position, they helped to formalize the separation of religion and the state. The *ulema* knew where real power resided and, whatever their theological reservations, backed these new rulers.

Muslim High Culture

The significant literary, artistic, architectural, and scientific legacies of the Abbasids attest to the cultural and intellectual vitality of the early Islamic centuries. Wealthy merchants, officials, and landholders supported a brilliant cultural efflorescence that we can barely hint at here. Intellectuals preserved and transmitted the knowledge and culture of earlier civilizations—Greek, Roman, and Indian. They also made fundamental contributions to science, philosophy, and medicine. Abu Nasr al-Farabi (872–950), called the second master (Aristotle being the first), explored the interplay of intellect and imagination in the creation and maintenance of civic virtue, and Abu Ali al-Husayn ibn Sina (980–1037) attempted to reconcile science and revelation (see Reading 3). Among the creative intellectuals flourishing in Islamic societies we find many non-Muslims, such as the Jewish philosopher, physician, and Talmudist Musa ibn Maymun (Moses Maimonides, 1135–1204), who lived and worked in Muslim Spain and Cairo, where he made major contributions to the strong rationalist strain of thought in the portion of the world dominated by Islam.

Wealthy patrons of scholarship in the Abbasid and other Muslim empires maintained large libraries housing vast collections of manuscripts. Educational institutions became accessible (through scholarships funded by pious foundations) to all groups in these highly literate societies in which the ability to read and master the *Quran* had great importance. When the immense corpus of learning produced and preserved in the Islamic world reached Christian Europe starting in the twelfth century, it astounded readers and helped shape Western scientific, theological, and philosophical discourse for centuries.

Although the Abbasid caliphate had fragmented by the mid-tenth century, the murder of the dynasty's last caliph (see Reading 6b) and the destruction of Baghdad by the Mongols came in 1258. Disintegration at the imperial center did not lead to cultural decay, curtailment of commerce, or barbarism as it did in Europe after the earlier fall of the Roman empire. In Chapter 2 we examine the post-Abbasid centuries of the Middle East and other regions of the Islamic world.

Sufism

In addition to asserting the teachings of *Sunni* Islam and the articulation of legal systems, the Abbasid society and its successors also produced and maintained Islamic mysticism, or *Sufism,* whose adherents sought ways to reach God through intense religious experience. One of the earliest *Sufis,* the eighth-century poet Rabia al-Adawiyya, expressed in her writings (see Reading 4) profound love for God. She rejected the material world for the higher joy of God-centered reverence, as did later *Sufi* masters, male and female. *Sufism* eventually spread all over the Islamic world in the form of sainthood cults formed to honor pious *Sufi* sages. In later periods *Sufi* disciples established lodges (*tariqas*) where they practiced and taught their particular mystical rites. As the Abbasid empire fragmented into smaller Muslim states, networks of *Sufi* lodges, and pilgrimages to shrines of saints, created bonds among Muslims across political frontiers. Most *Sufis* turned away from asceticism but still sought intense mystical experiences. In the early sixteenth century *Sufism* actually gave rise to a major *Shiite* dynasty—the Safavid—as we show in Chapter 3.

Besides meditation and prayer, *Sufis* and some members of the *ulema* who joined their ranks also saw other ways to achieve communion with God. The famous theologian and *Sufi* Abu Hamid al-Ghazzali (1058–1111) evoked the "hidden fire" of music and dance as a route to divine ecstasy. Earlier, the Spanish Muslim theologian Ali ibn Ahmad ibn Hazm (994–1063), though not a *Sufi,* expressed appreciation of the ways in which humans can link their earthly love to love of God.

The *Sufi* orders not only led Muslim men and women to God, mysticism also provided through the widespread networks of *tariqas* solace and guidance in the turbulent and disaster-filled world of the thirteenth and fourteenth centuries, which Reading 6 reveals. Mysticism had rejuvenated Islam in a period of crisis. The *tariqas* also helped peasants organize local agriculture and integrated the rural population into a revitalized belief system, deepening religion's hold on the population.

1. The *Quran* and Other Islamic Texts

Muslims believe that the *Quran* (Koran), the sacred book of Islam, revealed to the Prophet Muhammad in the Arabic language over a twenty-two-year period beginning in 610, is the timeless word of God. Most Muslims, viewing the scripture as a guide for life, own a copy of the *Quran* and many memorize it in childhood.

Some of the Prophet's immediate followers committed to memory the *suras* (chapters) of the *Quran* as Muhammad spoke them. Others transcribed his utterances. According to Islamic tradition, the Caliph Uthman (d. 656) had an official text prepared, the Arabic *Quran* that has come down to us, a book using powerful and eloquent language. The selections we present here in English translation give a flavor of its exalted expression as well as its attention to matters of everyday life.

Excerpts from the *sira,* or *Life of the Prophet of God,* by ibn Ishaq (704–767), appear in the second section of this Reading. Composed by the grandson of a convert to Islam, this work comes to us in a later abridged edition written by ibn Hisham (d. 833). The *sira* incorporates oral traditions revealing a "chain of transmitters" (*isnad*), much as the *hadiths,* or traditions of the Prophet, do. For easier reading, we have omitted most of the transmitters' names. The habit of naming sources and using direct speech makes it possible to evaluate the texts critically and also enlivens the subject matter, giving us narratives filled with both historical fact and God-given miracles.

The third part of Reading 1 consists of reported sayings and actions of the Prophet Muhammad, known as "Islamic Traditions," or *hadiths* in Arabic. Muslim scholars have collected and commented on them since Umayyad times. The *hadiths* presented here come from a collection gathered by al-Bukhari (810–870), a Persian from Central Asia, which has had great influence over *Sunni* Muslims' lives.

By early Abbasid times there also emerged a penal code administered by state officials, including the *muhtasib* who regulated public markets and businesses as well as aspects of public morality. We conclude Reading 1 with a selection of these regulations.

The *Quran:* Creation*

God created the heavens and the earth—a real creation. Let Him be exalted above all false worship.

He created man from a drop of sperm—man who is brazenly contentious; the live-stock also He created on your behalf, for the warmth and other uses, as well as the food, you have of them. . . . Your Lord is truly gracious and compassionate.

Things beyond your knowledge He has created also.

It is for God to indicate what the right path is; there are some that go astray. Had God willed He had surely guided all of you aright.

---

*From Kenneth Cragg, *Readings in the Qur'ân: Selected and Translated With an Introductory Essay* (London and San Francisco: Collins, 1988), pp. 99–100, 121–22, 169, 179, 229–30, 265, 303–5, 308, 311–15, 338–39. Rearranged. Minor changes in capitalization and punctuation made by the editors. American spellings adopted. By permission.

It is He who sends down rain from heaven for you to drink and to water the trees of your pasture. . . . The night and the day He has made to serve your ends. Sun, moon, and stars are all recruited to His command.

He has also set the mountains firm on the earth that it may be solid under you. There are rivers and tracks for you so that you may find your way, landmarks too, and the stars by which men are piloted.

Shall He, then, who created, be on a par with that which does not? Will you not realize? Were you set to count up the mercies of God you would not be able to number them. God is truly forgiving and merciful.   *Sura* 16

The *Quran:* The Last Day of Judgment

The Day of decision has its appointed time decreed—the Day when the trumpet is sounded. In throngs you will come; the heaven will be opened, its gates turning; the mountains will be carried away and dissolve like a mirage; *Jahannam* [hell] will lie in wait like an ambush, a place for the rebellious and their haunt for long years, where they shall taste no cool water nor refreshing drink but only boiling waters and bitter tears—their due requital.

They were not looking for their reckoning but totally rejected Our revelations. Everything We had ledgered in a book. "Taste, then, your retribution— a retribution which, on Our part, can only intensify!"

For those who truly fear God there is sure triumph, sheltered gardens and vineyards, buxom companions and a cup of overflowing delight. No idle talk will be heard there and no deceiving. Such is your . . . Lord's recompense, a bounty and a reckoning from the Lord of the heavens and of the earth and all within them, the all-merciful—He to whom they have no prerogative to speak on that Day when the Spirit and the angels stand rank on rank. Nor shall they address the all-merciful save him to whom He gives leave, saying only what is truth.   *Sura* 78

The *Quran:* The Prophets

We made the house (at Mecca) a place of sanctuary and security for the people, saying: "Make the place where Abraham prayed your house of prayer." Thus We made Our covenant with Abraham and Ishmael, that they should cleanse My house as a sanctuary for pilgrims and men of devotion to make the pilgrim circuit and do acts of worship and prostration.

Abraham and Ishmael built the foundations of the house, saying: "Lord, accept it at our hands, You who hear and know our hearts. Make us ever submissive to You and make our descendants a community of obedience to You. Show us our forms of devotion and turn to us in mercy. For You are the merciful One who turns again to men. Send among our people after us a messenger of their own kin, who will recite to them Your revelations, teach them the Book and the wisdom and purge them from evil. For You are ever powerful and wise."

Who but a fool would forsake the community of Abraham? We chose him in this present world; and in the world to come he will be among the righteous. . . .

To be rightly guided they say that you must be Jews or Christians. Say rather: "Ours is the community of Abraham, a man of pure worship. No polytheist he! Let your word be: 'We believe in God and in what has been revealed to us, and revealed to Abraham, Ishmael, Isaac, Jacob, and the tribes, and we believe in what was brought to Moses, to Jesus, and to the prophets, from their Lord. We do not distinguish between any of them and to God we make submission.'" If they believe in accordance with this faith of yours, then are they truly guided. But if they turn away from it they are plainly in schism. God who hears and knows all will see you through in all your dealings with them. *Sura* 2

People of the Book, do not go to unwarranted lengths in your religion and get involved in false utterances relating to God. Truly, Jesus, Mary's son, was the messenger of God and His word—the word which He imparted to Mary—and a spirit from Him. Believe, then, in God and His messengers and do not talk of three gods. You are well advised to abandon such ideas. Truly God is one God. Glory be to Him and no "son" to Him . . . their one and only guardian. *Sura* 4

The *Quran:* God's Revelation to Muhammad

It is We who have communicated the Qur'ān to you from above in gradual sequence. So await with patience what your Lord determines. Do not yield to any among them who is an evildoer or an unbeliever. Remember the Name of your Lord morning and evening; prostrate yourself to Him by night and celebrate His praise all the long night.

These men are in love with this fleeting world and put behind them the harsh reality of doom's day. *Sura* 76

The *Quran: Jihad,* or Struggle for the Faith

If you obey God and His messenger, He will not let you forfeit any of your deeds. For God is forgiving and merciful. Believers are those who, having believed in God and His messenger, do not doubt further but strive in the way of God (*Jihād*) with their possessions and their persons. These are the ones who are truly sincere. *Sura* 49

Fight in pursuit of the way of God those who fight against you but do not provoke hostility. God has no love for those who embark on aggression. Slay them where ever you encounter them and drive them out from places whence they have driven you. Subversion is a worse thing than slaughter. Do not do battle with them, however, in the vicinity of the sacred mosque unless they are warring with you there. If they fight you, slay them; such are the deserts of those who deny the faith. But if they desist God is certainly forgiving and merciful.

Fight them until there is no more subversion and religion is wholly God's. If they desist, hostility is at an end save for those who commit evil. Things sacrosanct allow of retaliation, so if in the sacred month let it be in the sacred month. Whoever makes aggression against you, take up hostilities in the same measure against them, fearing God. Know that God is with those who fear Him.

Going to war is prescribed for you, though it is to you a hateful thing. Yet it may well be that something you hate is nevertheless good for you, just as it can happen that you set your heart on what is bad for you. Knowledge in these things is God's, not yours.

They put questions to you about going to war in the sacred month. Say: "To go to war in that month is a serious matter, but—in God's sight—it is an even graver thing to forbid entry to the path of God, to deny the faith, to ban the sacred mosque and to throw out its people." Subversion is more heinous than slaughter. They will not cease waging war against you until—if you are able—they make you turn back from your religion. Should any of you in fact turn back from his religion and die as a recreant from faith—the doings of all such will come to naught in this present world and in the next they will be denizens of the Fire eternally. Those who have believed, who have emigrated and striven in the path of God, can anticipate the mercy of God, who is ever forgiving and merciful.   *Sura* 2

. . . [T]hose who take up retaliatory action when wronged are in no way culpable. It is only those who deal wrongfully with people who are to be reprehended—those who flout the right and commit outrage in the land. There is for them a grievous retribution. And whoever exercises patience and practices forgiveness—that is the staying power which masters things.   *Sura* 42

The *Quran:* Society and Law

Woe to those who act fraudulently, who exact their full measure when in receipt from others, yet give short measure when they reckon out or weigh out for others. Do such people not realize that they will be raised to life again for the great Day—the Day when mankind will stand before the Lord of all being?
     Sura 83

They inquire from you about intoxicants and games of chance. Say: "In both there is great evil, as also some advantage for mankind. The evil is greater than the benefit."

They ask you what they should lay out in charity. Say: "All you generously can." So God makes His signs clear to you so that you may ponder how they bear on this world and the next.   *Sura* 2

Believers! Eat of the good things with which We have provided you and give thanks to God—if indeed it is His worshippers you are! However, carrion, blood, and the meat of swine are prohibited to you as well as that over which any other name than God's has been invoked. But if anyone is driven by necessity, without deliberate intent and not going beyond his need, there will be no sin incurred by him. God is forgiving and merciful. *Sura 2*

The *Quran:* Marriage and Family

... [T]ake to wife such women as may seem good to you, that is, two, three, or four, and if you fear that you cannot treat them equitably, then one only.... Give women their marriage portion [bride-price] as a free-will gift. But if they freely give back part of it to you take it with happy satisfaction. *Sura 4*

It is not lawful for you to reclaim possession of anything you have given to your wives. *Sura 2*

Men shall have a share in what parents and close relatives leave behind and women have a share in what parents and close relatives leave behind, whether it be little or large, a share is laid down. *Sura 4*

Tell the believers who are men to be chaste in their looking and to keep their sexual impulses under control. ... And tell the believing women-folk to be chaste in their looking and to keep their sexual impulses under control, not parading their charms beyond what is chastely seen but drawing their veils over their bosoms. Let them not display their charms except to their own husbands, or fathers, or sons, or husband's sons, their brothers, brother's sons or sister's sons, or their own women-folk, the slaves in their charge, or their male servants who are without sexual capacity, or children ignorant of the embarrassment of women's nakedness. *Sura 24*

Women on being divorced must let three menstrual periods pass without cohabiting. ... During this interlude their husbands have every right to take them back again if they desire to be reconciled. The wives also have rights of their own comparable to those their husband has over them, in all fairness, while men's rights take precedence over theirs. God is all strong and all wise.

When you have divorced your wives and they have attained their term, do not hinder them from taking husbands for themselves if satisfactory agreement has been reached between them. *Sura 2*

Ibn Ishaq's *Sira,* or Biography of the Prophet Muhammad (eighth century)*

The First Converts: Khadīja ... was the first to believe in God and His Apostle, and the truth of the message. By her, God lightened the burden of the Prophet. He never met with contradiction and charges of falsehood, which saddened him,

---

*The excerpts from Ibn Ishaq's *Sira* are found in John Alden Williams, ed., *Islam* (New York: Washington Square Press, 1963), pp. 50, 53–55, 72–73, and 114–15. Notes deleted. American spellings adopted. Bracketed material added by the editors. By permission.

but God comforted him by her when he went home. She strengthened him, lightened his burden, proclaimed his truth, and belittled men's opposition. May God Almighty have mercy on her!

'Alī son of the Prophet's uncle Abū Ṭālib was the first male to believe in the apostle of God, to pray with him and to believe in his divine message, when he was a boy of ten. God favored him in that he was brought up in the care of the Apostle before Islam began. . . .

[*The Night Visit*]: The following account reached me from . . . Umm Hānī', daughter of Abū Ṭālib. It is pieced together in the story that follows, each one contributing something of what he was told about what happened when he was taken on the night journey.

Al-Hasan said that the Apostle said: "While I was sleeping . . . Gabriel came and stirred me with his feet . . . he brought me out of the door . . . and there was a white animal, half mule, half donkey, with wings at its sides with which it propelled its feet."

Qatāda said that he was told the Apostle said: "When I came to mount him he shied. Gabriel placed his hand on its mane and said, 'Are you not ashamed, O Burāq, to behave this way? By God, none more honorable before God than Muhammad has ever ridden you before.' The animal was so ashamed that he broke out in a sweat and stood still so that I could mount him."

In his story al-Hasan said: "The Apostle and Gabriel went their way until they arrived at the temple in Jerusalem. There he found Abraham, Moses, and Jesus among a company of the Prophets. The Apostle acted as their leader in prayer. Then he was brought two vessels, one containing wine and the other milk. The Apostle took the milk and drank it, leaving the wine. Gabriel said: 'You have been rightly guided, and so will your people be, Muhammad. Wine is forbidden you.'"

One of whom I have no reason to doubt told me on the authority of Abū Saʿīd al-Khudrī; I heard the Apostle say, "After the completion of my business in Jerusalem a ladder was brought to me finer than any I have ever seen. It was that to which the dying man looks when death approaches. My companion mounted it with me until we came to one of the gates of heaven called the Gate of the Watchers. An angel called Ismāʿīl was in charge of it, and under his command were twelve thousand angels, each having twelve thousand under his command."

A traditionist who had got it from one who had heard it from the Apostle told me that the latter said, "All the angels who met me when I entered the lowest heaven smiled in welcome and wished me well except one, who said the same things but did not smile or show the joyful expression of the others. When I asked Gabriel the reason he told me that if he had ever smiled before or would smile hereafter he would have smiled at me, but he does not smile because he is Mālik, the Keeper of Hell. I said to Gabriel. . . . "Will you not order him to show me Hell?" And he said, "Certainly! O Mālik, show Muhammad Hell.""

Thereupon he removed its covering and the flames blazed high into the air until I thought they would consume everything. So I asked Gabriel to order him to send them back to their place, and he did."

In this tradition Abū Saʿīd al-Khudrī said that the Apostle said: "When I entered the lowest heaven I saw a man sitting there with the spirits of men passing before him. To one he would speak well and rejoice in him saying 'A good spirit from a good body' and of another he would say 'Faugh!' and frown. . . . Gabriel told me this was our father Adam, reviewing the spirits of his offspring; the spirit of a believer excited his pleasure, and the spirit of a disbeliever excited his disgust.

"Then I saw men with lips like camels; in their hands were pieces of fire like stones which they used to thrust into their mouths and they would come out of their posteriors. I was told that these were those who sinfully devoured the wealth of orphans.

"Then I saw men like those of the family of Pharaoh with such bellies as I have never seen; there were passing over them as it were camels maddened by thirst when they were cast into Hell, treading them down, and they were unable to move out of the way. These were the usurers.

"Then I saw men with good fat meat before them side by side with lean stinking meat, eating the latter and leaving the former. These are those who forsake the women which God has permitted them, and go after those He has forbidden.

"Then I saw women hanging by their breasts. These were those who had fathered bastards on their husbands.

"Then I was taken up to the second heaven and there were the two maternal cousins, Jesus Son of Mary and John son of Zakariah. Then to the third heaven and there was a man whose face was as the moon at the full. This was my brother Joseph son of Jacob. Then to the seventh heaven and there was a man sitting on a throne at the gate of the Immortal Mansion. . . . Every day seventy thousand angels went in not to come back until the resurrection day. Never have I seen a man more like myself. This was my father Abraham."

The *Hadith:* Traditions of the Prophet*

. . . A man asked permission to speak to the Prophet, and when the Prophet saw him he said, "Unhappy the brother of his clan! Unhappy the son of his clan! (What a bad fellow!)" Then when the man sat down the Prophet looked cheerfully on him and spoke kindly to him. When the man went away, "ʿAʾisha said, 'Messenger of God, when you saw him you said this and that, then to his face you were cheerful and kindly!" And the Messenger of God said, "Why, ʿAʾisha,

---

*The *hadith* and social regulations are from John Alden Williams, ed., *Islam* (New York: Washington Square Press, Inc., 1963), pp. 72–73 and 114–115. Notes deleted. By permission.

when have you ever seen me act grossly with people? Verily, the worst place on the resurrection day in the sight of God will be that of the man whom people avoided fearing his Mischief."

A woman came to the Prophet and said, "My mother vowed to go on the pilgrimage, and died before fulfilling it. Should I make the pilgrimage in her place?" He said, "Yes, do it. If your mother had had a debt, would you have paid it?" She said, "Yes." "Then pay what she owes, for God is more worthy than anyone that we should keep our promises to Him."

We took some women captives, and in coition practiced withdrawal . . . so as not to have offspring from them. We asked the Messenger of God about this and he said, "Is that what you did?" Then he said three times, "There is not a soul who is to be born for the day of resurrection, but that it will be born." [This *hadīth* is used today to overcome objections to birth control.]

Social Regulations

Market Regulations: The *muhtasib* must order (transporters of goods) if they stay long in one place to unload the pack animals, for if the animals stand with loads, it will hurt them, and that is cruelty. The Messenger of God has forbidden cruelty to animals. The *muhtasib* should order the people of the market to keep it clean of filth which collects in it and will hurt the people . . . and he should allow no one to spy on his neighbors from the roofs or through windows, or men to sit in the paths of women needlessly; whoever does something of this sort must be corrected by the *muhtasib*.

Money Changers: Earning a living by changing money is a great danger to the religion of him who practices it; indeed there is no preserving his religion for him, except after knowledge of the Law so as to avoid falling into forbidden practices. It is incumbent on the *muhtasib* to search out their market and to spy on them, and if he finds one of them practicing usury or doing something illegal in his money-changing, to punish him.

Barber-Surgeons: . . . They must carry with them tools for circumcision, razor and scissors, for circumcision is a religious obligation for men and for women according to the generality of men of learning. . . . Our guide is what is related of the Prophet—the blessing of God and peace be on him—when he said to a man who had become a Muslim, "Get rid of the long hair of paganism, and be circumcised," and because also cutting off a part of the body is a part of God's right on us . . . like the cutting off the hand of a thief. If this is established, then circumcision for a man consists of cutting off the foreskin, and for a woman in (clitoral excision: [this is] practiced chiefly by [the] Shāfiʿī school). So it is obligatory for men and women to do this for themselves and their children, and if they neglect it, the Imām may force them to do it for it is right and necessary.

Ship-Men: Owners of ships and boats shall be prevented from loading their vessels above the usual load, for fear of sinking. For the same reason the *muhtasib* must forbid them to sail during windstorms. If they carry women on the same boat with men there must be a partition set between (men and women).

Punishments: Know that the first order of the *hisba* is prohibition, the second admonition and the third deterring and restraining. Deterring is for the future, punishment for the past, and restraining for the present and current. It is not for one of the subjects [common people] to do anything more than restrain. . . . What goes beyond stopping illegal acts . . . pertains to the authorities.

Admonition is useless from one who does not admonish himself, and we say that one who knows his words will not be accepted, because the people know of his delinquency should not undertake the *hisba* by admonishing, since there is no good in his admonishment. How shall one who is not himself honest make others honest? . . .

The second stage is putting the fear of God (in the culprit) and threatening him with physical punishment until he is deterred from what he is doing.

The third is reviling him and upbraiding him with rough words, though not (libelously) but with words that do not count as moral excess, such as "Libertine!" "Stupid!" "Ignorant! Will you not fear God?" "Loose of morals!" and that sort of thing, for if he is a libertine he is stupid—if he were not, why would he offend God?

2. *Shiite* and *Sunni* Views on Political Legitimacy

Most *Sunni* Muslims believe that the Prophet Muhammad died without setting forth rules of succession for leadership over the *umma*, the Islamic community he founded. Conflict erupted during the following century over who would become the rightful caliph, or *Imam* (leader of the community of believers), leading Muslims to elaborate contrasting theories of legitimacy.

Three main positions emerged. *Sunni* Muslims believed in hereditary succession for caliphs based on descent from Muhammad's clan, the Quraysh, and also stressed the need for new caliphs also to obtain community allegiance. We present the *Sunni* position in the first part of this reading. Another group claimed that Muhammad in fact had chosen as head of the *umma* his cousin and son-in-law Ali (see Reading 1), who in fact did become the fourth caliph. This group became known as Ali's partisans, *Shii* in Arabic, or, in common usage, *Shiites*. (See the second part of this reading and the introduction to this chapter.) On one level the *Shiites* stress the legitimacy of rule of only Ali's descendants. But for one important strain of *Shiite* belief it also involves Ali's "hidden" twelfth descendant, called the "hidden *Imam*." Followers of this branch of *Shiite* Islam, predominant in today's Iran, expect this *Imam* to appear on earth to establish a reign of justice as a prelude to God's final reckoning.

Kharajites took a third position. They believed that rulers should be chosen irrespective of hereditary claims by the *umma* and could be changed as new needs arose. Eventually the *Kharajites* became a minority movement within Islam. The more numerous *Sunnis* dominated the caliphate while the *Shiites* formed oppositional movements and a few independent dynasties, as we show in Chapter 2.

A. Abd al-Hasan Ali al-Mawardi, On Choosing a Caliph (eleventh century)*

The following excerpt from the writings of the celebrated jurist is translated into English under the title *The Powers of the Sultanate* and sets forth a *Sunni* conception of the caliphate. Al-Mawardi (974–1058) stresses the contractual basis for this institution: choice of caliphs from the Quraysh lineage, followed by community consent. Al-Mawardi, who served as an official of the Abbasid Caliphate in Baghdad, maintained that only the caliph could grant political legitimacy, and thereby supplied a rationale for the widespread practice of otherwise independent rulers seeking confirmation of their authority from the caliphs in Baghdad.

The Imamate: God, whose power be glorified, has instituted a chief of the Community as a successor to Prophethood and to protect the Community and assume the guidance of its affairs. Thus the *Imamate* is a principle on which stands the bases of the religious Community and by which its general welfare is regulated, so that the common good is assured by it. Hence rules pertaining to the *Imamate* take precedence over any other rules of government.

The *Imamate* is placed on earth to succeed the Prophet in the duties of defending the Religion and governing the World, and it is religious obligation to give allegiance to that person who performs those duties.

Abū Hurayra [a companion of the Prophet Muhammad] related that the Prophet, on whom be God's blessing and peace, said, "Other rulers will govern you after me. The pious will govern you with his piety, and the libertine with his immorality. Hear them both, and obey them in all that conforms with the truth. If they do well, it is to their credit and yours, but if they do evil, it will be to your credit and their discredit."

Thus the obligatory nature of the *Imamate* is established, and it is an obligation performed for all by a few, like fighting in a holy war, or the study of the religious sciences, and if no one is exercising it, then there emerge two groups

*From John Alden Williams, ed., *Themes of Islamic Civilization* (Berkeley, Los Angeles, London: University of California Press, 1971), pp. 84–87. Bracketed material added by the editors. Arabic words italicized. By permission.

from the people; the first being those who should choose an *Imām* for the Community, and the second those who are fitted to be *Imām*, of whom one will be invested with the *Imamate*. As for those of the community who do not belong to either of these two categories, there is no crime or sin if they do not choose an *Imām*. As to these two categories of people, each of them must possess the necessary qualifications. Those relating to the electors are three: . . . Justice, in all its characteristics. . . . Knowledge, sufficient to recognize who is worthy to be the *Imām* by virtue of the necessary qualifications. Judgment and wisdom to conclude by choosing the best person, who will best and most knowledgeably direct the general welfare.

As for those persons fitted for the *Imamate*, the conditions related to them are seven: . . . Justice in all its characteristics. . . . Knowledge requisite for independent judgment (*ijtihād*) about revealed and legal matters. . . . Soundness of the senses in hearing, sight, and speech, in a degree to accord with their normal functioning. . . . Soundness of the members from any defect that would prevent freedom of movement and agility. . . . Judgment conducive to the governing of subjects and administering matters of general welfare. . . .Courage and bravery to protect Muslim territory and wage the *jihād* against the enemy. . . . Pedigree: he must be of the tribe of Quraysh, since there has come down an explicit statement on this, and the consensus has agreed. . . . The Prophet said, "The Quraysh have precedence, so do not go before them," and there is no pretext for any disagreement, when we have this clear statement delivered to us, and no word that can raise against it.

There are ten things incumbent on the *Imām* as matters of the common interest. . . . He must maintain the Religion according to the principles established and agreed upon by the earliest Muslims (*salaf al-umma*), and if an innovator appears, or someone with dubious opinions who deviates from those principles, then he must clarify matters by logical proofs, and show him the correct way, and finally apply the rules and punishments to which he is bound, that religion may be preserved from disorder, and the Community from stumbling. . . . He must apply legal judgments for litigants, and stop contention among plaintiffs, so that equity reigns, without aiding the oppressor or weakening the oppressed. . . . He must guard Islamic territory and protect what is sacrosanct, so that people may gain their bread and move from place to place secure from any threat to life and property. . . . He must apply the punishments of the Law, so as to secure God's prohibitions from violation, and preserve the rights of God's servants from attack or destruction. . . . He must fortify the marches [frontiers] with adequate garrisons and deterrent power, so that the enemy may not appear due to neglect, committing misdeeds or shedding the blood of any Muslim or confederate. . . . He must struggle with holy war against those who have been invited to join Islam and rejected it, until they either convert or enter into the status of tribute-paying non-Muslim subjects, to make victorious the truth of God over every (other) religion. . . . He must collect the taxes on conquered territories and the poor-tax in conformity with the Law as written and interpreted, without fear or oppression. . . . He must administer the outlays and proper expenditures of the public treasury, without lavishness or niggardliness, and with punctuality. . . . He must see to it that trustworthy and loyal men are delegated to look after the offices and the monies under his control. . . . He must himself oversee matters and examine the circumstances, in order to direct the affairs of the Community and safeguard the Religion, and not delegate his authority seeking to occupy himself with pleasures or devotion, for a loyal person can yet turn traitor, and a faithful commander can yet deceive.

B. Allama al-Hilli, On the *Shiite Imamate* (between the end of the thirteenth century and beginning of the fourteenth century)*

> For *Shiites, Imams* descend in a bloodline from the fourth Caliph Ali, and are guided by God, therefore infallible and sinless theocratic leaders. Jamal al-Din Hasan ibn Yusuf al-Hilli (1250–1326), popularly known as Allama al-Hilli, was born in Iraq eight years before the Mongols sacked Baghdad (see Reading 6) and lived most of his life under Mongol rule. In Chapter 2 we show that, although they brought bloodshed and destruction to the Middle East, the Mongol invaders also revived international trade and the Islamic culture in which *ulema* such as al-Hilli could discuss the fine points of Islamic law, theology, and political theory. In the early 1300s al-Hilli moved to the Mongol il-Khanid court in Iran and influenced its ruler to convert to *Shiite* Islam. There he conducted debates with the leading *Sunni* theologians of his day. A prolific writer, he reputedly produced hundreds of books, some eight of which have become the standard classics of *Imami Shiism.*

He who is worthy of the *Imamate* is a person appointed and specified by God and His Prophet, not any chance person; it is not possible that there be more than one person at any one period who is worthy of it. Men have disagreed as to whether or not the *Imamate* is . . . [necessary]. Whoever has known dark experiences and has examined political principles knows of necessity that whenever men have among them a chief and a guide whom they obey, who restrains the oppressor from his oppression and the unjust man from his injustice and along with that leads them to rational principles and religious duties, and restrains them from corruptions which cause the destruction of order in their worldly affairs, and from the evils which result in wretchedness in the world to come, so that every individual might fear that punishment, then because of this they will draw near to soundness and depart from corruption. . . . Hence the

---

*From al-Hilli, *The Eleventh Chapter,* translated by William McElwee Miller (London: The Royal Asian Society, 1928), pp. 52–81. Bracketed material added by the editors.

Imamate is *lutf* [what God does, directly or indirectly, to make it easier for people to obey the divine will].

[There are] those who hold that it is incumbent upon men to appoint a ruler to guard their persons from harm. And we say that we have no quarrel with them as to the *Imamate's* being a protection from harm. But our quarrel is about their saying that [the act of appointing the *Imām*] has been bestowed upon men, for in this case there would be an actual conflict between God and men regarding the appointment of *Imāms,* and it would result in harm, whereas what is sought is the decrease of harm.

It is necessary that the *Imām* be immune to sin [really, free from error, otherwise he would also need an *Imām,* or spiritual guide] and that is impossible. And also if he committed sin, he would lose his place in men's hearts, and the value of his appointment would be nullified. And because he is the guardian of the law, in which case he must be immune to sin . . . which no one perceives but God the most high. Hence . . . the *Imām* must be appointed by God, not by the people. Agreement has been reached that in appointing the *Imām* the specification can be made by God and His Prophet, or by a previous *Imām* in an independent way (without the voice of the people). [There is disagreement over] whether or not his appointment can be in a way that is other than specification (by God and the Prophet). He who knows the unseen make[s] it known. And that comes about in two ways: (1) by making it known to someone immune to sin, such as the Prophet, and then he tells us of the *Imām's* immunity to sin and of this appointment; (2) by the appearance of miracles wrought by his hand to prove his veracity in claiming the *Imamate. Sunnis* say that whenever the people [*umma*] acknowledge any person as chief, and [give the *baya* or allegiance, they] are convinced of his ability and his power increases, he becomes the *Imām.*

The *Imām* [must] be absolutely the best of the people of his age, because he takes precedence over all [or he is above everyone else]. And if there were among them one better than he then the worse would have to take precedence over the better, and that would be evil.

The *Imām* after the Messenger of God is ʿAlī ibn Abī Tālib [d. 661]. And he is the best for two reasons: (1) he is equal to the Prophet. And the Prophet is the best, hence his equal is also the best; (2) the Prophet had need of him, and of no one else of the Companions and kindred, in his prayer. And he who is needed is better than anyone else. . . . [T]he word of the Prophet regarding him [was], "ʿAlī is the best judge of you all." He [also] is the most ascetic of men after the Prophet of God. Hence it comes about that he is the *Imām,* for the most ascetic is the best.

A matter of importance—the Twelfth *Imām* [Muhammad ibn Hasan al-Mahdi al-Muntanzir, in occultation since 874] is alive and the thought that it is unlikely that anyone like him should remain alive is false. And the cause of his being hidden is either some advantage which God has kept to Himself, or else the number of his enemies and the paucity of helpers.

O God, hasten his joy, and cause us to behold his victory and make us his helpers and his followers, and sustain us with his obedience and his good pleasure, and protect us from his opposition and his anger.

3. Abu Ali al-Husayn ibn Sina [Avicenna], The Ideal Muslim Intellectual (eleventh century)*

When the Abbasid empire broke into small competing states, brilliant intellectuals such as Abu Ali al-Husayn ibn Sina (980–1037) found many rulers willing to patronize their scholarship. The political instability resulting from the weakening of Abbasid authority did not stifle the tradition of cultural and intellectual exchange among Islamic cities and centers of learning. Born in a village near the Central Asian city of Bukhara, ibn Sina continuously traveled in search of knowledge and work. In the course of his voyages he distinguished himself as one of the most famous physicians, intellectuals, and men of science in the world, and Europeans continued to teach from his celebrated writings on medicine up to the eighteenth century. Not only did he master the many texts of ancient thinkers in Arabic translations, but he also added to knowledge in the fields of law, theology, philosophy, optics, astronomy, medicine, poetry, and philology. The following selection from ibn Sina's autobiography refers to the remarkable Arab intellectual and musical theorist Abu Nasr al-Farabi (870–950), also a Central Asian who studied in Abbasid Baghdad. Known mainly as a preserver and transmitter of ancient Greek philosophy, al-Farabi attempted to reconcile the Greek philosophical tradition with Islamic teachings. In this reading ibn Sina recounts his great debt to al-Farabi. He also refers to the *Shiite* Ismailis who ruled over Egypt from 869 to 1171 and sent missionaries throughout the Muslim world to convert people to their sect. One of his students who transcribed this biography added the reference to his drinking wine, which would cause ibn Sina problems with the *ulema*.

My father was a man of Balkh [one of the four capitals of the Central Asian region of Khurasan. Today Balkh lies within Afghanistan], and he moved from there to Bukhara during the days of [Prince] Nuh ibn Mansur [976–997]; in

---

*From A. J. Arberry, "Avicenna: His Life and Times" in G. M. Wickens, ed., *Avicenna: Scientist and Philosopher* (London: Luzac & Company, 1952), pp. 9 and 11–17. Bracketed material added by the editors.

his reign he was employed in the administration, being governor of a village-center in the outlying district of Bukhara. . . . I was also born there and after me my brother. Later we moved to Bukhara, where I was put under teachers of the Koran and of letters. By the time I was ten I had mastered the Koran and a great deal of literature, so that I was marveled at for my aptitude.

Now my father was one of those who had responded to the Egyptian [*Shiite*] propagandist (who was an Ismaili); he and my brother too had listened to what they had to say about the Spirit and the Intellect, after the fashion in which they preach and understand the matter. They would therefore discuss these things together, while I listened and comprehended all they said; but my spirit would not assent to their argument. . . . [T]hey began to invite me to join the movement, rolling on their tongues talk about philosophy, geometry, Indian arithmetic; and my father sent me to a certain vegetable seller who used the Indian arithmetic [and algebra], so that I might learn it from him.

Then there came to Bukhara a man called Abu Abd Allah al-Natili who claimed to be a philosopher; my father invited him to stay in our house, hoping that I would learn from him also. Before his advent [arrival] I had already occupied myself with Muslim jurisprudence, attending [studying with] Isma'il the Ascetic; so I was an excellent inquirer, having become familiar with the methods of postulation and the techniques of rebuttal according to the usages of the canon lawyers. I now commenced reading the *Isagoge* [Porphery's Introduction to the *Organon* of Aristotle] with al-Natili: when he mentioned to me the definition of genus, as a term applied to a number of things in answer to the question "What is it?" I set about verifying this definition in a manner such that he had never heard. He marveled at me exceedingly, and warned my father that I should not engage in any other occupation but learning; whatever problem he stated to me, I showed a better mental conception of it than he. So I continued until I had read the straightforward parts of [Aristotle's] *Logic* with him; as for the subtler points, he had no acquaintance with them.

From then onward I took to reading texts by myself; I studied the commentators, until I had . . . mastered . . . Logic. Similarly with Euclid['s *Elements of Geometry*] I read the first five or six figures with him; and thereafter undertook on my own account to solve the entire remainder of the book.

I now occupied myself with mastering the various texts and commentaries on natural sciences and metaphysics, until all the gates of knowledge were open to me. Next I desired to study medicine, and . . . [proceeded] to read all the books that had been written on this subject. Medicine is not a difficult science, and naturally I excelled in it in a very short time, so that qualified physicians began to read medicine with me.

The next eighteen months I devoted entirely to reading; I studied Logic once again, and all the parts of philosophy. During this time I did not sleep one night through, nor devoted my attention to any other matter by day. I prepared a set of files; with each proof I examined I set down the syllogistic premises and put them in order in the files, then I examined what deduction might be drawn

from them. I observed methodically the conditions of the premises, and proceeded until the truth of each particular problem was confirmed for me. When
I found myself perplexed by a problem, or could not find the middle term of
any syllogism, I would repair to the mosque and pray, adoring the All-Creator
until my puzzle was resolved and my difficulty made easy. At night I would return home, set the lamp before me, and busy myself with reading and writing;
whenever sleep overcame me or I was conscious of some weakness, I turned
aside to drink a glass of wine until my strength returned to me; then I went
back to my reading. If ever the least slumber overtook me, I would dream of
the precise problem which I was considering as I fell asleep; in that way many
problems revealed themselves to me while sleeping. So I continued until I had
made myself master of all the sciences.

I was now a master of Logic, natural sciences and mathematics. I therefore
returned to metaphysics; I read the *Metaphysics* [of Aristotle], but did not understand it and was baffled by the author's intention; I read it over forty times
until I had [learned] the text by heart. Even then I did not understand it or
what the author meant, and I despaired within myself, saying, "This is a book
which there is no way of understanding." But one day at noon I chanced to
be in the bookseller's quarter and a broker was there with a volume in his
hand which he was calling [auctioning] for sale. He offered it to me, but I
returned it to him impatiently, believing that there was no use in this particular science. However he said to me, "Buy this book from me; it is cheap,
and I will sell it to you for four dirhams. The owner is in need of the money."
So I bought it, and found that it was a book by Abu Nasr al-Farabi *On the Objects of the Metaphysics.*

I returned home and hastened to read it; and at once the objects of that book
[by Aristotle] became clear to me, for I had [learned] it all by heart. I rejoiced
at this, and upon the next day distributed much in alms to the poor in gratitude to Almighty God.

4. Rabia al-Adawiyya al-Qaysiyya, A Woman's Voice in *Sufi* Poetry (eighth century)*

In many religious traditions there are those who seek special knowledge or experience of God. Within Islam, this role is played mainly by the *Sufis,* who seek communion with the deity. *Sufis* do not believe, as do mystics of other faiths, that God actually dwells within human beings. The word *"Sufi"* derives from the Arabic word for wool (*suf*), relating to the coarse clothes worn by those who, more than a millennium ago, renounced the material world.

Sufism opened its ranks to women, but more men than women became *Sufi* leaders. In the early days of the Islamic empires, women attended *Sufi* meetings and sources mention sanctuaries where women, led by female religious teachers, or *shaykhas,* could pursue the mystical path to enlightenment.

Rabia al-Adawiyya al-Qaysiyya of Basra (c. 717–801) became a renowned *Sufi* saint. Sold into slavery in childhood, her aura of holiness induced her Muslim master to free her. She rejected marriage and followed an ascetic life, preaching voluntary poverty, patience, penitence, gratitude, and complete dependence on God. Her love for God was so complete, she reportedly said, that it left no room in her heart for hate.

Later *Sufis* organized lodges in various parts of the Muslim world from where they spread the teachings of their *Sufi* masters. They also acquired land for the upkeep of their orders, and most of them renounced the asceticism that had become the hallmark of Rabia's devotion to God.

My peace, O my brothers, is in solitude,
And my Beloved is with me alway[s],
For His love I can find no substitute,
And His love is the test for me among mortal beings,
When-e'er His Beauty I contemplate,
*He is my "*mihrāb*" [a niche in the front of every mosque],*
towards Him is my "qibla"
[toward Mecca, the direction in which Muslims pray.]
If I die of love, before completing satisfaction,
Alas, for my anxiety in the world, alas for my distress,

---

*From Margaret Smith, *Rābia the Mystic* A.D. *717–801 and Her Fellow-Saints in Islam* (Amsterdam: Philo Press, 1928; reprinted 1974), pp. 12, 28, 98, 102, and 142. Notes deleted. Bracketed material added by the editors. By permission.

O Healer (of souls) the heart feeds upon its desire;
The striving after union with Thee has healed my soul,
O my Joy and my Life abidingly,
Thou wast the source of my life and from Thee also came my ecstasy.
I have separated myself from all created beings,
My hope is for union with Thee, for that is the goal of my desire.

O my Joy and my Desire and my Refuge,
My Friend and my Sustainer and my Goal,
Thou art my Intimate, and longing for Thee sustains me,
Were it not for Thee, O my Life and my Friend,
How I should have been distraught over the spaces of the earth,
How many favors have been bestowed, and how much hast Thou
*   given me.*
Of gifts and grace and assistance,
Thy love is now my desire and my bliss,
And has been revealed to the eye of my heart that was athirst,
I have none beside Thee, Who dost make the desert blossom,
Thou art my joy, firmly established within me,
If Thou art satisfied with me, then
O Desire of my heart, my happiness has appeared.

I have made Thee the Companion of my heart,
But my body is available for those who desire its company,
And my body is friendly towards its guests,
But the Beloved of my heart is the guest of my soul.

I have loved Thee with two loves, a selfish love and a love
*   that is worthy (of Thee),*
As for the love which is selfish, I occupy myself therein
*   with remembrance of Thee to the exclusion of all others,*
As for that which is worthy of Thee, therein Thou raisest
*   the veil that I may see Thee.*
Yet is there no praise to me in this or that,
But the praise is to Thee, whether in that or this.

5. Abu al-Rayhum Muhammad ibn Ahmad al-Biruni, A Muslim Scholar Examines Hinduism (1030)*

A l-Biruni (973–1050), born in Ghazna in southern Afghanistan, became a great
eclectic savant who excelled in mathematics, astronomy, natural science, history, and geography. Over his lifetime he produced more than one hundred scholarly works. He spoke Arabic, Persian, Turkish, and learned Hebrew, Greek, Syriac,
Sanskrit, and several dialects of India, studying the latter while accompanying
Mahmud the Ghaznavid (998–1030) and his immediate heirs on their victorious
warring expeditions to northern India.

Al-Biruni's study of India, an excerpt from which appears below, is based
on firsthand observations, interviews, and a careful reading of Sanskrit texts.
He concluded that educated Hindus believe in a monotheistic God and follow
the Vedas and other scriptures, which helped pave the way for Muslims to grant
Hindus protected status as *dhimmi*. His belief in Islam's superiority over Hinduism, a recurrent theme in the text, helps us to understand some of the ideological underpinnings of the centuries-long domination by Muslim rulers in India
of the Hindu majority. It also helps explain the determination of Muslims to
separate themselves from Hindus when the British gave India its independence
(see Reading 16).

The . . . Hindus entirely differ from us in every respect, many a subject appearing intricate and obscure which would be perfectly clear if there were more
connection between us. The barriers which separate Muslims and Hindus rest
on different causes.

First, they differ from us in everything which other nations have in common.
And here we first mention the language, although the difference of language
also exists between other nations. If you want to conquer this difficulty (*i.e.* to
learn Sanskrit), you will not find it easy, because the language is of an enormous range, both in words and inflections, something like the Arabic calling
one and the same thing by various names . . . and using one and the same word
for a variety of subjects. . . . For nobody could distinguish between the various
meanings of a word unless he understands the context in which it occurs, and
its relation both to the following and the preceding parts of the sentence. The

*From Edward C. Sachau, ed., *Alberuni's India: An Account of the Religion, Philosophy, Literature,
Geography, Chronology, Astronomy, Customs, Laws and Astrology of India about* A.D. *1030* (London:
Routledge and Kegan Paul, 1888), pp. 17–24, 27, and 112–13. Text rearranged. Bracketed mate-
rial added by the editors.

Hindus, like other people, boast of this enormous range of their language, whilst in reality it is a defect.

Secondly, they totally differ from us in religion, as we believe in nothing in which they believe, and *vice versa*. On the whole, there is very little disputing about theological topics among themselves; at the utmost, they fight with words, but they will never stake their soul or body or their property on religious controversy. On the contrary, all their fanaticism is directed against those who do not belong to them—against all foreigners. They call them *mleecha, i.e.* impure, and forbid having any connection with them, be it by intermarriage or any other kind of relationship, or by sitting, eating, and drinking with them, because thereby, they think, they would be polluted. They consider as impure anything which touches the fire and the water of a foreigner; and no household can exist without these two elements. Besides, they never desire that a thing which once has been polluted should be purified. . . . They are not allowed to receive anybody who does not belong to them, even if he wished it, or was inclined to their religion. This, too, renders any connection with them quite impossible, and constitutes the widest gulf between us and them.

In the third place, in all manners and usages they differ from us to such a degree as to frighten their children with us, with our dress, and our ways and customs, and as to declare us to be devil's breed, and our doings as the very opposite of all that is good and proper. By the by, we must confess, in order to be just, that a similar depreciation of foreigners not only prevails among us and the Hindus, but is common to all nations toward each other.

[T]he repugnance of the Hindus against foreigners increased more and more when the Muslims began to make their inroads into their country . . . leaving to the people their ancient belief, except in the case of those who wanted to become Muslims. All these events planted a deeply rooted hatred in their hearts.

Now in the following times no Muslim conqueror passed beyond the frontier of Kabul and the river Sindh until the days of the Turks when . . . the Hindus became like atoms of dust scattered in all directions. . . . Their scattered remains cherish, of course, the most inveterate aversion toward all Muslims. This is the reason, too, why Hindu sciences have retired far away from those parts of the country conquered by us, and have fled to places which our hand cannot yet reach, to Kashmīr, Benares, and other places. And there the antagonism between them and all foreigners receives more and more nourishment both from political and religious sources.

Hindus believe that there is no country but theirs, no nation like theirs, no kings like theirs, no religion like theirs, no science like theirs. They are haughty, foolishly vain, self-conceited, and stolid. They are by nature niggardly in communicating that which they know, and they take the greatest possible care to withhold it from men of another caste among their own people, still much more, of course, from any foreigner. According to their belief, there is no other country on earth but theirs, no other race of man but theirs, and no created beings besides them have any knowledge or science whatsoever. Their haughtiness is such that, if you tell them of any science or scholar in Khurāsān and Persia, they will think you to be both an ignoramus and a liar. If they traveled and mixed with other nations, they would soon change their mind, for their ancestors were not as narrow-minded as the present generation is.

At first I stood to their astronomers in the relation of a pupil to his master, being a stranger among them and not acquainted with their peculiar national and traditional methods of science. On having made some progress, I began to show them the elements on which this science rests, to point out to them some rules of logical deduction and the scientific methods of all mathematics, and then they flocked together round me from all parts, wondering, and most eager to learn from me, asking me at the same time from what Hindu master I had learnt those things, whilst in reality I showed them what they were worth, and thought myself a great deal superior to them, disdaining to be put on a level with them. They almost thought me to be a sorcerer.

The belief of educated and uneducated people differs in every nation; for the former strive to conceive abstract ideas and to define general principles, whilst the latter do not pass beyond the apprehension of the senses, and are content with derived rules, without caring for details, especially in questions of religion and law, regarding which opinions and interests are divided.

The [educated] Hindus believe with regard to God that he is one, eternal, without beginning and end, acting by free will, almighty, all-wise, living, giving life, ruling, preserving; one who in his sovereignty is unique, beyond all likeness and un-likeness, and that he does not resemble anything nor does anything resemble him. . . . [T]hose who march on the path to liberation, or those who study philosophy and theology, and who desire abstract truth . . . are entirely free from worshipping anything but God alone, and would never dream of worshipping an image manufactured to represent him.

Chapter II

From the Coming of Steppe Peoples to the Age of Gunpowder Empires

Introduction

The Eurasian steppe, a three-thousand-mile-long zone of temperate grassland and semiarid, treeless plains, long the home of Turkish and Mongol herders, horsemen, and warriors, stretches from the lower Danube basin to Central Asia and Mongolia. The inhabitants of these regions began their migrations and incursions into western Asia and Europe long before the era of the Prophet Muhammad. We begin this section by focusing on the last cycle of such migrations and invasions of nomads, from the tenth century to the early fifteenth century, which brought Turkic-Mongol peoples deep into China, northern India, Central Asia, and the Middle East. There then emerged relatively stable empires—the Ottoman, the Safavid, the Mughal—which attained their cohesiveness partly because of their military use of gunpowder.

Ibn Khaldun and Historical Cycles

The thoughtful Muslim observer, renowned scholar, and statesman Abd al-Rahman ibn Khaldun (1332–1406) witnessed not only Turkish migrations and Mongol invasions into the Middle East but also nomadic movements into his native North Africa. Drawing on these experiences, he developed a theory of historical cycles in which successful nomadic assaults on vulnerable urban-centered societies create new dynasties, which in time grew luxurious, soft, and weak, and become attractive targets for the next wave of energetic, warlike people from the deserts and steppes who invade and take over enfeebled states. And then the cycle begins again. Ibn Khaldun offered this interpretation in his *Muqaddama* or *Introduction* to world history, a selection from which we present in Reading 7.

Ibn Khaldun's cyclical historical scenario contains more than an element of plausibility. The Byzantine and Persian empires had fallen to Arabian tribes, and the Turks and Mongols had come out of the steppes of Central Asia and taken over the former Abbasid empire. Later Turkish peoples would impose Ottoman rule on the Abbasid successor states. But modern scholarship suggests a far more complicated pattern than ibn Khaldun's: many dynasties fell because of strife among the sons of even strong leaders. Even the Abbasids found it necessary to relinquish direct administrative controls over much of their once-extensive domains to warrior chieftains who, over time, became independent of the imperial center and set themselves up as rulers in their own right—often taking the title of *amir* (prince or commander); *khan* (chief, ruler, or local governor); or *sultan* (holder of power).

The separate Turkish Seljuk dynasties, which ruled over Anatolia, Syria, and Persia starting in the eleventh century, exemplified this type of state. Turkish soldiers fought against the Greek Orthodox Byzantine empire, reducing its Asian territory to an ever-smaller corner of northwestern Anatolia. (In 1094 the Byzantine emperor called on fellow Christians in Europe for help in fighting off Muslim incursions, which soon brought crusading knights to Anatolia and the Middle East.) Although operating independently, Seljuk rulers continued to acknowledge the religious authority of the Abbasid caliphs in Baghdad. Among the Seljuks' major accomplishments were the granting of tax collection rights to military officers and the creation of a network of state-supported Muslim schools, or *madrasas*—the latter undertaken on the initiative of the noted Seljuk *wazir* (government minister) al-Hasan ibn Ali, known to history as Nizam al-Mulk (1018–1092). These *madrasas* trained young religious scholars for government positions and employment as notaries, teachers, and in other learned professions. The *ulema*, who comprised the faculty of these schools, taught an orthodox version of *Sunni* doctrines that standardized these beliefs and thereby mitigated political fragmentation of the period. Much later, in the present era, corrupted versions of these Islamic schools arose in Pakistan, Afghanistan, and elsewhere to preach the necessity of *jihad* against perceived foreign enemies and also against Islamic states allied with the West.

The Fatimid Dynasty: An Independent Caliphate from North Africa

Of all the states that emerged as the Abbasid caliphs lost their worldly power, the *Shiite* Fatimid dynasty (909–1171), originating in *Ifriqiya* (today's Tunisia), set up a rival caliphate. This dynasty claimed descent from Ismail (d. 740), seventh of what some *Shiites* believe constitute the true lineage of *imams* or heirs of Ali (d. 661), husband of the Prophet's daughter Fatima (d. 633), from whom the Fatimid dynasty took its historical name. In 969 the Fatimids moved their capital eastward into Egypt, and later they expanded their territory into the Fertile Crescent. Production of sugar, rice, citrus fruits, and other agricultural commodities in the Fatimid regions, along with profits of interregional trade, allowed the erection of the magnificent imperial city of Cairo, where art and learning flourished at a high level. The still-existing al-Azhar mosque and its affiliated college became one of the most prestigious educational institutions in the Islamic world.

In Syria and Palestine the Fatimids defeated the Seljuks and almost immediately faced the European crusaders who were sent by Pope Urban II (c. 1042–1099) to restore the Holy Land to Christian control. The crusaders vanquished the Fatimids and in 1099 conquered Jerusalem. When the Europeans occupied the Syrian coast and countryside, they massacred many of the residents, forced Muslim leaders to flee into exile, and transformed the remaining rural inhabitants into serfs (for Middle Easterners' views of the crusaders see Reading 6a). Although the crusades loom large in European medieval lore, they exerted little impact on the Islamic world. The military leader of the Kurdish Ayyubid dynasty, Salah al-Din (Saladin, c. 1138–1193), who had earlier defeated the Fatimids in Egypt, imposed unity on the Arabs and then drove the crusaders from Jerusalem in 1187.

The Mamluk Slave Dynasty

A new dynasty, the Mamluks (1250–1517), removed the last remaining crusader states and developed a military using enslaved men purchased in Central Asia and later from the Caucasus. After conversion to Islam, these men received training to become elite soldiers. At the conclusion of this training they were freed, served in the Mamluk armed forces, and, if politically astute and good soldiers, could rise to military and political leadership. Regulated by Islamic law (*sharia*), which encouraged manumission and required that slaves be treated with justice and kindness, the Mamluk system of military "slavery" did not rest on any notions of racial inferiority. Thus it differed greatly from the later system of African slavery prevalent in the Atlantic world.

The Mamluks took firm control of Syria, Egypt, and western Arabia and consolidated a *Sunni* state centered at Cairo. Their regime lasted four centuries and made perhaps its most important contribution in halting the advance of the invading Mongol armies in the mid-thirteenth century. Unable to repel the early-sixteenth-century Ottoman invasion of Egypt, Ottoman sultans allowed the Mamluks to retain local power over their lands and private armies. When Napoleon invaded Egypt in 1798 the forces he met and vanquished in the Nile Valley consisted of Mamluk warriors who still owed formal allegiance to the Ottoman sultan and paid him yearly tribute.

Mongol Invasions

Led by the Mongol chieftains Genghis Khan (c. 1162–1227) and his grandson Hulegu (1217–1265), the Mongols attacked the Middle East and other targets using explosives and other gunpowder weapons derived from Chinese technology. To compensate for the disparity between their small population base of 2 million and their world-conquering aims, these invaders used terror tactics to intimidate populations in the path of their advance and augmented their ranks by recruiting Turkish soldiers as they took over more and more of Central Asia. Defeating several of the Seljuk vassals in Anatolia, the Mongols prepared the way for the later rise of Ottoman power there. Moving through Persia, they slaughtered agriculturalists and city dwellers and instituted a practice, which later dynasties followed, of forcibly resettling artists and artisans in other parts of their vast domains. The Mongols also brought talented handcraftsmen from China into their Central Asian and Middle Eastern territories. In 1258

Hulegu's troops laid siege to Baghdad, massacred many of its residents, and executed the last Abbasid caliph (see Reading 6b). Fourteen years later the Mongols wiped out the main Persian strongholds of a violent Ismaili *Shiite* movement—the Assassins—known for murdering their political adversaries. Only Mamluk military power, as we have mentioned, saved the Syrian coast and North Africa from these conquerors.

The Mongols founded the il-Khanid state, which ruled Iran and Iraq for a century (1256–1353), during which time they embraced Islam. Despite the initial violence of their conquest, this dynasty, as had others before it, encouraged long-distance east-west trade and reintegrated the Middle East into the larger Eurasian commercial world.

Nevertheless, the disasters continued. In the mid-fourteenth century the fearful bubonic plague destroyed one-third of the Middle East's population (see Reading 6c). Later that century another nomadic group, the Tartars, led by their Muslim leader, Timur, invaded. Conquering Afghanistan, Persia, Iraq, and Syria, Timur also attacked Anatolia and defeated an Ottoman army at Ankara in 1402, taking the reigning sultan prisoner. Timur's simultaneous military campaigns in China diverted him from further conquest in the Middle East. Rulers of the dynasty he founded (the Timurid, 1370–1506) forcibly transported Middle East artisans and scientists to the capital at Samarkand (in present-day Uzbekistan), bringing additional Muslim culture to Central Asia. In Timurid domains many former nomads turned to agriculture. As the Timurids declined four new political formations arose to fill the resulting political vacuum. These were a revived Ottoman empire in the western part of the Middle East, most of North Africa, and in the Balkans, the Safavid *Shiite* state in Iran, a short-lived state in Uzbekistan, and the *Sunni* Mughal empire in parts of Afghanistan and India.

Just as the power of invading hordes from the steppes reached its pinnacle, the sedentary states began to use gunpowder weapons more efficiently in defense against nomadic cavalry. After Timur, further assaults from the Central Asian steppes tapered off and such new states as the Ottomans, Safavids, and Mughals no longer had to fight off nomadic invaders, and could thus establish long-lasting empires.

Rise of the Ottoman Empire

Although the Safavid and Mughal dynasties date from the early sixteenth century, the Ottomans (1281–1924), centered in Anatolia, first emerged two centuries earlier. Following Hulegu's thirteenth-century invasions, a local Turkish chieftain, Osman (1259–1326), founded a small state on the borders of the Byzantine empire. The Osmanli dynasty (anglicized as Ottoman) continued the Seljuk project of gradually converting the Anatolian Greek Orthodox inhabitants to Islam. The Ottomans also began their conquest of the Balkans, in southeastern Europe. They defeated a Serb coalition at the battle of Kosovo (1389), the echoes of which still reverberated six hundred years later when Yugoslavia fragmented in the 1990s. Using light artillery and siege machinery, their armies began attacking the well-fortified Byzantine capital, Constantinople. Under the leadership of Sultan Mehmet II (1429–1481), they finally captured the city in 1453. The Ottomans renamed it Istanbul, which served for the next five centuries as their capital. Realizing the danger in leaving imperial military power in the hands of armed units loyal to tribal lineages, the Ottomans introduced a new recruitment system (the *devshirme*), which provided "slaves" to staff major parts of the imperial army and administration. Under this institution, which bears no relationship to the Mamluk slave system, Ottoman recruiters took young Christian boys from the Balkans as a form of taxation, brought them to the capital, and converted them to Islam. There they received excellent educations. Some of the most gifted became military officers in the elite *Janissary* corps. Others, if they demonstrated superior intellectual capacity, joined the royal court as pages to the sultan and his ministers. Those with the most talent could later receive important posts in the imperial ministries.

Unencumbered by competing loyalties and owning no significant property, the *Janissaries* initially provided a major source of reliable military manpower. These armed forces enabled the Ottomans to extend their sway to the gates of Vienna and to bring Iraq, Syria, and most of North Africa under imperial control. They also fought frequent wars against the *Shiite* Safavids to the east and the Spanish empire to the west.

Ottoman rulers gave minor nobles the right to collect and retain taxes on designated rural lands in return for military service and for supplying local troops. Sultans forced many members of the landed Anatolian military aristocracy to resettle in the Balkans. There they remained isolated from the local population and lost their importance and their ability to threaten Istanbul's rule. The Ottomans also created a sophisticated state bureaucracy. Officials carried out surveys of crop yields in order to determine taxation rates. The legal scholars who staffed the judiciary, headed by the supreme jurist, the *sheikh al-Islam,* officiated in small-town and city courts and ruled on cases concerning land, water rights, and issues of personal status.

After the Ottomans conquered Constantinople, Mehmet II created the *millet* system to integrate the city's large Christian population into the empire. More broadly, the state granted local autonomy to the protected communities of Christians and Jews (the *dhimmi*) living within Ottoman domains. The sultan designated the chief leader of each religious group to head his community, gave him authority to establish schools and other cultural institutions, and permitted minorities to continue speaking their own languages. This official also collected state taxes and determined how much each person in the community under his authority paid. Army barracks near the quarters of these *millets* offered protection. In some parts of the empire the minority populations lived in separate areas. In others, such as Jerusalem, they lived alongside Muslims.

The empire reached its pinnacle of strength and authority under Sultan Suleiman the Lawgiver (1494–1566). The imperial court authorized the construction of superb mosques throughout its domains; it also patronized scientists, artists, and historians. The extensive land-based Ottoman empire matched and sometimes surpassed the power of the newly formed states of Europe. Only gradually, as we show in Chapter III, did Europeans overtake Islamic states.

Before competition with Europe set in, the Ottoman Middle East had evolved a vibrant regional economy based upon local agriculture and trade. Most Ottoman subjects, except those in cities like Istanbul, Aleppo, Damascus, Cairo, Tunis, and Algiers, lived in rural areas, where the differences between town and country remained less pronounced than in Europe. Urban residents cultivated gardens and thus produced some of their own food. By the sixteenth century Istanbul and Cairo became the cultural centers of the empire. Other cities flourished along local and long-distance trade routes, which the state kept safe from brigands. Large marketplaces drew buyers and sellers who paid revenues to government officials, which contributed to imperial wealth.

The Safavids in Persia

Farther to the east the Safavid state originated from a *Sufi* order in Azerbaijan established by Safi al-Din (1252–1334), a *Shiite* master whose teachings spread widely through the regions of the vast Timurid empire. Ismail (1486–1524), a later master of the same *Sufi* order, which had become a formidable military force, embraced Twelver *Shiism* (see the introduction to Chapter I, and Reading 2b), conquered Tabriz in 1501, and then the rest of Persia. Taking the title of *shah* (king), he founded the Safavid dynasty that lasted into the eighteenth century. Since most of its population embraced *Sunni* Islam, early Safavid *shahs* expelled the *Sunni ulema* and brought in a new *ulema* corps from southern Lebanon and Iraq that energetically encouraged conversion to *Shiism*. By the nineteenth century the Persian *ulema* had organized themselves into a hierarchical body unique in the Islamic world. Led by elderly prestigious scholars known as *ayatollahs*, this organization became self-perpetuating as new *ayatollahs* were nominated by their predecessors. Once they attained this high status they commanded devoted followings, controlled the country's religious endowments, and intermarried with the well-to-do merchant families.

Ismail's descendant, Shah Abbas I (1571–1629), continued support for the *Shiite* clergy, erected a magnificent capital city, Isfahan, and consolidated the Safavid state by combining military and economic strategies. On the military side, he formed a slave army drawn from Georgian and Armenian captives, integrated this force with regular tribal levies, and armed both groups with muskets. This enabled the *shah* to stabilize his western frontier adjoining Ottoman domains and to turn eastward to conquer Kandahar in Afghanistan (see Reading 8).

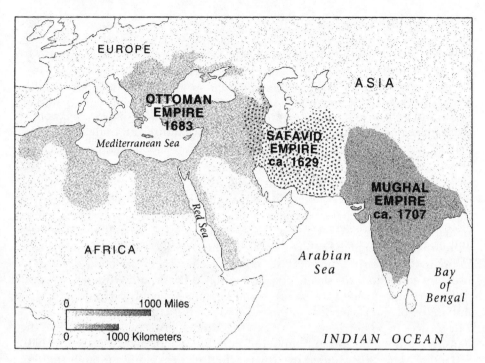

The Ottoman, Safavid, and Mughal Empires

Safavid armies received pay from the lands formerly held by local lords but now transformed by the *shah* into crown territories. Shah Abbas also assigned new tax farms to selected officers who, for a time, remained loyal to the crown. Playing off combinations of petty lords against the larger ones, he further weakened the landed aristocracy—as all of the major gunpowder rulers attempted to do. With British backing, he expelled the Portuguese from Hormuz on the Persian Gulf and expanded Safavid trade with India—a process that gave the British commercial advantages. By the late seventeenth century new competitors had been drawn into the lucrative Persian trade, including Dutch and French merchants, who competed with the British. Most of them operated through Armenian middlemen. Eventually, these Europeans came to dominate the seaborne trade with Persia. The inability of Shah Abbas's successors to prevent this competition anticipated the weaknesses that would undermine the Safavid dynasty in the early eighteenth century. Nor could they prevent local officials from engaging in extortion and diversion of tax revenues. In 1722 an attack by Afghan troops from Kandahar toppled the Safavid state. In Chapter III we describe the formation toward the end of the eighteenth century of the successor Qajar dynasty in Persia.

The Mughals in India

To the east of Safavid domains, Uzbek tribesmen had driven the warrior-poet Babur (1483–1530) from his ancestral home north of the Amu Darya (Oxus) River. At first he established a kingdom in Afghanistan from which he raided the densely populated, fertile plains of northern India. Using portable artillery and musket-wielding infantry, Babur defeated the sultan of Delhi in 1526 and a confederation of Hindu kings the following year. Thus began the 350-year Mughal dynasty, which, despite its name, had more Turkish than Mongol characteristics. But after his death Babur's heirs failed to hold on to the imperial legacy and fled to Safavid domains. It fell to Babur's grandson Akbar (1542–1605) to reconquer the Indian territory Babur had won. A remarkable ruler, Akbar transformed the Mughal administrative and military systems and continued some of the taxation policies of the Mughals' predecessors in north India. Historian John F. Richards writes that the "Mughal Empire was one of the largest centralized states known in pre-modern world history"; it "far outstripped in sheer size and resources its two rival early modern Islamic empires—Safavid Persia and Ottoman Turkey." Akbar's vision of what this empire could become—a land of Hindu and Muslim amity, of intermarriage and integration of the Hindu *Rajput* rulers (warrior princes from northern India) into the Mughal government—matched the empire's scale and offered a model of enlightened autocracy at its very best.

Under Akbar the Mughal dynasty reached its peak and, although some of his successors conquered new territory in southern India, signs of strain already began to appear. For one thing, the Muslim Mughal emperors always ruled over an overwhelmingly Hindu population. When some of Akbar's successors retreated from his attempts to reconcile religions, they alienated local Hindu and Sikh leaders (who formed a new sect of Hindusim in 1500). Nor could Mughal rulers manage the problem of succession to the throne contested by their sons and other claimants eager to rule. The Mughals also shared with their Ottoman and Safavid contemporaries the inability to prevent local power holders from retaining for themselves ever-increasing amounts of the imperial tax revenues. Some of these difficulties arose from the contradiction between the large territory controlled by the gunpowder empires and the growing contention with the Europeans.

Society and Culture in the Gunpowder Empires

As mentioned earlier, the Ottoman, Safavid, and Mughal empires encompassed vast territories. Agricultural production supplied immense wealth for the rulers. Local and long-distance trade flourished as well, supplementing the land taxes and sales of produce grown on royal domains. All three states adopted mercantilism, the system whereby governments sponsored and regulated enterprise, which also characterized Europe in the sixteenth and seventeenth centuries. Rulers of these three empires built large workshops (see Reading 11c) and encouraged others holding state monopolies to do so as well. Locally crafted rugs, porcelain, silk, jewelry, and other valued products of skilled labor found their way to regional and overseas markets. The imperial regimes' mercantilist economic policies encouraged the cultivation of such cash crops as cotton, flax, wool, and dyes, which the states usually taxed at higher rates than locally consumed foodstuffs. Revenues kept flowing into the central imperial treasuries.

When the Portuguese seized Goa on India's west coast in 1510 in order to interrupt and divert the profitable Indian Ocean trade, they succeeded in taking some of the east-west luxury trade away from Muslim and other Asian merchants. But these local traders often found ways to circumvent threatening Portuguese ships and to discover safe alternative routes that allowed them to retain a major share of the commerce moving eastward from the Indian Ocean. Where and when the Portuguese, and later the Dutch, proved to be overpowering adversaries, their local competitors developed new markets for new products and thus countered the European competition. The Portuguese and more so the Dutch, with their firm hold on the strategic Straits of Malacca, exercised control over the East Indian pepper trade, but Asian merchants readily substituted other spices and commodities in demand in the Middle East and farther west. Ottoman traders dramatically expanded the regional sales of Yemeni coffee, sweetened by locally grown sugar. Bengalis in the eastern Mughal empire developed a flourishing silk industry as did the inhabitants of the Anatolian city of Bursa. These luxury textiles, along with cheap cotton cloth produced in India, compared favorably with Chinese textiles, the high shipping costs of which made locally produced goods economically competitive. And in the eighteenth and nineteenth centuries these Muslim states began switching to the production of foodstuffs and raw materials intended for Western manufacturers and consumers, thus becoming peripheral areas serving Europe's fast-growing economy.

Art and culture flourished in the Muslim empires, aided by state sponsorship and patronage from rich merchants and landlords who lived refined and cultured lives. They covered the walls and floors of their houses with tightly woven silk and wool carpets of intricate design whose weavers bequeathed a precious legacy to their present-day successors. Both the Ottomans and Mughals experienced a genuine renaissance in miniature painting, ceramics, and jewelry manufacturing, as well as in the production of fine iron and steel ware. Artists decorated illustrated manuscripts with paintings of astonishing beauty, which, despite Islam's prohibition against representation of human bodies, portrayed the lives of the nobility in great detail. All three empires erected in their cities architectural works of great elegance: the Ottoman mosques with their tall, thin minarets; the cobalt blue tiles of Safavid mosques, domes, and public buildings; and the majestic Taj Mahal in Agra, India, built by a Mughal emperor in memory of his beloved queen. All of the Middle East, the Ottoman Balkan regions, Central Asia, and India shared in the economic prosperity and artistic creativity of the sixteenth and seventeenth centuries.

Warfare

Gunpowder transformed warfare in the era of the Ottoman, Safavid, and Mughal empires. The use of musket-bearing infantry and light artillery gave great advantages to states that mastered the new military technologies. Rulers of previously vulnerable urban areas and sedentary agricultural regions who adopted the new weapons could ward off further invasions from the steppes. As a result, nomadic assaults tapered off and wars tended to be fought between states.

The long-lasting Ottoman, Safavid, and Mughal empires provided centuries of relatively benign Muslim rule in the Middle East, North Africa, South and Central Asia. But while these Islamic gunpowder states still functioned, rapidly changing Europe in the eighteenth and nineteenth centuries posed a set of fundamental challenges to the Islamic world, which we explore in Chapter III.

6. Disasters Strike the Muslim World

I n this reading we group together texts that describe three calamities that befell the Muslim world: the European Crusades leading to their conquest of the Syrian coast, including Palestine, starting at the end of the eleventh century in the first reading; the Mongol conquest of Baghdad in the mid-thirteenth century in the second; and the ravages caused by the bubonic plague epidemic in the mid-fourteenth century in the third.

A. Usamah ibn Munquidh, An Arab Perspective on the Crusades (c. 1175)*

Although the Crusades did not exercise a major influence on the Middle East, they did help shape later perceptions of European-Arab relations. Over a period of two centuries between 1095 and 1291 a series of nine crusades brought knights and an assortment of adventurers and holy zealots from Europe intending to wrest control of the Holy Land—and especially the city of Jerusalem—from the Muslims. Only the First Crusade (1095–1099) succeeded in establishing long-lasting European footholds in Syria, including Palestine. The later crusades fortified already

---

*From *An Arab-Syrian Gentleman and Warrior in the Period of the Crusades: Memoirs of Usamah ibn-Munquidh,* translated by Philip K. Hitti (New York: Columbia University Press, 1929), pp. 60–61, 93, and 169. Bracketed material added by the editors. Notes deleted. By permission.

existing European settlements, and brought in fresh troops to help maintain garrisons. The longer crusaders stayed in the Middle East, the more they tended to appreciate the achievements of Muslim civilization. Newcomers, fired with crusading spirit, wanted primarily fame and fortune and the destruction of Muslim enemies rather than mutual accommodation or friendship. Each time that amicable relations developed between crusading communities and their Muslim neighbors, newly arrived crusaders would disrupt the pattern and reignite religious animosities.

In this reading we present the views of Usamah ibn Munquidh (1095–1188), "a Syrian-Arab gentleman and warrior," who describes events of the Second and Third Crusades during the mid- and late twelfth century and recalls both hostile and peaceful encounters with crusaders over his long lifetime. The disunity of the Muslim rulers of Syria and Egypt facilitated the crusaders' conquests. The Muslim leader Salah al-Din (Saladin) drove the crusaders from Jerusalem in 1187, and a little more than a century later the last remaining crusaders in Syria were forced to return to Europe.

I attached myself to the service of al-Malik al-'Ādil Mûr-al-Dîn (may Allah's mercy rest upon his soul!). He entered into correspondence . . . with a view to letting my wife and children, who had lingered in Egypt and had been treated with benevolence, start on their journey. Al-Ṣāliḥ sent back the messenger and gave as excuse the fact that he feared for their safety from the Franks. He also wrote to me, saying: . . . If thou dost feel that the personnel of the palace cherish ill feeling towards thee; then proceed to Mecca, where I shall deliver to thee a communication granting thee the governorship of the city of Uswān [Aswan, in southern Egypt]. . . . I shall then let go to thee thy wives and thy children.

I consulted al-Malik al-'Ādil and sought his opinion and he said: "O Usāmah, thou wert so glad to get rid of Egypt with its rebellions that thou didst believe the day when it came, and now thou wantest to return to it! Life is too short for that. I shall communicate with the king of the Franks [King Baldwin III of Jerusalem (1142–1162)] in order to secure a safe-conduct for thy family, and I shall then send someone to bring them hither." Accordingly Nūr-al-Dīn . . . dispatched a messenger and secured the safe-conduct of the king, with the cross on it, good for both land and sea.

This safe-conduct I sent with one of my servants, who carried also a letter from al-Malik al-'Adil and my letter to al-Malik al-Ṣāliḥ. Al-Ṣāliḥ transported my family on one of his private boats to Dimyāt, provided them with . . . money and provisions . . . and gave them the proper recommendation. From Dimyāt they sailed in a Frankish vessel. As they approached 'Akka [Acre] where the king (may Allah's mercy not rest upon his soul!) was, he sent, in a small boat, a few men who broke the vessel with their axes under the very eyes of my people. The king mounted his horse, stood by the coast and pillaged everything that was there.

One of my retainers came swimming to the king, taking the safe-conduct with him, and said, "O my lord the king, is this not thy safe-conduct?" "Sure enough," replied the king. "But this is the usage for the Muslims. Whenever one of their vessels is wrecked near a town, the people of that town pillage it." "Art thou going, then, to take us captive?" inquired my retainer. "No," replied the king. The king (may Allah's curse be upon him!) then put them in a house, had the women searched and took everything they all possessed. In the vessel were jewelry, which had been entrusted to the women, clothes, gems, swords, weapons and gold and silver amounting to about thirty thousand *dīnārs*. The king took it all. He then sent my people five hundred *dīnārs* and said, "This will see you home," though they were no less than fifty persons, men and women.

At that time I was in the company of al-Malik al-'Ādil in the land of King Mas'ūd [sultan of Iconium in present-day Turkey]. . . . The safety of my children, my brother's children, and our harem made the loss of money which we suffered a comparatively easy matter to endure—with the exception of the books, which were four thousand volumes, all of the most valuable kind. Their loss has left a heartsore that will stay with me to the last day of my life.

The Franks (may Allah render them helpless!) possess none of the virtues of men except courage, consider no precedence or high rank except that of the knights, and have nobody that counts except the knights. These are the men on whose counsel they rely, and the ones who make legal decisions and judgments.

Among the Franks are those who have become acclimatized and have associated long with the Muslims. These are much better than the recent comers from the Frankish lands. But they constitute the exception and cannot be treated as a rule.

B. Rashid al-Din Fazlullah (1247?–1318), The Mongol Conquest of Baghdad (thirteenth century)*

Being a political counselor to the Mongols had its risks as Rashid al-Din learned when he got caught up in dynastic squabbles and was executed in Tabriz by the last of the il-Khanid monarchs. Born into a family of Jewish doctors, Rashid al-Din converted to *Sunni* Islam. Taking up the profession of his father, he became court physician and minister in the government of the most capable ruler of the il-Khanid dynasty, Ghazan Khan (r. 1295–1304). Taking a leading role in the Mongol efforts to strengthen royal authority, revive commerce and agriculture, and stimulate public morality, the chronicler became privy to many secrets of state that he included in his histories. After Ghazan's successors converted to *Shiite* Islam, Rashid al-Din fell into disgrace, leading to his death.

---

*From Rashiduddin [Rashid al-Din] Fazlullah, *Jami' u't-tawarik* (*Compendium of Chronicles*), *A History of the Mongols*, part two, translated by W. M. Thackston (Cambridge, MA: Harvard University Department of Near Eastern Languages and Civilizations, 1999), pp. 487–99. Bracketed material added by the editors. By permission.

His account of the sack of Baghdad in 1258 by Genghis Khan's grandson Hulegu (1217–1265) contains morbid details of the Mongols' cold-blooded ferocity. Millions perished in Iran, Iraq, Anatolia, and large parts of Central Asia in this onslaught. Many more were wiped out by Mongol invasions of China and surrounding countries. Only the rigorously trained and disciplined soldiers of the Mamluk dynasty saved most of Syria and all of Egypt and the rest of North Africa from Hulegu's conquering armies. By killing the last ruling Abbasid caliph, the Mongols put a final end to that dynasty.

On the 9th of *Rabi'* II 655 [April 26, 1257] Hulegu Khan arrived in Dinawar on his way to Baghdad. From there he withdrew and went to Tabriz. . . . An emissary was sent to the caliph bearing threats and promises, saying, "When the Heretics' fortresses [belonging to the Assassins, a violent *Shiite* sect] were conquered we sent emissaries to request assistance from you. . . . In reply you said that you were in submission, but you did not send troops. Now, a token of submissiveness and allegiance is that you assist us with troops when we ride against foes. You have not done so, and you send excuses.

"No matter how ancient and grand your family may be, and no matter how fortunate your dynasty has been . . . is the brightness of the moon [the reigning caliph al-Mustasim, r. 1242–1258] such that it can eclipse the brilliance of the sun [Hulegu]?' Talk of what the Mongol army has done to the world and those in it from the time of Genghis Khan until today may have reached your hearing from common and elite, and you may have heard how, through God's strength, they have brought low . . . dynasties . . . all of whom were families of might and majesty.

"Previously we have given you advice, but now we say you should avoid our wrath and vengeance. Do not try to overreach yourself or accomplish the impossible, for you will only succeed in harming yourself. The past is over. Destroy your ramparts, fill in your moats, turn the kingdom over to your son, and come to us. . . . If our command is obeyed, it will not be necessary for us to wreak vengeance, and you may retain your lands, army, and subjects. If you do not heed our advice and dispute with us, line up your soldiers and get ready for the field of battle, for we have our loins girded for battle with you and are standing at the ready. When I lead my troops in wrath against Baghdad even if you hide in the sky or in the earth . . . I shall bring you down . . . I shall not leave one person alive in your realm, and I shall put your city and country to the torch. If you desire to have mercy on your ancient family's heads, heed my advice. If you do not let us see what God's will is."

In reply the caliph said, "Young man, you have just come of age and have expectations of living forever. You have . . . pass[ed] prosperously and auspiciously in dominating the whole world. You think your command is absolute. . . . Since you are not going to get anything from me, why do you seek [anything]? You come with strategy, troops, and lasso, but how are you going to capture a star [the caliph]? Does the prince not know that from the east to the west, from

king to beggar, from old to young, all who are God-fearing and God worshipping are servants of this court and soldiers in my army? When I motion for all
those who are dispersed to come together, I will deal first with Iran and then
turn my attention to Turan [in Central Asia], and I will put everyone in his proper
place. Of course, the face of the earth will be full of tumult, but I do not seek
vengeance or to harm anyone. I do not desire that the tongues of my subjects
should either congratulate or curse me because of the movement of armies,
especially since I am of one heart and one tongue with the *Qa'an* [Hulegu's
brother the Great Khan Mongke (r. 1251–1259)] and Hulegu. If, like me, you
were to sow seeds of friendship, do you think you would have to deal with my
moats and ramparts and those of my servants? Adopt the path of friendship and
go back to Khurasan [in Central Asia]."

Hearing the caliph's ill-considered words, Hulegu Khan flew into a rage and
. . . sent a message saying, "God the eternal elevated Genghis Khan and his progeny
and gave us all the face of the earth, from east to west. Anyone whose heart
and tongue are straight with us in submission retains his kingdom, property,
women, children, and life. . . . He who contemplates otherwise will not live to
enjoy them."

The Mongol army swarmed in like ants and locusts from all directions, forming
a circle around the ramparts of Baghdad and set . . . up a wall. . . . On Friday
the 25th of *Muharram* [February 1] the Ajami Tower was destroyed. On Mon-
day the 27th [February 3] the Mongol soldiers proceeded overwhelmingly against
the ramparts opposite the Ajami Tower. . . . Their liege men went up, and by
evening they had secured the whole of the tops of the eastern walls. . . . Hulegu
had ordered bridges built above and below Baghdad, boats made ready, cata-
pults installed, and guards stationed.

[T]he caliph and his three sons . . . came out on Sunday the 4th of *Safar* 656
[February 10, 1258]. With him were three thousand dignitaries of the city. He
approached Hulegu *Khan,* and the *padishah* [Hulegu] did not exhibit any
anger but asked after his health kindly and pleasantly. After that he said to the
caliph, "Tell the people of the city to throw down their weapons and come out
so that we may make a count." The caliph sent word into the city for it to be
heralded that the people should throw down their weapons and come out. The
people disarmed themselves and came out in droves, and the Mongols killed
them.

On Wednesday the 7th of *Safar* [February 13] the pillage and general massacre began. In one fell swoop the army went into the city and burned everything except a few houses belonging to Nestorians [Christians whose lives the
Mongols had spared because they belonged to the same religion as Hulegu's
senior wife, Doquz Khatun (d. 1265)] and some foreigners.

On Friday the 9th of *Safar* [February 15] Hulegu Khan went into the city to
see the caliph's palace. He settled into the Octagon Palace and gave a banquet
for the commanders. Summoning the caliph, he said, "You are the host and we
are the guests. Bring whatever you have that is suitable for us." The caliph, thinking

he was speaking seriously, trembled in fear. . . . He was so frenzied that he couldn't tell the keys to the treasuries one from another and had to have several locks broken. He brought two thousand suits of clothing, ten thousand *dinars*, precious items, jewel-encrusted vessels, and several gems. Hulegu Khan paid no attention and gave it all away to the commanders and others present. "The possessions you have on the face of the earth are apparent," he said to the caliph. "Tell my servants what and where your buried treasures are." The caliph confessed that there was a pool full of gold, in the middle of the palace. They dug it up, and it was full of gold, all in . . . ingots.

An order was given for the caliph's harem to be counted. There were seven hundred women and concubines and a thousand servants. When the caliph was apprised of the count of the harem, he begged and pleaded, saying, "Let me have the women of the harem, upon whom neither the sun nor the moon has ever shone."

"Of these seven hundred, choose a hundred," he was told, "and leave the rest." The caliph selected a hundred women from among his favorites and close relatives and took them away.

Hulegu Khan . . . [t]he next morning . . . ordered Su'unchaq to go into the city, confiscate the caliph's possessions, and send them out. The items that had been accumulated over six hundred years were all stacked in mountainous piles. . . . Most of the holy places like the caliph's mosque . . . were burned. Hulegu Khan decamped from Baghdad on Wednesday the 14th of *Safar* [February 20] on account of the foul air . . . and camped in the village of Waqaf-u-Jalabiyya.

The caliph was summoned. . . . At the end of the day on Wednesday the 14th of *Safar* 656 [February 20, 1258], the caliph, his eldest son, and five of his attendants were executed in the village of Waqaf . . . and the reign of the House of Abbas came to an end.

C. Ahmad al-Maqrizi, The Bubonic Plague in Syria and Egypt (fourteenth century)*

Born into a well-off Cairo family, al-Maqrizi received a traditional religious education from the best scholars of his day, afterward working as a magistrate, professor, and administrator. From 1408 to about 1418 he lived in Damascus. Upon returning to Cairo, he renounced all his public posts and dedicated the rest of his life to writing history. He has bequeathed to us numerous volumes on the historical geography of Cairo and the history of Egypt's Muslim dynasties. A

*From Ahmad ibn ʿAli al-Makrizi, *kitab al-sulūk li-maʿrifat duwal al-mulūk* (The Guide to the Knowledge of Dynasties and Kings), 4 vols., ed. by M. Mustafa Ziada, vol. II, part III (Cairo: Association of Authorship, Translation and Publishing Press, 1958), pp. 779–86. Translated from the Arabic by Hamid Irbouh. Bracketed material added by the translator. By permission of the translator.

prolific writer, he left other works on economics, religious affairs, and biography. Readers, however, need to exercise some caution as they read al-Maqrizi's text. The best estimates of the population of Cairo in 1340 done by Michael Dols in his fascinating book *The Black Death in the Middle East* (1977) fix the numbers between 500,000 and 600,000 inhabitants. Al-Maqrizi speaks of 900,000 dead in a two-month period, clearly an exaggeration. Despite this very real shortcoming, the description he offers provides a rare window into the depths of the calamity, which, according to Dols, killed an estimated 30 to 40 percent of the Middle Eastern population.

News reached [Cairo from Syria] that the plague in Damascus had been less deadly than in Tripoli, Hama, and Aleppo. From . . . [October 1348] death raged with intensity. 1200 people died daily and, as a result, people stopped requesting permits from the administration to bury the dead and many cadavers were abandoned in gardens and on the roads.

In New and Old Cairo, the plague struck women and children at first, then market people, and the numbers of the dead augmented. . . . The [ravages of the] plague intensified in . . . [November] in [New] Cairo and became extremely grave during *Ramadan* [December], which coincided with the arrival of winter. . . . The plague continued to spread so considerably that it became impossible to count how many died. . . .

In [January 1349], new symptoms developed and people began spitting up blood. One sick person came down with internal fever, followed by an unrestrained need to vomit, then spat blood and died. Those around him in his house fell ill, one after the other and in one or two nights they all perished. Everyone lived with the overwhelming preoccupation that death was near. People prepared themselves for death by distributing alms to the poor, reconciled with one another, and multiplied their acts of devotion.

None had time to consult doctors or drink medicinal syrups or take other medications, so rapidly did they die. By [January 7th,] bodies had piled up in the streets and markets; [town leaders] appointed burial brigades, and some pious people remained permanently at places of prayer in New and Old Cairo to recite funeral orations over the dead. The situation worsened beyond limits, and no solution appeared possible. Almost the entire royal guard disappeared and the barracks in the sultan's citadel contained no more soldiers.

Statistics of the dead from funerals in Cairo during . . . [November and December] attained 900,000. . . . There were 1,400 litters on which they carried the dead and soon even they did not suffice. So they began carrying dead bodies in boxes, on doors taken from stores and on plain boards, on each of which they placed two to three bodies.

People began searching for *Quran* readers for funerals, and many individuals quit their trades to recite prayers at the head of burial procession[s]. A group of people devoted themselves to applying a coat of clay to the inner sides of the graves. Others volunteered to wash corpses, and still others to carry them.

Such volunteers received substantial wages. For example, a *Quran* reader earned 10 *dirhams:* the moment he finished with one funeral, he ran off to another. A body carrier demanded six *dirhams* in advance, and still it was hard to find any. A gravedigger wanted 50 *dirhams* per grave. But most of them died before they had a chance to spend their earnings.

Family celebrations and marriages no longer took place. . . . No one had held any festivities during the entire duration of the epidemic, and no voice was heard singing. In an attempt to revive these activities, the *wazir* [prime minister] reduced by a third the taxes paid by the woman responsible for collecting dues on singers. The call to prayer was suspended at many locations, and even at the most important ones, there remained only a single *muezzin* [caller to prayer].

The drum batteries before most of the officers' quarters no longer functioned, and the entourage of a commander [who controlled a thousand men] was reduced now from about fifteen to three soldiers.

Most of the mosques and *zawiyas* [*Sufi* lodges] were closed. It was also a known fact that during this epidemic no infant survived more than one or two days after his birth, and his mother usually quickly followed him to the grave.

At [the end of February], all of Upper Egypt was afflicted with the plague. . . . According to information that arrived . . . from . . . other regions, lions, wolves, rabbits, camels, wild asses and boars, and other savage beasts, dropped dead, and were found with scabs on their bodies.

The same thing happened throughout Egypt. When harvest time arrived, many farmers had already perished [and no field hands remained to gather crops]. Soldiers and their young slaves or pages headed for the fields. They tried to recruit workers by promising them half of the proceeds, but they could not find anyone to help them gather the harvest. They threshed the grain with their horses [hoofs], and winnowed the grain themselves, but, unable to carry all the grain back, they had to abandon much of it.

Most craft workshops closed, since artisans devoted themselves to disposing of the dead, while others, not less numerous, auctioned off property and textiles [which the dead left behind]. Even though the prices of fabric and other such commodities sold for a fifth of their original value . . . they remained unsold. . . . Religious texts sold by their weight, and at very low prices.

Workers disappeared. You could not find either water carriers, or launderers or servants. The monthly salary of a horse groom rose from 30 to 80 *dirhams*. . . . This epidemic, they say, continued in several countries for 15 years.

7. Abd al-Rahman ibn Khaldun, Effective Rule and Dynastic Cycles (1375–1379)*

In any epoch ibn Khaldun (1332–1406) would deserve the accolade Renaissance man, a person of many talents and diverse interests. Combining knowledge of Islam with military acumen and an understanding of statecraft, he was one of the geniuses of the age. An itinerant professional statesman and diplomat, he started out from his native Tunis and served in high posts for a variety of Muslim princes.

This selection comes from his most widely read book, the *Prolegomena* (*Muqaddima*), or *Introduction,* to his *Universal History* (written between 1375 and 1379). As did some of the Greek and Roman historians before him, ibn Khaldun viewed history as a pattern of repeating cycles. Like a modern social scientist, he verified his theories through careful observation and objective research into the past. In order to understand the "glue" that held communities and states together, ibn Khaldun devised the concept of *asabiya* (or social solidarity), which refers to the tight mix of lineage relationships and cultural ties that bind rulers to their subjects.

. . . Human society having . . . been achieved and spread over the face of the earth, there arises the need of a restraining force to keep men off each other in view of their animal propensities for aggressiveness and oppression of others. Now the weapons with which they defend themselves against wild beasts cannot serve as a restraint, seeing that each man can make equal use of them. . . . The restraint must therefore be constituted by one man, who wields power and authority with a firm hand and thus prevents anyone from attacking anyone else, i.e., by a sovereign. Sovereignty is therefore peculiar to man, suited to his nature and indispensable to his existence.

According to certain philosophers, Sovereignty may also be found in certain animal species, such as bees and locusts, which have been observed to follow the leadership of one of their species, distinguished from the rest by its size and form. But in animals Sovereignty exists in virtue of instinct and divine providence, not of reflection aiming at establishing a political organization. . . .

---

*From *An Arab Philosophy of History: Selections from the Prolegomena of ibn Khaldun of Tunis*, translated from the Arabic by Charles Issawi, 2nd ed. (Princeton, NJ: The Darwin Press, 1987), pp. 100–180. Rearranged, and notes deleted. American spellings adopted. Bracketed material added by the editors. By permission.

It is maintained by some that rule can be founded on a Divine Law, commanded by God and revealed by Him to a man whom He has so endowed with outstanding qualities that other men willingly and unfeigningly obey him and surrender themselves to him. But this proposition cannot be demonstrated: for human society can exist without such a Divine Law, merely in virtue of the authority imposed by one man or of the Social Solidarity which compels the others to follow and obey him. And it is clear that the People of the Book and those who have followed the teachings of the prophets are few in comparison with the pagans, who do not have a book and who constitute a majority of the inhabitants of the world. And yet these pagans have not only lived but have founded states and left monuments. And until this day they form societies in the extreme northern and southern zones. Their condition is therefore not one of anarchy, i.e., of men left to themselves without restraint, for such a condition cannot possibly exist. . . .

Social solidarity is found only in groups related by blood ties or by other ties which fulfill the same function. This is because blood ties have a force binding on most men, which makes them concerned with any injury inflicted on their next of kin. Men resent the oppression of their relatives, and the impulse to ward off any harm that may befall those relatives is natural and deep rooted in men.

If the degree of kinship between two persons helping each other is very close, it is obviously the blood tie, which, by its very evidence, leads to the required solidarity. If the degree of kinship is distant, the blood tie is somewhat weakened but in its place there exists a family feeling based on the widespread knowledge of kinship. Hence each will help the other for fear of the dishonor which would arise if he failed in his duties towards one who is known by all to be related to him.

The clients and allies of a great nobleman often stand in the same relationship towards him as his kinsmen. Patron and client are ready to help each other because of the feeling of indignation which arises when the rights of a neighbor, a kinsman, or a friend are violated. In fact, the ties of clientship are almost as powerful as those of blood. . . .

The end [purpose] *of social solidarity is sovereignty.* . . . [E]very human society requires a restraint, and a chief who can keep men from injuring each other. Such a chief must command a powerful support, else he will not be able to carry out his restraining function. The domination he exercises is Sovereignty, which exceeds the power of a tribal leader; for a tribal leader enjoys leadership and is followed by his men whom he cannot however compel. Sovereignty, on the other hand, is rule by compulsion, by means of the power at the disposal of the ruler.

[Now rulers always strive to increase their power], hence a chief who secures a following will not miss the chance of transforming, if he can, his rule into sovereignty; for power is the desire of men's souls. And sovereignty can be secured only with the help of the followers on whom the ruler relies to secure the acquiescence of his people, so that kingly sovereignty is the final end to which social solidarity leads. . . .

Kingship and dynasties can be founded only on popular support and solidarity. The reason for this is, as we have seen before, that victory, or even the mere avoidance of defeat, goes to the side which has most solidarity and whose members are readiest to fight and to die for each other. Now kingship is an honored and coveted post, giving its holder all worldly goods as well as bodily and mental gratifications. Hence it is the object of much competition and rarely given up willingly, but only under compulsion. Competition leads to struggle and wars and the overthrow of thrones, none of which can occur without social solidarity.

Such matters are usually unknown to, or forgotten by, the masses, who do not remember the time when the dynasty was first established, but have grown up, generation after generation, in a fixed spot, under its rule. They know nothing of the means by which God set up the dynasty; all they see is their monarchs, whose power has been consolidated and is no longer the object of dispute and who do not need to base their rule any more on social solidarity. . . .

It is of the nature of states that authority becomes concentrated in one person. This is because, as we have said before, a state is founded upon solidarity. Now solidarity is formed by the union of many groups, one of which, being more powerful than the rest, dominates and directs the others and finally absorbs them, thus forming an association which ensures victory over other peoples and states. . . .

This wider union and solidarity will be achieved by some group belonging to a leading family; and within that family there is bound to be some prominent individual who leads and dominates the rest. That person will therefore be appointed as leader of the wider group, because of the domination enjoyed by his house over the others.

And once this leader is so appointed, his animal nature is bound to breed in him feelings of pride and haughtiness. He will then disdain to share with any one his rule over his followers; nay, he will soon think himself a God, as human beings are wont to do. Add to this the fact that sound politics demands undivided rule, for where there are many leaders the result is confusion, and if there were other gods than God in the universe, there would be chaos.

Steps are therefore taken to curb the power and to clip the wings and weaken the solidarity of the other groups, so that they shall not aspire to dispute the power of the ruler. The ruler monopolizes all power, leaving nothing to others, and enjoys alone the glory derived therefrom.

And this process may be achieved by the first king of the dynasty, or it may only come about under the second or the third, according to the power and resistance offered by the groups; but come about it certainly must. . . . Know, then, that the use of the ruler to his subjects lies not in his person, his fine figure or features, his wide knowledge, his excellent penmanship or the sharpness of his intellect, but solely in his *relationship to them.* For kingship and rule are relative terms, implying a certain relation between two objects: the ruler being the possessor of his subjects and the manager of their affairs. The ruler is, then, he who has subjects and the subjects are those who have a ruler, the ruler's relationship to his subjects being one of possession.

If this possession, and the consequences flowing from it, be excellent [i.e., if proper use is made of it] the object of rulership is perfectly fulfilled. For if [the power arising from] possession be applied in a just and beautiful way, the interests of the subjects will be promoted; if on the other hand it is applied in an evil and oppressive way, the subjects will suffer much harm and may even perish.

Now the excellence of rulership arises out of gentleness. For if the king is harsh, prone to inflict heavy punishments, always searching for the defects of his subjects and enumerating their misdeeds, they will be seized by terror and humiliation and will seek to protect themselves from him by lying, trickery and deceit until these qualities become ingrained in them and ruin their character. They may desert him in wartime, thus imperiling the country or else may conspire to kill him, ruining the state and its defenses. And if such a condition should persist, their solidarity will be weakened and with it the very basis of protection of the state.

Should the ruler however be gentle with his subjects and willing to overlook their shortcomings, they will have confidence in him, rely on him for protection, love him, and be prepared to fight unto the death against his enemies, thus bringing about a general improvement in conditions.

As for the requirements of good rule, they are that the ruler defend his subjects and be generous towards them. Defense is indeed the *raison d'être* of rulership, while generosity is one aspect of the ruler's gentleness towards his subjects and one means by which he can increase their welfare; it is also one of the chief ways of gaining their affection.

Now it is rare to find gentleness in men who have keen intelligence and awareness; rather is it to be found among the duller people. For an intelligent ruler is apt to impose upon the subjects more than they can bear, because he sees further than they, and can, thanks to his intelligence, foresee the consequences of any act or event; all of which spells ruin to the subjects. This is why he [i.e., Muhammad], peace be upon him, said: "Follow the pace of the weakest among you." This is why, also, the Lawgiver does not require excessive intelligence [in a ruler] . . . for this may lead to oppression, misrule and the driving of the people beyond what they are accustomed to.

It has thus been shown that intelligence and foresight are defects in a politician, for they represent an excess of thought, just as stupidity is an excess of stolidity. Now in all human qualities both extremes are reprehensible, the mean alone being commendable: thus generosity is the mean between extravagance and niggardliness, and courage between rashness and cowardice, and so on, for other qualities. And that is why those who are extremely intelligent are described as "devils" or "devilish" or something analogous. . . .

[G]enerally speaking, it is rare that the age of the state should exceed three generations, a generation being the average age of an individual, that is forty years. . . . [T]he first generation still retains its nomadic roughness and savagery, and such nomadic characteristics as a hard life, courage, predatoriness, and the desire to share glory. All this means that the strength of the solidarity uniting the people is still firm, which makes that people feared and powerful and able to dominate others.

The second generation, however, have already passed from the nomadic to the sedentary way of life, owing to the power they wield and the luxury they enjoy. They have abandoned their rough life for an easy and luxurious one. Instead of all sharing in the power and glory of the state, one wields it alone, the rest being too indolent to claim their part. Instead of aggressiveness and the desire for conquest we see in them contentment with what they have. All this relaxes the ties of solidarity, to a certain extent, and humility and submissiveness begin to appear in them; yet they still retain much of their pristine spirit because of what they have seen and remembered of the previous generation, with its self-confidence, pursuit of glory, and power to defend and protect itself. They cannot entirely give up all these characteristics, even though they have abandoned some of them. They still hope to regain the conditions prevailing in the previous generation, or even have the illusion that these virtues are still to be found in them.

As for the third generation, they have completely forgotten the nomadic and rough stage, as though it had never existed. They have also lost their love of power and their social solidarity through having been accustomed to being ruled. Luxury corrupts them, because of the pleasant and easy way of living in which they have been brought up. As a result, they become a liability on the state, like women and children who need to be protected. Solidarity is completely relaxed and the arts of defending oneself and of attacking the enemy are forgotten.

They deceive people by their insignia, dress, horse-riding and culture; yet all the while they are more cowardly than women. If then a claimant or aggressor appear, they are incapable of pushing him back. Consequently, the head of the state is compelled to rely on others for defense, making extensive use of clients and mercenaries, who may to some extent replace the original free warriors. . . .

8. Shah Abbas and Emperor Jahangir Debate the Persian Conquest of Kandahar (1622)*

U sing customary stylized and flowery language to describe the raw and brutal process of conquest, the Safavid Shah Abbas I (1571–1629) here informs his fellow monarch, Mughal emperor Jahangir (1569–1627), that Safavid forces

*From the *Jahangirnama: Memoirs of Jahangir, Emperor of India,* translated, edited, and annotated by Wheeler M. Thackston (Oxford, U.K., and New York: Oxford University Press, 1999), pp. 383–85. Notes deleted. Bracketed material added by the editors. By permission.

have taken the city of Kandahar in present-day Afghanistan. The Mughals in India and the Safavids in Persia had long fought over this city at the crossroads of Central Asian trade routes. Babur, the founder of the Mughal empire, had taken it in the sixteenth century. Jahangir, Babur's grandson, furious at the Persian conquest, had no choice at the time but to accept what had happened. Shut out of Central Asian trade through Kandahar, the Mughals turned instead to the sea, developed a powerful merchant marine, and expanded India's overseas commerce considerably, so what began as a catastrophe ended positively. Mughal India prospered under Jahangir's rule, but squabbles among his sons, who also attacked him, weakened the dynasty. Shah Abbas expanded Persian territory considerably, not only at Mughal expense but also in wars with the Ottomans, even temporarily taking the city of Baghdad.

Letter from the Shah of Persia

. . . It will have been reflected upon the knowledgeable heart and celestial mind of that brother as dear to me as life itself that during the events occurring in Iran after the inevitable death of His Highness the late Shah, certain territories departed from the control of those attached to this saintly family. When this supplicant at the divine court became occupied with affairs of state, all ancestral territories were wrenched from the hands of opponents with divine assistance and the good offices of friends. Since Kandahar was under the control of those appointed by your exalted dynasty, we considered them as our own and did not harass them, waiting for you to attend to the transference in a spirit of cooperativeness and brotherliness, like your mighty fathers and forefathers. When you neglected this, we repeatedly requested it by letter and message, by allusion and openly, thinking that perhaps in His Majesty's exalted view this miserable territory was not worth contending over and that he would order it given over to the representatives of this family, resulting in the elimination of the taunts of enemies and detractors and cutting-short the long tongues of the envious and fault-finders. This matter was put into abeyance, and when this was learned among friends and enemies and no reply either positive or negative was received from you, it occurred to us to take a hunting tour in Kandahar, thinking perhaps by this means my renowned brother's appointees, in view of the close and amicable relations that exist between us, would greet our retinue and meet us, and once again the firm foundations of amity on both sides would be apparent to the world and cause a cessation to the prattle of the envious and detractors. We set out on this tour without arms or armaments. When we reached the district of Farah . . . we dispatched an imperial rescript to the governor of that place informing him of our intention to make a hunting tour in Kandahar in order that he might receive us as guests. We . . . sent a message to the governor and *amirs* who were in the fortress, saying, "There is no difference between His Majesty the *Padishah* Shadow of God and our regal self. We consider any district that exists each other's. We are setting out in that direction on a tour. Let nothing be done that would cause consternation." Not hearing the contents of our conciliatory message truly and not maintaining the customs of friendship and unity, he exhibited contumacy. We arrived in the vicinity of the fortress and once again summoned the above-mentioned nobleman. Having said to him what advice had to be said, we sent him off and ordered our divinely assisted soldiers not to set foot near the fortress for ten days. Our advice profited not. They persisted in their opposition. Since it was impossible to have more forbearance than this, the *Qizilbash* [Turcoman nomadic] army, despite the lack of armaments, occupied itself with the subjugation of the fortress; and in a short period of time they had reduced towers and ramparts to the ground and brought the defenders to the point of asking for amnesty. Maintaining the connection of affection that has been observed from olden days between these two exalted lines and treading the path of brotherliness that was again so strongly reaffirmed in the days of that monarch's princehood between Your Majesty and our regal self that it was the object of jealousy of all rulers on the face of the earth, we pardoned their faults as required by innate manliness, enveloped them in favor, and sent them off to that exalted court. . . . Truly the basis of inherited and acquired amity and friendship on our part is too strong and firm to be damaged by the occurrence of some events . . . that happen by destiny. "Between us and thee there will be no custom of cruelty; there will be nothing but the path of love and fidelity." It is hoped that on your part too such pleasing conduct will be followed and that you will disregard certain trivial matters. If there has been any anxiety, please be so kind as to do away with it. Keep the garden of eternal spring of unity and concord green and fresh, and concentrate your exalted mind upon affirming the bases of agreement and concord, which maintain the harmony of persons and nations. Know that all our protected realm belongs to you, and kindly inform anyone you wish that it will be turned over to him without opposition. . . . More would be longwindedness. May your highly exalted banner be always and ever embraced by divine protection.

Reply from the Mughal Emperor

. . . That shah of Jamshedian might, whose army is like the stars, whose court is like the celestial sphere, who is worthy of the crown of the Chosroë's, scion of the Alavid house, offspring of the Safavid family, has, without provocation or cause, caused to wither the garden of amity, friendship, brotherliness, and unity, which should not have been clouded by the dust of contention until the end of time. Apparently the custom of unity and loyalty between rulers of the world used to be so firmly founded upon fraternal amity that they swore on each other's heads, and with such perfect spiritual intimacy and corporeal comradeship that a spirit could not come between them—much less territory or property. . . . "Alas for our unbounded love." The arrival of your amicable letter apologizing for "touring and hunting" in Kandahar . . . has assured us of the health of your angelic self. Roses of joy and glee have blossomed in the face of the auspicious age. May it not be hidden from the world-adorning mind of that exalted brother that until the arrival of your messenger . . . at this magnificent court no expression of a desire for Kandahar had ever been made. During the time we were occupied by a hunting tour of the happy vale of Kashmir, the temporal rulers of the Deccan shortsightedly stepped off the highway of obedience and subservience and took the path of rebellion. It was therefore incumbent upon our imperial mind to chastise the shortsighted, and the victory-emblazoned banners descended to the seat of the sultanate, Lahore; and we assigned our worthy son Shahjahan an invincible army to go against the wretches. . . . We were headed for the seat of the caliphate in Agra when Zaynal Beg arrived and delivered the friendly correspondence of that adorner of the royal throne. Taking that amulet of friendship as a good omen, we set out for the seat of the caliphate in Agra in order to repel the evil of enemies and wrongdoers. In that pearl-dripping letter no expression of a desire for Kandahar was made. Zaynal Beg expressed it orally. In reply we said, "We begrudge nothing to that brother. God willing, after completing the Deccan affair we shall grant you leave in a fashion befitting auspiciousness. Since you have traversed vast distances, rest a few days in Lahore from the travail of the road, for we shall summon you." After arriving in Agra, the seat of the caliphate, we summoned the aforementioned in order to grant him permission to depart. . . . [W]e set forth for the Punjab, our minds eased by victory, and were turning our attention to sending the aforementioned off. After certain necessary items of business were taken care of, we started because of the hot weather for Kashmir. . . . [w]e summoned Zaynal Beg to give him leave and to go with him and show him ourselves the delightful beauty spots of that pleasure garden one by one. At that point news arrived that that brother had come to conquer Kandahar—something that had never occurred to us. We were astonished. What could have caused him to go there himself in conquest, disregarding our friendship and brotherliness? Although the informants were reliable, we could not believe it. After the news was verified . . . we immediately ordered Abdul-Aziz Khan not to cross our brother, for the fraternal link was still strong, and we would not trade our degree of unity and loyalty for all the world. It would have been appropriate, given our friendship, to wait until the emissary arrived, for an amicable settlement of the claim might have been made. To have committed such an outrage before the emissary's arrival—upon whose shoulders will the people of the world lay the blame for breaking pacts and oaths and a breach of manliness and virtue? May God keep and preserve you at all times.

9. Suraiya Faroqhi, Ottoman Women's Lives (2000)*

A member of the Faculty for Cultural Sciences at the Institute for History and Culture in Munich, Germany, Professor Faroqhi knows the Ottoman archives well. Writing on peasants (from which we present a selection in Reading 11a), artisans, and women, she has produced a series of books, which describe in rich detail Ottoman daily life. Her most interesting finding in this selection on Ottoman women, based on inheritance records in *kadi* (*qadi*) courts conducted by religious judges, is that very few Anatolians practiced polygamy in the eighteenth and nineteenth centuries. Those who did lived at the upper aristocratic levels of society.

In Ottoman society it was rare for anyone to remain unmarried all their lives. Marriages were arranged by parents, although young men were sometimes able to escape such arrangements if they were not to their liking, by moving elsewhere. Young girls and women had fewer options. There are very few references in the *kadis'* registers to women who agreed to elope, and only slightly more to women who pleaded that they had been married as minors and now, having come of age, wished to dissolve the marriage. According to religious law it was possible for a Muslim man to marry a non-Muslim woman, although the opposite was not permitted and the children of "mixed" marriages were considered Muslims. Such marriages were quite common, particularly in frontier districts or in areas with a large non-Muslim population. . . .

Despite all the impediments, there are examples of Ottoman women who played an active part in representing the family interests even while their husbands were alive. We know of an action brought by a Christian woman who lived in a village near the central Anatolian town of Kayseri in the mid-eighteenth century. Her son-in-law had very probably murdered her daughter, and there was also a dispute regarding certain valuables. Whatever the facts of the matter, the plaintiff took the issue as far as Istanbul. Another case, involving a Muslim woman from a family of the central Anatolian élite, dates from the same period. In connection with some unfathomable affair, the woman's husband had been arrested and she as plaintiff campaigned actively for his release. Clearly, some energetic women did find opportunities to step out from the shadows of their male relatives. The ways in which they contrived to do this would be worth investigating in their own right.

---

*From Suraiya Faroqhi, *Subjects of the Sultan: Culture and Daily Life in the Ottoman Empire,* translated from the German by Martin Bott (London and New York: I. B. Tauris, 2000), pp. 102–4, 112–13. Notes omitted. By permission.

Recent studies of the Ottoman institution of marriage have shown how much the significance of polygamy had previously been overestimated. It is hard to provide figures, as we do not have a complete list of all the inhabitants of a town, both male and female, with appended information concerning their personal status. However, it is clear enough from the evidence of all the inheritance cases brought before the *kadi*, the records of which fill many pages in the registers, that polygamy was relatively uncommon. In the complete lists of heirs which form an important part of the relevant documents, there are few references to two wives, although widows were each entitled to a part of the inheritance and thus were bound to show up in the inheritance records. This finding has been confirmed so often that we must regard monogamy as the norm for the families of Anatolian townswomen.

Divorces were more frequent, and the husband could divorce his spouse unilaterally and without explanation at any time. We also know that some marriages were dissolved on the initiative of the woman. In such instances the husband would expect to be more or less handsomely remunerated for his consent. At the very least, any woman who desired divorce because (to use the official expression) "there is a lack of good understanding between us" would have to give up the financial benefits which normally would have accrued to her at the termination of her marriage. If the divorce were instigated by the husband, the wife had the right to a sum of money, agreed at the time of the marriage, and three months' alimony. Often, a woman seeking divorce would agree to pay her husband an additional sum of money. This form of separation was thus available only to affluent women.

In the early eighteenth century, polygamy was rather frowned upon among the well-to-do families of Istanbul described by Lady Mary Wortley Montagu (1689–1762). The wife of the English ambassador reported that the husband of one of her friends had recently taken a second wife. As a result, he lost his moral standing among his first wife's women friends and his first wife herself refused to allow him into her room. Such attitudes perhaps stem from the fact that many women of eminent families regarded the marriages of Ottoman princesses as their model. High officials who were offered the hand of a princess in marriage had to separate themselves from their previous partners, both wives and slaves. Their marriage to the princess would remain monogamous.

Attempts by eminent Ottoman ladies to impose monogamy on their husbands must have followed from the special circumstances of the eighteenth and early nineteenth centuries, when the princesses exercised a particularly strong influence on Istanbul high society. Exceptional cases apart, princesses had not possessed this standing in the sixteenth century, nor did they do so under the neo-absolutist regime of Sultan Abd ul-Hamid II ([r.] 1876–1909). A study of the institution of Istanbul marriage from 1880 onwards, based on quantitative data, has shown that, by this time, polygamy was virtually confined to palace society and to religious officials. It hardly existed among the merchants and artisans. Unlike ordinary townswomen, ladies of superior rank thus appear to have enjoyed only limited success in their attempts to impose monogamy. . . .

It must have been very difficult for young people from high-ranking families to meet potential partners from their own social class. Among the "ordinary" people in the towns, on the other hand, the cramped circumstances of their everyday lives doubtless created certain opportunities. Young people among the peasants and nomads could encounter one another more easily, at work in the fields, gardens or pastures.

In many areas, non-Muslim women dressed like the Muslims. Whether or not they left their face uncovered depended on the area and sometimes on the individual's status in life.

Unmarried women who lived alone were rare in Ottoman towns. However, widows quite often chose not to enter the household of a male relative. In the Balkan provinces in particular, Ottoman tax regulations accorded a special status to a woman managing her deceased husband's farm. In the central Anatolian trading town of Tokat as well, around 1640 there were many households for which the tax collectors entered the name of a woman. They, too, must therefore have been recognized as the heads of their households. A widow received only a small part of her husband's estate, the lion's share going to the children of the deceased. On marrying, the husband had to pledge to his wife a sum of money in the event that he divorced or predeceased her, which in the case of death, had to be paid before the rest of the estate could be divided. Careful husbands or fathers sometimes gave money to their wives or daughters during their own lifetimes, or nominated them as administrators of a family foundation from which they then drew a salary. However, even these incomes were often insufficient and many widows probably sought to remarry as quickly as possible. If this were not possible and there were children to care for, the woman would have to find some way of earning money.

There were limited opportunities available. Things were easiest for the woman who had a cash sum which she could lend or otherwise invest. Some women, no doubt from merchant backgrounds, even became involved in trade. Some invested their money as "silent partners." This could be done via the partnership contracts known as *mudaraba,* which involved the silent partner entrusting her money to a traveling merchant. . . . Women trading on a smaller scale were more common, supplying affluent women with textiles and jewelry, as well as bringing with them the latest news. . . .

There was little chance of a widow who had to support herself finding a position as a servant in a well-to-do household, because many affluent women possessed slaves. Often acquired while still very young, these girls would eventually be granted their freedom and allowed to marry. Another factor was a custom which persisted until the early twentieth century and which in Ankara can be traced back as far as the sixteenth. A poor family would send a daughter to become a servant in a wealthy household when she was still a young girl. There she would be brought up and supported while carrying out duties which varied according to her age. When she was ready to marry, the family which employed her would provide her dowry. At the beginning of her service it would have been agreed whether her parents or the family for which she worked were to select her husband. In most cases this agreement seems to have been an oral one, but occasionally it would be entered in the *kadi*'s register.

Adult women who needed to earn money, and who did not have enough capital to become small-scale traders, thus had to resort to manual work. As in many parts of early modern Europe, women were not generally admitted to guilds, and this made it even harder for them to gain a foothold in such a trade. However, it is noticeable that many of the looms on which mohair was woven in Ankara during the seventeenth century were located in homes rather than in workshops. It seems likely that in such cases the craftsman's wife would, as a member of his family, assist him in his work, if she were not a weaver herself. Women, some of whom were in the pay of a merchant, were engaged above all in spinning mohair yarn.

Chapter III

Contradictions of Modernity: Imperialism and Social Change

Introduction

During the nineteenth century the Ottoman and Qajar states introduced parliamentary systems, upgraded their administrative structures, and expanded their military forces. These reforms strengthened their abilities to remain independent of European control while allowing them to mobilize their populations to join in the processes of global commercialization then under way. The reforms also responded to and stimulated further demand for increased popular participation in public life—as happened in Europe and America at the same time.

Regions that had fallen under imperial domination, such as India and parts of the Maghreb, however, entered the modern world in a much different way—as colonial dependencies. Czarist Russian conquests dismantled traditional Muslim states in Central Asia and put them under central imperial control. As the Russian regime itself began participating in the world capitalist system, and as railroads extended into Turkestan and the Kazakh regions, state officials and local entrepreneurs pulled these areas into a wider commercial network. They turned lambskins, wool, silk, and carpets into desirable export products; encouraged cotton production; and settled nomads on agricultural lands. While Russian merchants and government bureaucrats may have profited from these changes, the peasantry and local artisans remained poor. Whatever the region and whoever ruled, the contradictions of modernity stood out starkly—wealth for those who controlled land and the networks of trade, poverty and degradation for others.

Limits of Change in the Muslim World

The changes that took place in nineteenth-century Muslim societies, such as the granting of rights to subjects (see the Ottoman *Tanzimat* decrees, Reading 10), the initiation of land reform, and administrative and military upgrading, did not substantially change the processes of handicraft production. Few businesses adopted industrial machinery (see Reading 11c). Artisans continued to produce consumer goods in traditional ways, and local private investors tended to put their money into urban and rural real estate rather than into industry. Those people living under colonial rule most often found themselves locked out of the global race for industrial wealth and power in the nineteenth century.

Earlier, Europeans had taken over the East Indies, Central Asia, and Mughal India, as we indicated in Chapter II. Algeria, in Ottoman North Africa, a major Muslim territory taken over by France in 1830, is something of a special case.

The French promoted the fiction that it was not a colony at all, but an integral part of metropolitan France. French agricultural entrepreneurs soon arrived and imported large quantities of tractors and other farm machinery, making production on their large holdings among the most modern in the world of that period. As happened elsewhere, most Algerian landholders and day laborers benefited little from these transformations.

Not until the twentieth century did riches come to the Middle East in the form of revenues from the new petroleum industry, as Chapter VI shows. But this wealth, accumulating slowly at first, resulted from initiatives from outside the region and did not lead to sustained development, except for the oil sector. Such Islamic states as the Ottoman and Mughal empires had expanded by creating vast land-based dominions, which had greater fixed costs than the European seaborne empires. To sustain their agricultural and commercial wealth, these Muslim states required massive, expensive administrative and fiscal structures. Not only did they find it time-consuming and necessary to construct complex administrative systems to collect taxes from agricultural producers and long-distance traders, they also had to maintain huge armed forces to defend their far-flung territories. By the late eighteenth and early nineteenth centuries these costs had become onerous, especially for the besieged Ottomans.

Muhammad Ali, His Successors in Egypt, and the Suez Canal

Egypt presents an instructive case study of how Western, in particular British, interests restricted economic and social change. In Chapter II we mentioned Napoleon Bonaparte's initially successful 1798 invasion of Egypt and Syria, which were then provinces of the Ottoman empire. The Ottomans and the British defeated this French expedition, causing Napoleon to abandon his army and return to France. Muhammad Ali (1769–1849), an experienced and successful Albanian military officer, then arrived in Egypt as Ottoman commander of a brigade of fellow Albanian soldiers and proceeded to subdue the French soldiers left behind. He also reorganized the Mamluk armed forces whom the French had just trounced. Recognizing his success in both these tasks, the sultan appointed him governor of Egypt. In that position, Muhammad Ali initiated the most energetic attempt at state-sponsored industrialization of any Islamic region up to that time. He also transformed the military and introduced educational reform for his officer corps. Muhammad Ali carried out these changes in a highly authoritarian, mercantilist manner.

He began by importing Western technology and advisers who trained Egyptians in the professional and technological skills needed to industrialize the country and revamp the military. This ambitious domestic program of economic and military reform attracted the attention of the Ottoman sultan who sent Muhammad Ali to subdue dissidents in Arabia and the Sudan. But when he exceeded these orders and moved troops into Syria he no longer acted as an underling but as a rival of the sultan. British political leaders at the time did not wish to see Ottoman power undermined, nor did they want to face Egyptian industrial competition. The British therefore backed the Ottoman ruler by using military force against Muhammad Ali. Along with Ottoman forces, they defeated Muhammad Ali's armies and navy, as well as his ambitious plans. (Fifteen years later, during the Crimean War [1853–56], the British, then acting in conjunction with the French, would again prop up the Ottoman empire.) Europeans preferred weak states with their economic role limited to producing grain and raw materials to feed and clothe Europeans and supply their manufacturing enterprises. Backed by Great Britain, the sultan granted Muhammad Ali and his progeny hereditary rule in Egypt in order to curb any of his and his dynasty's future territorial and industrial ambitions.

At this juncture geography—the mere 100 miles of Egyptian territory separating the Red Sea from the Mediterranean—became destiny. Ferdinand de Lesseps (1805–94), a French diplomat who had served in Egypt, dreamed of building a canal through Suez, and his friendship with one of Muhammad Ali's sons assured him of receiving the concession. Its unequal terms, typical of agreements between Europeans and nonindustrialized states, greatly favored the Suez Canal Maritime Company, requiring that Egypt supply the labor and most of the capital for constructing the canal.

On the basis of glowing prospects, Muhammad Ali's successors obtained huge loans from European banks. By the time the canal opened in 1869, the Egyptians had paid the bulk of the construction costs: £11.5 million of the total £16 million. To pay back the loans, Muhammad Ali's grandson Ismail Pasha (1830–95), who had presided over the brief Egyptian cotton boom brought about by the American Civil War, sold his shares in the Suez Canal Company to the British government in 1875. Because of ballooning debts, Egypt could not draw any of the promised royalties until a half century later. Many Egyptians believed that the Europeans had swindled them.

In order to raise money—much of which went into Egypt's new and expensive mass educational programs, modeled on European schools—Ismail continued to borrow large sums at inflated rates. In 1876 Egypt defaulted on its debt in the same year the Ottoman government did. Ismail now had to place the country's finances in the hands of a joint British-French Debt Commission. Loss of economic autonomy quickly led to diminution of political authority. When Ismail attempted to dismiss a few of the debt commissioners in order to regain control over Egypt's finances, the European powers forced the sultan to remove him.

A popular uprising followed Ismail's ouster and the installation of his more pliant son, Tawfiq Pasha (1852–92). Led by army colonel Ahmad Urabi Pasha (1839–1911), one of the few Egyptian officers of peasant ancestry, the insurgents demanded a constitution, a diminution of the ruler's power, and restoration of Egypt's right to determine its own spending and budget priorities. The peasantry saw Urabi as the leader to free them from the immense burden of taxation, and he also won backing from the army and a group of reformist notables.

Fearing an intensification of the uprising, the British responded in 1882 with a classic exercise of gunboat diplomacy: the shelling of the seacoast city of Alexandria by an offshore naval squadron, followed by a military occupation of the Canal Zone. Claiming that they would soon withdraw, the British stayed for seventy-four years. For trying to defend his country against British conquest, Colonel Urabi suffered exile for life, but his struggle did not cease. As we show in Chapters IV and VII, Egyptians in the early years of the next century sought constitutional government and organized mass movements to demand independence.

The West's Advantages

The Muslim world lacked anything comparable to the vast wealth that flowed into Europe from their seaborne empires in Africa, the Americas, and South and East Asia. These riches had helped finance the initial entry of the Portuguese, Dutch, and Spanish into the 4,000-mile-wide Indian Ocean trading system, where the British and French later became dominant. Prior to 1500, Middle Eastern, Indian, Indonesian, and Malaysian merchants had been the main intermediaries in this flourishing Euro-Asian trade. But, as we have shown at the end of the introduction to Chapter II, Muslim merchants had succeeded in circumventing European blockades as well as in breaking commercial monopolies. These same investors and entrepreneurs, however, found insuperable obstacles to establishing modern factory production. Since Europeans controlled access to industrial technologies (limiting availability to potential competitors, as they did with Muhammad Ali), they did not allow most technically weaker countries to make use of them.

The fortunes of the Muslim world and the industrializing nations dramatically diverged during the nineteenth century. Reaping the benefits of strong state structures and much earlier scientific and commercial revolutions, the West created the social, technological, and financial conditions for the industrial revolution that transformed people's lives all over the globe. The Muslim world, with its extensive land-based resources, well-developed local and international trade networks, and booty from territorial conquest, had flourished for centuries because these three main sources of wealth allowed most Islamic states to keep taxes relatively low.

The Mughal empire deviated from this practice. Their fiscal agents collected enormous revenues from the large rural population of India, which they controlled. With these revenues they created a huge bureaucracy whose members enjoyed high incomes. As a result, the empire hummed with handicraft industries, which provided ample goods for both domestic administrators and foreign markets. With very low labor costs, the Mughals had few incentives to industrialize. Over time even this wealthy Muslim empire found itself lagging behind the European countries already embarked on their industrial transformations.

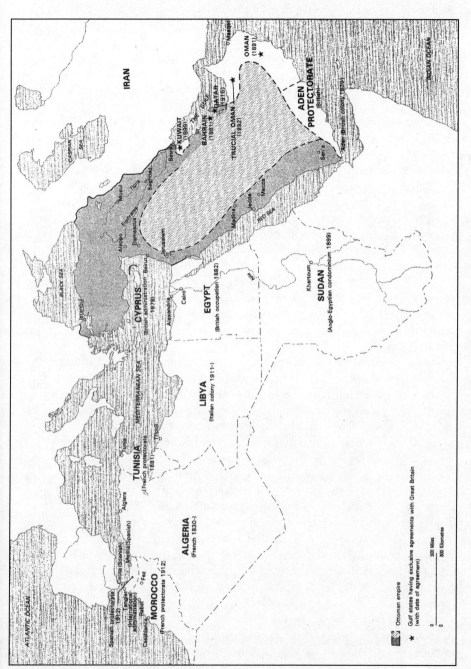

Expansion of European Empires before 1914

By the late eighteenth century Middle Easterners began noticing and responding to the effects of this divergence. In the leading industrial and commercial
nation, Great Britain, the regimentation of the factory system permeated society, including the military. Precision weapons, disciplined soldiers, and better
military training gave the Europeans crucial advantages as they began taking
over Muslim lands. By 1757 the British began their conquest of Mughal
India, and later in the century Russian empress Catherine the Great (1729–
96) seized the Crimea from the Turks, expelling large numbers of Crimean
Tartars into Ottoman domains. In the nineteenth century her descendants
seized such formerly Persian territories as Georgia and Baku lying between
the Black and Caspian seas.

Rulers who maintained sprawling, multiethnic, independent states remained
on the defensive, guarding shrinking territory. For example, when the Ottomans had to quit the Balkans during the nineteenth and early twentieth centuries after a series of costly wars, they lost some of the most prosperous regions
of their empire, where they had invested heavily in regional markets and artisanal
workshops. To compensate for such catastrophic losses and to meet rising
expenses, they and other Muslim rulers had to raise revenues by borrowing
from European bankers and granting foreigners concessions to develop natural
resources in return for large payments and promises of future royalties. Most
sovereigns also had to increase taxes just to stay afloat. Defensive expenditures on military modernization, reform, and foreign advisers demanded ever-
expanding revenues.

European pursuit of free trade and open markets, aggressively applied to the
Muslim world and other regions of the globe, tied increasing numbers of agriculturalists and merchants to the world economy, initially bringing them new
prosperity. Yet crises overseas, such as great economic depressions and stock
market crashes, now also brought havoc to a wider circle of Muslims participating in a worldwide system, which they no longer controlled. Locally, when droughts
hit, Muslim rulers no longer had the capacity to prevent European commercial agents from exporting local food grains. Open door treaties imposed by
European powers in the 1820s and 1830s had fixed tariffs at artificially low rates.
This made it difficult, if not impossible, for sultans and shahs to raise export
tariffs precipitously and thereby stop scarce wheat and other cereals from leaving
their ports. Western as well as Muslim sovereigns had to feed their populations during droughts, so these heads of state had to import foodstuffs to compensate for the shortfalls at much higher prices than the cost on local markets.
When tax collectors demanded higher revenues to pay for such calamities—as
well as needed reforms to counter foreign intrusion—they often provoked rebellions, which had to be put down by military forces at great expense, leading
to further spiraling costs and social dislocation.

Unequal competition took place on the political as well as on the economic
level. As European power extended into the Islamic world and also into other
areas of the world, extraterritoriality (granting of legal privileges to foreigners

and their local agents) became one of the ways in which that power found expression. Ottoman sultans and other monarchs had concluded agreements called capitulations with some of the mercantile Italian city-states and European kings in the fifteenth century. Such agreements allowed representatives from these countries to reside in their territory and to settle disputes involving Europeans on the basis of European legal principles. Over time these capitulations became a series of entering wedges by which the West extended its economic and political domination of regions that fell into the orbit of one or another European empire. And when nationalism arose among those dominated peoples, the capitulations provided targets for resentment, as did the displays of power and authority by Europeans and their local agents.

The Ottomans Try Reform

By 1839 many, but not all, Ottoman subjects sensed they were falling behind in a race with the West. The need to call on British assistance in dealing with Muhammad Ali the year before overcame the conservative opposition within the empire. The brutal 1826 massacre of the *Janissary* corps on orders of Sultan Mahmud II (1785–1839) removed a major obstacle to change. With them out of the way, the Ottoman army could establish new, more efficient infantry units and its officers could receive training in modern weaponry. But the destruction of the *Janissaries* also had a downside: no other group could play their role as spokesmen for the discontented artisans and the lower-level *ulema* hurt by the reform policies. Without them, no comparable powerful voice existed capable of articulating widespread grievances, including those against reform policies that in the popular imagination seemed to mimic the West and undermine traditional values.

The main reform efforts centered about the complex package of civil, economic, educational, and political decrees issued between 1839 and 1876 known as the *Tanzimat,* or reordering. Brought about by Ottoman bureaucrats familiar with developments in the West, the *Tanzimat* reforms aimed at creating a centralized Ottoman administration complete with a Council of Ministers and an agency to promote justice. Assuring the upper echelons of the *ulema* that they would have a place in the new order and that their sons could attend the new schools to train administrators and professionals gave the reform cause powerful allies. The reform decrees proclaimed the inviolability of subjects' lives and the protection of their property. The *Tanzimat* reformers also regularized tax assessments and collections, secured land titles, revamped the courts, and removed some of the arbitrariness in the conscription of soldiers. (We present two of the most important of these decrees in Reading 10.)

The *Tanzimat* land reform of 1858 deserves close attention. As Suraiya Faroqhi shows in Reading 11a, before the land reform peasants enjoyed hereditary tenure on vacant state lands, the availability of which made it possible for previously landless youth and ambitious peasants to relocate and establish rights over the unclaimed tracts, but they did not own the land on which they worked. Under the new law the state distributed small plots to landless rural dwellers in Anatolia, a policy not implemented in outlying provinces. Urban notables and rural gentry in the Fertile Crescent circumvented the intent of these reforms by bribing imperial officials to obtain vast agricultural estates. The land received by rural dwellers in Anatolia helps explain the determination with which their descendants fought off Greek invaders eager to gain territory from the defeated Ottoman empire after World War I, which we discuss in Chapter IV.

The new 1876 Ottoman constitution brought the *Tanzimat* to its climax, but two years later this experiment in expanded participation in government came to a screeching halt. The autocratic Sultan Abd al-Hamid II (1842–1918) suspended the constitution but continued certain reforms in a highly dictatorial manner. Construction of telegraph and railroad lines more closely linked parts of the shrinking, but still far-flung, empire. Education became more widely available and newspaper and book publishing expanded dramatically, though government censors restricted the content of courses and publications. Professional schools offered training for prospective lawyers, physicians, and teachers while military academies employed Prussian instructors to teach the arts of war. And wars continued to drive Ottoman power from the Balkans as Bosnia, Serbia, Montenegro, Romania, Cyprus, and part of Bulgaria became severed from the empire. These defeats, combined with local uprisings and the ongoing debt crisis, impelled the sultan to clamp down at home and to align himself internationally with Imperial Germany. As Chapter IV shows, the Ottoman empire joined the central European alliance of Germany and the Austro-Hungarian empire when war broke out in 1914.

Young Ottomans and Young Turks

Although the Ottomans lost territory during the waning years of the *Tanzimat,* they still ruled over a multiethnic and a religiously diverse empire. The "Young Ottomans," a group of intellectuals led by journalists, advocated breaking down the religiously based *millets* (discussed in the introduction to Chapter II) and bringing all citizens under direct state control. Opposed to authoritarianism and convinced of the benefits of Islamic culture (in its broadest, most inclusive form) as a potential unifier of diverse people, these reformers believed that such liberal institutions and practices as parliaments and constitutions, and extending rights to all citizens, would give people a stake in keeping the empire alive and prosperous.

The Balkan war of 1878 pulled the Ottoman empire toward greater state control and more autocratic rule, since trying to win the wars entailed massive mobilization of resources and men. War usually has the nefarious effect of silencing domestic opposition. So it did in the Ottoman empire when Sultan Abd al-Hamid II ended constitutional rule in 1878 and reverted to tried and tested authoritarianism.

A generation later both Western-trained army officers and young professionals trained in new schools, calling themselves "Young Turks," overthrew the sultan and made all subsequent Ottoman rulers follow their orders. Mustafa Kemal (1881–1938), who joined this movement, would soon become the founder of the new state, Turkey, that emerged after the Ottoman empire's demise following World War I. The pressures of the last Balkan War of 1912 and the Great War of 1914–18 brought to power those Young Turks who favored centralizing and Turkifying what remained of the empire, thereby alienating many Arabs who before this had shared power with the Turks in governing the empire. Some of these Arabs, such as the *Sharif* Husayn of Arabia, whose ambitions we examine in Chapter IV, sought alliances with the British to fulfill their own dynastic ambitions; others began formulating plans for creating a future unified state. The postwar League of Nations mandate system, which allocated Arab territory to Britain and France, created new states that conflicted with the aspirations of these Arab nationalists.

Persia under the Qajar Dynasty

During its 130-year existence, the Qajar state (1794–1925) experienced humiliating treatment at the hands of the Russians and the British. Trying to play off one power against the other, Qajar shahs (kings) handed out lucrative concessions to various Western businessmen and agreed to capitulation agreements like those the Ottomans had arranged with European states. Popular outcries against domination by the West reached near-revolutionary levels in the 1890s, when one Qajar ruler gave a monopoly on tobacco sales to a British financier that seemed particularly disadvantageous to Iran, and then had to cancel the concession a short time later. The successful tobacco boycott showed what an aggrieved populace backed by energized *ulema* could do. But the underlying problems remained: crippling debt, encroachment by the Russians and British, and inept and oppressive royal administration. Iran and neighboring Afghanistan (and other regions as well) found themselves caught in European rivalries played out in the Middle East, Central Asia, and South Asia. The British sought to safeguard India and obtain commercial advantages wherever possible, and the czarist Russian government attempted to gain a warm-water outlet to the Mediterranean Sea and consolidate its hold over Central Asia.

During the brief interlude between the fall of the Safavids (1722) and the rise of the Qajar dynasty in 1794, those *ulema* who remained in Persia and had not fled to *Shiite* communities in Iraq demonstrated their independence from the state. When Qajar rulers took over they could not deprive these *ulema* of the control they exercised over religious and charitable endowments, which brought them close to the basic needs of the population. Thus, the *ulema* strengthened their positions in Persia and remained a force with which the state authorities had to reckon through the end of the nineteenth century. In the Ottoman empire the situation differed greatly: the state had nationalized many religious establishments, thereby weakening the *ulema* and reducing their independence before the twentieth-century attainment of Turkey's national independence, in which the *ulema* played little role.

By the early twentieth century the Qajar shah granted his subjects a constitution with a consultative assembly, the *majlis,* but these internal reforms could not guarantee genuine independence. In 1907 the British and Russians formalized their long-standing agreement to divide Iran into "spheres of influence," the Russians in the north, the British in the south. The dynasty's days were numbered. Shortly after World War I a Persian military officer took power, ousted the Qajars, and established a new dynasty, the Pahlevi. (In Chapter IV we discuss other aspects of this 1907 Anglo-Russian Entente relating to Afghanistan.) The new ruler, Reza Khan (c. 1878–1944), changed the country's name to Iran, signifying the land of the Aryans, its pre-Islamic conquerors. This signaled the new shah's intention to weaken the hold of Islam in his kingdom. In subsequent sections we discuss later developments in Iran.

The British *Raj* Supplants the Mughal Empire

Farther east the Muslim Mughal empire ruled an overwhelmingly Hindu population, out of whose agricultural and handicraft labor came the legendary wealth controlled by imperial officials. But many Hindu untouchables, outcasts in their own society, converted to Islam to seek opportunities not permitted by caste restrictions. Thus the Muslim population of India grew both through conquest and by promising freedom from caste restraints, creating a polyglot civilization that managed to survive and flourish despite major cultural and social differences among its inhabitants. The arrival of Europeans disrupted the equilibrium between diverse communities, since the newcomers sought local support in order to establish footholds and commercial positions in the Indian Ocean region and threw their weight behind their respective Indian supporters. Each European power had its favorite allies and used them to enhance influence and weaken their competitors.

The British *Raj* evolved from the British East India Company, founded in 1600 to challenge the aggressive Dutch trade monopoly in the East Indies. After the British failed to dislodge the Dutch from their bases in Southeast Asia, the company concentrated its efforts on gaining profitable trade concessions in Mughal India. The resulting wars for domination of India, especially the battles between the British and the French, exacerbated traditional local rivalries. They also became deadlier than ever before because the newcomers added new, efficient guns and imposed discipline on local troops who joined their militias.

The impressive scale of British imperial rule matched that of the Mughals. Like the forts, monuments, and mosques built by Mughal emperors, imposing British public buildings in New Delhi, Lahore, Bombay, Calcutta, and other urban centers symbolized the power that lay behind the new system of British control. Ruling through Indian administrators and princes, the British collected substantial taxes from the population and recruited plentiful and cheap labor and soldiers for new agricultural and industrial projects and their military. Indian soldiers became the mainstay of overseas wars and police operations. Many of them saw action in the Middle East and in Europe during the twentieth century's world wars. The high level of exploitation, and the favoritism shown to Hindus over Muslims by the British, provoked early resistance from the subject peoples. After the Sepoy mutiny in 1857, when Indian soldiers serving Britain rebelled, the British government assumed direct control over India and ended the Mughal dynasty.

Widespread dissatisfaction with colonial rule affected not only India but also other areas under European control. Nationalists in late-nineteenth- and early-twentieth-century Egypt organized mass demonstrations in favor of independence, and in the French colonies of Southeast Asia and North Africa rebellions also simmered. Discontent in India gave rise to a modern Indian nationalist movement whose leaders tried to convince the British to grant self-government. But the colonial authorities showed no inclination to make any more than minor concessions. Partly in recognition of the many Indians who had served in the British army in World War I, the London government enacted the Government of India Act in 1919, which established an Indian parliament with authority over sanitation, education, and agriculture. Other, more important matters such as control of the military remained in the hands of British officials. Earlier that same year a British general ordered his troops to fire on an unarmed gathering of Indian nationalists protesting the act in the northern Indian city of Amritsar, killing hundreds.

The Amritsar massacre marks a turning point. Masses of Indians, outraged at the killings and generally angered by British colonial policies, now had a leader in Mohandas K. Gandhi (1869–1948), who had just returned from the British colony of South Africa where he had developed a strategy of dramatic nonviolent resistance to oppression. Calling this new strategy *satyagraha* (holding to the truth), he joined forces with other nationalists in the Indian National Congress, which he dominated in the 1920s. Gandhi promoted boycotts of British manufactured goods and organized campaigns of civil disobedience involving millions of followers. However, as we show in Chapter IV, Indian Muslims, fearing minority status in an independent India, opted for a separate Muslim state.

The Coming World Wars

Britain remained the overlord of the Arab Middle East until after World War II, but did not contest czarist Russia's territorial aims in Central Asia. In Persia the shared Russo-British sphere of interest remained in force at least through World War I. But after its defeat in the 1905 war with Japan, Russia withdrew from the rivalry for Afghanistan, but opposed outright British occupation of its territory. Thus, the British and Russians formally agreed to a "protectorate" over Afghanistan, which did not impinge on the interests of either power. In accordance with imperialist power politics of the day, neither Britain nor Russia consulted with the Afghans or Persians when disposing of their territory. When he learned about it, Amir Amanullah (1898–1960), Afghanistan's ruler, tried to prevent the establishment of a protectorate over his domains and provoked a confrontation with the British. Fearful of again getting embroiled in another war there, the British acknowledged Afghanistan's independence in 1919, and that country joined the League of Nations. But Aminullah's plans to carry out reforms in Afghanistan (see Reading 15a) alienated his more conservative countrymen, who forced him to abdicate and flee. Afghanistan reverted to its tribal ways for another generation.

Thus, the British and czarist Russians had resolved their differences over the Muslim East by the early twentieth century. A parallel set of imperial rivalries that nearly brought France and Great Britain to war over their competing claims in Africa was settled amicably, and an alliance system (the *Entente*) was formed, binding Russia, France, and Britain together in opposition to newly developed German power and its own expansionist aims. When war broke out in 1914, the Ottoman and Austro-Hungarian empires joined Germany. Later the United States joined the *Entente* in World War I. The outcome of that war brought defeat for Germany and destruction of the two empires allied with it. In addition, the czarist Russian empire (on the *Entente* side) was overthrown by its internal enemies and did not survive the war. We deal with this great conflict and its aftermath in Muslim lands in Chapter IV.

10. Decrees from the Ottoman *Tanzimat*

The nineteenth-century Ottoman reform movement, known as the *Tanzimat* (reordering), drew on both traditional Muslim critiques of political authority and ideals of the European enlightenment. It also grew out of previous efforts by Ottoman officials to centralize state institutions and create a modern army. Although the British exerted great diplomatic pressure on the Ottomans to institute the legal reforms associated with the *Tanzimat,* many farseeing Ottoman subjects also welcomed the opportunity to undertake this administrative reorganization and to check the unbridled powers of the monarchy. Rather than simply an effort to appease European powers, concern for human rights prompted Ottoman statesmen to draft the documents presented here.

Major changes followed as part of this fundamental reform movement. The framers of the *Tanzimat* introduced new penal, maritime, and commercial codes;

abolished slavery and torture; attempted to institute a new tax system; created a nondenominational, secular judicial system; reorganized the provincial administration; and formed a streamlined military officer corps to lead a new conscript army. Wide-ranging social legislation and programs addressed problems of land tenure, communications, industry, public health, and primary schools for boys and, later, for girls. Higher education also got a boost. Supported by intellectuals and a lively press, as we describe in Chapters IV and VII, the foundation of representative legislative bodies at the central and provincial levels culminated in 1876 with the declaration of a constitutional monarchy and the transfer of powers to a parliament. However, Sultan Abd al-Hamid II, sensing Europe's heightened threat to Ottoman stability, shut down parliament and suppressed the constitution, ushering in three decades of continued autocracy. Despite this, educational and military reform continued in Ottoman domains.

A. The *Gulhane* Proclamation (1839)*

This proclamation, the opening paragraphs of which we present here, signed in the Rose Chamber (*Gulhane*) of the sultan's palace, committed the Ottoman monarchy to put all the state's efforts into transforming the empire's political and social order. Although written in terms of past practices, it set the tone for future progressive political reforms. In an age when slaves or bonded laborers worked the plantations of the Americas, this proclamation guaranteed equal rights before the law for all persons regardless of ethnicity or creed. Following the examples of the French and American revolutions, the proclamation set forth the principles that allowed effective executive and legislative power to pass from the monarch to the bureaucracy and representative bodies.

All the world knows that in the first days of the Ottoman Monarchy, the glorious precepts of the Koran and the Laws of the Empire were always honored. The Empire in consequence increased in strength and greatness, and all her subjects, without exception, had risen in the highest degree to ease and prosperity. In the last 150 years a succession of accidents and divers causes have arisen which have brought about a disregard for the sacred code of Laws, and the Regulations flowing therefrom, and the former strength and prosperity have changed into weakness and poverty; an Empire in fact loses all its stability so soon as it ceases to observe its Laws.

These considerations are ever present to our mind, and, ever since the day of our advent to the Throne, the thought of the public weal, of the improvement of the state of the Provinces, and of relief to the peoples, has not ceased to engage

*From Edward Herslet, *The Map of Europe by Treaty*, 4 vols. (London: Butterworth, 1875–1891), vol. II, pp. 1002–5. American spellings adopted.

it. If, therefore, the geographical position of the Ottoman Provinces, the fertility of the soil, the aptitude and intelligence of the inhabitants are considered, the conviction will remain that, by striving to find efficacious means, the result, which by the help of God we hope to attain, can be obtained within a few years. Full of confidence, therefore, in the help of the Most High, assisted by the intercession of our Prophet, we deem it right to seek by new institutions to give to the Provinces composing the Ottoman Empire the benefit of a good Administration.

These institutions must be principally carried out under three heads, which are:

1. The guarantees insuring to our subjects perfect security for life, honor, and fortune.
2. A regular system of assessing and levying Taxes.
3. An equally regular system for the levy of Troops and the duration of their service.

From henceforth, therefore, the cause of every accused person shall be publicly judged in accordance with our Divine Law, after inquiry and examination, and so long as a regular judgment shall not have been pronounced, no one can, secretly or publicly, put another to death by poison or in any other manner.

No one shall be allowed to attack the honor of any other person whatsoever.

Each one shall possess his Property of every kind, and shall dispose of it in all freedom, without let or hindrance from any person whatever; thus, for example, the innocent Heirs of a Criminal shall not be deprived of their legal rights, and the Property of the Criminal shall not be confiscated.

These Imperial concessions shall extend to all our subjects, of whatever Religion or sect they may be; they shall enjoy them without exceptions. We therefore grant perfect security to the inhabitants of our Empire, in their lives, their honor, and their fortunes, as they are secured to them by the sacred text of our Law.

As all the Public Servants of the Empire receive a suitable salary, and that the salaries of those whose duties have not, up to the present time, been sufficiently remunerated, are to be fixed, a rigorous Law shall be passed against the traffic of favoritism and of appointments (*richvet*), which the Divine Law reprobates, and which is one of the principal causes of the decay of the Empire.

B. An Ottoman "Bill of Rights" (1856)*

> Often thought of as a sop to European negotiators who worked out the text of the Treaty of Paris ending the Crimean War (1853–56), this *Hatt-i Humayan* (Imperial Edict) constitutes another part of the *Tanzimat*'s Bill of Rights. Reaf-

---

*From Edward Herslet, *The Map of Europe by Treaty,* 4 vols. (London: Butterworth, 1875–1891), vol. II, pp. 1243–49. American spellings adopted. Bracketed and italicized material added by the editors.

firming the principles of the *Gulhane* decree of 1839, this act demonstrated clearly the willingness of the Ottoman state to embrace its non-Muslim populations as full citizens. Besides reorganizing and democratizing Jewish and Christian community organizations, non-Muslims could serve on the Ottoman Council of State, which reviewed the most important affairs of the realm, and as judges of the Supreme Court.

It being now my [the sultan's] desire to renew and enlarge still more the new Institutions ordained with the view of establishing a state of things conformable with the dignity of my Empire and . . . by the kind and friendly assistance of the Great Powers, my noble Allies, . . . The guarantees promised on our part by the Hatt-i Humayan of Gulhane, . . . are today confirmed and consolidated, and efficacious measures shall be taken in order that they may have their full and entire effect.

All the Privileges and Spiritual Immunities granted by my ancestors . . . , and at subsequent dates, to all Christian communities or other non-Muslim persuasion established in my Empire under my protection, shall be confirmed and maintained.

Every Christian or other non-Muslim community shall be bound . . . to examine into its actual Immunities and Privileges, and to discuss and submit to my Sublime Porte [the Ottoman government] the Reforms required by the progress of civilization and of the age. . . . The ecclesiastical dues, of whatever sort or nature they be, shall be abolished and replaced by fixed revenues of the [Orthodox Christian] Patriarchs and heads of communities. . . . In the towns, small boroughs, and villages, where the whole population is of the same Religion, no obstacle shall be offered to the repair, according to their original plan, of buildings set apart for Religious Worship, for Schools, for Hospitals, and for Cemeteries.

Every distinction or designation tending to make any class whatever of the subjects of my Empire inferior to another class, on account of their Religion, Language, or Race, shall be for ever effaced from the Administrative Protocol.

As all forms of Religion are and shall be freely professed in my dominions, no subject of my Empire shall be hindered in the exercise of the Religion that he professes. . . . No one shall be compelled to change their Religion . . . and . . . all the subjects of my Empire, without distinction of nationality, shall be admissible to public employments. . . . All the subjects of my Empire, without distinction, shall be received into the Civil and Military Schools of the Government. . . . Moreover, every community is authorized to establish Public Schools of Science, Art, and Industry.

All Commercial, Correctional, and Criminal Suits between Muslims and Christians or other non-Muslim subjects, or between Christians or other non-Muslims of different sects, shall be referred to Mixed Tribunals. The proceedings of these Tribunals shall be public: the parties shall be confronted, and shall produce their witnesses, whose testimony shall be received, without distinction, upon oath taken according to the religious law of each sect.

The organization of the Police . . . shall be revised in such a manner as to give to all the peaceable subjects of my Empire the strongest guarantees for the safety both of their persons and property. . . . Christian subjects, and those of other non-Muslim sects, . . . shall, as well as Muslims, be subject to the obligations of the Law of Recruitment. The principle of obtaining substitutes, or of purchasing exemption, shall be admitted.

Proceedings shall be taken for a Reform in the Constitution of the Provincial and Communal Councils, in order the ensure fairness in the choice of the Deputies of the Muslim, Christian, and other communities, and freedom of voting in the Councils.

As the Laws regulating the purchase, sale, and disposal of Real Property are common to all the subjects of my Empire, it shall be lawful for Foreigners to possess Landed Property in my dominions.

The Taxes are to be levied under the same denomination from all the subjects of my Empire, without distinction of class or of Religion.

A special Law having been already passed, which declared that the Budget of the Revenue and Expenditure of the State shall be drawn up and made known every year, the said law shall be most scrupulously observed.

[We omit provisions on banks, roads, and canals—eds.]

Such being my wishes and my commands, you, who are my Grand Vizier, will, according to custom, cause this Imperial *Firman* to be published in my capital and in all parts of my Empire; and will watch attentively, and take all the necessary measures that all the orders which it contains be henceforth carried out with the most rigorous punctuality.

11. Social and Economic Change in the Ottoman Empire

As the introduction to this section has shown, enormous internal and external pressures weighed on the subjects as well as on the rulers of the Ottoman empire during the nineteenth century. The empire lost more than half its territory (see Map p. 73), its industrialization lagged, disease and famine ravaged its population, and many who could would migrate to the Americas. Meanwhile millions of mainly Muslim refugees entered its shrinking territory from regions annexed by the European powers or newly become independent territories in the Crimea, the Caucasus, and the Balkans.

This Reading shows that despite these handicaps, Middle Easterners struggled to advance. The region obtained modern transportation (railroads, ships, canals), communications (the telegraph), and educational systems (primary and secondary schools, colleges, professional schools). As Hanna Batatu shows in this Reading, part b, the Ottomans restructured their government, reducing the power of *sheikhs* and increasing political centralization. Urban centers changed most. Istanbul began to look like a European city. Its residents (Muslims, Christians, and Jews) adopted full or modified Western dress, and households took on European family patterns. Muslim merchants profited from still-flourishing internal trade routes, while non-Muslim merchants—the Jews of Baghdad, the Greeks of Izmir, the Armenians of Istanbul, and the Maronites of Beirut—expanded into European and Indian markets (see Alexander Scholch's description of European trade with Palestine in part d of this reading). As guilds declined, a new workforce emerged and some women found employment in industrial factories. As Suraiya Faroqhi reveals in part a, these transformations also affected agricultural populations.

A. Suraiya Faroqhi, Ottoman Peasants (2000)*

The scant records available regarding the daily life of Ottoman peasants makes it extremely difficult to generalize about their conditions. Professor Faroqhi, whom we identify in the headnote to Reading 9, uses court archives and other sources to give a panorama of the Ottoman rural world of Anatolia and the Balkans from the sixteenth century through the nineteenth century. (In Reading 9, she illuminates the social and economic lives of Ottoman women.) Here she shows that the availability of uncultivated but fertile land gave peasant farmers and handicraft producers the opportunity to earn their livelihoods, without being forced into serfdom, as was happening in Russia at the time.

At the end of the fifteenth and throughout the sixteenth century the farmers of Anatolia and the Balkan provinces lived in social circumstances that varied considerably from place to place and region to region. Nevertheless, with respect to their relationships with the Ottoman state, there were more similarities than differences. A farm (*çift*) worked by a single family or household (*hane*) constituted the usual economic unit. Additional labor, required at harvest time, probably was obtained through mutual help between neighbors, as is still the custom in certain areas of Turkey.

Ottoman peasants did not own their own land; absolute ownership rested with the state, and peasants were merely hereditary tenants. Only the sons enjoyed the unqualified right of inheritance, but other family members, especially daughters, could take over the farm in the absence of sons. According to the provisions (*kanunname*) of the southern Anatolian province of Karaman, dating from the year 1584, it would be unjust to eject from a farm the family of a peasant

*From Suraiya Faroqhi, *Subjects of the Sultan: Culture and Daily Life in the Ottoman Empire* (London and New York: I. B. Tauris, 2000), pp. 53–55 and 57–59. Notes deleted. American spellings adopted. By permission.

leaving no son; in his lifetime the deceased had, after all, invested his labor. Daughters did, however, have to pay a special fee in order to be granted the right to inherit, a fee also demanded of other family members such as nephews or grandchildren. The heirs were not always willing to pay; towards the end of the sixteenth century, for example, a bitter dispute ensued in a village of northern Anatolia when the family of a minor, who was about to inherit from his grandfather, resisted paying the initiation fee that was demanded.

Usually peasant levies were collected by an individual granted the appropriate authority and known as *timar*-holder by the Ottoman central government. In return, the individual in question would be expected to undertake military and sometimes also administrative duties. To what extent the *timar*-holder (*sipahi*) was involved in everyday agricultural business depended on local circumstances and no doubt also on his personal interests. A sultan's decree of 1648 was directed at those peasants who maintained that the *sipahi*'s only authority over them was that of levying taxes; the peasants were instructed to treat the *timar*-holder as their master. On the other hand, many of these holders of tax prerogatives were kept away from the villages in their jurisdiction by their military duties. Moreover, the holders of such "military fiefs" could themselves be exchanged by the central government at any time and moved to some remote province of the empire. It was therefore difficult for them to construct a personal power base.

Nevertheless, tensions between *timar*-holders and peasants were more or less inevitable. One source of conflict concerned the peasants' obligation to transport the corn taxes that they owed the *sipahi* to the nearest market. This market was often so distant that valuable working time was lost. In many provinces there was a rule that this duty should not require more than one day, but the extent to which this rule was actually adhered to is not known. Moreover, the *sipahi* might also insist that the corn be transported to a city, since the prices there were higher, even though a village market would have been nearer. Another problem arose from the distribution of the harvest; most of the holders of tax prerogatives required the peasants not to collect the corn from the fields until they themselves had taken their share. If a *sipahi* were delayed or, as the peasants sometimes supposed, if he failed to appear out of malice, the harvest would rot in the fields or be devoured by mice. If the villagers did not wait to clear the fields, they could expect to be fined.

Another contentious issue involved peasants seeking the consent of the *sipahi* to leave their villages to seek work in a city, or try their luck in another region. In times of population growth many holders of tax prerogatives must have granted their consent to migration in order to rid "their" village of landless young peasants. Often unable to marry, these village boys were regarded as trouble-makers. However, many peasants left their land without permission, and the *sipahi* sometimes caught up with them years later. In fact, despite such risks, migration was often possible because in case of doubt the burden of proof lay with the *sipahi*, and incomers who paid their taxes regularly were naturally very welcome among their neighbors in the towns. If necessary it was possible to come to an arrangement with the *kadi,* who would decree that the person in question had lived for so many years in the city that he need not leave. Many conflicts must nevertheless have arisen from this issue, however difficult they are to discern from the dry and unemotional style of the relevant *kadi* records.

Most rural conflicts in Anatolia were, however, alleviated somewhat by the fuzzy borders between nomadic and sedentary peoples. In many areas the peasants would move their families and animals to the high pastures in summer, while many largely nomadic groups would do some farming at their winter lodgings. Thus, not only did nomads settle and become peasants quite easily, but the opposite could also occur. Most areas were very sparsely populated, increasing the options open to country people. As it was possible thus to evade the issue, conflicts between peasants and *sipahis* did not lead to the peasants' revolts characteristic of the middle ages and early modern Europe.

Although some "estates" in the hands of non-peasants developed in the eighteenth century, particularly along the Balkan coasts, the vast majority of peasants worked family farms. Many of these non-peasant holdings, which were often quite small, belonged to members of the local administration, who had profited from their intermediary position to acquire land. If the Ottoman central government demanded taxes *en bloc* from a whole province, as it often did, there was scope for profitable manipulation of the assessment of individual villages and families. Certain villages might be treated leniently and the shortfall made up from the others. In such cases the official charged with assessing the villages could expect a reward from the beneficiaries as well as winning grateful followers for himself. Further potential for profit lay in the conversion of peasant crop taxes into money— perhaps by selling them to export merchants, and forwarding the cash to Istanbul. Money-lending was also widespread, despite its contravention of the Islamic prohibition on demanding interest payments. Many members of the provincial upper classes who, particularly from the second half of the eighteenth century, also sponsored buildings and decorative painting, were thus very much market-oriented. Yet the real source of their wealth remained political.

Those villagers who farmed the property belonging to the eighteenth- and early nineteenth-century rural gentry were in an altogether inferior legal position to peasants inhabiting a typical *timar* of the sixteenth century. In the earlier period, peasants at least had security of tenure so long as they farmed the land properly. This was, however, denied them, or at least limited, in those areas in which much of the land had been swallowed up by the estates of the local gentry. Peasants ended up as day-laborers or sharecroppers, and their quality of life sank accordingly. However, this process differed significantly from the "second serfdom" introduced into central and eastern Europe from the sixteenth century onwards, to which it is often compared. For the landed aristocrats of eastern Europe who reduced the farmers on their estates to serfs could count on the support of the crown. By contrast, this was not the case in the Ottoman territories. Recognizing that the gentry was taking over farmland, the central government saw this as a problem to be dealt with at some suitable opportunity. However, the sultan always refused to grant a legal basis to the subordination of agricultural laborers to their masters.

Be that as it may, the peasants of remote mountain areas had many more economic options than the tied sharecroppers of the plains. Many worked as mule drivers, and as trade with Vienna and Leipzig began to flourish in the eighteenth century, many such drivers became haulage contractors or cattle-dealers. In addition, these villagers would also sell the products of local craftsmen. Trade was thus by no means the monopoly of the towns; certain sectors of rural society also profited from the opportunities which were opening up.

In the Ottoman realm the divide between town and country was in general much less rigid than it was in many areas of medieval Europe. Just as there were country merchants, so there were many townspeople who earned their livelihoods from their gardens and vineyards, where they often spent several months during the summer. This semi-agricultural way of life was still evident even in the middle of the twentieth century. During the late 1940s, in a medium-sized central Anatolian town such as Akşehir, most craftsmen and retailers were unable to support themselves from their businesses alone and had to cultivate their gardens. During the harvest the shops would be deserted; only an apprentice might perhaps remain, while the owners busied themselves with their farming activities. In fact, many towns in other Mediterranean regions also possessed this semi-rural character; well into the twentieth century, many Sicilian townsmen still relied on agriculture.

In cultural terms, though, the divide between town and country was clearer than it was in economic matters. Written culture . . . was largely confined to the towns and was accessible only to a small section of rural society. Mosques were not built in large numbers in Anatolian villages until the nineteenth and twentieth centuries. Most villagers who could read and write had probably learned to do so in the nearest town or in a dervish [*Sufi*] convent. Registers of pious foundations of the second half of the sixteenth century, which also list the existing schools, only record a very few such establishments in the countryside. Moreover, there is no evidence that large numbers of schools were founded in villages between the seventeenth and nineteenth centuries, although this did happen in many small towns. For these reasons our sources are so scanty that a cultural history of the rural population can, in general, really begin only in the nineteenth century.

B. Hanna Batatu, Political Centralization in Iraq and Kurdistan (1978)*

Ottoman reformers of the *Tanzimat* attempted to create stable institutions that would allow them to provide services efficiently and police and tax diverse

---

*From Hanna Batatu, *The Old Social Classes and the Revolutionary Movements of Iraq* (Princeton, NJ: Princeton University Press, 1978), pp. 73–8. Notes deleted. Bracketed material added by the editors. By permission.

populations. In the rural areas of Anatolia these reforms strengthened peasants' legal title to the lands they had farmed for centuries. In other regions far from Istanbul Ottoman policies produced unintended results. In this selection from his monumental study of Iraq's social and political history, the late Georgetown University professor Hanna Batatu (1926–2000) showed that, in response to land reforms, old tribal aristocrats and urban merchants throughout Iraq laid claim to large tracts of land, depriving the rural poor of most of their property. In the south near Basra and in the region surrounding Baghdad, however, intense competition for peasant labor allowed rural dwellers to sell their produce and buy the goods they needed on the open market instead of through their tribal *shaikhs* (leaders) as they had done previously. This gave them a degree of freedom outside of their tribes. *Shaikhs,* while losing influence over the peasants, nevertheless became wealthy landowners, rich but estranged from the groups that had once supported their leadership. The efforts to undo these changes would create turmoil in Iraqi politics and society for generations afterward.

In the nineteenth century, new forces came to disturb the *shaikh,* shatter his isolation, decompose his military leagues, and undermine his self-sufficient communal domain.

The new forces had their source ultimately in the increasing entanglement of the Ottoman Empire in the meshes of the world of capitalism, but more immediately in the ensuing spirit of change that had taken hold of Ịstanbūl and that brought in its wake the extinction of the Janissaries in 1826, the establishment of a new conscripted army, the end of the virtually independent Georgian Mamlūk dynasty of Baghdād in 1831, the reincorporation of the Iraq province into the parent empire, the new land laws of 1858, steam navigation on the Tigris, telegraphic communications, the centralized *wilāyah* [Ottoman province] system, the dynamic and enterprising governor of Baghdād Midḥat Pasha (1869–71), and the Young Turk Revolution of 1908.

The *shaikh* felt all this in the direct pressure by the Turkish government to break his position and destroy the cohesion of his tribe, and in the indirect but far more potent influence of remoter forces—those of the world market—brought near to him by the new river communications.

According to the Ottoman conception, all the land, apart from some *mulk* [private property] and *waqf* holdings [belonging to religious endowments], was *mīrī,* that is, belonged to the state. Its effective occupiers held it, in theory, under lease from the ruling authority. In 1858 a new land code embodied this conception, but at the same time introduced a new kind of tenure, known as *ṭāpū,* by providing, with the retention of the right of ultimate ownership of the land by the state, for the grant of a legal and heritable right of usufructuary possession to individuals.

The new code arose from the same determination that marked tribal policy in Iraq and that sought to Ottomanize the tribal world: that is, to strengthen the central Ottoman administration at the expense of shaikhly power. For this purpose the code provided a new means: the creation from among the tribesmen of a large number of small landowners. But things turned out differently in practice, although the Turks went far in undermining tribalism.

Thus from about the middle of the nineteenth century, the Turks succeeded in obtaining a hold over the powerful Muntafiq confederation by setting the dominant Saʿdūns against one another and farming out the Muntafiq country to the highest bidder among them. At one point they tried to take away a large chunk of the lands under their control, but had to abandon this course. Finally, in 1871, their great governor Midḥat Pasha induced a number of Saʿdūn chiefs to accept the new Ottomanizing policy. The bait was their conversion from mere tribute-receiving *shaikhs* into regular *ṭāpū* holders of the lands of the Muntafiq tribes. This split the Saʿdūn family into Ottomanizers and exponents of the old tribal principles. But much more serious was the implicit dispossession of the rank-and-file tribesmen from the land in which they had a communal tribal right, and their conversion into mere tenants. Thus vast areas of land supporting many tribes became in effect the fiefs of the Saʿdūns who, with the advance of cultivation, grew very wealthy on their rents until about the turn of the century, when their tribesmen acquired large numbers of modern rifles and gradually refused to pay anything. The Saʿdūns now split up the tribes, leasing the land to each small sectional chief independently of the head *shaikh*. In this manner they were able to collect a fraction of their rents until a few years before the First World War, when many of the tribesmen declined payment altogether. The working of all these forces had the effect of fracturing the Muntafiq confederation into numerous mutually hostile tribes, themselves decomposing into a multitude of independent sections and subsections.

Ottoman initiative also led to the breaking of the power of the Khazāʿil, "the kings of the Middle Euphrates," although the drying up in the 1880s of the Hillah Shaṭṭ [a shallow lake] on which they had much of their cultivation, contributed to their decline.

The fate of the Banī Lām was milder than that of the Khazāʿil, but Banī Lām lost its influence over the Albū Muhammad and the other tribes of the ʿAmārah area. The agricultural lands, which had once suffered from its exactions, became after 1883 *saniyyah,* that is, the personal property of the Ottoman sultan, who, however, found it impracticable to lease his estates to any but the shaikhly stratum. On the other hand, the authority of this stratum was weakened by frequent redistribution of the estates between the various members of the dominant tribal families. This excited bitter jealousies, forestalled shaikhly combinations, but gave rise to ceaseless disturbance.

Divisions also overtook Zubaid, Dulaim, and, to a lesser extent, the Shammar confederation. Their component tribes and main sections tended to become virtually independent.

In the Kurdish belt, the principalities of Bahdinān, Sorān, and Bābān were destroyed between 1837 and 1852, but Ottoman rule remained tenuous, and real power fell to the *aghas* [chiefs] and *begs* [lords] of the constituent tribes and the chiefs of the mystic paths. Into the same hands passed also the bulk of the land in this area. More often than not, the *ṭāpū* records were compiled . . . at the dictation of *aghas* whose greed outweighed all other considerations.

More far-reaching than the actions of the Turks was the impact on the *shaikhs* and their leagues of the use of steamers on the Tigris. Most affected, particularly after the opening of the Suez Canal in 1869, were the tribes of the lower section of the river and on the Shaṭṭ-il-ʿArab. By the end of the nineteenth century, the subsistence economy of these tribes had to no little degree given way to a market-oriented economy. The *shaikh*, who hitherto had had limited opportunities to exploit his tribesmen, began in his new status as *ṭāpū* or leaseholder to view them in a new way, that is, as a source of profit. The tribal peasant became of greater worth to him than the fighter-tribesman. Fortunately for the peasant, he was not tied to the soil. When unhappy, he moved to the service of another *shaikh* or to the lands of nonresident landlords from Baṣrah, or sought work in the new town of ʿAmarah or in the city of Baṣrah itself, so that there developed the unfamiliar phenomenon of big *shaikhs* competing against each other for peasants. This led to the intermixture of tribes and to increasing instances of *shaikhs* landlording alien tribesmen. It was also possible now for individual peasants, particularly in Baṣrah province, to sell their share of the produce and buy their own needs from the local market, when previously exchange of tribal produce occurred only through the *shaikh*. Similar processes developed in country districts neighboring Baghdād and a number of other towns so that here, as in parts of Baṣrah province, riverine peasants bore allegiance to no *shaikh*, and the territorial rather than the tribal connection was predominant.

The legacy of the Turks was, therefore, a tribal system generally enfeebled and, on the Shaṭṭ-il-ʿArab and in areas adjacent to the cities, in a state of advanced decomposition. The decline of the political and military power of the *shaikhs, aghas,* and *begs* was unmistakable. The military confederations and principalities were destroyed. In their place arose a multitude of antagonistic tribes and tribal sections. . . . Many of these sections were practically free from the authority of the parent tribe. On the other hand, the groundwork was laid for the economic growth of the *shaikhs* and *aghas* by the granting or leasing to them or the registering in their name, through fraud or bribery, of vast estates supporting many tribes or whole villages, tribal and nontribal, in utter disregard of the prescriptive right of rank and file tribesmen or nontribal cultivators. This new economic power of the *shaikhs* and *aghas* was, however, in its essence a concealed threat to their very historical existence, for it was alienating them from the only real source of their power: their tribe. It was substituting for the life-renewing, patriarchal and blood relationships—where these existed—the new subversive relationships of production. This ultimately was to lead to the undoing of the *shaikhs* and *aghas*.

C. Donald Quataert, Manufacturing Workshops (1994)*

In this reading Donald Quataert, professor of Ottoman history at the State University of New York at Binghamton, tackles the complex issue of why the Ottomans failed to industrialize in the nineteenth century. He demonstrates that the government introduced legislation in the last decades of the century that abolished internal customs duties, granted tax exemptions for imported machines, and generally stayed out of the way of capitalists investing in new plants. In actuality, officials often acted in ways that undercut such reforms: customs officials charged duties despite laws on the books abrogating them; government ministers tended to favor the agricultural sector over industry because large export markets existed for Ottoman produce; and it seemed more productive to import very cheap industrial goods from nearby industrial countries rather than to establish substitute industries that initially would produce expensive and relatively shoddy products.

Protecting local industries had also become nearly impossible because of open door treaties, such as the one imposed on the Ottoman empire by Great Britain in 1838 that prohibited the levying of high tariffs on imported manufactured goods, the standard way industrializing countries safeguarded their nascent industries. Ever since the British forced Muhammad Ali, ruler of Egypt, to dismantle his factories the message from abroad seemed clear enough. As Afaf Lufti al-Sayyid Marsot shows in her 1984 study *Egypt in the Age of Muhammad Ali*, Europe would not tolerate any serious industrial competition. Fear of losing jobs in handicraft industries mobilized a good part of the working population to protect their old tried and tested techniques rather than adopt new methods that might reduce the workforce to unskilled laborers. Despite the roadblocks that prevented Ottoman industrialization in the nineteenth century, the new Republic of Turkey, freed of external constraints and having centralized its government, in the 1930s invested heavily in state-sponsored modern industries and created large numbers of factories (see Reading 15b).

Foreigners were fond of blaming government corruption, inefficiency and ineptitude for the underdevelopment of Ottoman manufacturing during the nineteenth century, by which they meant the general absence of mechanized factories. There were plenty of Ottoman laws promoting industrialization although most of these came quite late, after 1870. These often remained dead

---

*From Donald Quataert, "Ottoman Manufacturing in the Nineteenth Century," in Donald Quataert, ed., *Manufacturing in the Ottoman Empire and Turkey, 1500–1950* (Albany: State University of New York Press, 1994), pp. 90–3. Notes deleted. By permission.

letter; tax exemptions, for example, were without effect when customs officials collected the duties anyway. Laws providing for duty-free import of all machines installed in a new factory had been on the books since 1873, and were renewed regularly thereafter. In addition, orders from 1876 freed Ottoman industrial products from both internal and external customs duties. Some historians have pointed to the apparent correlation between the various enactments of duty-free legislation and the bursts of factory founding that did occur. In this analysis, by implication, Ottoman industrialization would have been more successful if only government legislation had been more enlightened and consistent.

Two brief comments seem appropriate here. First, it is true that government policy focused on agriculture rather than manufacturing. But the assumption that such a comparative lack of emphasis on industrial development spelled the presence of a backward, unenlightened government is unfair. Rather, we need to consider that segments of the bureaucracy perceived that there were advantages in having cheap industrial imports. Powerful policy-making elements did not favor import substitution policies. This is a perfectly rational option. In common with most of the world outside of nineteenth-century Europe and the United States (and Japan), "neither markets nor input supplies were attractive and therefore it was more profitable to supply manufactured goods from outside than to make them in the country concerned." Overall, the steady fall in the price of manufactured goods and, for much of the period except 1873–1896, the reverse pattern for agricultural commodities, pushed Ottoman entrepreneurs and workers towards the agrarian sector at the expense of the industrial. Second, the role of state policy has been vastly exaggerated by both contemporary observers during the nineteenth century and my colleagues in Ottoman history. While state policy certainly was significant, its importance was not unlimited. The eight percent internal duty on goods shipped from one point to another certainly did hurt factory owners who were trying to establish broad internal markets. But, government policy was not the critical factor in the formation of Ottoman cotton yarn factories, or for that matter, the general pace and tempo of Ottoman industrialization.

Rather, we should look at the host of other factors that severely circumscribed policy-making options. In the realm of politics, we need to remember that Britain was the dominant power until the 1870s, and actively sought to prevent the development of rival manufacturers. When Britain, in the 1830s, destroyed Mohammed Ali Pasha, the Egyptian dynasty builder, the lesson was made clear. He had been pursuing industrialization in order to develop his power base in Egypt and the British quite deliberately dismantled his considerable accomplishments to remove the threat to their Middle Eastern markets. Instead, Britain during its industrial hegemony sought to permit only free trade. From the perspective of international politics, Ottoman industrial development was not a viable option for Istanbul planners.

The absence of security in the early years of the nineteenth century certainly discouraged the large capital investment needed for a factory and all its equipment, so readily visible and subject to predation by bandits and marauders. The lack of water resources certainly was critical in many areas. It should be recalled that water power played a crucial role in early American and European manufacturing and steam did not replace water power until late in the nineteenth century. This water option simply was not available in most of the Ottoman world.

The comparative sparseness of the Ottoman population depressed manufacturing potential as well. Relatively low population densities, in the absence of countervailing factors, meant an overall shortage of workers that discouraged the massing of labor power so necessary to factory life. Not coincidentally, most factories emerged in the relatively more densely populated areas such as the European provinces, and Istanbul and Izmir. Low densities also reduced the possibilities for labor-intensive industrial activities, although these were present. Also, the population of twenty-six million was very thinly scattered over the territorially vast Ottoman Empire. Nor was the total potential market terribly large; compare, for example, the Ottoman population to that of contemporary Qing China, that held some 350 million persons. And finally, the small and scattered Ottoman population and its proximity to Europe made Ottoman manufacturing more vulnerable to Western interference than its Chinese contemporary.

Factory formation, moreover, was retarded by the actions of the Ottoman populace; Ottoman workers, entrepreneurs, and the population at large, passively and actively resisted the formation of many factories. Elite groups including state officials participated, at least sometimes. There was considerable publicly expressed concern, for example, about the air and water pollution that a factory might bring. Such objections have a face value but they surely camouflaged the fear of economic competition as well. In 1875, for example, entrepreneurs sought to found a water-powered yarn factory in the town of Niaousta. The Salonica provincial administrative council, that had jurisdiction, carefully stated the conditions under which the factory could be built. In particular, it would not be permitted to interfere with the livelihoods of town dwellers. Because women had been producing wool yarn in workshops of the town since olden times, the factory therefore could produce only cotton yarn. Nor could the factory diminish the water supplies needed for the local gardens, orchards, and fields. There was a similar popular and official response when a British subject opened an Izmir factory for printing muslin. Some local Armenian manufacturers, whose factory offered a similar product, protested and Istanbul consequently ordered the new factory to close. Sometimes the evidence of resistance is unclear. On a number of occasions, a newly opened factory caught fire and was destroyed. Was this active resistance, or merely the result of carelessness or the hazards of the age? For example, a fez factory, built in Salonica in 1908–9, burned down almost immediately and was not rebuilt. At Trabzon, a British firm bought and imported the machinery for a cotton and woolen weaving plant "but while in store a fire damaged them greatly so that most of the parts will have to be renewed." Other known examples of resistance include that of Uşak where, in the early 1890s, two capitalists tried to erect a wool spinning factory for carpet making. In the face of strong protests from local residents who feared the loss of hand spinning jobs, the government denied the concession. Wool yarn factories later were built at Uşak anyway, only to be sacked and burned by angry hand spinners in March 1908. But they did reopen. At Adana, a knitting factory "was burnt down and never started again." Resistance, that included factory burning, however, did not prevent the emergence of a major cluster of steam-powered factories, to reel silk, in the Bursa district during the 1850s. Nor can we trace the general absence of factories to Ottoman machine breakers, however fascinating they were.

D. Alexander Scholch, European Trade with Palestine (1982)*

Throughout the nineteenth century much of the Middle East remained rural, producing agricultural goods for the global market: high-quality cotton from Egypt; rice and silk from Iran, Anatolian Bursa, and Lebanon. Palestine produced olive oil, specialty grains, and the highly prized Jaffa oranges for European consumption.

Professor Alexander Scholch of Essen University in Germany shows how the Palestinian rural population entered the world market with new, local cash crops.

The produce of southern Palestine was mainly exported through Jaffa, that of the northern part of the country through Haifa and Acre. With regard to the *Jabal* Nablus [the Nablus hills], it is difficult to ascertain how much of its produce destined for export went to Jaffa and how much to Haifa. Furthermore, Acre was the main port for that part of the Hauran grain which was not consumed within Syria.

Jaffa's main export commodities through the period 1856–82 were (in a changing order of priority which will be explained): wheat, barley and durra [millet]; sesame; olive oil and soap; oranges, other fruits and vegetables. The main buyers were France, which took the largest share of the sesame and a considerable part of the olive oil, grain and, for a time, cotton; Egypt, which imported most of the soap as well as olive oil, fruits and vegetables; and England, which took nearly all of the durra and a considerable share of the wheat and barley. Grain, fruits, vegetables and soap were also shipped to northern Syria, Asia Minor, Greece, Italy and Malta.

---

*From Alexander Scholch, "European Penetration and the Economic Development of Palestine, 1856–1882," in Roger Owen, ed., *Studies in the Economic and Social History of Palestine in the Nineteenth and Twentieth Centuries* (Carbondale, IL: Southern Illinois University Press, 1982), pp. 12–17. Notes deleted. American spellings adopted. Bracketed material added by the editors. By permission.

The most important export commodities of Haifa and Acre were wheat, barley, durra, sesame and olive oil. Wheat went to Italy (for the pasta), France, England and Greece, and also to Lebanon and Asia Minor; barley was sent to Lebanon, and also to England and France; durra mainly to England and France; sesame nearly exclusively to France, olive oil to Egypt, France and Asia Minor. In some years cotton was exported to France. The greater part of the wheat shipped from Acre came from the Hauran. . . .

The stimuli from external markets will be illustrated by the example of cotton-growing. . . . Northern and central Palestine (the district of Acre and the *Jabal* Nablus) were traditionally among the most important cotton-growing districts of Syria. Nearly all of the cotton which was not processed locally or marketed in central Syria, notably in Damascus, was exported to France. From 1852, however, French demand for sesame (for oil extraction) increased strongly. Agricultural production was therefore concentrated on this commodity. It was easy to convince the peasants to do so as the growing of sesame required much less labor than that of cotton and as the sesame seed was less dependent on the weather. Furthermore, after the outbreak of the Crimean War [in 1853] and the suspension of the grain supply from South Russia, there was suddenly a great demand for wheat and barley. Thus the export of cotton was brought to a standstill.

A new reorientation took place, however, when the price of raw cotton rose towards the end of the 1850s—because of higher English demand, and then again after the outbreak of the American Civil War. As a result, in the spring of 1863, agriculturalists in northern Palestine sowed three times the amount of cotton they had grown in the preceding year. Even the remote and swampy corner round Lake Hula was affected by the boom.

A similar development took place in the district of Jaffa. French demand for sesame, the rise of grain prices during the Crimean War, and the beginnings of a regular export of oranges in the late 1850s, had brought cotton-growing to a standstill there as well. Instead, orange groves were expanded in the area surrounding the town, while grain and sesame was grown in the hinterland. In an attempt to reverse this trend, the Cotton Supply Association of Manchester and British consular agents on the spot (Finn in Jerusalem and Kayat in Jaffa) tried to stimulate a revival of cotton-growing. Egyptian and American seed was sown on a trial basis in various parts of southern Palestine with excellent results. But only the high prices of the American Civil War were able to revive cotton-growing and export on a large scale. In 1863 the area sown with cotton in southern Palestine was four times as large as in 1862, and this in spite of the fact that none of the seed which the Ottoman authorities are alleged to have ordered to be distributed actually reached the area. Consul Kayat reported that seven villages in the district of Jaffa had reserved two-thirds of their arable land, on which they had formerly mainly grown sesame, for cotton. As a result exports increased by nearly ten times over the preceding year and some merchants had to import gins as the less sophisticated local machines could not cope with these quantities. In 1864 there was hardly any village in the district which did not sow cotton on a considerable part of its land, and there was a further six-fold increase in production. Even the Bedouin took part in this profitable undertaking. The reversal set in with the collapse of prices in the autumn of 1864 . . . with the end of the American Civil War, and with a plague of locusts in 1865 and 1866. The export of cotton came to an end at the beginning of the 1870s.

Finally, some remarks on the Jaffa orange have to be made. Regular export began after the Crimean War, mainly organized by the Greek coastal shippers. In 1856 the average annual yield was already put at 20,000,000 oranges. Two decades later, in 1873, there were 420 orange groves in the vicinity of Jaffa, yielding 33,300,000 oranges annually. One-sixth of them were consumed in Palestine, the rest were shipped to Egypt and Asia Minor on Greek ships. From 1875, Jaffa oranges were also exported to Europe (Russia, Austria, Germany and France) on a significant scale. This long-range trade increased markedly when the oranges were packed more carefully and exported in boxes. For shipping to Europe only the egg-shaped and thick-skinned *shamutis* were suitable, leaving the round and smaller *baladis* to be sold on the local and regional markets. The volume of the 1880 harvest was 36,000,000 oranges. And in his report for the year 1881, the British Consular-Agent remarked that orange gardens were now regarded as the best form of capital investment where annual net returns of 10 per cent on invested capital could be expected.

12. Jamal al-Din al-Afghani, Plan for Islamic Unity (1884)*

Jamal al-Din al-Afghani (1839–97) holds a critical place at the center of modern Islamic thought and activism. His tireless advocacy of Islamic modernism, his appeals to Muslims to master science and technology, and his opposition to European imperialism set an example that many other Muslims followed while he lived and after he died. He voyaged widely, attempting to rally Muslims in favor of pan-Islamic unity while attacking corrupt rulers whom he blamed for many of the ills that had befallen their countries. While in Paris, Afghani, along with his Egyptian disciple Muhammad Abduh (1849–1905), edited a short-lived but influential publication, *al-Urwah al-Wuthqa* (The Indissoluble Bond), where this essay

*From Jamal al-Din al-Afghani, "Islamic Union" (from *al-Urwah al-Wuthqa*, 1884), in Jacob Landau, *The Politics of Pan-Islam: Ideology and Organization* (Oxford, U.K.: Clarendon Press, 1990), appendix B, pp. 318–20. Notes deleted. American spellings adopted. Bracketed material added by the editors. By permission.

was first published. It may have been written or dictated by Afghani, or composed by Abduh under Afghani's influence. While later living in Persia Afghani opposed the Qajar ruler's grant of a tobacco concession to a British entrepreneur, and was expelled. Later he lived in the Ottoman empire where the sultan employed him to undermine British influence over other Muslim lands.

"Obey Allah and His Messenger and do not quarrel with one another, lest you fail and die." (Quran 8:48)

The dominions of Islam stretched between the furthest point west to Tonkin, on the borders of China, in a breadth between Fezzan in the north and Sarandib south of the Equator. Muslims inhabited [these] continuous and contiguous lands, which they ruled invincibly. Great kings reigned over them and administered most of the globe with their swords. None of their armies was routed, none of their flags was lowered and none of their words was contradicted. . . . Their cities were well populated and solidly constructed, competing with the world's cities in the industry of the inhabitants and their originality. . . . [When] their Abbasid Caliph spoke, the Chinese Emperor would obey him and the greatest Kings in Europe would tremble.

The Muslim navies ruled unrivalled in the Mediterranean Sea, the Red Sea, and the Indian Ocean, being predominant there until recently; their opponents had to yield to the power that defeated them. Muslims abound nowadays in those lands inherited from their forefathers; their number is no less than 400 millions. Individually, their hearts are replete with the tenets of their religion; they are more courageous than their neighbors and better prepared to die. In this, they are the strongest people in their contempt for worldly life and the most unconcerned with vain glories, since the Koran reached them. . . . Every Muslim perceives himself personally involved whenever a group of Muslims is subjugated by foreigners.

This has been the case [both] formerly and nowadays. However, the Muslims have come to a halt, retarded in knowledge and industry, after having been teachers to the world. Their countries started losing the lands on their periphery, although their religion forbids them to yield authority to their opponents. . . . [C]onflict among their princes had caused disunity, so that Muslims failed to oppose the aggression of their enemies. . . . This is what happened to the Muslim princes, along with shameful losses brought about by their disunity in wars in which no nation could have competed with them [otherwise]. However, corruption penetrates the souls of those princes, over time. . . . This is what brought down the Muslims of Spain and destroyed the pillars of the Timurid [Mughal] Sultanate in India, erasing its remains. The British established their government there on this Sultanate's ruins. . . . Agreement and co-operation for strengthening Islamic rule are among the pillars of the Islamic religion; belief in them is a basic doctrine for Muslims, requiring neither a teacher to preach it, nor a book to confirm it. . . . Were it not for their misguided princes, eager for domination, Muslims east and west, north and south, would have joined a common appeal. For preserving their rights, the Muslims need only to turn their thoughts towards their own defense and agree on common action, when necessary, and merge their hearts in a joint feeling about the dangers threatening their nation.

Looking at the Russians, one notices three characteristics. They are lagging in the arts and sciences behind the rest of Europe's nations, their lands have no natural resources (if there are, nobody can exploit them for industry), and they are abjectly poor. None the less, focusing their thoughts on the defense of their nation, agreeing on its development, and joining their hearts have created a state capable of shaking the whole of Europe. The Russians do not own factories required for most instruments of war, which does not prevent them from obtaining them; the arts of war are less developed in Russia, which does not prevent them hiring officers from other nations to instruct their armies—so that their military forces have acquired awesome strength and an aggressive power feared by European states.

So what has prevented us from resembling others in a matter which is simple for us and which we strongly desire—to preserve our nation's honor, to grieve for what hurts it, and to co-operate to defend a total union against whomsoever attacks it? Those responsible for preventing the movement of thoughts and the rise in enthusiasm are [the princes] sunk in luxury, seeking succulent food and soft bedding . . . who have become a yoke on the necks of Muslims, barring these lions from rising to attack—rather, rendering them a prey to foxes. There is no refuge except in Allah.

O people, descendants of the brave and the noble, has the tide turned against you and has the time for despair come? No, no, may Allah forbid the loss of hope! From Edirne to Peshawar, there is an uninterrupted sequence of Islamic states, united in the religion of the Koran, numbering no less than 50 millions, distinguished by courage and bravery. Should these not agree between themselves on defense and attack, as have all the other nations? Were they to agree between themselves, this would be no innovation [*bida'*], for co-operating is one of the pillars of their religion. Has apathy stricken their senses, so that they are insensitive to one another's needs? Should not each consider his brother with the Koranic precept of "the Muslims are brethren," so that they set up together the union to stem the waves threatening them from all sides?

I am not implying that one person ought to rule all [Muslims]; this is difficult, perhaps. I do hope, however, that the Koran would be their ruler and religion the focal point of their union; that every leader would do his utmost to preserve the others, since his own life and survival depends on them. Not only is this a pillar of religion, but a necessity, also. The time for an agreement has come! The time for an agreement has come!

Chapter IV

The Two World Wars and Their Aftermaths

Introduction

The First World War drew not only much of Europe into conflict but parts of the Islamic world as well. A major Middle Eastern power—the Ottoman empire—fought on the side of Germany and Austria-Hungary (the three forming the "Central Powers" alliance). As Chapter III showed, the Ottomans backed the losing coalition mainly because of the history of prewar territorial encroachments against it by Great Britain, France, and czarist Russia (who made up the Allied, or *Entente,* side in the war). The European countries embroiled in war drafted and recruited soldiers and replacements from their colonies for their own workers fighting on the front. Many of these colonial peoples were Muslims who came to the battlefields and cities of Europe from India and Africa. Large numbers of Central Asian Muslims also fought in the czarist armies. One national group particularly affected by the war, the Christian Armenians, lived in the path of these Russian armies. Seen as favoring the czarist coalition, uprooted from their homes by Ottoman troops, and sent on forced marches out of the war zone, this population found itself subjected to severe hardship. Turks carried out massacres of Armenians throughout the empire. Those who could do so escaped abroad (see Reading 14).

On whatever side, few Europeans could conceive of "Orientals" or "natives" in any commanding role in wartime, or as citizens of independent states afterward. For example, when facing the Turkish-led Ottoman forces in the Middle East, the British expected to triumph easily. But the Ottoman armies mounted well-planned and -executed (if unsuccessful) offensives against the British stronghold in Suez. Under a young army colonel, Mustafa Kemal (mentioned in Chapter III as a rising figure in the Young Turk movement), Ottoman forces decisively repulsed the 1915 Allied attack on the strategic Dardanelles Straits. Elsewhere, Middle Easterners, North Africans, Central Asian Muslims, and both Hindu and Muslim Indians played important roles in the eventual Allied victory, and, as we shall mention, in the postwar struggles as well.

The German state's location in central Europe dictated the necessity of fighting a two-front war. On the eastern front the Germans trounced czarist Russia, initially a member of the coalition whose other members—Great Britain and France—fought more than three years of static trench warfare in western Europe. The defeated Russians made a humiliating separate peace with the Germans and withdrew from the fighting in March 1918, four months after the revolutionary Bolsheviks took power. The United States in April 1917 had belatedly joined the *Entente* forces fighting on the western European front, contributed supplies and food staples, and helped inflict the decisive defeats on the Central Powers that compelled their surrender in November 1918.

Postwar Realities and the Imposed Peace Settlements

The war's impending end brought into play secret agreements negotiated a few years earlier by Britain, France, and czarist Russia to carve up and annex Ottoman territory. With Russia embroiled in a civil war that followed its Bolshevik revolution, Britain and France carried through as much of the expansionist program as they could manage to do in face of a new postwar reality: the unexpected resurgence of Turkish power, which we dicuss later in this Introduction. The Europeans encouraged Arabs to join them in the war against the Ottomans (see Readings 13a and b), and, for reasons that we mention later, Arab troops fought alongside British forces in Syria, Palestine, and Iraq.

On the eve of the war, Arabs within the Ottoman empire had become restive under Turkish rule—especially after the Young Turks created the centralized state we discussed in Chapter III and those leaders favored a version of nationalism that discriminated against Arab subjects. When war broke out, British officials, aware of this discontent, sought Arab allies to help defeat the Ottomans. The main British official in the region, Sir Henry McMahon (1882–1969), high commissioner for Egypt, conducted negotiations on behalf of his country. He contacted the Hashemite leader in Arabia, Husayn ibn Ali (1853–1931), whose title, *sharif,* marked his descent from the Prophet Muhammad. Husayn had served as Ottoman-appointed governor of Muslim holy sites in Arabia, but as his correspondence with McMahon shows (see Readings 13a and b), he agreed to join the British for a suitable reward: an extensive kingdom for himself and his descendants where Britain would have significant economic and military privileges. Despite the vagueness of McMahon's assurances, Husayn, his sons, and their Arabian soldiers fought alongside Western troops.

The Hashemites did receive rewards: confirmation of Husayn's control of central Arabia; creation of a state to the east of the Jordan River for one of Husayn's sons, Abdullah; and a state in Syria for Faysal, another son. Except for Jordan, a Hashemite state to this day (see Reading 26a), all the other territorial gains won by the Arabs proved fleeting: Husayn soon lost Arabia to the Saudis; the French took Syria and deposed Faysal. Soon afterward the British placed Faysal on Iraq's newly created throne, where he reigned for the rest of his lifetime. Iraqi nationalists eventually overthrew the dynasty.

While the World War I victors made these concessions to traditional Arab leaders, expectations arose widely among Arabs in former Ottoman territories for genuine independence. These hopes came in part from the worldwide emergence of nationalism, now heightened by wartime rhetoric of freedom and the stirring message of self-government promoted by the U.S. president, Woodrow Wilson (1856–1924). But the earlier Sykes-Picot agreement on dividing up former Ottoman possessions among Britain and France (see Reading 13c and Map p. 117) took precedence. We know about the secret British, French, and Russian plans to divide the Ottoman empire among themselves because the Bolshevik revolutionaries found them among the papers of the czarist regime they ousted and, defying diplomatic tradition, published them.

The Americans backed their wartime allies and supported the transfer of Iraq and Palestine to British control and Syria and Lebanon to the French. More Ottoman territory would have been taken (see Map p. 108) had not a strong Turkish state arisen after the war to protect Anatolia from Greek, Italian, and French territorial designs. The League of Nations' "mandate" system provided the fiction that these colonies would be prepared for self-government by their European overlords. Even so, and without considering the special prize awarded to the Jews—a "national home" in Palestine (see Reading 19a)—most of the Arab populations of the regions affected came away from World War I disillusioned and unwilling to accept the new colonial realities imposed on them.

These complex interacting events also defined an important, if fleeting, moment in Central Asian history. On taking power in Russia, the Bolsheviks repudiated the 1907 Russo-British agreement establishing spheres of influence in Persia and, with revolutionary and rhetorical zeal, declared the vast expanse of the old czarist empire freed from all imperial domination. In a bid to win over the mostly Muslim population of Central Asia and to undermine British rule in India, they backed a pan-Islamic program echoing back to Jamal al-Din al-Afghani a half century earlier (see Reading 12), but this whole effort soon collapsed. By the mid-1920s the Bolsheviks had defeated their internal enemies, thwarted external invasions, and began to assert control over the vast expanse of Central Asia.

The Arab Middle East Under the Mandate System

The British and French holders of the Middle Eastern mandates immediately discovered that they ruled over hostile populations. Only Transjordan (later renamed Jordan) remained quiescent. In Iraq, before Faysal's appointment as king, the British had pieced together a mandate state out of incompatible Kurdish, and Arab *Shiite* and *Sunni* regions. Iraqi nationalists objected, including some army officers who had served under Faysal in the war against the Ottomans. The Iraqis began to organize an armed opposition. Only after a bitter and costly struggle did the British defeat them. Faysal's accession to the throne served for a time to prevent further uprisings (see Reading 17).

The French got Syria, from which they created the separate state of Lebanon. Designed to favor the Maronite Christians over other Lebanese—the *Shiite* and *Sunni* Muslims, the Druze community (whose beliefs incorporate Islamic symbols along with gnostic and neo-Platonic tenets), and other Christians— mandate Lebanon encompassed more territory than the old Mount Lebanon district of Ottoman Syria. Faysal's ouster in 1920 from the territory adjoining Lebanon (which soon became the mandate state of Syria) caused revolts, which the French brutally suppressed. Ruled afterward by a small core of French bureaucrats and indigenous collaborators, Lebanon and Syria gained complete independence only after World War II.

In that war, having surrendered to the German invaders in 1940, France became a client state of the Third Reich. This greatly weakened France's hold over her colonies, and when British and American wartime forces later took over these territories, they stirred hopes for their eventual independence. However, General Charles de Gaulle (1890–1970), leader of the French anti-Nazi armed forces, had different ideas. He wanted to restore French imperial control everywhere, but pressure from Britain and the United States forced him to withdraw from Syria and Lebanon. Remnants of colonial practices persisting in postindependence Syria and especially Lebanon in the 1940s would create future problems.

The United States

The United States sought no Middle Eastern territory after World War I, but it did back the imperial ambitions of its British and French allies at the postwar peace conferences. When the Senate refused to ratify the World War I peace treaty in 1919, the United States temporarily withdrew from the formal arena of international diplomacy, and never joined the League of Nations. But this withdrawal did not really imply isolationism, as the country greatly extended its global economic power in the interwar years. By its participation in the 1928 "Red Line" petroleum agreement, the United States participated in developing the Middle East's oil fields. After World War II weakened French and British power, the United States become a member of the United Nations (successor to the failed League of Nations), and assumed during the Cold War years a dominant role in global affairs. Later chapters will explore these matters.

Changes in Turkey

Independence, crushed in the Arab territories, reasserted itself in Turkish domains directly after World War I. Under the leadership of Ottoman military commander Mustafa Kemal, the Turks repulsed a British invasion early in the war, then, defying the sultan's defeatism, they fought successfully to hold on to their Anatolian territories. Yet another invading force had arrived—Greeks seeking (with British and French backing) to conquer a substantial amount of Turkish territory. Armed peasants under Mustafa Kemal's leadership defended lands granted to their ancestors in the *Tanzimat* reforms six decades earlier (see the Introduction to Chapter III). By winning a resounding military victory over the Greeks, the Turks convinced the Allies to renegotiate a new settlement (the Treaty of Lausanne, 1923), which gave Turkey far more favorable terms than did the humiliating 1920 Treaty of Sévres.

Mustafa Kemal, now the acknowledged leader of the Turks, abolished both the sultanate and the caliphate and established an independent, secular republic, Turkey, with its capital at Ankara and he as its first president. A dictator, Kemal later took the name Ataturk (father of the Turks) and carried out many of the reforms that earlier *Tanzimat* reformers had introduced. Ataturk went beyond them to embrace emancipation of women, mass education, and industrialization (see Reading 15b). One early, prominent supporter of Ataturk's reforms, Turkish feminist Halidé Edib, soon perceived the tyrannical side of his rule and (as her essay in Reading 15c shows) broke with his regime (see also our discussion of their ongoing conflict in Chapter VII).

Persia and Afghanistan

Farther east, the Persian Qajar dynasty from its inception in 1779 had steadily lost territory. Czarist Russian pressure forced abandonment of Qajar claims on the Caucasus region, and the British compelled Persia to cede the agriculturally rich Herat area to Afghanistan. In the late nineteenth and early twentieth centuries, popular movements led by coalitions of secular nationalists and *Shiite* clergy agitated for and won a parliamentary regime. But the discovery of large oil fields there by British petroleum engineers in 1908 soon brought even greater foreign intervention. Already the Russians and British had divided Persia into spheres of influence. In 1911 a group of Russian-backed Persian politicians, with czarist military support, shut down the newly formed parliament, allowing imperial Russian influence to prevail. During the First World War Russians occupied the northern part of the country while the British, then allied with Russia, held the Gulf coast and the interior, including, at the end of the war, the oil fields in southwestern Persia. After 1918 the Anglo-Persian Petroleum Company granted the Qajar regime a small, steady income from oil revenues, which allowed that monarchy to survive for a few more years.

The war and its immediate aftermath brought major changes to Persia and Afghanistan. An intelligent but barely educated military commander, Reza Khan Pahlavi (c. 1878–1944), ousted the last Qajar shah, made peace with the Russian Communist government, changed the country's name to Iran, and established in 1925 the new (but short-lived) Pahlavi dynasty. Six years earlier, as mentioned in Chapter III, Great Britain had recognized Afghanistan's nominal independence, in return for which the Afghans had to accept the British-imposed Durand line, arbitrarily dividing the Pashtun ethnic community, as the country's border with India. Formal autonomy and membership in the League of Nations failed to bring stability to Afghanistan. Later chapters will explore Afghanistan's turbulent and costly role in Cold War and post–Cold War struggles.

Reza Shah disappointed many reform-minded Iranians, especially those who hoped for an effective parliamentary regime. Some of the *Shiite ulema* also opposed him, since the *shah* undermined their legitimacy by appointing secular-

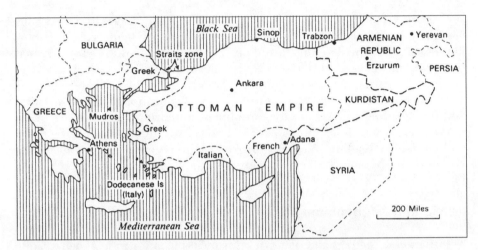

Plans for the Partition of Anatolia After World War I

ists to the government bureaucracy and by glorifying the pre-Islamic Persian past to the detriment of Islam. The failure of the shah's regime to win significant increases in oil revenues from the British also generated internal dissent. Deposed by invading British forces during World War II for his pro-Nazi sympathies and exiled to South Africa, Reza Shah abdicated in favor of his son, Muhammad Reza Shah (1919–80).

The new monarch embarked on a program of economic development favoring landholders and the military and aligned his country closely with the United States. The young shah emulated his father and imposed changes from the top down, while repressing the opposition. These oppositionists made up a diverse coalition, consisting of radical secular nationalists demanding greater democracy and nationalization of Iran's oil industry (see Reading 28a), those who resented Iran's subservience to the United States (the successor to British power in the region), as well as the disaffected *ulema* (see Reading 28b). The Pahlavis helped create the very alliance among social groups in Iran who—as Chapter VI will show—together toppled the dynasty in 1979. But this alliance divided soon afterward on the internal policies of the Islamic republic that replaced it (see Reading 28c).

In neighboring Afghanistan, a descendant of the royal Pashtun Durrani tribe, Muhammad Zahir Shah (1914–   ), became king in 1933 after the assassination of his father. Recognizing that he could not take dramatic steps to change his country against the will of traditional tribal leaders or the great powers, the monarch temporized during much of the four decades of his reign. Because of U.S. indifference to his pleas for assistance, Zahir Shah drew closer to the Soviet Union, which supplied arms and military training for Afghanistan's army. Yet the king remained fearful of Soviet power on his northern borders. As we shall see in Chapter VIII, some of this fear had good foundation. Even as the Cold War waned and the Soviet Union began its final disintegration, the regime in Moscow eventually invaded Afghanistan with disastrous consequences that reverberated well into the twenty-first century.

Egypt: Independence by Degrees

The British takeover of the Suez Canal and their occupation of Egypt in 1882 (see the Introduction to Chapter III) greatly stimulated the development of Egyptian nationalism. By the late nineteenth century several moderate nationalist parties coexisted but could do little to free the country from British domination or relieve the economic suffering of the peasantry, hurt by the decline in demand for Egyptian cotton. Focused on ending the British protectorate and winning political independence, the upper-class leaders of these parties generally ignored peasant grievances.

Although there was no combat in Egypt during World War I, Egyptians fought in the British armed forces against the Ottomans. Nationalist politicians hoped that at war's end they could send a delegation (*wafd*) to the peace conference and plead for independence. However, the British denied the leader of what would soon become the *Wafd* Party, Saad Zaghlul (c. 1850–1927), permission to leave, and then when he protested further they deported him. A national uprising in urban and rural areas resulted, which the British suppressed. Freed, Zaghlul and the *Wafdists* hoped for support from the Americans. But the United States preferred to recognize Britain's protectorate rather than champion Egyptian independence. A standoff resulted in Egypt: the nationalists remained committed to full self-government while their colonial overlords offered partial sovereignty— a parliamentary system in which Britain retained authority, not only over the Suez Canal but also over Egypt's communications and defense systems.

The agitation for genuine independence continued and expanded, leading the British in 1922 to grant the Egyptians a constitution, but one of still limited powers. These concessions intensified nationalist pressures on Great Britain to remove its troops. A three-way tug-of-war ensued among the *Wafd* Party, the king, and the British, bringing about the formal abrogation in 1936 of Egypt's status as a protectorate. But the continued presence of British military forces for another twenty years showed clearly where predominant power lay.

New groups entered the arena of struggle. In 1928 a Cairo elementary school teacher, Hasan al-Banna (1906–49), founded the Muslim Brotherhood, an organization that demanded a greater role for Islam in running the Egyptian state. Reading 32b sets forth al-Banna's program: reducing oppression, disease, and crime and promoting wholesome Islamic morality. Growing to a membership of half a million in the early 1930s, the Brotherhood appealed to many strata of society and challenged the nationalism of the *Wafd* and other secular parties. Al-Banna's movement also inspired many other Islamic radical organizations throughout the Islamic world, as we show in Chapter VII. Al-Banna himself became a personal dictator over the organization he had founded, accepting no criticism and demanding blind obedience from his followers. As the Muslim Brothers began to carry out assassinations, its members became targets of police roundups. Al-Banna was executed in 1949, probably by Egyptian police officials. The Brotherhood survived, and its conflicts with Egypt's secularist regime continue to the present day.

The Interwar Years

The European powers that received mandates from the League of Nations in the Arab portions of the former Ottoman empire had assumed the tasks of preparing the local populations for future self-government, but neither the League nor its main members showed any interest in carrying out these commitments. This failure caused a profound transformation in the Middle East and eventually in the rest of the Islamic world. Non-Muslims now controlled key portions of the Arab heartlands, and this generated great resentment, which persists even to the present day, although neither the mandates nor old-fashioned colonies exist there any longer. But through control of markets for Middle Eastern goods (especially oil), by its military bases scattered through the region, its support of Israel, and its powerful global cultural apparatus, the United States, which has replaced the mandate powers as the main external force in the region, continues to dominate. The last chapters of this book explore modern Islamic radicalism—derived in great measure from Egypt's Muslim Brotherhood—which in part, has arisen in reaction to continuing Western domination.

After World War I the holy sites of Mecca and Madina in the western portion of Arabia, known as the Hijaz, remained under the authority of the *Sharif* Husayn. But Husayn had formidable local rivals. Much earlier, the *Hanbali* religious reformer Muhammad ibn Abd al-Wahhab (1703–92), a champion of strict adherence to Muslim legal texts, had allied with the Saudi tribal rulers of a small Arabian market town. Animated by the strict *Wahhabi* teachings, the Saudis expanded their authority throughout Arabia, defeating Husayn's troops in 1924. Eight years later, Abd al-Aziz ibn Saud (1880–1953) became the first king of Saudi Arabia. Since then the Saudi dynasty has supervised the main Muslim holy sites and pilgrimage destinations in Arabia—a great honor and responsibility.

Also in the interwar period, U.S. firms discovered petroleum and invested in oil concessions in Saudi Arabia and in several other states in the Persian/Arab Gulf region, including Bahrain and Kuwait. We could hardly exaggerate the importance of petroleum and natural gas in shaping not only the modern Middle East but also the Caspian Sea regions of Central Asia. Chapter VI of this book deals with the politics and economics of oil production and its international distribution. Here, we need mention that several of the oil-rich Gulf states, especially Saudi Arabia, face the serious problem of how to reconcile the great wealth that petroleum production has created with the austere tenets of *Wahhabism*.

Along with oil, the Arab-Israeli crisis shaped the immediate pre- and post-war Middle East. As World War II approached, two main problems engulfed Palestine, as Chapter V explains: the growing desperation of the Arab Palestinian peasantry, leading during 1936–39 to a bitter revolt that British and Zionist armed forces suppressed; and the increasing misery among Zionists at the rising anti-Semitism in Nazi Germany that sent many Jews to their deaths. When that anti-Semitism reached the unbelievable levels of a holocaust, the postwar fate of Palestine was decided—both the United States and the U.S.S.R. would support and aid in the creation of a Jewish state in Palestine.

Besides its direct and indirect impact on Palestine, World War II also affected Muslim regions of the Middle East, southern Asia, and Central Asia. Given how Western countries used their victory in World War I to undermine Arab ambitions and extend their power and influence throughout the Middle East, it is significant that so few in the Muslim world defected to the Axis side—Fascist Italy, Nazi Germany, and Japan—in the next major world war. The overwhelming majority of Middle Easterners and South Asians sided with the Allies. We have already noted the removal of Iran's Reza Khan for pro-Axis sympathies. The British also thwarted a pro-German coup d'état in Iraq. Some nationalists in India, Palestine, Afghanistan, and other regions either acted as Axis propagandists or voiced pro-Axis positions. Most other leaders waited to see which side would win World War II and how best to press the new victors for liberation. Developments in India provide an example of how this strategy worked and at what cost.

India and Pakistan

Except for bitter battles in North Africa and struggles against the Japanese in Muslim areas of East Asia, little fighting took place in the Middle East or in other Islamic countries during World War II. That war nevertheless had enormous consequences for the region, one of the most important of which concerned the decolonization of the Indian subcontinent after decades of nationalist agitation. Would postcolonial India comprise one state or two? Attempts at agreement between Muslims and Hindus foundered. The Indian National Congress, jointly led by Mohandas K. Gandhi (1869–1948) and Jawaharlal Nehru (1889–1964), wanted a unified secular state. But the Muslim League, headed by Muhammad Ali Jinnah (1876–1948), opposed a state where Muslims would remain in a permanent minority. He called instead for the establishment of a Muslim state in northern India (see Jinnah's 1940 speech, Reading 16) and mobilized an overwhelming Muslim vote for partition in the 1946 elections for the all-India constituent assembly. Eager to terminate their colonial presence in India, the British agreed to partition and to the creation of a predominantly Muslim Pakistan with Jinnah as its first governor-general.

Horrifying communal strife accompanied partition. Jinnah's prediction that Muslims and Hindus could not live in the same country came true when one million people seeking sanctuary among their coreligionists ended up dead.

Seven and a half million Muslims fled India for Pakistan, and ten million Hindus went in the opposite direction. Leaders also perished: a Hindu ultranationalist angered by his victim's solicitude for Muslims assassinated Gandhi; and Pakistan's first prime minister, Liaquat Ali Khan (1895–1951), died at the hand of an Afghan Pashtun nationalist.

Crises developed almost immediately after independence over Kashmir, a northwestern region populated largely by Muslims and claimed by both Pakistan and India. Kashmir's Hindu ruler turned the province over to India and a war ensued, leading the United Nations to divide Kashmir between the two contending countries. Since 1948 conflicts have repeatedly erupted over the divided province, and recently Muslim activists from Kashmir have made deadly cross-border raids into India. India has accused Pakistan of collusion with the Kashmiris. This territorial dispute has taken on new seriousness since the late 1990s when both India and Pakistan exploded nuclear weapons.

Pakistan itself was divided at the 1947 partition of the Indian subcontinent into two predominantly Muslim regions a thousand miles apart: one territory curled around Afghanistan in the northwest that became West Pakistan with its capital at Karachi, the other in East Pakistan with its capital at Dacca. The mostly Bengali population in the east came to resent its subordination to West Pakistan, and a war resulted when the Indian army intervened on the side of the independence-seeking Bengalis. East Pakistan became Bangladesh, an independent country, in 1971.

Neither India nor Pakistan has maintained stability since independence. In Pakistan widespread political corruption, weak civil institutions, and seemingly insoluble territorial disputes have rendered it vulnerable to periodic takeover by military dictatorships. In India the National Congress Party has ruled for most of the first half century after independence, for much of that time under the Nehru dynasty. But Nehru's daughter, Indira Gandhi (1917–84), revealed a dictatorial streak during the so-called emergency period, from 1975 to 1977. After favoring a secular, multicommunal India hospitable to Muslims, Sikhs, and Hindus, Indira Gandhi and her son Rajiv (1944–91), who ruled after her, began catering to xenophobic Hindu nationalism. Religious nationalists (Sikhs in the case of Indira, Hindus in the case of Rajiv) assassinated both these members of the Nehru dynasty. These killings, and the political splits that preceded them, opened the way to political power for rightist Hindu groups such as the Bharatiya Janata Party (BJP), which defeated the Congress Party in elections in 1989 and 1998. At this writing BJP has emerged as the dominant political force in India, managing the tense confrontation with Pakistan over Kashmir as communal disputes over Hindu and Muslim holy sites roil domestic politics. Peering into the future of the Indian subcontinent and in such regions as Afghanistan and other populous Muslim nations in the Indian Ocean basin and East Asia's Pacific rim, we witness the growing incidence of communal strife, which, in a global age, increasingly affects all people in the world.

13. Conflicting Promises During World War I

All the documents in this reading are from the World War I period and they reveal the depth of the *Entente* powers' concern with the postwar settlement. They show Britain, France, and czarist Russia planning the division of the Ottoman empire and distribution of its parts to the victors. Those Arabs who had allied with Great Britain and France against the Turks willingly accepted great power protection, hoping to establish their own new states.

Selections a and b, excerpts from an extensive set of letters that defined delicate negotiating positions, were exchanged between an Ottoman official in Arabia, the *Sharif* Husayn ibn Ali, and the British High Commissioner in Egypt, Sir Henry McMahon. Husayn wanted a large Arab state encompassing Greater Syria (including Palestine) in exchange for sending his troops to fight against the Ottomans. Remaining vague about future commitments, McMahon sought to assure Husayn of British friendship. He makes clear that the British could not include in any hypothetical Arab state coastal Syria (including Lebanon), which the British were about to promise to the French in the secret Sykes-Picot Treaty of 1916 (see this Reading, part c). Nor could he offer Husayn Iraq, where the British had already discovered oil, although eventually one of Husayn's sons did ascend the throne of a newly established British-controlled state in Iraq (see Reading 17).

Meanwhile Zionism became entwined in the decisions over Arab lands. In 1917 the British government issued the Balfour Declaration (Reading 19a), endorsing the establishment in Palestine of a "national home for the Jewish people." Part V will further explore Palestinian/Arab and Zionists' responses as the great powers hammered out a postwar settlement.

A. *Sharif* Husayn ibn Ali, Desire for Arab Independence (1915)*

In this letter to Sir Henry McMahon, *Sharif* Husayn ibn Ali, Ottoman governor of the Hijaz, the region in Arabia containing the Muslim holy cities of Mecca and Madina, promised to support British war efforts and rebel against the Ottomans. In exchange he requested the creation of an Arab state in Middle Eastern territories that the Ottomans then controlled. In part b of this reading we give McMahon's reply.

---

*From Great Britain, *Parliamentary Papers*, Command No. 5957, House of Commons *Sessional Papers*, 1939, pp. 3–4. American spellings adopted.

July 14, 1915

To his Honor:

WHEREAS the whole of the Arab nation without any exception have decided in these last years to live, and to accomplish their freedom, and grasp the reins of their administration both in theory and practice; and whereas they have found and felt that it is to the interest of the Government of Great Britain to support them and aid them to the attainment of their firm and lawful intentions (which are based upon the maintenance of the honor and dignity of their life) without any ulterior motives whatsoever unconnected with this object;

And whereas it is to their (the Arabs') interest also to prefer the assistance of the Government of Great Britain in consideration of their geographical position and economic interests, and also of the attitude of the above-mentioned Government, which is known to both nations and therefore need not be emphasized;

For these reasons the Arab nation see fit to limit themselves, as time is short, to asking the Government of Great Britain, if it should think fit, for the approval, through her deputy or representative, of the following fundamental propositions, leaving out all things considered secondary in comparison with these, so that it may prepare all means necessary for attaining this noble purpose, until such time as it finds occasion for making the actual negotiations:

Firstly—England to acknowledge the independence of the Arab countries, bounded on the north by Mersina and Adana up to the 37° of latitude . . . [and] up to the border of Persia; on the east by the borders of Persia up to the Gulf of Basra; on the south by the Indian Ocean, with the exception of the position of Aden to remain as it is; on the west by the Red Sea, the Mediterranean Sea up to Mersina. England to approve of the proclamation of an Arab *Khalifate* of Islam.

Secondly—The Arab Government of the *Sherif* to acknowledge that England shall have the preference in all economic enterprises in the Arab countries whenever conditions of enterprises are otherwise equal.

Thirdly—For the security of this Arab independence and the certainty of such preference of economic enterprises, both high contracting parties to offer mutual assistance, to the best ability of their military and naval forces, to face any foreign Power which may attack either party. Peace not to be decided without agreement of both parties.

Fourthly—If one of the parties enters upon an aggressive conflict, the other party to assume a neutral attitude, and in case of such party wishing the other to join forces, both to meet and discuss the conditions.

Fifthly—England to acknowledge the abolition of foreign privileges in the Arab countries, and to assist the Government of the *Sherif* in an International Convention for confirming such abolition.

Sixthly—Articles 3 and 4 of this treaty to remain in vigor for fifteen years, and, if either wishes it to be renewed, one year's notice before lapse of treaty to be given.

Consequently, and as the whole of the Arab nation have (praise be to God) agreed and united for the attainment, at all costs and finally, of this noble object, they beg the Government of Great Britain to answer them positively or negatively in a period of thirty days after receiving this intimation; and if this period should lapse before they receive an answer, they reserve to themselves complete freedom of action.

B. Sir Henry McMahon, Qualifying British Pledges (1915)*

A month after receiving *Sharif* Husayn's letter, McMahon responded cautiously to the demands for an independent Arab state. Speaking for Great Britain, and aware of conflicting promises made or about to be made to allied states, he committed British support to Husayn in establishing a vaguely defined desert kingdom, carved out of greater Syria.

Although two of Husayn's sons did become monarchs in the Hashemite kingdoms of Iraq and Transjordan, both under British mandates, the *sharif* ended up losing control of Arabia to the Saudis who, as we have mentioned, with British backing, forcibly conquered the Hijaz in 1924 and established their kingdom eight years later. The British sought and found an even more compliant set of rulers in these desert-based Saudi tribal *sheikhs*.

The two districts of Mersina and Alexandretta and portions of Syria lying to the west of the districts of Damascus, Homs, Hama and Aleppo cannot be said to be purely Arab, and should be excluded from the limits demanded [for these sites, see the map, p. 117].

With the above modification, and without prejudice to our existing treaties with Arab chiefs, we accept those limits.

As for those regions lying within those frontier wherein Great Britain is free to act without detriment to the interests of her ally, France, I am empowered in the name of the Government of Great Britain to give the following assurances and make the following reply to your letter:—

(1) Subject to the above modifications, Great Britain is prepared to recognize and support the independence of the Arabs in all the regions within limits demanded by the *Sherif* of Mecca.

(2) Great Britain will guarantee the Holy Places against all external aggression and will recognize their inviolability.

---

*From Great Britain, *Parliamentary Papers,* Command No. 5957, House of Commons *Sessional Papers,* 1939, pp. 7–9. American spellings adopted. Bracketed material added by the editors.

(3) When the situation admits, Great Britain will give to the Arabs her advice and will assist them to establish what may appear to be the most suitable forms of government in those various territories.

(4) On the other hand, it is understood that the Arabs have decided to seek the advice and guidance of Great Britain only, and that such European advisers and officials as may be required for the formation of a sound form of administration will be British.

(5) With regard to the *vilayets* [provinces] of Baghdad and Basra, the Arabs will recognize that the established position and interests of Great Britain necessitate special administrative arrangements in order to secure these territories from foreign aggression, to promote the welfare of the local populations and to safeguard our mutual economic interests. . . .

I am convinced that this declaration will assure you beyond all possible doubt of the sympathy of Great Britain towards the aspirations of her friends the Arabs and will result in a firm and lasting alliance, the immediate results of which will be the expulsion of the Turks from the Arab countries and the freeing of the Arab peoples from the Turkish yoke, which for so many years has pressed heavily upon them.

C. The Sykes-Picot Agreement on Dividing up Arab Lands (1916)*

Sir Mark Sykes, a British colonial official, and François George Picot, his French counterpart, met secretly in wartime London over the course of several weeks in late 1915 and early 1916. Their negotiations concerned division of the postwar Middle East among the Allies at the war's end. Since czarist Russia was part of this alliance, both parties had to obtain the agreement of the Russian Foreign Minister, Sergei Sazanoff.

When in 1917 the Bolsheviks seized power in Russia, they found the secret documents that revealed the imperialist origins of World War I, a conflict described officially by the Allies as inspired only by their noble aims. The Bolsheviks published the full texts.

Here we present a contemporary summary of the key clauses of the Sykes-Picot agreement and a map that illustrates it. British Foreign Secretary Sir Earl Grey sent these in a letter in May 1916 to Paul Cambon, French ambassador to Great Britain. The terms of this agreement ran counter to some of the assurances only recently made to the Arabs by the Allies.

*From E. L. Woodward, ed., *Documents on British Foreign Policy, 1919–1939*, First Series, vol. IV (London: Her Majesty's Stationery Office, 1952), pp. 245–47. American spellings adopted. Bracketed material added by the editors.

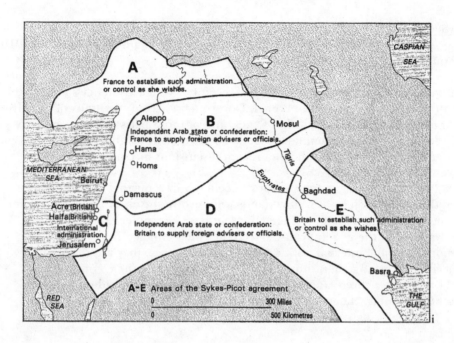

A

France to establish such administration or control as she wishes.

Aleppo

B

Independent Arab state or confederation: France to supply foreign advisers or officials.

Hama

Homs

Mosul

MEDITERRANEAN SEA

Beirut

Damascus

Tigris

Euphrates

Baghdad

Acre (British)

Haifa (British)

C

International administration

Jerusalem

D

Independent Arab state or confederation: Britain to supply foreign advisers or officials.

E

Britain to establish such administration or control as she wishes.

CASPIAN SEA

Basra

RED SEA

THE GULF

A–E Areas of the Sykes-Picot agreement

0 ——————————— 300 Miles

0 ——————————— 500 Kilometres

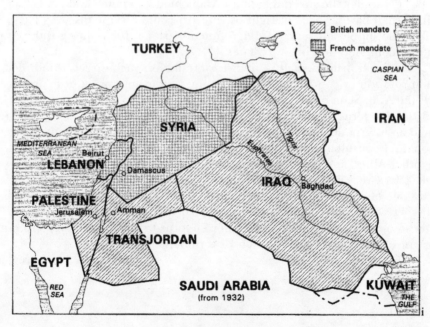

TURKEY

British mandate

French mandate

CASPIAN SEA

SYRIA

IRAN

MEDITERRANEAN SEA

Beirut

LEBANON

Damascus

Euphrates

Tigris

IRAQ   Baghdad

PALESTINE

Jerusalem

Amman

TRANSJORDAN

EGYPT

RED SEA

SAUDI ARABIA
(from 1932)

KUWAIT

THE GULF

The Sykes-Picot Agreement and the Mandates

(Secret.)

Foreign Office, May 16, 1916

Your Excellency [Cambon],

I have the honor to acknowledge the receipt of your Excellency's note of the 9th instant, stating that the French Government accept the limits of a future Arab State, or confederation of States, and of those parts of Syria where the French interests predominate, together with certain conditions attached thereto, such as they result from recent discussions in London and Petrograd on the subject.

I have the honor to inform your Excellency in reply that the acceptance of the whole project, as it now stands, will involve the abdication of considerable British interests, but, since His Majesty's Government recognize the advantage to the general cause of the the Allies entailed in producing a more favorable internal political situation in Turkey, they are ready to accept the arrangement now arrived at, provided that the co-operation of the Arabs is secured, and the Arabs fulfill the conditions and obtain the towns of Homs, Hama, Damascus, and Aleppo.

It is accordingly understood between the French and British Governments—

1. That France and Great Britain are prepared to recognize and protect an independent Arab State or a Confederation of Arab States . . . [see Map on p. 117] under the suzerainty of an Arab chief . . . France and . . . Great Britain shall have priority of right of enterprise and local loans. . . . [They] shall alone supply advisers of foreign functionaries at the request of the Arab State or confederation of Arab States.

2. . . . Great Britain, shall be allowed to establish such direct or indirect administration or control as they desire and as they may think fit to arrange with the Arab State or Confederation of Arab States. . . .

3. . . . [In Jerusalem and the region surrounding it] there shall be established an international administration, the form of which is to be decided upon after consultation with Russia, and subsequently in consultation with the other Allies, and the representatives of [Husayn] the *Sharif* of Mecca.

4. That Great Britain be accorded (1) the ports of Haifa and Acre, (2) guarantee of a given supply of water from the Tigris and Euphrates. . . . His Majesty's Government, on their part, undertake that they will at no time enter into negotiations for the cession of Cyprus to any third Power without the previous consent of the French Government.

[Grey]

14. Vahakn N. Dadrian, The Fate of the Armenians in World War I*

Scattered for centuries among the Ottoman and the Persian Safavid and Qajar empires, the Armenians (a Christian population) had usually served as useful subjects of sultans and shahs, managing much of the long-distance trade between Europe and the Middle East. But in the twentieth century Armenian aspirations for nationhood clashed with Ottoman aims. The Turks accused the Armenians of backing their enemy, czarist Russia. In this reading, Dadrian, director of genocide research at the Zoryan Institute in Cambridge, Massachusetts, argues on the basis of new data that the Turkish repression amounted to a conscious policy of genocide. Other scholars claim that the Armenians brought much of their suffering on themselves.

The historical debate over the "Armenian question" will doubtless continue as a hotly contested issue. Many Armenians who survived the wartime and postwar repression, expulsions, and killings ended up as citizens of the Soviet Armenian Republic, which became an independent country in 1991when the Soviet Union collapsed.

The wartime fate of the Ottoman Empire's Armenian minority continues to be controversial. The debate in the main revolves around the causes and nature of that fate. Some historians have alleged that what is involved is centrally organized mass murder—or, to use contemporary terminology, genocide. This school of thought maintains that the Ottoman authorities were waiting for a suitable opportunity to undertake the wholesale liquidation of the empire's Armenian population, and the outbreak of World War I provided that opportunity. The Committee of Union and Progress (CUP, or Unionists), who controlled the Ottoman government, they argue further, did in fact undertake this liquidation under cover of the war. Others, however, dispute these assertions, especially that of genocidal intent. This group maintains that Armenian acts of disloyalty, subversion, and insurrection in wartime forced the central government to order, for purposes of relocation, the deportation of large sections of the Armenian population. According to this argument, apart from those who were killed in "inter-communal" clashes—that is, a "civil war"—the bulk of the Armenian losses resulted from the severe hardships associated with poorly ad-

*From Vahakn N. Dadrian, "The Armenian Question and the Wartime Fate of the Armenians as Documented by the Officials of the Ottoman Empire's World War I Allies: Germany and Austria-Hungary," in *International Journal of Middle East Studies*, vol. 34, no. 1 (February 2002), pp. 59 and 71–77. Notes and German and Turkish texts deleted. Bracketed material added by the editors. American spellings adopted. By permission.

ministered measures of deportations, including exhaustion, sickness, starvation, and epidemics. In other words, this school of thought holds that the Ottoman Empire, in the throes of an existential war, had no choice but to protect itself by resorting to drastic methods; therefore, the tragic fate of the Armenians must be understood in the context of the dire conditions of World War I. These views are encapsulated in the formula that the noted Middle East historian Bernard Lewis has used—namely, the desperate conditions of "an embattled empire."

Even if one grants that the Armenians did provoke the authorities to any significant degree through acts of disloyalty and deserved severe retribution, the intensity and the scale of the retribution applied against them during the war raises valid questions about the plausibility of the argument. If the retaliation exceeded all bounds of commensurateness, had the characteristics of a predesigned general scheme that targeted an entire population rather than being random outbursts of impulsive violence directed against actual or suspected troublemakers, and if the tempo of destructiveness continued far beyond the elimination of the agents of provocation, then one has to consider other frameworks of explanation. The conclusions and judgments of German and Austro-Hungarian diplomats and military officers operating in various parts of the Ottoman Empire during the war provides such a framework of explanation.

On 12 November 1915, German Foreign Minister Gottlieb von Jagow relayed to his ambassador in Istanbul German Chancellor Hollweg's edict . . . decrying the Ottoman wartime policy of exterminating . . . Armenians. German Commander-in-Chief Field Marshal Paul von Hindenburg denounced that "policy of annihilation" . . . , which he said was being used as a means to solve "the Armenian question." . . . In the June 1915–October 1918 period, four successive German ambassadors explicitly characterized the anti-Armenian measures as devices to "solve the Armenian question through annihilation"; of these, three quoted directly [Ottoman] Interior Minister Tālat to this effect. Austria-Hungary's ambassador, Johann Pallavicini, after a meeting with Tālat, informed Vienna that "through scandalous measures . . . the Armenian question has been solved." Karl Count zu Trautmannsdorff-Weinsberg, deputy to Ambassador Pallavicini, in a 30 September 1915 report likewise spoke of a meeting with Tālat, who "with a certain gratification" told him that there were no more Armenians in Erzurum. The deputy then lamented the fact that "unheard-of horrors" . . . are being perpetrated and that "the extermination of the Armenian race is all but achieved."

Several German consuls and vice-consuls, stationed in the interior of the land, and therefore close to the scenes of the unfolding extermination campaign, underscored the historical antecedants of that campaign and consistently reiterated the theme: "solving the Armenian question" was the underlying, but actually overriding purpose of the campaign.

In examining the wartime fate of Ottoman Armenians to portray it as accurately as possible, the "why" of that fate was treated as an inseparable part of the problem. The historical aspect of the "why" needs to be completed, however, by the consideration of the contemporary dimension of the problem. Reverting to the time frame of World War I, one needs to add to the "why" the adverb "now," and ask the ancillary question: why now [1915]? German and Austro-Hungarian documents answer that question on two levels. Nearly all of them reiterate time and again that the conditions of the war, with all its crises, emergencies, and exigencies, were used effectively to initiate and implement the campaign of extermination. In other words, by harnessing its manifold opportunities, the war was rendered functional. . . .The most explicit and authoritative answer to the question "why now?" is provided, however, by Interior Minister Tālat, whom German ambassador Wolff-Metternich identified as the principal architect of the extermination campaign. In an effort to secure the cooperation of the German government, he informed Berlin that "the work that is to be done must be done now; after the war it will be too late."

The other . . . issue here is the alliance with the Central Powers serving as a shield . . . to block or obviate outside interference in the extermination operations. . . . In one of his most important "confidential" reports, a veteran diplomat, Germany's Aleppo Consul Walter Rössler, declared that "there can be no doubt . . . that the authorities are utilizing . . . the alliance with the Central Powers for the purpose of resolving the Armenian question."

[A careful examination of German and Austro-Hungarian archives shows] that, despite varying [Ottoman] attempts at coverups and outright denials, the wartime anti-Armenian measures were not only carefully planned by the central [CUP] authorities, but were also intended to destroy wholesale the victim population, a destruction process to which they [the German and Austrian officials] had become the reluctant witnesses. Their uniform conclusion about the nature of the wartime fate of the Armenians acquires special validation from an extraordinary source identified with the Ottoman camp: General Mehmed Vehip, commander-in-chief of the Third Army and an ardent CUP member. Given his background, Vehip's testimony reflects not only authority but also a singularity in purpose. Departing from the established path of most other CUP leaders, including high-ranking military officers, he testified with candor. One can only infer from the tone injected in the text of his account that he was indignant at what he learned and observed. Lewis Einstein, special assistant at the American Embassy in Istanbul during the war, describes Vehip as "a chivalrous soldier." At the request of the Mazhar Inquiry Commission, which in the postwar period conducted a preliminary investigation to determine the criminal liability of the wartime Ottoman authorities in the matter of Armenian deportations and massacres, Vehip prepared a deposition . . . on 5 December 1918. After providing a host of details, Vehip offered his "summary conviction" . . . as follows:

> The Armenian deportations were carried out in a manner utterly unbecoming to [our sense of] humanity and civilization and inimical to the honor of the government. The murder and annihilation of the Armenians

and the plunder and expropriation of their possessions were the result of
the decisions made by the Central Committee of *Ittihad ve Terakki* [CUP]. . . .
These atrocities occurred under a program that was determined upon and
involved a definite case of willfulness. They occurred because they were
ordered, approved, and pursued first by the CUP's [provincial] delegates
and central boards, and second by governmental chiefs who had [ignored]
the law, had pushed aside their conscience, and had become the tools of
the wishes and desires of the [*Ititihadist*] *ceimiiyet* [council]. . . .

Vehip's pungent testimony attests not only to the calamitous fate of the Armenians, but also to the fact that not all military authorties approved the scheme
that brought about that fate. In fact, tensions and antagonism often existed between the high- ranking CUP operatives pushing for the implementation of that
scheme and the high-ranking military and civilian officials who resisted and were
even counterposed to it. Some of these men were dismissed; others were reas-
signed; and still others were killed outright or by ambush. . . .

It is this futility [of protest] that accents the inexorability and meticulous-
ness with which the anti-Armenian scheme was organized and was brought to a
successful end.

Based on the evidence supplied by a host of officials from Imperial Germany
and Imperial Austria-Hungary, the Ottoman Empire's wartime allies, the following conclusion becomes inescapable. Through the episodic interventions
of the European Powers, the historically evolving and intensifying Turko-Armenian
conflict had become a source of both anger and frustration for Ottoman rulers
and elites driven by a xenophobic nationalism. A monolithic political party that
had managed to eliminate all opposition and had gained total control of the
Ottoman state apparatus efficiently took advantage of the opportunities provided by World War I. It purged by violent and lethal means the bulk of the
Armenian population from the territories of the empire. By any standard of
definition, this was an act of genocide.

15. Challenges to New Nations:
Afghanistan, Turkey, and
the Fertile Crescent

Immediately after the First World War Afghan and Turkish leaders introduced
reforms to transform their societies profoundly. These measures took hold
in Turkey (see this Reading, part b) since they reinforced trends already begun
in the nineteenth-century Ottoman empire (see the Introduction to Chapter III

and Reading 10). Some Turks, such as the feminist writer Halidé Edib, while supporting reforms, objected to the dictatorial way in which the president of Turkey, Mustafa Kemal, implemented them (see part c). In Afghanistan the attempted introduction of far-reaching reform programs led to the overthrow and exile of King Amanullah Khan (1892–1960) and Queen Soraya in 1929, since many Afghans viewed the royal couple's plans for the country, some of which we present in part a, as alien to their own traditions and rejected them. In Syria, after World War II, where Arab nationalism took hold as local populations looked for ways to unify in order to rid themselves of what they saw as new imperialist domination, Michel Aflaq created the *Baath* party and formulated its ideology, a summary of which we present in part d of this Reading. Baathists later took power in Syria and Iraq and established competing dictatorial states, each attempting to unify their fellow Arabs at the others' expense.

A. Queen Soraya, The Liberation of Afghan Women (1922)*

Queen Soraya's proposals for women's education presented here entailed an important part of the reform program for Afghanistan championed by her husband, who believed that "religion does not require women to veil their hands, feet and faces or enjoin a special type of veil. Tribal custom," he continued, "must not impose itself on the free will of the individual." He also deemed international recognition important, and Amanullah managed to get Afghanistan admitted to the League of Nations after gaining British acknowledgment of his country's independence in 1919. Amanullah adopted a new legal code and introduced new styles in dress, which allowed women in Kabul to go unveiled. He also encouraged people to wear Western clothing. In keeping with his generation's views about inducing change, reformers naively thought that if they forced or encouraged people to change their external dress that would lead to changes in their mentalities. It took some time for those favoring transformation to realize that change occurs in more complex and subtle ways. Amanullah's educational reforms, expressed here by Queen Soraya, became another visible symbol of the royal couple's attempt to impose foreign values and institutions on a very traditional country. Soraya's father, Mahmud Tarzi (1865–1933), one of Afghanistan's leading nationalists and reformers, served as an important adviser to the king and encouraged his son-in-law to take major risks. Amanullah and Soraya visited several European countries and while overseas spent time with Mustafa Kemal in Turkey. Traditionalists, including members of the Afghan *ulema,* used the royal couple's attachment to European models to attack them, contribut-

---

*Afghanistan Royal Proclamation by Queen Soraya (1922), in Senzil K. Nawid, *Religious Response to Social Change in Afghanistan, 1919–1929: King Aman-Allah and the Afghan Ulama* (Costa Mesa, CA: Mazda Publishers, 1999), pp. 221–22. Bracketed material added by the editors. By permission.

ing to Amanullah's loss of tribal support. Key tribal components of the armed forces deserted him so that in 1929 the king and queen had to flee into exile in Italy. They never returned to Afghanistan.

To my dear sisters, the inhabitants of Kabul and its vicinity:

The following provisions have been ratified for your welfare and that of your daughters and are herewith announced for your information. . . . A man and a woman together form the complete human being, as the survival of both is essential for the continuation of the human race. Thus, the responsibilities of life have been divided between men and women. Women are in charge of raising children, preparing food and managing the household, and men are responsible for earning a living and providing for the family. If we examine their respective roles carefully, we see that the responsibilities of women are even more difficult than those of men, particularly in the area of child care, which means that without acquiring proper education herself, it is virtually impossible for a woman to properly fulfill this most important responsibility in life. Women are in charge of bringing up the future generation, the most important responsibility in life. If we deprive women of education, we have, in effect, incapacitated half of our body and have destroyed our subsistence with our own hands.

It was not in vain that *Hazrat* Muhammad (may peace be upon him) made the acquisition of knowledge obligatory for both men and women without ascribing any special privilege [to men] when he said, "to gain knowledge is the religious duty of all Muslim men and women." The Muhammadan law (*shar'-i-mostafawi*) allows a woman to become a *qazi* [religious judge], and it is obvious that in order to reach that rank one has to go through years of study with a great master and acquire a great deal of knowledge. This proves that [in Islam] education is considered equally important for women. In the days when literacy had become common among Muslims and educational centers were established throughout the Muslim world, many women like men became famous scholars, *mohadithas* (specialists of *hadith*), literary persons, and artists.

[We omit several examples cited by Queen Soraya.]

There are many examples of highly educated and famous women scholars, teachers, and saints in Islamic history, and there are many examples of women who demonstrated great bravery in war. In short, it is rational and legally proper for women to acquire knowledge.

In response to an urgent need, two girls' schools . . . were established last year in . . . Kabul. However, since neither of these schools could accommodate more students, and the first one was a little too far from the city, both schools were merged in Golistan Saray, which has superior rooms and can house 800 students. In this way all female students will be able to meet in one place, where their expenses for clothing, food, veils, and books will be paid by the government on an equal basis. A number of skilled teachers will be recruited from inside the country and from abroad to teach classes in home economics, child development, sewing, knitting, and cooking. Since the regular girls' school will recruit only young girls between the ages of six and ten, a vocational school has been established for adult women to provide professional training in sewing, cooking, and making artificial flowers. The purpose of this school is to help women learn new skills and become financially independent in order to release themselves from total financial dependence on their husbands or their families. By the end of the year 1301 [1922], the students who graduate with the first, second or third rank in any of the above professions will receive awards of 1000, 700, and 400 rupees, respectfully. . . . In addition, by learning a skill that will help them earn money, women will become assets to their husbands. The vocational women's school . . . is also housed in Golistan Saray and is awaiting the attendance of ambitious and high-minded sisters.

Qualified teachers will receive good salaries and, in addition, will render a service to the educational program of our beloved country.

By means of his proclamation, I inform you that whosoever wants to register . . . or would like to apply for a teaching position should send her resume to the director . . . for permission and benefit from sources of knowledge and information. At this stage, students will be placed in different classes according to the level of their achievement.

B. Mustafa Kemal, Design for a Modern Secular Turkish State (1925)*

An enthusiastic champion of modernity, Kemal introduced sweeping changes in the new Turkish state, which a popular upsurge of nationalism he led had created. He, like Amanullah in Afghanistan (see part a, this reading), believed that changing externals (even clothing and headgear) would lead to internal personal transformations. So Kemal banned the fez for a modern brimmed hat that made it difficult for men to place their heads to the ground in prayer. His motives derived from a fierce secularism allied to enthusiastic pursuit of modernism. Similar impulses lay behind Kemal's reform of language, replacing Arabic script with letters derived from European languages and reducing the number of words in common usage, which had the advantage of rapidly expanding literacy in Turkey, but also the disadvantage of cutting off modern Turkey from the region's rich and diverse Ottoman past. Kemal's willingness to make that sacrifice is evident in his removal of the country's capital from the ornate, history-drenched city of Istanbul to the stark, inland provincial city of Ankara. Determined to start anew and bury the past, Kemal also renounced Turkish irredentist claims on former imperial territories, even those with predominantly Turkish-speaking peoples.

*From Mustafa Kemal, "An Exhortation to Progress," from the Istanbul daily newspaper *Ashham,* September 1, 1925, translated from the Turkish in *Living Age* (New York), vol. 327 (October 31, 1925). Bracketed material added by the editors. Arabic and Turkish words italicized.

By doing that he saved Turkey from many costly wars, which would have consumed it for decades and would have wasted scarce resources.

Kemal certainly believed that Turkey could and should transform itself into a modern country as quickly as possible and toward that end he founded new state-run industries and made provision for a multiparty political system after his own dictatorship ended with his death in 1938. People feared him in Turkey, but many also admired him for his strong hand in wrenching the country out of its past. Not all agreed with his methods, however. Halidé Edib (1883–1964), the outspoken Turkish reformer, while endorsing many of Mustafa Kemal's goals, broke with him over his dictatorial rule (see part c, this reading). Four years before his death, Kemal received from the Turkish National Assembly a new surname for himself, an apt title—Ataturk (father of the Turks).

The object of the revolution . . . is to give to the citizens of the Republic a social organization completely modern and progressive in every sense. It is imperative for us to discard every thought that does not fall in line with this true principle. All absurd superstitions and prejudices must be rooted out of our minds and customs.

It is shameful for a civilized nation to expect help from the dead. Let the worthy occupants of . . . tombs rest in the happiness which they have found in a religious life. I can never tolerate the existence, in the bosom of a civilized Turkish society, of those primitive-minded men who seek material or moral well-being under the guidance of a *sheik,* possibly blind and hostile to the clear light of modern science and art.

Comrades, gentlemen, fellow countrymen! You well know that the Republic of Turkey can never be a country of dervishes and *sheiks* and their disciples. *The only true congregation is that of the great international confraternity of civilization.* To be a real man it is necessary to do what civilization commands. The leaders of the *tekkés* (Muslim cloisters, [*Sufi*] shrines, or "monasteries") will comprehend this truth, which will lead them voluntarily to close those institutions as having already fulfilled their destiny.

The Government of the Republic possesses a bureau of religious affairs. This department includes a numerous staff of *imams* (priests), *muftis* (chief priests), and scribes. These functionaries are required to have a certain standard of knowledge, training, and morality. But I know that there are also persons who, without being entrusted with such functions, continue to wear priestly garb. I have met many among them who are unlearned, or even illiterate. Yet they set themselves up as guides for the nation! They try to prevent direct contact between the Government and the people. I should like to know from them from what and from whom they have received the qualities and attributes which they arrogate to themselves.

It is said that we Turks have a national costume. However that may be, whatever we wear is certainly not of our own invention. The fez is of Greek origin. Very few of us would be able to say what constitutes a national costume. For example, I see in this crowd a man who is wearing a fez wound round with a green turban. He has on a vest with sleeves, and over that a coat like my own. I cannot see what he is wearing below that. What sort of clothing is that anyway? How can a civilized man consent to make himself ridiculous in the eyes of everyone by decking himself out in such outlandish garb? All employees of the Government, and all our fellow citizens, will have to reform such anachronisms in their dress.

By her great achievements the Turkish nation has proved that she is a nation essentially revolutionary and new. Even before these last few years we have entered upon the path of progress. But all our efforts to advance remained relatively futile. The reason we failed was that we did not pursue our purpose with method. It must be clearly recognized, for instance, that human society is made up of the two sexes. Is it possible for one half of society to progress while the other half is neglected? It is imperative that man and woman march together along the way of progress at the same time and in the same step. We may note with satisfaction that we at last appreciate this necessity. Let us look straight at this question, then, and face the consequence with courage.

C. Halidé Edib [Adivar], Dictatorship and Reform in Turkey (1929)*

> Written some years after Mustafa Kemal wrote his account of Turkey's transformation (this Reading, part b), this essay by an ardent feminist and Kemal's onetime close friend offers a more nuanced and critical view. One of Turkey's major novelists, Halidé Edib gained further fame as a patriot, giving impassioned speeches in 1919 when a Greek army invaded Anatolia, and even serving as a noncombatant in the Turkish army. Edib and her distinguished Turkish physician husband Adnan lived in exile until after Ataturk's death, when they returned to Turkey. She then taught English literature at Istanbul University. Her publications include her *Memoirs* (1926), *The Turkish Ordeal* (1928), and several works of fiction.

In the interplay of political parties in Nationalist Turkey, the Kurdish revolt, which took on a grave aspect in 1925, proved a trump card for the extremists in the People's Party to use against the Progressive Republicans. They argued that the clause in the program of the Progressive Republicans advocating freedom of thought had encouraged the insurgents and strengthened the rising. The instigation of the Kurdish rising was attributed to foreign intrigue, and political anxiety was fanned almost into panic at the possibility of another armed struggle.

---

*From Halidé Edib, "Dictatorship and Reforms in Turkey," *Yale Review* XIX (September 1929), pp. 27–44. American spellings adopted. Bracketed material added by the editors. By permission.

[W]hat is of supreme interest is the change of a democratic state, of five years' standing, into a dictatorial one without even an altering of the form or the closing of the National Assembly. . . . Mustafa Kemal Pasha possessed the lightning power of seizing favorable circumstances at the right moment. After all, the Turkish dictatorship was not and is not unique in the world. The postwar world favors dictatorship. Bitterly disillusioned about the old institutions which were not sufficient to stop the great catastrophe of 1914, it seeks something new. The old broke down, crushing what was good as well as what was rotten. The new generation is morbidly impatient to see a new world rise overnight. Hence such words as "liberalism" and "freedom of thought," which lead to a slow growth, are now out of favor in politics. The mob cry of the world is for "spontaneous generation," a sudden, artificial, spontaneous human generation—a process that will turn men into the desired shape with the desired behavior and thought. Hence there has never been so much emphasis on "doing" instead of "thinking" as there is today. Dictatorships have the appearance of "doing" all the time, whether they accomplish lasting changes and effect internal reconstruction or not. Accordingly, they are the latest fashion in politics.

There is no other country which stands in need of "doing" more than Turkey. In such a country a strong, centralized government, if not a dictatorship, with stabilized forces backing it, is inevitable and perhaps necessary. This fundamental psychology of the present world including Turkey will tend to create and to maintain strong, centralized government in Turkey, although the dictatorial form is a passing phase.

But the continuation under the dictatorial regime of 1925 to 1929 in Turkey of reforms—some of them begun long ago—and especially the nature of these reforms, are more interesting and profitable to consider than the terrorist methods by which they are supposed to have been made possible.

This process of reform has been going on for nearly a century, but within the last twenty years it has moved with tremendous rapidity. The story in the Western press, usually the outcome of the most superficial and hurried observation after a pleasant Mediterranean trip, is that Turkey was changed overnight from an Eastern into a Western country. This view is more than superficial; it is false. Whether the recent reforms could have been carried out by other than terrorist methods is a question to be seriously discussed. And there is no doubt that in time they were bound to be carried out—but whether in three years or in thirteen or thirty years, no one can tell. Naturally, one includes among those which were sure to come only the fundamental reforms that will last. The nature of the leading reforms effected by the dictatorial régime in Turkey confirms, as will be shown, the assumption that they are the continuation of Westward movements long under way and are not any sudden departure from the main line of progress which the Turks have taken.

The first and most spectacular of these was the so-called "hat law," passed in 1925. It was also the most futile and superficial in comparison with the others which followed. But it was the *only one* which accomplished a change overnight even in outside appearances. In a week it made the Turks don European hats (the only part of the city-dweller's outfit which was still un-Westernized) and made them look like Westerners, although the manner in which it was accomplished was utterly un-Western. The Westernization of Turkey is not and should not be a question of mere external imitation and gesture. It is a much deeper and more significant process. To tell the Turk to put on a certain headdress and "get civilized" or be hanged, or imprisoned, is absurd, to say the least. The opposition of individuals among the men on the street, really much more Westernized than the people who carried the measure through, had a note of wounded self-respect rather than an objection to the wearing of hats. Among all the recent measures, this was the most seriously opposed in the country itself. Any opposition to the hat law was labeled as reactionary. The interesting fact connected with the substitution of the hat for the Turkish fez is that of all the changes of the last four years it attracted the greatest attention in the Western world. The many fundamental changes taking place in Turkey have been either unnoticed or criticized, or treated as unimportant items of foreign news in Western papers. But the moment the Turks put hats on their heads, the general cry in the West was, "at last the Turks are civilized; they wear hats." Hence those who enacted the hat law might say: "We have killed a few, and imprisoned a large number, but it was good psychology: has anything in the past brought Turkey so into the limelight? Has anything brought the Turk nearer to the European in the European mind?"

In Turkey, the first substantial result of the hat law was that it enriched European hat factories at the expense of the already impoverished Turks. Broadly one can say that the hat law could not have passed in 1925 without a régime of terror. The Islamic reactionaries, the liberals, the people who understand the spirit of the West were all opposed to it for different reasons. What would otherwise have happened is this: a very small number of Turks who had worn hats in the summer in Constantinople would have gradually increased, and in a generation the hat-wearers would have been in a majority in the cities. But the Turkish peasant would have stuck to his old headdress.

The adoption of the Swiss code in place of the Islamic family law in 1926 was an act of a much more serious nature. This could have been put through without much coercion, although there would have been some bitter criticism.

The prevalent journalistic stuff published in the West about Turkish women, declaring that they were freed from harems in thousands, that their veils were lifted, and that they were first allowed to enter public life as a result of this law, is both absurd and untrue. All Turkish men of the progressive type, regardless of the political party to which they belonged, especially from 1908 on, have been in favor of the progress of women and have helped to give them rights and opportunities—educational, economic, and social. From the moment Turkish women entered the economic field there has been no discrimination whatever of the kind which European feminists complain of. Women in Turkey have always received the same salaries or wages as the men, and the fact of their being married or unmarried has never hampered them in their search for work. Lately, women have also had good facilities for education. In 1916 the University of Istanbul opened its doors to them, and among the large number of students who have been sent to Europe, especially to Germany, there were a considerable number of women. Naturally, the Great War gave these movements a practical turn. The governmental departments as well as financial houses and trades then had to employ a great number of women. Not only in the big cities but also in smaller places women were forced to take up some trade and go to work in order to support their families. As breadwinners they became vital and important to the nation as a whole. The large amount of public work which women were thus obliged to do led to a natural social freedom and did away entirely with their partial seclusion in the majority of cities.

A very significant event of the Young Turk régime was the passing of a revised family law in 1916. The Islamic law concerning women had two weak points: polygamy and divorce. In the cities the right of polygamy, outside of the court circle and that of the conservative rich, was not widely exercised. General public opinion banned it, and urban economic conditions were making it an impossibility for a Turk to have even a single wife. But in certain rural districts, especially in Eastern Anatolia, the scarcity of men and the scarcity of labor both led men to take more than one wife whenever they could do so. As to divorce, a man had the right, up to 1916, to repudiate his wife at any moment while a woman had to go to court and prove certain things before she could obtain a divorce.

Before that time, the family law had been within the special jurisdiction of the *Sheih-ul-Islam,* then the judicial head of the Islamic religion in Turkey; and the extreme conservatives as well as the religious bodies were opposed to any change in this situation. The family belonged with religion, they argued, and a change might lead to the entire disintegration of society. Nevertheless, in 1916, the Islamic courts were placed under the authority of the Ministry of Justice, and the family law was revised in favor of women—in the spirit of Islam, although the execution of the law was no longer subject to its control. Marriage in Islam is a mutual contract between man and woman, and the revised law interpreted marriage from that particular point of view. Women were allowed to insert into their marriage contracts every right, including that of divorce. From that time on, educated Turkish women could, and did in a small number of cases, take advantage of this freedom under the law, but the vast number of uneducated women naturally could not profit by it.

A year after the Sultan's government had been abolished in Constantinople, it was seriously discussed whether the revised family law of 1916 should be restored with or without alterations. In 1924 the National Assembly took up the question, and it aroused great interest especially among the women of the cities, and of Constantinople in particular. At a large meeting of women in the Nationalist Club, a committee of women was chosen to study the situation and send a petition to the National Assembly. . . . This committee made a study of the family laws of Sweden, France, England, and Russia, and having found the Swedish law most desirable, sent a translated copy with a petition attached to it to the National Assembly. . . . Their petition at the time had no definite result. But there was a group of very keenly interested young deputies who worked for the adoption of a Western code rather than the restoration of the revised family law of 1916. Mahmoud Essad Bey, the deputy from Smyrna, who became Minister of Justice in 1925, was one of the leading spirits in this movement. In 1926 the new law following the Swiss code was passed. It can be termed, perhaps, one of the two most significant and important changes that have taken place during the dictatorial régime. This particular law will mean the final social unification of the Turks with the European nations, since it gives the Turkish family that kind of stability which constitutes the Western ideal of the family. The decision to adopt the Swiss law, which is entirely Western, instead of to revise and alter the old Islamic family law, which could have made marriage a freer if a less stable institution and brought it nearer to the present Russian law, was one more triumph in Turkey of the Western ideal over the Eastern ideal, and one of more importance for the future than is presently realized.

The educational rights that Turkish women have gained are no longer questioned even by the smallest minority, and the sphere of their work has been constantly widening. It is perhaps a blessing that they have not obtained the vote. Thus they have been protected from the danger of being identified with party politics, and their activities outside the political world could not be stopped for political reasons. [Turkish women received the right to vote in 1934.]

In the Turkish home, women continue to be the ruling spirit, more so, perhaps, because the majority contribute to the upkeep by their labors. At the present time, offices, factories, and shops are filled with women workers in the cities; and in addition to their breadwinning jobs, and sometimes in connection with them, women have interested themselves in child welfare and hygiene, and in organizing small associations to teach poor women embroidery, sewing, weaving, and so on. The favorite profession of Turkish women today, after teaching, is medicine. All this is the city aspect of the situation. In the rural districts, women still continue to live their old life with its old drudgery, and will continue to live under these conditions until a more up-to-date agricultural system is adopted and the rudiments of education can be taught them. It would not be an underestimate to say that something like ninety percent of the Turkish women are very hard workers; the question is not how to provide more work for them but how to train them better for their work and to give them more leisure. The small percentage of the idle rich (much smaller in Turkey than elsewhere) do on a miniature scale what the idle rich of other countries do. Unfortunately, Turkey is judged by the life and attitude of these idlers, who are conspicuous to the eyes of the traveler, rather than by the hard-working majority.

In 1928 the clause in the Turkish constitution which declared Islam the state religion was abolished. This act was again the culmination of a process that had been going on for a number of years. As far back as 1908 the Young Turks had adopted a definite policy tending to the separation of church and state. The Turkish sociological writer Zia Keup-Alp first openly argued for the necessity of taking the *Sheih-ul-Islam* out of the cabinet, as a step towards secularization—

he wanted the *Sheih-ul-Islam* to be in a position like that of the other heads of churches in Turkey, the Patriarchs. Zia Keup-Alp was then one of the influential members of the Central Committee of the Young Turk Party, and under him an active campaign for the secularization and nationalization of Islam in Turkey was carried on. The Koran was then translated into Turkish for the first time. He constantly championed the idea of religious reform, believing that a change in the direction of progress and enlightenment in the West had come after the Reformation, and that neither Turkey nor any other Islamic nation could progress or live without a deep reform in Islam.

The change of the Turkish alphabet from the Arabic to the Latin characters is as important as the adoption of the Swiss family law in its future significance. Although this change was not made until last year [1928, when the Turks unveiled their new alphabet], it was the result of a much earlier movement affecting not only the alphabet but the language. . . . The desire to purge and purify and to nationalize the language, the desire to free it from the artificial superstructure of Arabic and Persian, was both articulate and general.

In March, 1929, the law of Maintenance of Order—the law which made a party dictatorship possible in Turkey, without an altering of the Constitution, and merely by a use of a constitutional sanction for dictatorship—was abrogated. But the momentum of the last four years, plus the temperament, the self-interest, and the conviction of certain minds that a dictatorship is the thing, is still prolonging its oppressive atmosphere. In form Turkey is bound to stay a republic. The traditional forces are so much destroyed and discredited that the revival of the sultanate is an impossibility. Whether military figures, with a party behind them, can assume a dictatorial power for very much longer will depend on what is going on in the world in general and in Europe in particular. Will there be a future united, though not uniform, Europe? If one could solve the sorry riddle of European destiny, one could clearly answer the question, Whither Turkey?

D. Michel Aflaq, Purifying the National Ideal: *Baath* Ideology (1959, revised 1963)*

Cofounder of the *Baath* Party and certainly its main ideologist, Aflaq drew on earlier pan-Arab thought and his own experiences to develop the outlook presented here. Readers should note the *Baath*'s anti-Communism and anti-Marxism, its semimystical evocation of nationalism, and the determination to use force against its enemies. Born to a Greek Orthodox Christian family in Damascus, Aflaq

*From Michel Aflaq, *For the Sake of the Ba'th* (Beirut, 1959; 2nd ed., 1963), translated from the Arabic, as excerpted and edited by Kemal Karpat in *Political and Social Thought in the Contemporary Middle East,* revised and enlarged ed. (New York: Praeger, 1982), pp. 145–47, 151–53. Rearranged. Bracketed material added and Arabic words italicized by the editors. By permission.

studied in Paris where he briefly joined the French Communist Party. Aside from his ideological pronouncements, Aflaq did not influence decision making in either the Syrian or the Iraqi Baathist states once Hafez al-Asad and Saddam Husayn assumed power.

The Arab *Ba'th* is a unique movement that undertakes neither to disguise problems nor to treat them superficially; it sees itself as reflecting the soul of the nation and her various needs. When we say that this is [a] revolutionary movement [we] must first of all forge the essence of the nation and rekindle in the Arab personality its strength to fight and to shoulder the responsibilities of life, we also have in mind the recovery by Arab thought of its aptitude for seeing things directly, freely, without artifice or imitation. Arab thought will then be in line with the laws of nature and of life; it will be able to understand problems in their true perspective and organize its work in a creative manner. In saying this, we have in view our great mission which is to lead the Arabs, individually and collectively, toward this healthy state of thought and mind.

Communist socialism is limited. It is based, in effect, on an economic philosophy, Marxism, whose economic and historical conceptions nowadays cannot stand up to true scientific criticism. In addition, we observe that this Communist socialism is difficult to achieve and does not correspond to the reality we know. In fact, it can only succeed through world revolution. *Ba'th* socialism is flexible and is not tied by artificial economic laws. In addition, it can be easily achieved and corresponds to reality, for it consists simply in a fair and healthy economic reorganization of Arab society. This socialism will be achieved when Arabs take charge of their own destiny and free themselves from imperialism and feudalism.

We consider that the Communist Party is a destructive force, for two reasons. The first resides in its deceptive socialism which promises the Arab people all they direly need, at the same time trying to drag it into the clutches of another state, Russia. The second reason is its internationalism [forcing every Communist country to promote world revolution].

If we come to power in Syria, we will abolish the differences between the privileged classes and the others; we will ensure justice, at the same time preparing ourselves to perfect our work. Perhaps we shall not be able to give the people all they desire; perhaps even we shall take a part of what they need, in order to equip the army and ensure the success of the *coups d'état* in all the Arab countries. Socialism cannot be achieved in Syria alone, for Syria is a small state with limited resources. It cannot be achieved, because imperialism and the pressure exerted by all the other Arab countries make the total success of socialism just as difficult there. That is why our socialism will only be able to gain definite recognition in the framework of a single Arab united state—that is to say, when the Arab people are freed, and when the impediments that oppose the success of socialism, such as imperialism, feudalism, and the geographical frontiers created by politics, are removed.

The National Socialism of Germany and of Italy is linked to Nazi and fascist philosophy, based on the idea of racial superiority and on the difference between peoples, i.e., on the superiority of one kind over another and their right to dominate the world. These philosophies likewise establish differences between nationals of the same nation, which leads to the dictatorship of an individual or of a class. True socialism cannot succeed in such a system.

Ba'th socialism is inspired by its own philosophy, does not despise other nations, and does not aim at domination. It is an end in itself, to procure economic and social benefits that are easily achieved.

There is no doubt that within the same nation there is a struggle between those who own the means of production and those who do not. But even within the same nation, it is not possible to view this struggle in the literal and arbitrary manner proposed by Marxism. To begin with, we have rejected internationalism in the Marxist sense and have advocated a free cooperation among independent socialist countries. Hence we accept the links binding us Arabs to other nations and we admit the possibility of meeting together on equal terms, not under the orders of an organization like Communism. This latter course has led, as you know, to the subjection of all the working classes to the Soviet Union, where they act as mere agents of Soviet policy.

Hence, our advocacy of free cooperation among independent socialist countries is more realistic and appropriate. Within the Arab world, we have tackled the problem in a manner that differs from Marxism: We have postulated the national problem as an indivisible whole and have not, like the Marxists, merely isolated the economic aspect, namely, the conflict between the owners and those who do not own. Our problem is much more extensive than this: It is a problem of a nation that is fragmented and partly colonized. Fragmentation is the major obstacle in its path of progress. It is also a problem of a backward nation—in mentality, in its economy, in politics, and in everything. We must build everything anew. Thus, we have placed the Arab nation to one side and all who attempt to retard its progress, to another. The capitalists and feudalists are not the only enemies of the Arabs; there are also the politicians who cling to this state of fragmentation because it serves their own interests; there are, in addition, those who submit to the imperialists, in one form or another, and finally, those who fight ideas, education, evolution, enlightenment, toleration, and the independence of our homeland. All these men we have placed on one side and the Arab nation on the other. Therefore, we do not claim to have divided our nation into two or more classes, on the Marxist pattern. We maintain that a man of religion, for example, who sows the seeds of religious fanaticism and is poor, is as detrimental to society as the capitalists and feudalists who exploit workers and peasants.

Nevertheless . . . the economic problem is essential. If we are to justify our leniency toward exploiters and reactionaries by using nationality as an excuse, we would deprive our struggle of its vital nerve. This conflict between the masses who are deprived of ownership and the exploiting class, which hinders all development and is deaf to all appeals to the national interest, is in fact beneficial and should not frighten us, since it will lead to national resurgence. From the liberation of the poor masses will issue forth the virtuous Arab citizen who is capable of understanding his nationalism and of achieving its ideals, since nationalism loses all its significance if it exists alongside injustice, poverty, and privation.

The matter is not as easy as you might suppose. . . . We must guard against the deceptive boasts of interested men who falsely advocate the national interest and merely wish to protect their skins when, in attempting to influence us, they ask: "Are we not all of one nation?" The Ba'thists must be on their guard against such guile. Nationalism as currently understood in our homeland or in the West is, for the most part, a negative and illusory concept permeated with reactionary and exploitationist beliefs. It is our duty to strip away this mask of negativism and deception. Nor need we be afraid of this, because a core will always remain after we have purified the nationalist idea. This core may be something very simple and insubstantial but it is nevertheless essential. Nationalism, in truth, is not vanity, is not fanaticism vis-à-vis other nations, is foreign to all material interests of a certain class, and is, in fact, humanism itself manifested and realized in one living reality: the nation.

Therefore, we accept only the positive aspects of nationalism, having cast aside all fanaticism and superficialities. Nationalism is the spiritual and historical bond between members of a nation, whom history has stamped in a special manner and has not isolated from the rest of humanity. History gave those members of a nation a distinctive character and a distinctive personification of humanity so that they might become active parts of this latter, creating and interacting with the whole. . . . [N]ationalism . . . is not built upon malice toward other nations or toward our fellow-citizens. The struggle we have created within our nation is not vicious but beneficial. Love, in reality, is a hard thing. For when we love our nation and our fellow-Arabs and wish them a prosperous future and a dignified life, we do not shrink from the use of force against all who attempt to hinder our progress and our evolution.

16. Muhammad Ali Jinnah, Divide India; Create Pakistan (1940)*

The collapse of the Mughal empire left a sizable Muslim population in British India, but one far short of a majority except in the northwest and northeast regions of the country. As the sentiment for independence from colonial-

---

*Excerpt from Muhammad Ali Jinnah's presidential address delivered at the All-India Muslim League meeting in Lahore, March 1940, in Jamil-Ud-Din Ahmad, ed., *Some Recent Speeches and Writings of Mr. Jinnah*, 3rd ed. (Lahore: Sh. M. Ashraf, 1943), pp. 152–56. American spellings adopted.

ism grew, the question came up of whether or not Hindus and Muslims could coexist in a postcolonial unitary state. In this 1940 speech the leading Muslim nationalist, Jinnah (1876–1948), voiced the conviction that no such coexistence was desirable, or even possible.

Denying that he offered a communalist argument based on cultural incompatibility, Jinnah nevertheless argued that people who do not intermarry, or eat in each other's homes, or share the same literature, must live in separate states. This invocation of almost instinctual separation provides an example of what sociologists call the "self-confirming prophecy"—believing in something that most people dismiss as impossible to achieve and speaking, publishing, and acting on that belief, helping to bring about the predicted situation that might otherwise not have happened.

In seeking a Muslim state in India separate from the predominantly Hindu one (both came into existence seven years after this speech), Jinnah failed to anticipate that the same alleged incompatability that prevented living together at peace in the same state might also lead to strife between Hindus and Muslims living in adjoining states. Jinnah died in the midst of the mutual slaughter that followed independence on August 15, 1947, as did the Hindu leader, Mohandas K. Gandhi (1869–1948), who very reluctantly favored partition of India with Muslims and Hindus living in separate states.

The problem in India is not of an inter-communal character but manifestly of an international one, and it must be treated as such. If the British Government are really in earnest and sincere to secure peace and happiness of the people of this subcontinent, the only course open to us all is to allow the major nations separate homelands by dividing India into "autonomous national states." There is no reason why these states should be antagonistic to each other. On the other hand the rivalry and the natural desire and efforts on the part of one to dominate the social order and establish political supremacy over the other in the government of the country will disappear. It will lead more towards natural good-will by international pacts between them, and they can live in complete harmony with their neighbors. This will lead further to a friendly settlement all the more easily with regard to minorities by reciprocal arrangements and adjustments between Muslim India and Hindu India, which will far more adequately and effectively safeguard the rights and interests of Muslims and various other minorities.

It is extremely difficult to appreciate why our Hindu friends fail to understand the real nature of Islam and Hinduism. They are not religions in the strict sense of the word, but are, in fact, different and distinct social orders, and it is a dream that the Hindus and Muslims can ever evolve a common nationality, and this misconception of one Indian nation has gone far beyond the limits and is the cause of most of your troubles and will lead India to destruction if we fail to revise our notions in time. The Hindus and Muslims belong to two different religious philosophies, social customs, literatures. They neither intermarry nor interdine together and, indeed, they belong to two different civilizations which are based mainly on conflicting ideas and conceptions. Their aspects on life and of life are different. It is quite clear that Hindus and Muslims derive their inspiration from different sources of history. They have different epics, different heroes, and different episodes. Very often the hero of one is a foe of the other and, likewise, their victories and defeats overlap. To yoke together two such nations under a single state, one as a numerical minority and the other as a majority, must lead to growing discontent and final destruction of any fabric that may be so built up for the government of such a state.

The present artificial unity of India dates back only to the British conquest and is maintained by the British bayonet, but the termination of the British regime, which is implicit in the recent declaration of his Majesty's Government, will be the herald of the entire break-up with worse disaster than has ever taken place during the last one thousand years under Muslims. Surely that is not the legacy which Britain would bequeath to India after 150 years of her rule, nor would Hindu and Muslim India risk such a sure catastrophe.

Muslim India cannot accept any constitution which must necessarily result in a Hindu majority government. Hindus and Muslims brought together under a democratic system forced upon the minorities can only mean Hindu *raj*. Democracy of the kind with which the Congress High Command is enamored would mean the complete destruction of what is most precious in Islam.

Muslims are not a minority as it is commonly known and understood. One only has to look round. Even today, according to the British map of India, 4 out of 11 provinces, where the Muslims dominate more or less, are functioning notwithstanding the decision of the Hindu Congress High Command to . . . prepare for civil disobedience. Muslims are a nation according to any definition of a nation, and they must have their homelands, their territory and their state. We wish to live in peace and harmony with our neighbors as a free and independent people. We wish our people to develop to the fullest our spiritual, cultural, economic, social and political life in a way that we think best and in consonance with our own ideals and according to the genius of our people. Honesty demands and the vital interests of millions of our people impose a sacred duty upon us to find an honorable and peaceful solution, which would be just and fair to all. But at the same time we cannot be moved or diverted from our purpose and objective by threats or intimidations. We must be prepared to face all difficulties and consequences, make all the sacrifices that may be required of us to achieve the goal we have set in front of us.

[This is] the task that lies ahead of us. Do you realize how big and stupendous it is? Do you realize that you cannot get freedom or independence by mere arguments? The intelligentsia in all countries in the world have been the pioneers of any movements of freedom. What does the Muslim intelligentsia propose to do? I may tell you that unless you get this into your blood, unless you are prepared to take off your coats and are willing to sacrifice all that you can and work selflessly, earnestly and sincerely for your people, you will never realize your aim. Friends, I therefore want you to make up your mind definitely and then think of devices and organize your people, strengthen your organization and consolidate the Muslims all over India. I think that the masses are wide awake. They only want your guidance and your lead. Come forward as servants of Islam, organize the people economically, socially, educationally and politically and I am sure that you will be a power that will be accepted by everybody.

17. Peter J. Sluglett and Marion Farouk-Sluglett, Divide and Rule in British-Controlled Iraq (1991)*

The artificial boundaries and the joining together of disparate peoples with different religious beliefs and ethnicities in the Middle Eastern mandates created by the League of Nations in the early 1920s, as the Introduction to this chapter shows, intensified divisions within and among the states carved out of Ottoman territory. Iraq was one of these states. It contained a significant portion of the region's Kurdish population, who hoped to unite with Kurds in Iran, Syria, and Turkey to form a Kurdish state. But the Turks and the British found it in their interests to keep the Kurds from unifying in a single state. (see Map p. 141)

The Kurds in Iraq sat on some of the richest oil reserves in the Middle East in the northern Mosul region, and no controlling power would agree to give up those revenues. The British played off the various Iraqi groups against one another and thereby assured continuing strife even after the formal disbanding of colonial authority. The picture presented here of Iraq applies to many other fragile nations that originated in the post–World War I era, when most of the Middle East was under direct Western domination. In this case, the British placed Hashemite Prince Faysal (Faisal) I (1885–1933) on the Iraqi throne in 1921 after the French expelled him from Syria a year earlier. His grandson Faysal II (1935–58) and the young king's prime minister Nuri al-Said (1888–1958) both were killed in the army coup d'état of 1958 that overthrew the monarchy.

Peter J. Sluglett, professor of history at the University of Utah, and the late Marion Farouk-Sluglett, who taught at the University College of Wales, Swansea, U.K., together wrote *Iraq Since 1958: From Revolution to Dictatorship* (1990). He is presently doing research on the urban history of the Middle East.

*From Peter Sluglett and Marion Farouk-Sluglett, "Iraq," in *Tuttle Guide to the Middle East* (Boston, Rutland, VT, and Tokyo: Charles E. Tuttle Co., 1992, © 1991), pp. 84, 86–88. Foreign words italicized. Bracketed material added by the editors. American spellings adopted. By permission.

* * *

The modern state of Iraq was created in 1920, as part of the peace settlement after the First World War. The victorious Allies divided the Arab provinces of the former Ottoman Empire between them; Britain, which had been in occupation of the provinces of Basra and Baghdad for most of the war, and Mosul by the end of the war, was appointed mandatory power under the new system of international trusteeship established by the League of Nations.

Although parts of the country had been united under a single government at various times in the past, the entity which emerged in 1920 had had no previous independent existence as a nation state. Britain imported a king, Faisal, the son of *Sharif* Husain [Husayn] of Mecca, and endowed Iraq with a constitution and a bicameral legislature. The mandate, a form of indirect rule where Arab ministers and officials were closely supervised by British advisers whose advice had to be taken, came to an end in 1932, when Iraq was admitted to the League of Nations as an independent state. By this time Britain had secured Iraq's present northern boundary, had made sure that the concession for oil exploration and exploitation was given to the Iraq Petroleum Company, a conglomerate of British, Dutch, French and United States oil interests, and had created a social base for the monarchy by confirming "suitable" tribal leaders in full possession of what had previously been the customary holdings of "their" tribes. In addition, Britain retained military bases in Iraq and continued to exercise strong political and economic influence.

In 1941, a group of Iraqi officers led a short-lived resistance movement against Britain which resulted in a second British occupation until the end of the war. Between 1945 and 1958 the country was governed by a succession of 24 cabinets, most of which contained combinations of the same handful of individuals, often headed by the veteran pro-British politician Nuri al-Sa'id. Genuine opposition parties were banned for most of this period, which meant that there was little room for the development of a democratic tradition. Many Iraqis believed that the country's most urgent need was national independence, which would be followed by economic development and social reforms, both of which were being blocked or denied by the monarchy and its British sponsors. At the same time the state was almost universally seen as the "natural" vehicle to carry out these reforms and to implement the development so urgently needed. This kind of thinking, usually but not always associated with "socialism," had wide currency elsewhere in the Middle East in the post-war period and was by no means unique to Iraq.

During and after the Second World War, members of the rising middle classes were expanding their investments in manufacture, commerce and real estate, a process which accelerated in the 1950s when oil began to make a major impact on the economy. Although oil revenues were still modest, they were sufficient to finance the expansion of the bureaucracy, the educational system and other services, and this increase in government expenditure had a generally stimulating effect on the economy.

Private capital continued to be concentrated in the hands of some 25 families, many of whom had controlling interests in several different kinds of business. Between them, these families controlled more than half of all private corporate commercial and industrial wealth. Far below them in status and wealth were medium-to-small property-owners, religious dignitaries and local notables, wholesale and retail merchants, manufacturers, owners of workshops and repair shops, petty traders and so on, as well as the newly emerging intelligentsia of professionals, lawyers, army officers and civil servants. This latter group, together with large sections of the urban poor, felt acutely aware of the exclusive nature of the political system and came to form the core of the independence movement in the 1940s and 1950s. The beginnings of a working class were also emerging particularly in the large foreign-owned enterprises such as the railways, Basra port and the Iraq Petroleum Company. Because of its close links with the independence movement, organized labor developed into an effective political force in the years preceding the [1958] revolution.

Ethnic and Sectarian Divisions

On another level, in spite of the far-reaching effects of these changes, Iraq society contained, and continues to contain, elements which had never been combined in an independent and separate polity. Then as now, the population was divided into a variety of overlapping categories, including social and ethnic origin, religious sect, occupation, and regional and tribal background. Apart from the Christian (3.6%) . . . communities, some 95% of Iraqis are Muslims. About a quarter of the Muslims are Kurds, who are mostly *Sunni* Muslims; the remaining three-quarters are Arabs. The Arab Muslims are divided into *Sunnis* and Twelver *Shias,* the latter forming the largest single religious community in the country.

Iraqi censuses do not provide details of sectarian affiliation, but as the two sects (*Sunni* and *Shia*) live in distinct parts of the country (apart from Baghdad and Basra, which are mixed) it is possible to make some broad generalizations. The *Shias* form 52% of the total Muslim population, and, perhaps more significantly, 70% of the Arab Muslim population. Southern Iraq is predominantly *Shia,* while the center, west and north of the country are mainly *Sunni.* The main shrines of Twelver *Shiism* (also the "state religion" of Iraq's neighbor Iran) are located in Iraq, at Najaf, Karbala, Samarra, and Kadhimain, a district of Baghdad. These shrines are major centers of religious learning as well as the traditional residences of the spiritual leaders of the worldwide Twelver *Shia* community.

As the Ottoman Empire was a *Sunni* institution, what state educational facilities existed in Iraq were mainly for *Sunnis;* in addition, *Shias* were both disinclined to enter, and not recruited into, government service. Furthermore, before the First World War most *Shias* were concentrated either in the countryside away from the centers of government or in the shrine towns, which had a fairly independent existence. Hence, when the new state was created in 1920,

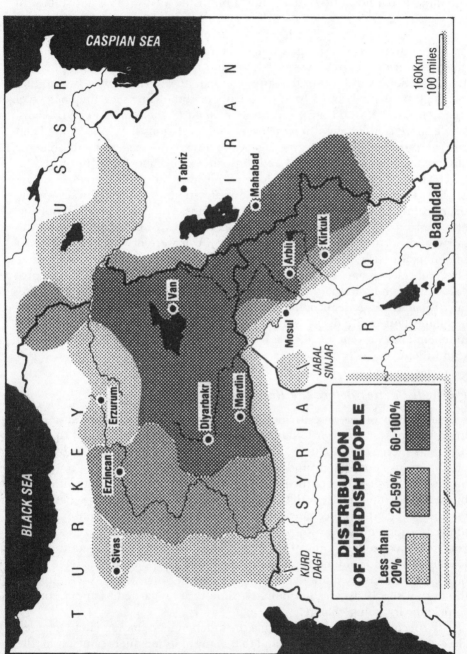

Distribution of the Kurdish People

very few *Shias* entered government service, a situation which changed only with the rapid expansion of (secular) education in the 1940s, 1950s and 1960s. In consequence, the *Shias* "started off" by being under-represented politically. This tendency has continued, and has been compounded by other factors such as an increasingly repressive state, which reinforces communal identity, the exclusive nature of the regime since 1968, and the continuous deterioration in Iraq's relations with Iran. In the latter context, however, it should be said that although Iraqi and Iranian *Shias* are members of the same sect, Iraqi *Shias* feel themselves to be Arab Iraqis, and Iranian *Shias* feel themselves to be Iranians. While there is a certain affinity between *Shias* relations have not always been cordial, and there is also a degree of rivalry between the religious establishments at Qom and Mashhad [in Iran] and those at Karbala and Najaf [in Iraq].

The population is also divided along ethnic lines. About 72% are Arabs, 23% are Kurds—there are also Kurdish communities in Iran, Syria and Turkey—while the remaining 5% consist of Turcomans, Assyrians, Armenians and other smaller ethnic groups. The Kurds form a compact majority of the population in the north and north-west of the country. Most Kurds were originally members of semi-nomadic tribes, but constraints on cross-frontier movements and other economic factors have encouraged sedentarization and wider educational provision, urban migration and various political developments have tended to reduce tribal ties. In general, both the sectarian and ethnic divisions were becoming less important in the decades preceding the 1958 revolution, as the national independence movement acted as a crucial unifying factor and helped to transcend them.

Political Parties Before the Revolution

For a variety of reasons, no liberal democratic party was able to muster anything like mass support or to build up an effective machinery under the mandate and monarchy (1920–58). Such parties as existed tended to be loose organizations centered around prominent personalities. After the mid-1920s most of the leading Iraqi participants in the Arab Revolt, in company with Faisal himself, made their peace with the mandatory power (unlike their Syrian counterparts . . .) and had become dependent on Britain for the maintenance of the status quo and their own positions within it. As long as they remained in control it was virtually impossible for an effective pluralistic democratic system to emerge, and no genuine opposition party could gain power through the ballot box. As a result, constitutional democracy had become widely discredited by the end of the 1950s and the military came to be regarded as an acceptable vehicle for initiating change.

It is a peculiarity of Iraqi politics that the independence movement functioned almost exclusively underground, and that many of its members came under the influence of the Communist party (founded in 1934), which organized almost all the mass demonstrations and strikes of the 1940s and early 1950. After Jamal

Abdal Nasser's rise to power in Egypt in 1952, the pan-Arab nationalists and the Ba'thists also began to gain influence, especially among the *Sunni* population. Before Nasser, partly because of Iraq's ethnic and communal heterogeneity, pan-Arabism had made little headway; Iraqi nationalism had a far wider appeal. Even in the late 1950s there was no Nasserist party as such, and the Ba'th, founded in Syria [see Reading 15d] and brought to Iraq by Syrian school-teachers in the early 1950s, had only 300 members in 1955, the year when Saddam Husain joined.

Chapter V

Arabs and Zionists Struggle Over Palestine

Introduction

The struggle between Palestinians and Zionists began in the 1890s, when the Ottoman empire controlled the Fertile Crescent, a region that encompassed Iraq and Syria and included Palestine. In this chapter we begin with the situation in Ottoman Palestine, and then describe the origins of modern Zionism. World War I gave control of Palestine to Great Britain, which allowed Zionist settlers there to create a "national home" much to the distress of the Arab residents. Unrest and rebellion in the interwar years impelled Britain to abandon Palestine after World War II. We then narrate the establishment in 1948 (during a war between Zionists and Arabs) of the state of Israel and the more than half a century of conflict that followed and still rages.

Palestine's Land and People

Ottoman authorities, determined to prevent communal strife at Palestine's holy sites (sacred to Muslims, Jews, and Christians), placed portions of Palestine under the jurisdiction of the Ottoman interior ministry in Istanbul, while the Nablus and Acre districts came under the control of the governor of Beirut. The sultan and wealthy local families owned about one-third of the land on which Arab cultivators worked. Peasants also farmed collectively owned fields, allocated to them by village elders. In the mid-nineteenth-century reform period (see Reading 10) Ottoman rulers attempted to distribute land, but many peasants, fearing the burden of taxation that came with ownership, preferred to have land registered in the names of trusted local notables who could bargain with tax collectors. Much of this land eventually passed into the hands of the heirs of the old local notables, who hired landless day laborers or sharecroppers. Land grievances thus predated twentieth-century problems in Palestine.

Muslim and Christian Arabs made up 80 percent of the 738,000 inhabitants of prewar Palestine. About 85,000 Jews, mostly elderly, lived mainly in Jerusalem. There they kept alive the religious yearning, exemplified in many Jewish pious texts, that one day Jews living in the Diaspora outside of Palestine would return to Zion, the Holy Land, to await the arrival of the Messiah. This small community kept a presence at the city's Western or "Wailing" Wall, the remnant of the ancient biblical temple that the Romans destroyed in the first century C.E. They prayed there and lamented their dispersal. From Palestine they sent emissaries yearly throughout the Diaspora to collect funds to support the community and to pray with the Jews they met for their return to Zion.

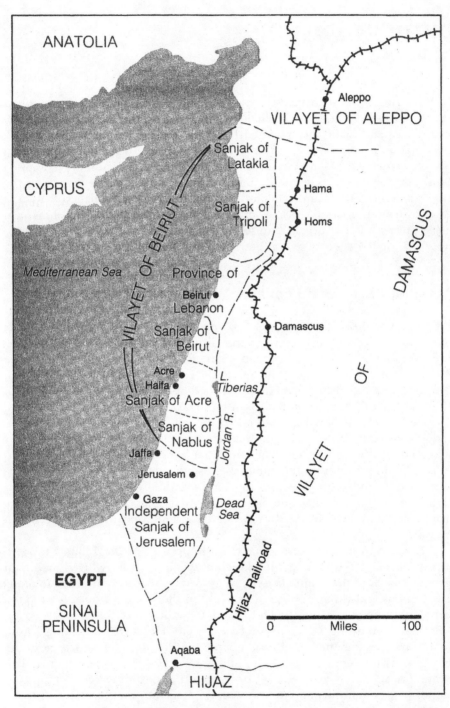

ANATOLIA

VILAYET OF ALEPPO

Aleppo

Sanjak of
Latakia

CYPRUS

Hama

Sanjak of
Tripoli

Homs

Mediterranean Sea

Province of

VILAYET OF BEIRUT

Beirut

Lebanon

DAMASCUS

Sanjak of
Beirut

Damascus

Acre

Haifa

Sanjak of Acre

L.
Tiberias

Sanjak of
Nablus

Jordan R.

Jaffa

Jerusalem

Gaza

*Dead
Sea*

VILAYET

Independent
Sanjak of
Jerusalem

OF

EGYPT

SINAI
PENINSULA

Hijaz Railroad

0   Miles   100

Aqaba

HIJAZ

Ottoman Palestine and Syria

After remaining stable for centuries, the population of Palestine increased by several thousand as Jews established new Zionist settlements there during the last decades of the nineteenth century. By contrast, over 90 percent of the Palestinian Arabs descended from families residing there for centuries and only about 8 percent arrived recently. Migration or death during World War I reduced the Jewish population by a quarter, the Muslims by 6 percent, and the Christians by 13 percent.

Having little connection to the older Jewish community in Palestine, modern Zionism arose in response to the upsurge of European anti-Semitism and had few roots in the Middle East. Its founder, Theodor Herzl (1860–1904), a Viennese journalist, became incensed when a powerful anti-Semitic political movement took power in his city. He also reacted strongly against government-sponsored anti-Jewish riots (pogroms) in eastern Europe and the French government's false accusation of a Jewish army officer, Alfred Dreyfus (1859–1935), of selling military secrets to the Germans. Herzl believed that for the protection from such persecution, European Jews had to migrate to a land of their own. In 1896 he published *The Jewish State* (see Reading 18a), and created the World Zionist Movement. After Herzl's early death, the British Zionist Chaim Weizmann (1874–1952) and others carried on Herzl's work. Palestinian Arabs and Muslim intellectuals followed this movement from its inception in the late nineteenth century and vocally opposed land sales to Zionists and Zionist settlements (see Readings 18b and c).

Modern Zionism arose in an age of nationalism, but it differed from other nationalist movements in that the Jewish Zionists wished to create a state where thousands of years earlier Jews had ruled over a kingdom. Expelled by the Romans, the Jews lived scattered in a Diaspora where they possessed no territory to establish a Jewish nation. They therefore had to first locate and claim such territory and then build a state on it by the ingathering of Jewish people scattered throughout the world. All other nationalisms consolidated fragmented national territory and constructed states where the population already lived; the main task for them consisted of mobilizing national sentiment and consolidating small political units into a more or less unified central state, as Italy, Germany, and Japan had recently done.

Since the Jews could not follow this route, Herzl's *Jewish State* showed them an alternate path: first, to gain the backing of a great power, which would grant them sovereignty over a territorial base somewhere on earth. That power would then protect the fledgling community as it grew and developed. (As it turned out, Britain, and later the United States, provided the Zionists these services.) Secondly, they had to operate gradually. Since Jewish migrants would come from distant lands, to regions where they would meet hostile populations, they had to proceed slowly without revealing their long-range goal. Mainly they had to build the institutions of their settlements piece by piece, until their communities could leap into statehood.

Great Britain, Zionism, and the Arabs

Herzl had tried unsuccessfully to convince the Ottoman sultan to allow Jewish immigrants to settle in Palestine and began seeking a Jewish homeland in South America or Africa. But the Zionist movement he founded refused to consider any alternative to Palestine. Before World War I many thousands of Zionist immigrants did reach Palestine, as we have mentioned. But when that war pitted Great Britain against the Ottoman empire, geopolitical considerations moved Zionist plans much closer to realization.

When Ottoman forces attacked the British stronghold at the Suez Canal from bases in Palestine, the London government realized Palestine's strategic importance and sought ways to retract an earlier promise to the French to allow them to include most of Palestine within a future Syrian state. Also, Britain's ally, czarist Russia, faring badly against the German assault, seemed on the verge of pulling out of the war. The British Foreign Office conceived of attempting to win backing from Russian Jews by promising them a "national home" in Palestine, hoping that they would use their influence to keep Russia fighting. That hope never materialized, since czarist Russia ceased to exist in 1917, when the Bolshevik revolutionaries triumphed and made a humiliating separate peace with the Germans—who eventually lost the war because of defeats elsewhere.

The British promise took the form of the November 2, 1917, letter from Foreign Secretary Arthur James Lord Balfour (1848–1930) to British Zionists assuring them that the government viewed "with favor the establishment in Palestine of a national home for the Jewish people" (Reading 19a). Britain did not consult Arab leaders about this momentous shift in policy, known as the Balfour Declaration. The Arabs remained skeptical of the phrase in that declaration saying "nothing shall be done which may prejudice the civil and religious rights of the existing non-Jewish communities," and did not accept British assurances that a "national home" would not become a Jewish state.

After the war, when the victors translated the Sykes-Picot agreement (Reading 13c) into League of Nations mandates, the Balfour Declaration became a formal part of Britain's Palestinian mandate. However, when the British quickly severed the desert area east of the Jordan River (Transjordan) from the Palestine mandate, they stipulated that the Balfour Declaration did not apply to Transjordan, which the British gave to one of the sons of the *Sharif* Husayn of Arabia.

Arabs categorically opposed the Balfour Declaration and British control of Palestine, but the Zionists welcomed both. Mandate regulations provided little opportunity for the Arab majority lawfully to protest or resist establishment of the Jewish home, or for the Zionists to transform that home into a nation, except by extralegal methods. Zionists and the Arabs eventually resorted to war against each other and against the British as well.

Zionists and Palestinians Under British Authority

To Herzl's two strategic principles (great power backing and gradualism) another Zionist, David Ben-Gurion (1886–1973), provided a third requirement: that everyone coming into the new state-in-the-making had to learn and speak Hebrew, the national language. This requirement put everyone at the same disadvantage since they all, including religious scholars and rabbis, had to learn the living language, not only its liturgical form. Ben-Gurion also understood, following Herzl, that the new migrants also had to build institutions for statehood and social solidarity in order to succeed when the moment for creating the state arrived. A Polish Jew, Ben-Gurion migrated to Palestine in 1906 and rose to power in two of the major institutions Zionists created—the *Histadrut* Labor Federation and the Jewish Agency, responsible for bringing Jewish immigrants to Palestine. (In 1948 he became Israel's first prime minister.) A third agency, the Jewish National Fund (JNF), working closely with the other two, handled land purchases.

Arab opposition to Jewish settlement developed early. Prior to World War I and in the postwar mandate years, the land question became the main point of contention between Zionists and Arabs. Financed by Diaspora Jewry, the JNF bought up land in Palestine under regulations that provided that it would forever belong to the *yishuv*. Arabs saw Jewish land purchases as expropriation of territory rightfully theirs. Furthermore, wishing to depend only on Jewish labor, settlers ejected Arab rural workers, provoking strikes and accelerating Palestinian dispossession and proletarianization. As the Palestinian rural economy weakened in the 1920s, the *yishuv* acquired more land. After 1929 the JNF increasingly obtained fertile tracts from local Palestinian landowners who needed money to transform wheat fields into orchards. Yet the Zionists never controlled more than 8 percent of the total mandate territory—about 20 percent of its fertile land.

When Palestine's British-controlled administration took shape, initial Arab unwillingness to participate ensured the smaller Jewish community of disproportionate influence on how to spend tax revenues, the bulk of which came from the far more numerous Arabs. Palestinians received fewer jobs and less credit, agricultural aid, and welfare benefits. Economic hardship in the 1920s and '30s inflamed Arab resentment toward the British, the Zionists, and the Arab landlords who continued selling land. But class divisions and clan rivalries often inhibited the Palestinans from acting collectively on their grievances. Two leading Arab families of Jerusalem, the Nashashibis and the al-Husaynis, competed for dominance, and the British attempted to co-opt one prominent militant, Muhammad Amin al-Husayni (1895–1974), whom they appointed *mufti* (head religious official) of Palestine in 1921. Eventually al-Husayni enjoyed a large budget and wielded considerable power, but he never abandoned his pursuit of Palestinian goals.

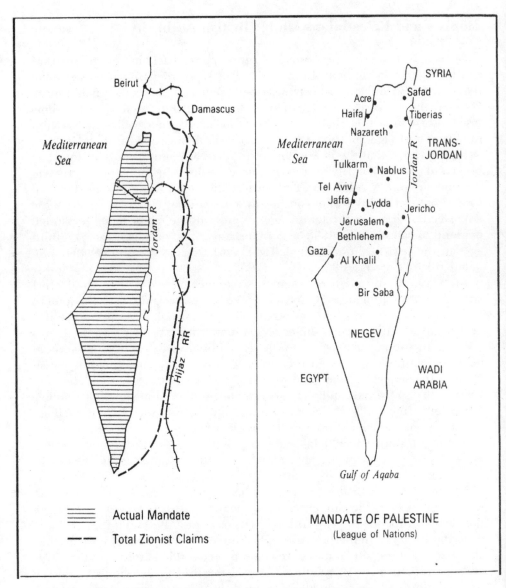

Beirut

Damascus

*Mediterranean
Sea*

Jordan R.

Hijaz RR

SYRIA

Acre   Safad
Haifa   Tiberias
Nazareth
TRANS-
JORDAN

*Mediterranean
Sea*

Tulkarm   Nablus

Tel Aviv
Jaffa   Lydda
Jericho
Jerusalem
Bethlehem
Gaza
Al Khalil

Bir Saba

NEGEV

EGYPT

WADI
ARABIA

Gulf of Aqaba

Jordan R.

≡≡≡ Actual Mandate

– –   Total Zionist Claims

MANDATE OF PALESTINE
(League of Nations)

Zionist Claims and the Palestinian Mandate

Flare-ups and Revolt

In 1929 a flare-up took place when *yishuv* members attempted to bring chairs, benches, and screens (the latter to separate men and women worshippers) to Jerusalem's Western Wall. Arabs opposed this violation of established custom, and deadly battles raged in Jerusalem and nearby towns. The British dealt with this and other incidents of unrest by cracking down, and by sending royal commissions to investigate. Reports of two of these commissions in 1929 and 1930 sought to remedy the underlying causes of the conflict, calling for an end to the eviction of Arab agriculturalists and a recognition of the limited "absorptive capacity" for further Jewish immigration to Palestine. Zionists rejected these recommendations and early in 1931 British Socialist prime minister Ramsay MacDonald (1866–1937) sided with them (see Reading 19c).

The 1937 Peel Commission report, issued in response to a major Arab revolt, recommended eventual partition of Palestine, with Zionists receiving enough territory to form a Jewish state after the termination of the mandate. (See Map p. 152) The Arabs repudiated the commission's conclusions (Reading 20b), while Zionists reluctantly agreed to them but hoped to increase the territory allotted them. In his account of the Arab revolt (Reading 20a), Ted Swedenburg shows that the insurgents mobilized poor urban dwellers and *fellahin* (peasants) around issues of social justice. Palestinians also attacked British pipelines that terminated at Haifa. Some Arab notables also joined the revolt, while others (especially the Nashashibi clan) collaborated with the British. Lacking weapons, its leaders killed early in the struggle, the movement went down to defeat in 1939 as Jewish militias joined British forces in crushing it. The British deported most Palestinian militants who had not died in the fighting. Some escaped, as did the *mufti* who spent much of World War II in Nazi Germany, where his radio broadcasts opposed the Allied efforts to defeat the Axis powers.

As war approached, the British, fearing further sabotage of Middle Eastern oil installations, issued another report—the 1939 White Paper (Reading 20c), which rejected partition and promised free elections and independence to Palestine after ten years. The British also imposed new restrictions on both Jewish immigration and Zionist land acquisition. Given the much larger Arab population, Palestinians would have dominated any unitary state. The Zionists, fearing this, demanded partition and greater immigration. Their determination greatly intensified as the Nazis murdered European Jews. They refused to countenance any other solution than unrestricted immigration and a Jewish state (see Reading 20d). They and the Palestinians (who refused to wait another decade for independence) and other Arabs rejected the White Paper.

Zionist Nation Building, War, and Statehood

Despite British attempts to limit Jewish immigration, Zionists circumvented barriers and smuggled thousands into Palestine. The *Histadrut* (General Federation of Jewish Workers) assisted this process in several ways: by founding settlements for the illegal immigrants, inculcating Zionist ideology and providing Hebrew instruction, managing cooperative enterprises, and directing a clandestine militia, *Haganah* (defense). The *Histadrut* did not admit Arab workers to membership nor arrange for equal pay scales (although it did establish an Arab affiliate). One of the organization's most active members, Ben-Gurion, also founded the *Mapai* political party, the ancestor of the Labor coalition and the dominant Zionist political force.

Labor Zionists faced an opposition "Revisionist" movement led by Russian-born Vladimir Jabotinsky (1880–1940), who wanted to establish a Jewish state on both sides of the Jordan River (see Reading 19d). Although Jabotinsky never broke with Great Britain, some of his militant followers founded illegal militias, the *Irgun Zvai Leumi* (National Military Organization) and *Lehi* (acronym for Fighters for the Freedom of Israel, or the Stern Gang), which attacked Arab civilians and British troops and officials. After Israeli statehood the Revisionists became the *Herut* (freedom) movement, a component of the rightist *Likud* (unity) bloc. Two *Likud* leaders, former *Irgun* commander in chief Menachem Begin (1913–92) and Stern Gang member Yitzhak Shamir (1914–), became prime ministers of Israel.

World War II brought a measure of prosperity, and also repression and an uncertain future to Palestinian Arabs. Labor scarcity and the need for supplies in nearby battle zones raised prices for agricultural goods and wages so that poor Arabs could improve their material condition. Much wealth went into educational opportunities for Palestinian youth, transforming them into the most educated of all Arabs. The British prohibited political organizing during wartime and kept many Palestinians in exile. Those allowed back had to abide by a ban on politics. Soldiers and other law enforcement officers searched homes at will, confiscated evidence, and arrested and held Palestinians indefinitely. Harsh laws remained in effect even after the creation of Israel. Continuing divisions among Palestinians prevented agreement on common plans for the postwar struggles ahead and allowed neighboring Arab states (organized since 1945 in the Arab League) to represent Palestinian positions. Since many of the Arab regimes still had colonial overlords dictating security and economic policy, Palestinians often nurtured suspicions of their Arab neighbors' good intentions.

The immigration question moved to the forefront in wartime as British authorities attempted to placate the Arabs by limiting land sales and curtailing the influx of Jews. Would-be immigrants faced mortal danger if they remained in Nazi-dominated Europe, but as persecution of Jews increased, so did British and Arab opposition to the augmented immigration stream. Great Britain, Canada, and the United States refused to accept Jewish refugees, increasing the focus on Palestine. Anguish over the Nazi extermination of six million Jews swung global opinion behind the Zionist cause and away from Arab plight. Arabs could find no compelling reason why the world community believed that Jewish suffering had to be rectified at Palestinian expense, and they searched unsuccessfully for ways to present their situation to a mostly unsympathetic world. Palestinians remained quiescent during the war, retaining the illusory hope for their own state once hostilities ended.

Jews worldwide backed Great Britain against Germany. About 30,000 Palestinian Jews fought in British wartime units, receiving valuable military experience and weapons, which they often retained. But some extreme Revisionists continued to attack the British despite the ongoing war. Although victorious, Great Britain emerged in 1945 weakened and unable to hold on to its empire. Besides withdrawing from India (see Reading 16), Britain turned the Palestine question over to the United Nations, the organization that replaced the League of Nations.

The UN Special Commission on Palestine issued two sharply differing sets of recommendations. The majority called for partition into Arab and Jewish states with Jerusalem as an international zone (see Map p. 190). The minority supported a federated state with autonomous Jewish and Palestinian areas. The Arabs rejected both, while the Zionists accepted the majority plan. On November 29, 1947, the UN General Assembly approved this plan and Arab forces attacked almost immediately.

Some 50,000 Arab troops—ranging from the crack forces of Jordan's Arab Legion to volunteer irregulars from various Arab countries—faced 30,000 battle-seasoned Jewish fighters, augmented by 20,000 volunteer war veterans from the Diaspora. France and Czechoslovakia supplied the Jews with armaments. Indirect military aid came from Jordan's King Abdullah, who kept the Arab Legion out of major battles in exchange for control over the Jordan River's West Bank and Arab Jerusalem after the war. In wartime, Israel declared its statehood. Victory came to the Jews by 1949 because of better staff work, the efforts of skilled and dedicated fighters, and the *yishuv*'s near total mobilization and unity of purpose. The full horror of the Holocaust also stirred worldwide support for the Zionists' victory.

Although few outside of the Middle East paid attention to the wartime exodus of Palestinian refugees, their situation eventually became a matter of contention. The official Zionist explanation concludes that Arab leaders encouraged their people to flee so that they could return after the expected Zionist defeat and resume their lives in Arab Palestine. By this account the Israelis bore no responsibility for Arab refugees, who by leaving forfeited their homes and property. A sharply divergent Palestinian view (shared in part by a new wave of Israeli scholars) argues that Israeli forces drove many of the 700,000 or more Palestinian refugees out of their country. The April 1948 slaughter by *Irgun* militias, operating with the approval and cooperation of *Haganah,* of the Arab residents of Deir Yasin, a village west of Jerusalem, not only impelled many Palestinians to flee, it seemed intended to do just that. Similar events, or threats, had the same effect of emptying many other Palestinian villages and towns.

Most Palestinians who fled their homes registered as refugees with the UN and found substandard housing in the crowded camps of the West Bank, the Gaza Strip, or in Jordan, Lebanon, and Syria. The UN General Assembly at the end of 1948 passed Resolution #194 (see Reading 21b), which called for the return of the Palestinians to their homes. Those deciding not to go back,

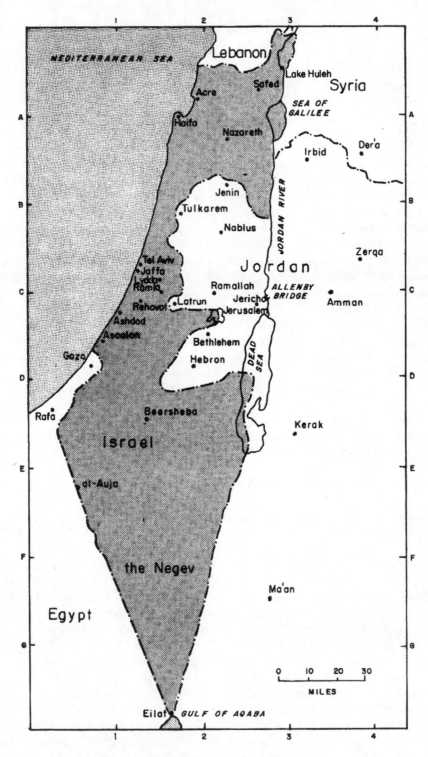

The Israeli-Arab Armistice Lines, 1949

the resolution added, should receive compensation for lost and damaged property. The problem remains unsettled.

Israel had a refugee problem of its own as displaced persons from Europe inundated the Jewish state. Zionists expected all or most Diaspora Jews to migrate to Israel, especially after the *Knesset* (Parliament) passed the 1950 Law of Return (Reading 21c), but this did not happen. Many Jews preferred living in North America or western Europe. The poorest, and most ideologically motivated, refugees, or those shut out of Western countries, moved to Israel. By 1951, 680,000 had arrived, most of them Ashkenazic Jews from Europe. Later Sephardic immigrants from North Africa and other Middle Eastern countries came in such large numbers that by 1961 they made up 45 percent of Israel's population. After the Israeli victory in the 1967 war even more Sephardic Jews flocked to Israel. Like Palestinian refugees, these Jewish migrants brought few possessions from their countries of origin. Those who arrived first took possession of Palestinian homes.

More War, More Suffering

Israel's next war, in 1956, resulted from the invasion of Egypt by British, French, and Israeli armies bent on punishing that country's leader, Jamal Abd al-Nasser (1918–70) for nationalizing the Suez Canal and for presuming to seek regional and world leadership. Israel had some additional reasons—the closing of the straits leading to the Red Sea and Nasser's support for the Palestinians. The U.S. government, seizing an opportunity to diminish British and French influence in the Middle East, forced the invaders to withdraw, and Nasser emerged a hero of the Arab world.

Two major wars then followed. Disputes over Jordan River water inflamed Israeli-Syrian tensions, and the Syrians warned Nasser that they expected an Israeli attack. The Tel Aviv government confirmed these fears by announcing its intent to change the Syrian regime. When the Soviets signaled Israeli troop movements, Nasser, as the leader of the Arab world, felt that he had to act. After requesting the withdrawal of UN troops stationed in the Sinai, he closed the Straits of Tiran to Israeli shipping, thereby provoking an Israeli attack. This 1967 war ended with a resounding Israeli victory over Egypt and Arab states allied with it. As a result Israel occupied Gaza, former Jordanian territory on the West Bank, and Syria's Golan Heights. Several hundred thousand more Palestinians came under Israeli control.

Another war broke out in 1973 when President Anwar al-Sadat (1918–81) ordered Egyptian armies to attack Israel, believing that after a cease-fire he could negotiate peace. Taken by surprise, the Israelis seemed headed toward defeat, until a massive U.S. airlift forced Egyptian troops to retreat. Sadat's scenario resulted in a bilateral treaty (Camp David I, brokered by U.S. president Jimmy

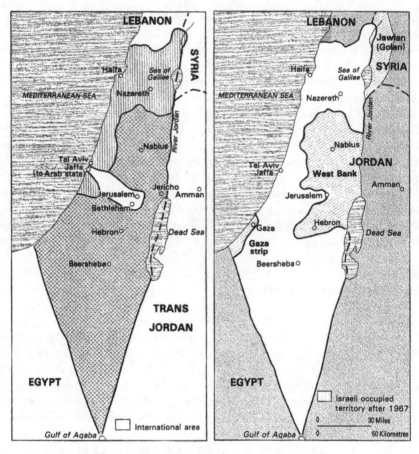

1937 Partition Plan/1967 Israeli Occupation

Carter [1924–   ]), which brought peace between Egypt and Israel but failed
to resolve the Palestinian-Israeli conflict.

For another two decades Israel nurtured the illusion that this conflict would
end by simply defining the Palestinians out of existence and by considering Jordan,
with its large Palestinian population, as all the state the Palestinians needed.
For years Israel refused to deal directly with Palestinians but only with Arab states,
and the *Knesset* passed a law forbidding diplomatic contact with Palestinians.
Even at the 1992 Madrid negotiations, Palestinians had to feign membership
in a Jordanian diplomatic delegation to join the talks. The Israelis also concluded
that the 1967 war had extinguished all Palestinian claims to property or homes
in the former mandate territory. The Palestinians realized that to regain attention they needed to build a fighting organization.

The Palestine Liberation Organization

Although a variety of groups claim to speak on behalf of the Palestinians, the Palestine Liberation Organization (PLO) has led the struggle for four decades, imposing itself as the body with which Israel and the world must deal to achieve peace. Other states too have intervened in the Palestinian question, especially those Arab countries that fought in 1948 and whose populations insisted that leaders not forget the Palestinian cause. When in the 1950s Palestinian groups formed to liberate their country, Arab leaders, fearful of provoking another war, moved to control and harness Palestinian militancy for their own strategic aims. The founding of the PLO in 1964 at a meeting in Cairo of the Arab League came at Nasser's initiative. He wanted to unify competing Palestinian factions and prevent the emergence of an independent and militant Palestinian organization. Other Arab leaders supported Nasser's approach.

The war in 1967 dramatically changed Middle Eastern political and social dynamics. Above all it brought all Arabs a sense of despair at their political and military impotence. The eloquent poem by Syrian poet Nizar Qabbani (1923–98) in Reading 22a captures this somber mood. Defeat discredited Arab secular regimes, who, dependent on repressive military force to control their own populations, could no longer presume to muzzle the PLO, whose importance grew along with its freedom to maneuver.

The Palestinians refashioned the PLO into an independent organization led by Yasir Arafat (1929–   ), a Jerusalem-born Muslim civil engineer who had organized guerrilla fighters to defend Palestinian bases in Jordan. His organization, *al-Fatah* (the conquest), dominant within the PLO, made him PLO chairman. Combining militancy with diplomacy, the PLO in 1974 won UN recognition and gradually modified its goals from creating a secular state over all of mandate Palestine to seeking a state over a more limited territory from which Israel would presumably agree to withdraw after negotiations. By the 1980s Arafat had marshaled the PLO leadership to formally recognize Israel's right to coexist with a future independent Palestinian state.

Israeli and U.S. political leaders wavered over Arafat's importance and legitimacy, sometimes inviting him to diplomatic summits, other times trying to disqualify him as the Palestinian interlocutor, even after Palestinians in 1996 overwhelmingly elected him president of the Legislative Council that governed the West Bank and Gaza. Islamic radicals in Palestine who owe primary allegiance to such organizations as *Hamas* (see Reading 24c) did not repudiate Arafat's leadership, nor do they follow it.

Israeli Society, Finance, and Foreign Policy

After statehood, besides focusing on absorbing Jewish immigrants, Israel made every effort to obtain foreign aid from Diaspora Jewry, and from supportive states.

Beginning modestly, U.S. financial and military assistance dramatically increased after 1971, reaching several billion dollars yearly by the end of the decade. (When Egypt made peace with Israel in 1979, it too enjoyed similar American largesse.) The U.S. Congress, often more favorable to the Jewish state than the executive branch, also extended generosity to Israel by guaranteeing loans or forgiving its debts. German reparations payments to Israel for Jewish victims of Nazi tyranny amounted to nearly eleven billion dollars between 1954 and 1982, with projections that Germany would eventually disburse several tens of billions of dollars more by 2030. Some of this money became available for the purchase of industrial equipment and such infrastructural projects as schools and roads. Access to diverse funding sources permitted Israel's agricultural and industrial growth and contributed to its prominence in information technology development. Its per capita wealth rose from $12,400 yearly in 1992 to about $18,000 a decade later—levels significantly higher than its near neighbors. But Israel's dependence on external funding has produced chronic inflation and high taxes needed to pay for the country's military and its extensive social services.

The military emerged early as one of the most important of Israel's institutions. Except for Arabs, Orthodox Jews, and married women, young people must complete military service before they can find jobs or advance politically. Single Jewish women join for limited military service, thereby freeing men for combat. The state also allows Orthodox Jews to enroll in the armed forces without actually serving, giving them full citizenship privileges—a concession to the religious parties.

Military industry makes up a significant portion of the Israeli economy. After the 1973 war, when massive shipments of American arms averted an Israeli setback, Israel increasingly manufactured its own armaments while continuing imports from the United States. These industries employ about 25 percent of Israel's population, and the country has become a major arms exporter, selling billions of dollars of military equipment yearly. Israel also has a secret nuclear arsenal, whose formal existence the state denies.

Israel's distrust of its neighbors and the importance ascribed to military concerns extend back even before the state formed. Signals of Arab moderation have met deep suspicion as mere tactical moves or "traps" camouflaging hostile intent. Relentless military policy—immediate armed retaliation and aversion to risky diplomatic initiatives—have not brought peace.

Although Ben-Gurion rhetorically called for a Jewish-Arab alliance, Israel preferred relying on its ties to the United States, and forming alliances with countries flanking the Arab world—Ethiopia, Pahlavi Iran, and Turkey. During the Cold War Israel backed the West against the Soviet Union, and earned Washington's designation as a major strategic partner. Even after the coming to power of Ayatollah Ruholla Khomeini (1900–89), an avowed enemy of the Jewish state (see Reading 28b), Israel continued to supply arms to Iran. Only recently have Israeli policy makers reconsidered their alliances and made clear their opposition to Iran's Islamic Republic. Turkey remains one of Israel's closest allies.

Peace with Egypt; War in Lebanon

An exception to Israel's anti-Arab "peripheral strategy" came in response to Egyptian president Sadat's 1977 peace initiative, which Israel's prime minister Menachem Begin welcomed. Both leaders, as we have mentioned, participated in negotiations hosted by President Jimmy Carter at Camp David, Maryland. After signing the peace agreement, Israel returned the Sinai Peninsula (captured in the 1973 war) to Egypt (after the occupiers had extracted most of its petroleum). The *Likud* government then claimed that Israel had no further obligations under UN Resolution #242 (see Reading 23a) to return other captured land. The Camp David agreement made Egypt into a nonbelligerent state, which stood aside when Israel invaded Lebanon in 1978 and 1982. Sadat's subsequent assassination highlighted the deep opposition in the Muslim world to any agreement that ignored Palestinian claims and that facilitated Israel's ability to make war elsewhere.

Menachem Begin's government attacked Lebanon in 1982 to eliminate PLO commandos and their allies who could raid Israel from bases there. No such assaults had taken place for months when Begin ordered Defense Minister Ariel Sharon (1928–   ) into action. The Israelis counted on the support of the right-wing Lebanese Phalange movement, composed largely of Maronite Christians. Acting with lightning speed after aerial bombardments, Israeli troops crossed into Lebanon and captured most of the country, including its capital city, Beirut. There, under Israeli occupation, Phalange militias massacred Palestinian civilians at the Sabra and Shatila refugee camps, which horrified the world. Palestinian combatants and their Lebanese allies suffered military defeat, forcing the PLO to withdraw from Lebanon and relocate to distant Tunisia. After dismissing Sharon because of the Sabra and Shatila atrocities, Begin resigned and retired from politics. *Likud* leader Yitzhak Shamir succeeded him.

Intifada I

After its defeat in Lebanon, the PLO faced several new situations: expulsion to North Africa; the end of the petroleum boom; reduced subsidies from oil-producing states; fewer jobs for Palestinians in the Gulf; and a drastic fall-off in remittances, which sustained many Palestinians on the West Bank and Gaza. In addition, great power interest in encouraging negotiations between Israelis and Palestinians seemed to have waned. These changes threw Palestinian militants back on their own resources, and in late 1987 an uprising (*intifada*) began (see Reading 24b). Managed by local activists from Palestine's civil society and directed against continued Israeli occupation of the West Bank and Gaza, the *intifada* also received direction from PLO leaders in Tunisia. Together they hoped to demonstrate that military defeat could not quench Palestinian nationalism. Indeed, when the United States. refused Arafat permission to attend a special 1988 UN session on Palestine in New York City, the world body rescheduled the event for Geneva where the Palestinian chairman read a text (some of which U.S. State Department personnel had drafted) in which he recognized Israel, while calling for a Palestinian state alongside it.

In the occupied territories the *intifada* mobilized masses of Palestinians, children as well as adults, who demonstrated, staged strikes, threw stones, and disseminated propaganda. PLO fighters mounted attacks on Israeli occupation forces and settlers. To divide the Palestinians, Israel initially backed the Islamic movement *Hamas* (which opposed the PLO's goal of establishing a Palestinian state on the West Bank and Gaza in favor of an Islamic state in all the former mandate territory; see Reading 24c). But when *Hamas* launched its own attacks against Israelis, government support apparently ceased. The PLO's tenacity enabled it to retain the backing of most Palestinians and gain augmented recognition in Europe, while U.S. diplomats initiated a new Middle Eastern peace process, which continued until the 1990–91 Gulf War.

In that war the PLO, which Iraq had earlier supported, refused to denounce Saddam Husayn, and Palestinians suffered for this unpopular stance. Kuwait expelled thousands of skilled Palestinian workers and administrators whose families depended on remittances. Also, Saudi Arabia stopped subsidizing the PLO. During the war Iraq fired several SCUD missiles into Israel, and Israel's armed forces complied with U.S. orders not to retaliate, lest Arab states withdraw from the American-led coalition, which held together for the six weeks of the war. At its conclusion U.S. president George H. W. Bush announced American determination to achieve a solution to the Palestinian/Israeli conflict as part of his rhetorical call for a "new world order" of harmony and justice (see Reading 27c).

Oslo

After the Second Gulf War the United States and the Soviet Union actually took joint steps to end the conflict over Palestine by summoning Israel and the Arab states to a peace conference in Madrid. These talks achieved no immediate success, but other regional and global pressures combined to restart the sputtering peace process. The collapse of the Soviet Union brought more than a million educated Soviet Jews to Israel, and Palestinians feared that these migrants would swell the Jewish settlements. When Prime Minister Shamir requested loan guarantees from the United States to assist in settling these new immigrants, President Bush agreed to help if Israel moved toward peace with the Palestinians, and curtailed settlements on the West Bank and Gaza. Shamir refused, but soon Laborite and former general Yitzhak Rabin (1922–95) became prime minister and he agreed to negotiate on the basis of a "land for peace" formula. The *Knesset* repealed the law banning Israeli contacts with the PLO, and soon the secret meetings began in Norway that would produce the 1993 Oslo Accords (see Reading 25a).

In principle the Oslo negotiators achieved a breakthrough, even though the accords themselves contained vague clauses that prevented achievement of a comprehensive agreement. The Palestinians formally abandoned armed struggle and accepted Israel's right to rule over 78 percent of mandate Palestine, and expected in return the remaining 22 percent (the West Bank, Gaza, and Arab East Jerusalem) to be placed under their control. Disputes soon arose over how much occupied territory Israel would retain, and whether land assigned to the Palestinians would compose a truly sovereign, contiguous state. Less than a year later Israel agreed to withdraw from the Gaza strip and the West Bank town of Jericho. A newly created Palestinian Authority, headed by Yasir Arafat, took over those evacuated territories. Soon a second Arab country, Jordan, signed a peace agreement with Israel.

The Assassination of Rabin and the Second *Intifada*

Momentum for a negotiated settlement halted when a Jewish religious fanatic assassinated Prime Minister Yitzhak Rabin at a pro-peace rally in Tel Aviv on November 4, 1995. Suicide bombers from the Islamic radical group *Hamas* had increased assaults on Israeli civilians, and a Jewish settler had machine-gunned twenty-nine Palestinian worshipers at a holy site in Hebron. It became apparent that a subculture of religious fanaticism lurked in Judaism as well as in Islam and that their mutual acts of vengeance could derail the Oslo process. But Israeli government policy on West Bank settlements, as Rabin had recognized (see Reading 25b), also played a role in prolonging and even worsening the conflict. The government began constructing a series of roads crisscrossing the West Bank that only Israelis could use (see Map p. 223). This seriously reduced Palestinian Authority territorial holdings and sliced it into unconnected segments.

After Rabin's death, and several waves of suicide bombings by *Hamas* and another radical group, Islamic *Jihad*, Benjamin Netanyahu (1949–) became prime minister. Despite his reputation as a hard-liner on the Palestinian question, he grudgingly went along with the Oslo momentum, ordering withdrawal of Israeli forces from much of Hebron, responding to U.S. president Bill Clinton's appeal that he meet with Arafat on U.S. soil. Arafat agreed to Israeli demands that the Palestinians consider removing objectionable passages in their National Charter (see Reading 22b). Netanyahu transferred some territory to the Palestinians just before the 1999 Israeli elections, which he lost to Labor Party leader and former army general Ehud Barak (1942–).

Barak began his brief tenure by withdrawing the last Israeli Defense Force (IDF) forces from Lebanon, and transferring another small part of the West Bank to Palestinian control. But continued Palestinian suicide bombings moved Israel's electorate rightward while the stalemate in progress toward statehood impelled the Palestinians closer to a renewed and more militant *intifada*. The

Clinton presidency drew to a close with one more attempt to revive the peace process, bringing Barak and Arafat again to Camp David. No authoritative text of these discussions exists, nor have the Israelis ever made clear precisely what territorial concessions they proposed there or at a follow-up meeting at Taba. One version suggests Barak made a generous offer that Arafat rejected. But since the Israeli leader had barely survived a no-confidence vote in the *Knesset,* and faced an impending election contest against Ariel Sharon, a formidable opponent pledged to overturn Oslo, Arafat had little incentive to make concessions. Nevertheless, he seemed ready to allow Israel to consolidate its West Bank settlements closest to the border and annex them to Israel. But time ran out in this hastily convened meeting before any definitive agreement could emerge.

A subsequent last-minute meeting between officials of Barak's government and the PLO took place at Taba (on the Egyptian-Israeli border) where a slightly more explicit (but still incomplete) blueprint for a Palestinian-Israeli peace agreement did emerge. At Taba Israel apparently acknowledged some degree of responsibility for the creation—and therefore the solution—of the Palestinian refugee problem. But once Ariel Sharon took office all possibility of negotiated peace evaporated. Although no longer in play, the Taba negotiations (see Reading 25c) represent the closest the parties have come to a comprehensive agreement.

Any Way Out?

By the time of Taba Ariel Sharon had taken his provocative tour of the *Haram al-Sharif,* on the Temple Mount in Jerusalem, which includes the Dome of the Rock sanctuary in Jerusalem, and the second *intifada* had broken out. Long in the making, this new uprising involved the dangerous adoption by PLO-linked organizations of the suicide-bombing tactics of *Hamas* and other Islamic radical groups. This brought down on the PLO, and Palestinians generally, fierce IDF responses—deadly tank and armored vehicle sweeps through Palestinian towns and refugee camps and targeted assassinations of Palestinian militants. The Sharon government held Arafat responsible for the new cycles of terror and counterterror, and has gained U.S. support for harsh crackdowns on Palestinians (see Reading 26f).

Persistently, Arafat holds on to his position despite heavy criticism even from some Palestinians impatient with his leadership or with his willingness to make concessions. As the interview with PLO official Marwan Barghouti (Reading 26c) demonstrates, no one credible will stand against him in elections.

Another solution proposed in early 2002 by Saudi Arabia's Crown Prince Abd al-Aziz, and accepted by the Arab League (see Reading 26d), has all but disappeared in the present turmoil in Israel and in the current Bush administration's campaign for a global struggle against terrorism. It offered recognition of Israel by Arab countries in exchange for complete Israeli evacuation of the West

Bank and Gaza. Combined with Palestinian pressure to end suicide bombings (see Reading 26e), steps by the Palestinian Legislative Council to establish a government responsible to it, and a revival of something like the Taba negotiations, peace may again appear on the agenda.

18. Zionism and Its Early Arab Opponents

T he secular Jewish Hungarian writer Theodor Herzl (1860–1904), reacting to heightened anti-Semitism in Europe, wrote a pamphlet titled *The Jewish State* in 1896, excerpted in part a of this reading. It served as a catalyst for the creation of the modern Zionist movement. As soon as it formed, Muslims responded negatively, as we see in two newspaper articles in parts b and c of this reading, by Rashid Rida (1865–1935), a leading Muslim reformer, and by an anonymous Ottoman official, who adopted the pseudonym "Tiberias."

A. Theodor Herzl, Zionism: The Vision of an Eventual Jewish State (1896)*

The Zionist movement that Herzl created differed from the Jewish religious tradition calling for the return of Jews to Zion (Israel) to await the appearance of the Messiah. Herzl proposed establishing a Jewish state wherever Jews could find sufficient land to accommodate those fleeing oppression and realized that in searching for such a site Zionists would have to get the backing of a great power. Requesting a home in Ottoman Palestine, Herzl heard directly from the sultan that European Jews could not reside there, where in 1890 some 500,000 Arabs already lived. Herzl then considered places in Latin America and Africa.

After he wrote *The Jewish State,* however, and after he had organized the World Zionist Organization, Herzl found that the largest group of his followers, those from eastern Europe, refused to consider any other site than Palestine. He acceded to these demands, and from then on the Zionist movement aimed at carving out a state in Palestine and nowhere else. During World War I the British, after having conquered Palestine, associated themselves with Zionism and supported the creation of a home there for the Jewish people—a promise enshrined in the Balfour Declaration (Reading 19a).

---

*From Theodor Herzl, *The Jewish State: An Attempt at a Modern Solution of the Jewish Question* (New York: American Zionist Emergency Council, 1946), pp. 85–96.

* * *

No one can deny the gravity of the situation of the Jews. Wherever they live in perceptible numbers, they are more or less persecuted. Their equality before the law has become practically a dead letter. They are debarred from filling even moderately high positions, either in the army, or in any public or private capacity. And attempts are made to thrust them out of business also: "Don't buy from Jews!"

Attacks in Parliaments, in assemblies, in the press, in the pulpit, in the street, on journeys—for example, their exclusion from certain hotels—even in places of recreation, become daily more numerous. The forms of persecutions vary according to the countries and social circles in which they occur.

Let us first settle the point of staying where we are. Can we hope for better days. . . ? I say that we cannot hope for a change in the current of feeling. And why not? Even if we were as near to the hearts of princes as are their other subjects, they could not protect us. They would only feel popular hatred by showing us too much favor. . . . The nations in whose midst Jews live are all either covertly or openly Anti-Semitic.

The whole plan is in its essence perfectly simple.

Let the sovereignty be granted us over a portion of the globe large enough to satisfy the rightful requirements of a nation; the rest we shall manage for ourselves.

The creation of a new State is neither ridiculous nor impossible. We have in our day witnessed the process in connection with nations which were not largely members of the middle class, but poorer, less educated, and consequently weaker than ourselves. The Governments of all countries scourged by Anti-Semitism will be keenly interested in assisting us to obtain the sovereignty we want.

The plan, simple in design, but complicated in execution, will be carried out by two agencies: The Society of Jews and the Jewish Company.

The Society of Jews will do the preparatory work in the domains of science and politics, which the Jewish Company will afterwards apply practically.

The Jewish Company will be the liquidating agent of the business interests of departing Jews, and will organize commerce and trade in the new country.

We must not imagine the departure of the Jews to be a sudden one. It will be gradual, continuous, and will cover many decades. The poorest will go first to cultivate the soil. In accordance with a preconceived plan, they will construct roads, bridges, railways and telegraph installations; regulate rivers; and build their own dwellings; their labor will create trade, trade will create markets and markets will attract new settlers, for every man will go voluntarily, at his own expense and his own risk. The labor expended on the land will enhance its value, and the Jews will soon perceive that a new and permanent sphere of operation is opening here for that spirit of enterprise which has heretofore met only with hatred and obloquy.

Let all who are willing to join us, fall in behind our banner and fight for our cause with voice and pen and deed.

Those Jews who agree with our idea of a State will attach themselves to the Society, which will thereby be authorized to confer and treat with Governments in the name of our people. The Society will thus be acknowledged in its relations with Governments as a State-creating power. This acknowledgment will practically create the State.

Should the Powers declare themselves willing to admit our sovereignty over a neutral piece of land, then the Society will enter into negotiations for the possession of this land. Here two territories come under consideration, Palestine and Argentine. In both countries important experiments in colonization have been made, though on the mistaken principle of a gradual infiltration of Jews. An infiltration is bound to end badly. It continues till the inevitable moment when the native population feels itself threatened, and forces the Government to stop a further influx of Jews. Immigration is consequently futile unless we have the sovereign right to continue such immigration.

The Society of Jews will treat with the present masters of the land, putting itself under the protectorate of the European Powers. . . . We could offer the present possessors of the land enormous advantages, assume part of the public debt, build new roads . . . and do many other things. The creation of our State would be beneficial to adjacent countries, because the cultivation of a strip of land increases the value of its surrounding districts in innumerable ways.

Shall we choose Palestine or Argentine? We shall take what is given us, and what is selected by Jewish public opinion. The Society will determine both these points.

Argentine is one of the most fertile countries in the world, extends over a vast area, has a sparse population and a mild climate. The Argentine Republic would derive considerable profit from the cession of a portion of its territory to us. The present infiltration of Jews has certainly produced some discontent, and it would be necessary to enlighten the Republic on the intrinsic difference of our new movement.

Palestine is our ever-memorable historic home. The very name of Palestine would attract our people with a force of marvelous potency. If His Majesty the Sultan were to give us Palestine, we could in return undertake to regulate the whole finances of Turkey. We should there form a portion of a rampart of Europe against Asia, an outpost of civilization as opposed to barbarism. We should as a neutral State remain in contact with all Europe, which would have to guarantee our existence. The sanctuaries of Christendom would be safeguarded by assigning to them an extra-territorial status. . . . We should form a guard of honor about these sanctuaries, answering for the fulfillment of this duty with our existence. This guard of honor would be the great symbol of the solution of the Jewish Question after eighteen centuries of Jewish suffering.

B. Rashid Rida, Pay Attention to Zionist Encroachment (1898)*

> Even before World War I Arab writers warned of Zionist aims to build a Jewish settler community in Palestine. The newcomers would purchase land, live in separate communities, replace Arabs with Jewish farm laborers, and reduce the Palestinians to a minority in their own land. We present here the viewpoint of Rida, who described Zionism as a form of European colonialism. This selection presents a portion of an article from Rida's influential Cairo newspaper, *al-Manar* (The Beacon), one of the earliest examinations of Zionism's impact on the Middle East.

Apathetic people, lift up your heads and see what is going on. Consider what [other] people and nations are doing. Pay attention to what is happening in your world. Does it please you that the newspapers around the globe are reporting that the impoverished of the most miserable people [the Jews], whom all governments are expelling from their countries, have so mastered [requisite] knowledge and civilization that they can come to your country, colonize it and transform its [former] masters into wage laborers and its affluent into paupers? . . . Think about this matter [of Zionist encroachment], and make it the subject of your conversations in order to find out whether it is just or unjust, true or false. If it becomes clear that you have neglected to defend the rights of your fatherland, and the interests of your nation and your religious community, reflect on and study, debate and examine the matter. It is more appropriate for contemplation than thinking about shortcomings, spreading slander, insulting those who are innocent. It is more worthy of discussion than making fun of and accusing your [Arab] brothers.

C. "Tiberias," Warning of Zionist Colonization (1910)**

> In the years after Rashid Rida's warning (part b, this reading), Zionist settlements began appearing in Ottoman Palestine. The anonymous author of this article, who called himself "Tiberias" (the name of a city in Roman Palestine), may have been Shukri al-Asali, subgovernor of Nazareth.

No one doubts that Zionist colonization, in other words foreign seizure of the land of Palestine, is based on political and economic matters which cannot be

---

*From Rashid Rida, *Khabar wa itibar* (News and Viewpoints), *al-Manar* (April 9, 1898), p. 108. Translated from the Arabic by Stuart Schaar.

**From "Tiberias," "Zionist Colonization: The Local Government's Propagation of It. Its Harmfulness to the State and Nation," *al-ittihad al-uthmani* (Ottoman Unity), [Beirut] no. 559 (July 9, 1910), p. 2. Translated from the Arabic by Rashid Khalidi. Bracketed material inserted by editors. By permission of the translator.

hidden from those with eyes to see; this is an economic party whose aim is to take possession of these great lands by the force of wealth spent freely to further this vital economic desire, whose result will be the shattering of the unity of the native farmers who have been oppressed over time. If we look at what happened to the al-Dalaika and al-Sbeih tribes and to others after their lands had been taken over by those traitors among the government officials who were working for [the Zionists] by grace of the money they spend freely, and knowing the harm caused by this seizure: the inhabitants become slaves to those who have ambitions in this land and deceived the nation at the outset, saying that they came to this country to help its people achieve happiness, to bring progress to the country and to invest their wealth in modern ways. The trick worked and they gained possession via this subterfuge, with the help of these traitors among the government employees. They use tricks and intrigues to oppress the native population and take their rights, until they are forced to emigrate and leave the country. Thus do they poison things until they become masters of the country, and have effective control over it. The government loses loyal subjects willing to risk their lives for the glory of the state, just as it loses our country.

This was the situation in the land of Palestine under the past government [of Sultan Abd al-Hamid II], and it sadly continues in the Constitutional era [the early Young Turk period], with the government showing laxness towards these dangerous matters, which may bring great catastrophes on the state. Since silence about such economic wars does not fit in this age, but is rather a terrible crime against the nation and the homeland, we call for the attention of the *vali* [governor] of Beirut, whose job it is to look into these vital economic matters. And we warn the *qaymmaqam* [subgovernor] of [the town of] Tiberias and those around him of these dangers, since the nation today is not like it was yesterday: it is lying in wait for those who betray the nation and the homeland, just as it is ready to fight this colonization with all its material and moral forces—and God favors goodness and integrity.

19. The Balfour Declaration and the Mandate Period

A combination of strategic motives produced the Balfour Declaration, presented in part a of this reading. The war highlighted the importance of Palestine and some British politicians thought that backing the Zionist cause in Palestine would win support from Jewish populations in Russia and the United States for the war effort.

For reasons set forth in part b of this reading, Arabs opposed the declaration and Britain's League of Nations mandate for Palestine. Part c reproduces a let-

ter written by British Prime Minister MacDonald in 1931 to Chaim Weizmann
that countermands earlier restrictions on Jewish immigration and reaffirms Britain's
commitment to the Balfour Declaration. Part d offers Vladimir Jabotinsky's testimony before the 1937 British Peel Commission in which he argued for opening up both sides of the Jordan River to "many millions" of Jewish immigrants
fleeing repression in Europe.

A. The Balfour Declaration: A Jewish Home in Palestine (1917)*

At the outset of World War I and continuing to 1917, France claimed possession of greater Syria, including Lebanon and Palestine. But when British troops
defeated Ottoman forces there and occupied it in 1917, they effectively extinguished France's claims to Palestine, while recognizing French control over Syria
and Lebanon.

Early in the war Zionist leaders approached British officials to get their support for their cause. At first the British paid scant attention, but by 1917 the London
government approved the Balfour Declaration, which Foreign Secretary Arthur
Balfour sent as a letter to Zionist leader Lionel Walter Lord Rothschild (1868–
1937). Great Britain's efforts to gain international support for its promise to the
Zionists (and at the same time legitimize British control of Palestine) achieved
success when the League of Nations approved the Palestine mandate.

The British also hoped that the declaration would bring approval from the
United States and especially from Russian Jews who might influence the Bolsheviks, a Marxist party that had just won power on a platform of opposition to the
war, not to abandon their allies. In March 1918, the Bolshevik government made
a separate peace with Germany. But the Americans, having joined the war as Britain's
ally, fulfilled London's expectations and approved the Balfour Declaration.

[London] 2 November 1917

Dear Lord Rothschild,

I have much pleasure in conveying to you, on behalf of His Majesty's
Government, the following declaration of sympathy with Jewish Zionist
aspirations which has been submitted to, and approved by, the Cabinet:

"His Majesty's Government view with favor the establishment in Palestine
of a national home for the Jewish people, and will use their best endeavors
to facilitate the achievement of this object, it being clearly understood that
nothing shall be done which may prejudice the civil and religious rights of
existing non-Jewish communities in Palestine, or the rights and political

---

*From *Mandate for Palestine Together With the Balfour Declaration* (Jerusalem, 1938), facsimile text.

status enjoyed by Jews in any other country." I should be grateful if you would bring this declaration to the knowledge of the Zionist Federation.

Yours sincerely,
Arthur James Balfour

B. The General Syrian Congress, Our Objections to Zionism and Western Imperialism (1919)*

Before the League of Nations endorsed the creation of mandate territories in the Middle East controlled by Britain and France, U.S. President Woodrow Wilson recommended sending a commission to survey Arab views on the question. Two prominent Americans, Harry C. King and Charles R. Crane, served on this commission. They arrived in Damascus on June 25, 1919. Their presence led the Syrians, provisionally ruled by the Hashemite *Amir* Faysal, son of the *Sharif* Husayn ibn Ali of Arabia, to convene a Congress in the Syrian capital to which the Syrians invited delegates from Lebanon and Palestine. The following document summarizes the Congress resolution adopted on July 2, which the Syrians presented to the King-Crane Commission. Although the commission issued a report favorable to Arab nationalism and to the Palestinian cause, its findings received scant attention. Despite Wilson's call for self-determination in some of his wartime utterances, he ignored the King-Crane report and accepted the Balfour Declaration (part a, this Reading) and the British/French imperial arrangements made in the Sykes-Picot agreement (see Reading 13c). Later developments would reveal that the Arabs misplaced their confidence in Wilson's "noble principles."

1. We ask . . . [for] complete political independence for [Greater] Syria . . . [encompassing Lebanon and Palestine].

2. We ask that the Government of this Syrian country should be a democratic civil constitutional Monarchy . . . safeguarding the rights of minorities, and that the King be the Emir Feisal, who carried on a glorious struggle in the cause of our liberation and merited our full confidence and entire reliance.

3. Considering the fact that the Arabs inhabiting the Syrian area are not naturally less gifted than other more advanced races and that they are by no means less developed than the Bulgarians, Serbians, Greeks, and Romanians at the beginning of their independence, we protest against Article 22 of the Covenant of the League of Nations, placing us among the nations in their middle stage of development which stand in need of a mandatory power.

---

*From the King-Crane Commission Report in *Foreign Relations of the United States: Paris Peace Conference, 1919*, 13 vols. (Washington, DC: U.S. Government Printing Office, 1942–47), vol. 12, pp. 780–81. Bracketed material inserted by the editors.

4. In the event of the rejection by the Peace Conference of this just protest for certain considerations that we may not understand, we, relying on the declarations of President Wilson, that his object in waging war was to put an end to the ambition of conquest and colonization, can only regard the mandate mentioned in the Covenant of the League of Nations as equivalent to the rendering of economical and technical assistance that does not prejudice our complete independence. And desiring that our country should not fall prey to colonization and believing that the American Nation is farthest from any thought of colonization and has no political ambition in our country, we will seek the technical and economical assistance from the United States of America, provided that such assistance does not exceed twenty years.

5. In the event of America not finding herself in a position to accept our desire for assistance, we will seek this assistance from Great Britain, also provided that this assistance does not infringe on the complete independence and unity of our country and that the duration of such assistance does not exceed that mentioned in the previous article.

6. We do not acknowledge any right claimed by the French Government in any part whatsoever of our Syrian country and refuse that she should assist us or have a hand in our country under any circumstances and in any place.

7. We oppose the pretensions of the Zionists to create a Jewish commonwealth in the southern part of Syria, known as Palestine, and oppose Zionist migration to any part of our country; for we do not acknowledge their title but consider them a grave peril for our people from the national, economical, and political points of view. Our Jewish compatriots shall enjoy our common rights and assume the common responsibilities.

8. We ask that there be no separation of the southern part of Syria, known as Palestine, nor of the littoral western zone, which includes Lebanon, from the Syrian country. We desire that the unity of the country should be guaranteed against partition under whatever circumstances.

9. We ask for complete independence for emancipated Mesopotamia [Iraq] and that there should be no economical barriers between the two countries.

10. The fundamental principles laid down by President Wilson in condemnation of secret treaties impel us to protest most emphatically against any treaty that stipulates the partition of our Syrian country and against any private engagement aiming at the establishment of Zionism in the southern part of Syria; therefore we ask the annulment of these conventions and agreements.

The noble principles enunciated by President Wilson strengthen our confidence that our desires emanating from the depths of our hearts shall be the decisive factor in determining our future; and that President Wilson and the free American people will be our supporters for the realization of our hopes, thereby proving their sincerity and noble sympathy with the aspiration of the weaker nations in general and the Arab people in particular.

We also have the fullest confidence that the Peace Conference will realize that we would not have risen against the Turks, with whom we had participated in all civil, political, and representative privileges, but for the violation of our national rights, and so will grant us our desires in full in order that our political rights may not be less after the war than they were before, since we have shed so much blood in the cause of our liberty and independence.

We request to be allowed to send a delegation to represent us at the Peace Conference to defend our rights and secure the realization of our aspirations.

C. James Ramsay MacDonald, Letter to Chaim Weizmann (1931)*

The introduction to this section has surely prepared readers for outbreaks of discord, conflicts, and inconsistencies in mandate Palestine. We document British wavering—sometimes leaning toward the Arabs, and at other times favoring the Zionists, especially on the issue of Jewish immigration. The 1930 White Paper took the former position, but when Socialist leader Ramsay MacDonald (1866–1937) became prime minister, he backed the Zionists, to the dismay of Arabs, who labeled this communication the "Black Letter."

[London] 13 February 1931

Dear Dr. Weizmann:

In order to remove certain misconceptions and misunderstandings, which have arisen as to the policy of his Majesty's Government with regard to Palestine . . . and also to meet certain criticisms put forward by the Jewish Agency . . . [we forward to you our] authoritative interpretation of the . . . White Paper of 1930 . . . [which] recognizes that the undertaking of the mandate is an undertaking to the Jewish people and not only to the Jewish population of Palestine. . . .

In carrying out the policy of the mandate the mandatory cannot ignore the existence of the differing interests and viewpoints. These, indeed, are not in themselves irreconcilable, but they can only be reconciled if there is a proper realization that the full solution of the problem depends upon an understanding between the Jews and the Arabs. Until that is reached, considerations of balance must inevitably enter into the definition of policy. . . .

[The] rights and position [of non-Jews] . . . are not to be prejudiced; that is, are not TO BE impaired or made worse. The effect of the policy of immigration and settlement on the economic position of the non-Jewish community cannot be excluded from consideration. But the words are not to

---

*From Great Britain, *Parliamentary Debates* [Hansard], February 13, 1931, vol. 248, cols. 751–57. Bracketed material inserted by the editors.

be read as implying that existing economic conditions in Palestine should be crystallized. On the contrary, the obligation to facilitate Jewish Immigration and to encourage close settlement by Jews on the land remains a positive obligation of the mandate and it can be fulfilled without prejudice to the rights and position of other sections of the population of Palestine. . . .

D. Vladamir Jabotinsky, Let Us Settle Palestine and Transjordan (1937)*

Jabotinsky (1880–1940), the founder of the Zionist "Revisionist Movement," evoked extreme hatred from his political foes and great devotion from his followers. The Revisionists separated from mainstream Zionism in 1935, arguing that the *yishuv* should not rely on the British to guarantee Jewish statehood in Palestine. Jabotinsky had earlier opposed Britain's creation of a separate Transjordan, insisting on retaining the original mandate terms, which for a very short period encompassed both Palestine and Transjordan. He and his followers also favored massive legal or illegal immigration of European Jews into an enlarged Palestine and direct action by armed Jews to impose a Zionist state over Palestine and Transjordan. His followers founded extralegal militia groups, including the *Irgun*.

[T]he term "Palestine" when I employ it will mean the area on both sides of the Jordan, the area mentioned in the original Palestine Mandate. That area is about three times the size of . . . Belgium. We maintain that the absorptive capacity of a country depends . . . on the human factor; . . . on the quality of its people or of its colonizers, and on . . . the political régime under which that colonization is either encouraged or discouraged.

We maintain and claim that Palestine is at the cross-roads of the . . . main arteries of this hemisphere. The road from the Cape to Cairo, passing through the Suez Canal and going up to Vladivostok or Moscow . . . is the main artery of the future by land. The sea route from Liverpool to Adelaide and Bombay . . . is the main water artery, and . . . in future, the air arteries. . . .

An area of Palestine's size populated at the rather modest density of . . . Wales, can hold eight million inhabitants; populated at the density of Sicily, it can hold twelve million . . . populated at the density of England . . . or of Belgium . . . it could hold eighteen million inhabitants. . . . Palestine on both sides of the Jordan today holds a population of about 1,600,000[;] the mar-

*From V. Jabotinsky, *Evidence Submitted to the PALESTINE ROYAL COMMISSION*, House of Lords, London, February 11, 1937 (London: New Zionist Press, 1937), pp. 9–13. American spellings adopted.

gin is rather very large, and the Zionist claim . . . that . . . Palestine is good for holding the 1,000,000 present Arab population, plus 1,000,000 . . . for their progeny, plus many millions of Jewish immigrants—and plus peace. . . . [W]e claim that area; and I think that disposes ultimately of any suspicion that, in our schemes, anybody of any Party dreams of displacing or of disturbing the present non-Jewish population.

We are facing an elemental calamity, a kind of social earthquake. Three generations of Jewish thinkers and Zionists . . . have come to the conclusion that the cause of our suffering is the very fact . . . that we are everywhere a minority. It is not the anti-Semitism of men; it is, above all, the anti-Semitism of things, the inherent xenophobia of the body social or the body economic under which we suffer.

[T]here are moments, there are whole periods in history when this "xenophobia of Life itself" takes dimensions which no people can stand, and that is what we are facing now. I do not mean to suggest that I would recognize that all the Governments concerned have done all they ought to have done; I would be the last man to concede that. I think many Governments, East and West, ought to do much more to protect the Jews than they do; but the best of Governments could perhaps only soften the calamity to quite an insignificant extent, but the core of the calamity is an earthquake which stands and remains.

We are not free agents. We cannot "concede" anything. Whenever I hear the Zionist[s], most often my own Party, accused of asking for too much— Gentlemen, I really cannot understand it. Yes, we do want a State; every nation on earth, every normal nation, beginning with the smallest and the humblest who do not claim any merit, any role in humanity's development, they all have States of their own. That is the normal condition for a people. Yet, when we, the most abnormal of peoples and therefore the most unfortunate, ask only for the same condition as the Albanians enjoy, to say nothing of the French and the English, then it is called too much. I should understand it if the answer were, "It is impossible," but when the answer is, "It is too much" I cannot understand it.

We have got to save millions, many *millions*. I do not know whether it is a question of re-housing one-third of the Jewish race, half of the Jewish race, or a quarter of the Jewish race; I do not know; but it is a question of millions. Certainly the way out is to evacuate those portions of the Diaspora which have become no good, which hold no promise of any possibility of a livelihood, and to concentrate all those refugees in some place which should *not* be Diaspora, not a repetition of the position where the Jews are an unabsorbed minority within a foreign social, or economic, or political organism. Naturally, if that process of evacuation is allowed to develop, as it ought to be allowed to develop, there will very soon be reached a moment when the Jews will become a majority in Palestine. I am going to make a "terrible" confession. Our demand for a Jewish majority is not our maximum—it is our minimum.

I have the profoundest feeling for the Arab case, in so far as that Arab case is not exaggerated. This Commission have already been able to make up their minds as to whether there is any individual hardship to the Arabs of Palestine as men, deriving from the Jewish colonization. We maintain unanimously that the economic position of the Palestinian Arabs, under the Jewish colonization and owing to the Jewish colonization, has become the object of envy in all the surrounding Arab countries, so that the Arabs from those countries show a clear tendency to immigrate into Palestine. I have also shown to you already that, in our submission, there is no question of ousting the Arabs. On the contrary, the idea is that Palestine on both sides of the Jordan should hold the Arabs, their progeny, *and* many millions of Jews. What I do not deny is that in that process the Arabs of Palestine will necessarily become a minority in the country of Palestine. What I do deny is that *that* is a hardship. It is not a hardship on any race, any nation, possessing so many National States now and so many more National States in the future. One fraction, one branch of that race, and not a big one, will have to live in someone else's State: well, that is the case with all the mightiest nations of the world. I could hardly mention one of the big nations, having their States, mighty and powerful, who had not one branch living in someone else's State. That is only normal and there is no "hardship" attached to that. So when we hear the Arab claim confronted with the Jewish claim; I fully understand that any minority would prefer to be a majority, it is quite understandable that the Arabs of Palestine would also prefer Palestine to be the Arab State No. 4, No. 5, or No. 6—that I quite understand; but when the Arab claim is confronted with our Jewish demand to be saved, it is like the claims of appetite versus the claims of starvation.

20. Palestine on the Eve of World War II

This reading contains four sections: part a, an essay by a modern scholar on the Palestinian Revolt (1936–39); part b, the negative reaction to the Peel Commission Report by Arab notables; part c, the British White Paper of 1939, which anticipated the war that Great Britain soon faced against Germany and its allies. Three years later, as World War II raged on several fronts and the Nazi massacres of the Jews had begun, a Zionist Congress convened in New York City to denounce the White Paper and demand unrestricted Jewish immigration to Palestine. The resolutions of this Congress make up part d of this reading.

A. Ted Swedenburg, The Palestinian Revolt, 1936–39 (1988)*

A complicated movement, fomented by others than the traditional Palestinian notables, the Palestinian Revolt was led by a new generation of grassroots leaders.
Swedenburg's essay, a preliminary version of his 1995 book *Memoirs of Revolt*,
describes this leadership as well as the intertwining of class factors and militant
nationalism in the revolt. After crushing it with the help of Zionist militias, the
British killed or exiled Palestinian leaders and left behind a defeated, resentful
Palestinian populace still hoping for an independent state as World War II began.
The postwar period did little to relieve Arab grievances. In defeat, those who had
revolted in 1936–39 bequeathed a political legacy to later generations of Palestinian nationalist militants, such as participants in later *intifadas* (uprisings),
described in Readings 24b and 26c.

The spark that ignited the explosion came from an independent organization
intimately connected to the peasantry and semi-proletariat created by the agrarian
crisis . . . [and] founded by radical Islamic reformer *Shaykh* 'Izz al-Din al-Qassam
[d. 1935]. A native of Jabla, Syria, and a key figure in the 1921 revolt against
the French, al-Qassam took refuge in Haifa after fleeing Syria under sentence
of death. A man of great religious learning who had studied at Cairo's al-Azhar,
al-Qassam was associated with the Islamic reform (*Salafiya*) movement, as well
as with certain *Sufi turuq* [mystical brotherhoods]. He quickly achieved prominence in Haifa as a preacher and teacher. Unlike other political activists in
Palestine, al-Qassam concentrated his efforts exclusively on the lower classes
with whom he lived. He set up a night school to combat illiteracy among the
casual laborers (recent migrants from rural areas) of Haifa shantytowns and
was a prominent member of the Young Men's Muslim Association. In 1929 al-
Qassam was appointed marriage registrar of Haifa's *Shari'a* court. The duties
of this office, which required that he tour northern villages, permitted him to
extend his efforts to the peasantry, whom he encouraged to set up growing and
distribution cooperatives.

Using his religious position, al-Qassam began to recruit followers from among
the *fellahin* (peasants) and the laborers of Haifa, organizing them into clandestine cells of not more than five persons. By 1935 he had enlisted 200, perhaps even 800, men. Many received military training, carried out after dark; all
were imbued with al-Qassam's message of strict piety, of struggle and sacrifice,

---

*From Ted Swedenburg, "The Role of the Palestinian Peasantry in the Great Revolt (1936–1939),"
in Edmund Burke III and Ira Lapidus, eds., *Islam, Politics and Social Movements* (Berkeley: University of California Press, 1988), pp. 189–94. Notes deleted. Bracketed material added by the editors. Arabic words italicized. By permission.

of patriotism, the necessity for unity, and the need to emulate early Islamic heroes. . . . [His] political activities . . . paralleled those of Hasan al-Banna [1906–49], founder of the Muslim Brothers (*al-Ikhwan al-Muslimin*) in Egypt [see Reading 32b]. . . . But while al-Banna attracted the new Egyptian petty bourgeoisie, al-Qassam focused on the recently dispossessed peasants working as casual laborers in the slums.

Al-Qassam's appeal to religious values was not simply a return to tradition or a retreat into the past, but instead represented a real transformation of traditional forms for revolutionary use in the present. He seized on popular memories of the Assassins [a violent *Shiite* organization that flourished between the late eleventh and mid-thirteenth centuries] and the wars against the Crusaders by invoking the tradition of the *fida'iyn* [individuals who sacrificed themselves for their faith by performing a violent act], the notion of struggle that involved sacrifice. His clandestine organization resembled that of a *Sufi* order: his followers grew their beards "wild" and called themselves *shaykhs*. . . .

[In] November 1935 . . . al-Qassam launch[ed] . . . a full-scale revolt. Accompanied by a small detachment of followers, he set out from Haifa with the aim of raising the peasantry in rebellion. An accidental encounter with the police led to a premature battle with the British military, however, and al-Qassam died before his rebellion could get off the ground.

Nonetheless, his example electrified the country. Independent radical organizations eulogized al-Qassam and gained new inspiration from his revolutionary project. Al-Qassam rapidly achieved the status of a popular hero, and his gravesite became a place of pilgrimage. His legacy also included the many Qassamites still at large and prepared for action, as well as militant nationalists who set up fresh political groupings in the towns and organized armed bands on the Qassam model. Urban radicals also redoubled their organizing in the villages in preparation for a new anti-British outbreak. In such a highly charged atmosphere, only a small event was needed to trigger an explosion. That incident occurred on 13 April 1936, when two Jews were murdered in the Nablus Mountains, perhaps by Qassamites. Following a wave of brutal reprisals and counter-reprisals, the government declared a state of emergency. In response, "national committees" led by various militant organizations sprang up in the towns and declared a general strike. The notables followed along, trying to retake control of the unruly movement. On 25 April all the Palestinian parties (including the Nashashibi's National Defense Party) met with the national committees and set up a coordinating body known as the Higher Arab Committee (H.A.C.), with Amin al-Husayni as its president. Although the H.A.C. grew out of the notables' move to regain their dominant position, nonetheless, as a merging of the independent radical groupings with the traditional leadership it was more representative than the old Arab Executive had been. The H.A.C. quickly declared that the general strike would continue until the British Government put an end to Jewish immigration to Palestine, and it restated the other basic national demands—the banning of land sales and the establishment of an independent national government.

[T]he revolt's focus rapidly shifted to the countryside. A conference of rural national committees convened in May and elaborated a specific peasant agenda, including a call for nonpayment of taxes and the denunciation of the establishment of police stations in villages at *fellahin* expense. . . . In mid-May, armed peasant bands in which Qassamites featured prominently appeared in the highlands. They were assisted by armed commandos in the towns and by peasant auxiliaries who fought part-time. Though connected to the urban national committees, in general these bands operated independently of the *mufti* and the H.A.C. From mountain hideouts they harassed British communications, attacked Zionist settlements, and even sabotaged the Iraq Petroleum Company oil pipelines of Haifa. This last activity posed a particular threat to British global hegemony, for in the 1930s Great Britain still controlled the bulk of Middle East oil and the Haifa pipeline was crucial to imperial naval strategy in the Mediterranean.

The towns, in a state of semi-insurrection, were finally brought under control by the British in July, which left the countryside as the undisputed center of revolt. In the following month Fawsi al-Qawuqji, hero of the Syrian Druze rebellion of 1925, resigned his commission in the Iraqi army and entered Palestine with an armed detachment of pan-Arab volunteers, declaring himself commander-in-chief of the revolt. Although the military effectiveness of the rebel movement was improved and al-Qawuqji was hailed as a popular hero throughout the country, he never managed to unite all the diverse bands under his command.

While popular forces fought the British in the countryside, the notables of the H.A.C.—only one of whom had been arrested—were negotiating with the enemy for a compromise to end the conflict. British authorities increased the pressure in late September by launching tough countermeasures—boosting their military force to 20,000, declaring martial law, and going on a new defensive. The H.A.C. was also constrained by the onset of the agricultural season: peasants wanted to resume work, but, more important, harvest season started in September on the plantations of wealthy citrus-growers. The H.A.C., preferring negotiations to mass mobilization, which threatened notable leadership, called off the six-month-old general strike on 10 October, with the understanding that the Arab kings (of Iraq, Jordan, and Saudi Arabia) would intercede with the British Government on the Palestinians' behalf and that the government would act in good faith to work out new solutions. A long interim period ensued. While notables pinned their hopes on a Royal Commission of Inquiry, activists and rebel band leaders toured the villages and purchased weapons in preparation for a new round of fighting.

In July 1937, the British Peel Commission published its recommendations for the partition of Palestine into Arab and Jewish states. Arab reaction was universally hostile; even the Nashashibi faction that had defected from the H.A.C. condemned the partition proposal. Feelings ran especially high in the Galilee, a highland region with few Jewish residents, which the plan of partition included in the proposed Jewish state. In September, following the assassination of the British district commissioner for Galilee (possibly by Qassamites), the second phase of the revolt erupted. British authorities responded by banning the H.A.C. and deporting or arresting hundreds of activists. The *mufti* managed to evade arrest by escaping to Lebanon in October. Shortly thereafter, fierce fighting broke out. With the notable leadership in exile or imprisoned, command now shifted decisively to the partisans in the countryside.

Rebel bands were most active in the Nablus and Galilee highlands, the areas of greatest popular resistance. The Jerusalem-Hebron region . . . was also an important center. In these districts the various bands set up their own court system, administrative offices, and intelligence networks. While peasants and ex-peasant migrants to the towns composed the vast majority of band leaders and fighters, young urban militants played important roles as commanders, advisers, arms transporters, instructors, and judges. Qassamites were particularly well represented at the leadership level. By taxing the peasantry, levying volunteers, and acquiring arms through the agency of experienced smugglers, the bands were able to operate autonomously from the rebel headquarters-in-exile set up by the notable leadership at Damascus. A network of militants in the towns, particularly from among the semi-proletariat, collected contributions, gathered intelligence, and carried out acts of terror against the British, the Zionists, and Arab *simsars* [intermediaries in trade] and collaborators.

In the summer and fall of 1938 the rebellion reached its peak. Some 10,000 persons had joined the insurgent bands, now sufficiently well organized for a handbook of instructions to be issued for their members. Commanders of the largest bands established a Higher Council of Command to enhance military coordination. Most of the Palestinian highlands were in rebel hands, and by September government control over the urban areas had virtually ceased.

Once rebels gained the upper hand in the towns, the peasant character of the revolt expressed itself even more clearly. Rebel commanders ordered all townsmen to take off the urban headgear, the fez, and to don the peasant head cloth, the *kafiya;* urban women were commanded to veil. This action was both practical, in that it protected rebels from arrest by the British when they entered the towns, and symbolic, in that it signified the countryside's hegemony over the city. Insurgents also instructed urban residents not to use electric power, which was produced by an Anglo-Jewish company. Few dared to disobey these orders. Large sums of money were extracted from wealthy city-dwellers as contributions to the revolt, and particularly large "contributions" were demanded from the big orange-growers and merchants at Jaffa who supported the Nashashibi opposition.

On 1 September, the joint rebel command issued a declaration that directly challenged the leading classes' dominance over the countryside. Although limited in scope, the declaration represented a social program that went beyond the merely "national" goals of the *a'yan* [notables]. In it the commanders declared a moratorium on all debts (which had so impoverished the peasantry and by means of which notables controlled agricultural production) and warned both debt collectors and land agents not to visit the villages. Arab contractors, who hired work teams for the construction of police posts in the villages and roads to facilitate access to rebel strongholds, were also ordered to cease operations. In addition, the statement declared the cancellation of rents on urban apartments, which had risen to scandalously high levels. This item was particularly significant in that, by linking the needs of peasants and urban workers, it revealed the new class alliance underpinning the revolt.

The rebels' interference with landlord-usurer control over the countryside and their demands for contributions from the wealthy constituted a "revenge of the countryside," which prompted thousands of wealthy Palestinians to abandon their homes for other Arab countries. Well-off Palestinians tended to view the rebels as little better than bandits. In part this charge was justified, for there were serious discipline problems within the rebel camp, despite the considerable advances the bands achieved in coordination and unity of purpose. For instance, clan or family loyalties occasionally interfered with the class or national interests of certain rebel commanders, who carried out petty blood-feuds under cover of nationalist activity. Some peasants were alienated by the coercive manner employed by particular leaders to collect taxes and by their favoritism toward certain clans. Moreover, although class divisions among the peasants were not well developed, villagers were by no means homogeneous in their class interests.

Most accounts of the revolt stress the internal problems faced by the rebels. Although such criticisms are exaggerated and detract from the rebels' positive accomplishments, they cannot simply be dismissed. The British and the Nashashibis were able to exploit the contradictions within the rebel movement through such means as the formation of "peace bands" in late 1938 to do battle with the rebels. Although representative primarily of the interests of landlords and rural notables, the peace bands were manned by disaffected peasants.

More important for British strategy than the peace bands was the signing of the Munich Agreement on 30 September 1938. This allowed Britain to free one more army division for service in Palestine and to launch a military counter-offensive. Is it possible that British Prime Minister [Neville] Chamberlain [1869–1940] signed the Munich Agreement not merely to appease Hitler momentarily but also to protect Britain's oil supply in the Mediterranean from "backward" but dangerous bands of peasants? It would be difficult to chart a clear cause-effect relation, but it is evident at least that for the British chiefs of staff, Palestine was a crucial strategic buffer between the Suez Canal and potential enemies to the north (Germany, Soviet Union) and was an indispensable link in land communications. With war looming on the horizon in Europe, Britain was seeking desperately to end the disturbances in Palestine.

In any event, the Munich Agreement had disastrous consequences not just for Czechoslovakia but for the rebellion in Palestine as well. By 1939 the rebels were fighting a British military force of 20,000 men as well as the R.A.F. In addition,

Orde Wingate [1903–44], a British officer, organized a counterinsurgency force of Jewish fighters known as the Special Night Squads to terrorize villagers and to guard the oil pipeline. The British counteroffensive increased pressure on the rebels and prompted further internal problems, such as abuses in collecting taxes and contributions and an upsurge in political assassinations.

However, the intensified military offensive was still not enough to finish off the rebellion, so the British launched a diplomatic one as well. In March 1939 the government issued a White Paper (see part c, this Reading) declaring that it was opposed to Palestine becoming a Jewish state, that Jewish immigration would be limited to 75,000 over the next five years, that land sales would be strictly regulated, and that an independent Palestinian state would be set up in ten years with self-governing institutions to be established in the interim. Although both the notables and the rebels rejected the White Paper, the Palestinian populace responded to it more favorably. Clearly, while it did not satisfy the maximum national demands, the White Paper represented a concession wrung from the British by armed resistance. Zionist reaction against the White Paper, by contrast, was much more virulent.

The revolt was gradually crushed by extreme external pressures and the resultant internal fracturing of the movement. After over three years of fighting, the intervention of substantial British military forces aided by the Zionists, and nearly 20,000 Arab casualties (5,032 dead, 14,760 wounded), the rebellion was finally subdued. In July the last major rebel commander was captured; once the war with Germany began in September 1939, fighting ended altogether. An entirely new set of circumstances on the international scene was to determine subsequent events in Palestine.

B. The Arab Response to the Proposed Partition of Palestine (1938)*

At the height of the Palestinian Revolt leaders of the Arab world met in Cairo to express their opposition to the British Peel Commission Report (1937), which proposed partitioning Palestine into two states. They also agreed that the 400,000 Jewish people then living in Palestine could stay there, but they opposed any further Jewish immigration. Since Hitler's rise to power in 1933, and with Europe on the verge of a general war, Zionist leaders had organized both legal and illegal Jewish immigration into Palestine and had no intention of stopping this movement. The resolutions of this Congress helped convince the British government to issue the White Paper of 1939 (part c, this Reading). War intervened and this plan never materialized.

---

*From *Resolutions of the Inter-Parliamentary Congress*, Cairo, October 7–11, 1938, pp. 5–7. American spellings adopted. Bracketed material added by the editors.

* * *

The Congress declared that Jewish Immigration which flowed into the country as a result of the Balfour Declaration was one of the worst calamities that ever befell Palestine. Since this Declaration has already been shown to be null and void, it constitutes a clear violation of the rights of the Arabs and therefore justice demands that the status prior to the Balfour Declaration should be re-established and that the principle of Jewish Immigration be acknowledged as *ultra vires* [the British going beyond their legitimate powers].

Nevertheless, this Congress, actuated by a genuine desire to co-operate with the British Government for the solution of the Palestine problem and for the maintenance of good relations between Great Britain on the one hand and Arab and Muslim Countries on the other, recommends that the people of Palestine should make a sacrifice by agreeing to accept in their midst the Jews who are already in Palestine. This must be, however, on the condition that further Zionist Immigration is definitely prohibited, so that the difficulties resulting from this immigration, which has caused great harm to the country, may not be further aggravated.

This solution, so favorable to the Jews, should be acceptable to the British Government because . . . the solution proposed justifies the assumption that Great Britain has fulfilled her promise to the Jews by having facilitated their immigration into Palestine. The result of this immigration has been that there is, at present, in Palestine, a population of over 400,000 Jews, numbers which constitute a fulfillment of the "favorable view" of the British Government towards the establishment in Palestine of a Jewish National Home.

Any other interpretation of the Balfour Declaration would mean that it was desired to make Palestine Jewish, which is contradictory even to the text of the Declaration itself (see Reading 19a). This attitude on the part of Great Britain would offend Christians and Muslims throughout the world, and would be resisted by the Arabs and the Muslims with all the power at their command.

The partition of Palestine is not less dangerous than Jewish immigration, nor is it compatible with the British Declaration that Great Britain entered the war in the East for the purpose of emancipating its peoples and the establishment of national governments in accordance with the wishes of the people. It is also inconsistent with the declaration that "the well-being and the development of such peoples form a sacred trust of civilization."

Partition would create in Palestine two neighboring hostile states between which it is impossible to imagine the possibility of an exchange of inhabitants, property and holy places, such as mosques, churches and cemeteries. Furthermore, partition would deprive the Arabs of their land, which constitutes the bulk of their wealth in the territory proposed to be ceded to the Jewish State. It would also deprive them of an outlet to the sea. The Jews, on the other hand, possess hardly any property of any value, and have no population, in the barren mountainous regions intended to form the Arab State.

In addition to what has been stated above, the Arabs do not recognize the legality of the Balfour Declaration, even if it only aimed at the establishment of a Spiritual Home for the Jews. How, then, would they acquiesce in the seizure by others of the best and the most fertile region of their country, while it is proposed that they themselves shall be relegated to the barren rocky regions where they would be starved and annihilated?

C. The British Government's White Paper on Palestine (1939)*

The British government issued this White Paper on the eve of World War II. It disavowed the Peel Commission's earlier recommendation of partition and called for eventual establishment of an independent and united Palestinian state. The Jewish Agency vehemently denounced and rejected this pronouncement on the grounds that it "denied the Jewish people the right to rebuild their national home in their ancestral country." The Arabs of Palestine, wishing for immediate independence, also denounced the 1939 White Paper.

The Royal Commission and previous Commissions . . . have drawn attention to the ambiguity of certain expressions in the Mandate, such as the expression "a National Home for the Jewish people," . . . [which are] a fundamental cause of unrest and hostility between Arabs and Jews. His Majesty's Government are convinced that . . . a clear definition of policy and objectives is essential. The proposal of partition recommended by the Royal Commission would have afforded such clarity, but the establishment of self-supporting independent Arab and Jewish States within Palestine has been found to be impracticable. It has therefore been necessary for His Majesty's Government to devise an alternative policy which will . . . meet the needs of the situation in Palestine. . . .

I. THE CONSTITUTION

. . . In light of these considerations His Majesty's Government make the following declaration of their intentions . . .

(1) The objective of His Majesty's Government is the establishment within ten years of an independent Palestine State in such treaty relations with the United Kingdom as will provide satisfactorily for the commercial and strategic requirement of both countries in the future. This proposal for the establishment of the independent State would involve consultation with the Council of the League of Nations with a view to the termination of the Mandate.

---

*From the Royal Institute of International Affairs, *Great Britain and Palestine 1915–1939*, 2nd ed. (New York: Oxford University Press, 1939), pp. 134–40. American spellings adopted. Bracketed material added by the editors.

(2) The independent State should be one in which Arabs and Jews share in government in such a way as to ensure that the essential interests of each community are safeguarded.

(3) The establishment of the independent State will be preceded by a transitional period throughout which His Majesty's Government will retain responsibility for the government of the country. During the transitional period the people of Palestine will be given an increasing part in the government of their country. Both sections of the population will have an opportunity to participate in the machinery of government, and the process will be carried on whether or not they both avail themselves of it.

(4) As soon as peace and order have been sufficiently restored in Palestine steps will be taken to carry out this policy of giving the people of Palestine an increasing part in the government of their country, the objective being to place Palestinians in charge of all the Departments of Government, with the assistance of British advisers and subject to the control of the High Commissioner.

[We omit details of the projected machinery of government—eds.]

(6) At the end of five years from the restoration of peace and order, an appropriate body representative of the people of Palestine and of His Majesty's Government will be set up to review the working of the constitutional arrangements during the transitional period and to . . . make recommendations regarding the Constitution of the independent Palestine State.

(7) His Majesty's Government will require . . . that . . . adequate provision has been made for:

(a) the security of, and freedom of access to, the Holy Places, and the protection of the interests and property of the various religious bodies.

(b) the protection of the different communities in Palestine in accordance with the obligations of His Majesty's Government to both Arabs and Jews and for the special position in Palestine of the Jewish National Home. . . .

II. IMMIGRATION

. . . It has been urged that all further Jewish immigration into Palestine should be stopped forthwith. His Majesty's Government cannot accept such a proposal. It would change the whole of the financial and economic system of Palestine and thus affect adversely the interests of Arabs and Jews alike. Moreover, in the view of His Majesty's Government, abruptly to stop further immigration would be unjust to the Jewish National Home. But, above all, His Majesty's Government are conscious of the present unhappy plight of large numbers of Jews who seek a refuge from certain European countries, and they believe that Palestine can and should make a further contribution to the solution of this pressing world problem. . . . [The Government offers] the following proposals regarding immigration.

(1) Jewish immigration during the next five years will be at a rate which, if economic absorptive capacity permits, will bring the Jewish population up to approximately one-third of the total population of the country. Taking into

account the expected natural increase of the Arab and Jewish populations, and the number of illegal Jewish immigrants now in the country, this would allow of the admission, as from the beginning of April this year, of some 75,000 immigrants over the next five years . . . .subject to the criterion of economic absorptive capacity.

[We omit details of the rate of permissible Jewish immigration—eds.]

His Majesty's Government are satisfied that, when the immigration over five years . . . has taken place, they will not be justified in facilitating, nor will they be under any obligation to facilitate, the further development of [t]he Jewish National Home by immigration regardless of the wishes of the Arab population.

III. LAND

The Administration of Palestine is required, under Article 6 of the Mandate, "while ensuring that the rights and position of other sections of the population are not prejudiced," to encourage "close settlement by Jews on the land," and no restriction has been imposed hitherto on the transfer of land from Arabs to Jews. The Reports of several expert Commissions have indicated that, owing to the natural growth of the Arab population and the steady sale in recent years of Arab land to Jews, there is now in certain areas no room for further transfers of Arab land, whilst in some other areas such transfers of land must be restricted if Arab cultivators are to maintain their existing standard of life and a considerable landless Arab population is not soon to be created. In these circumstances, the High Commissioner will be given general powers to prohibit and regulate transfers of land. These powers will date from the publication of this Statement of Policy and the High Commissioner will retain them throughout the transitional period.

The policy of the Government will be directed toward the development of the land and the improvement, where possible, of methods of cultivation. In the light of such development it will be open to the High Commissioner, should he be satisfied that the "rights and position" of the Arab population will be duly preserved, to review and modify any orders passed relating to the prohibition or restriction of the transfer of land.

D. The Biltmore Program (1942)*

David Ben-Gurion, head of the Jewish Agency, on a visit to New York City during the war in May 1942 for a conference of American Zionists, acted as the driving force behind the meeting at New York City's Biltmore Hotel, which issued this declaration. It reflected world Jewry's opposition to the British White Paper of

---

*Declaration adopted by the Extraordinary Zionist Conference, Biltmore Hotel, New York City, May 11, 1942, in Aaron S. Klieman and Adrian S. Kleiman, eds., *American Zionism: A Documentary History*, 15 vols. (New York: Garland Publishing Co., 1990–1991), vol. 9, pp. 14–5.

1939 (part c, this Reading). This program called for the establishment of a Jewish state in Palestine and open immigration for Jewish refugees seeking a haven from Nazi persecution and mass murder.

1. American Zionists assembled in this Extraordinary Conference reaffirm their unequivocal devotion to the cause of democratic freedom and international justice to which the people of the United States, allied with the other United Nations, have dedicated themselves, and give expression to their faith in the ultimate victory of humanity and justice over lawlessness and brute force.

2. This Conference offers a message of hope and encouragement to their fellow Jews in the Ghettos and concentration camps of Hitler-dominated Europe and prays that their hour of liberation may not be far distant.

3. The Conference sends its warmest greetings to ... the ... *Yishuv* in Palestine, and expresses its profound admiration for their steadfastness and achievements in the face of peril and great difficulties. The Jewish men and women in field and factory, and the thousands of Jewish soldiers of Palestine ... who have acquitted themselves with honor and distinction ... on [wartime] ... battlefields, have shown themselves ... ready to assume the rights and responsibilities of nationhood.

4. ... In the course of the past twenty years, the Jewish people have awakened and transformed their ancient homeland ... [and] their numbers [there] have increased to more than 500,000. They have made the waste places to bear fruit and the desert to blossom. Their pioneering achievements in agriculture and in industry, embodying new patterns of cooperative endeavor, have written a notable page in the history of colonization.

5. In the new values thus created, their Arab neighbors in Palestine have shared. The Jewish people in its own work of national redemption welcomes the economic, agricultural and national development of the Arab peoples and states. The Conference reaffirms the stand previously adopted at Congresses of the World Zionist Organization, expressing the readiness and the desire of the Jewish people for full cooperation with their Arab neighbors.

6. The Conference calls for the fulfillment of the original purpose of the Balfour Declaration and the Mandate which "*recognizing the historical connection of the Jewish people with Palestine*" was to afford them the opportunity, as stated by President Wilson, to found there a Jewish Commonwealth.

The Conference affirms its unalterable rejection of the White Paper of May 1939 and denies its moral or legal validity. The White Paper seeks to limit, and in fact to nullify Jewish rights to immigration and settlement in Palestine, and, as stated by Mr. Winston Churchill in the House of Commons in May 1939, constitutes "a breach and repudiation of the Balfour Declaration." The policy of the White Paper is cruel and indefensible in its denial of sanctuary to Jews fleeing from Nazi persecution; and at a time when Palestine has become a focal point in the war front of the United Nations, and Palestine Jewry must provide all available manpower for farm and factory and camp, it is in direct conflict with the interests of the allied war effort.

7. In the struggle against the forces of aggression and tyranny, of which Jews were the earliest victims, and which now menace the Jewish National Home, recognition must be given to the right of the Jews of Palestine to play their full part in the war effort and in the defense of their country, through a Jewish military force fighting under its own flag and under the high command of the United Nations.

8. The Conference declares that the new world order that will follow victory cannot be established on foundations of peace, justice and equality, unless the problem of Jewish homelessness is finally solved.

The Conference urges that the gates of Palestine be opened; that the Jewish Agency be vested with control of immigration into Palestine and with the necessary authority for upbuilding the country, including the development of its unoccupied and uncultivated lands; and that Palestine be established as a Jewish Commonwealth integrated in the structure of the new democratic world.

Then and only then will the age-old wrong to the Jewish people be righted.

21. The Creation of the State of Israel

The first two selections in this reading, both United Nations General Assembly documents, reflect the international organization's historic role as the successor to the League of Nations. Soon after the end of World War II the British evacuated Palestine and turned the question over to the United Nations. Part a gives the 1947 UN majority resolution #181 recommending partition of Palestine into two states, which Arabs rejected and Zionists accepted—although they wanted more than the 55 percent of the land allotted to them. War for control of Palestine then broke out, during which, in 1948, Israel declared its statehood. Its victory over the Arabs led to an influx of nearly 700,000 Jewish refugees from Europe and the Muslim world and an outflow of more than that number of fleeing Arab Palestinians.

A year after the General Assembly proposed its partition plan, the organization issued Resolution #194, which called for an Arab "Right of Return" to postmandate Palestine (see part b). But the fledgling UN had no power to enforce either of these resolutions, especially since Israel had determined to prevent Arabs who fled the war zones to return to their homes. These unresolved problems remain among the key issues more than a half-century later. So far the UN has proved as incapable as had the League of Nations in handling the Palestine question.

In 1950, the Israeli *Knesset* (parliament) passed its own Law of Return, which we reproduce in part c of this Reading.

A. UN General Assembly, the Partition Plan: Resolution #181 (1947)*

A majority of states in the UN General Assembly voted for this partition plan for Palestine on November 29, 1947. The resolution called for termination of the British mandate and the creation of two states: one Arab, the other Jewish (see Map p. 190). The city of Jerusalem was to enjoy special status under an international administration. Thirty-one countries voted in favor of this resolution (including both the United States and the Soviet Union). Seven countries voted against and sixteen abstained. The Zionists accepted the majority resolution, while the Arabs, who wanted a single state in Palestine dominated by the Arab majority, rejected it. Iran, India, and Yugoslavia offered another alternative at the time: one state in Palestine with Arab and Jewish zones.

The Termination of Mandate

The Mandate for Palestine shall terminate as soon as possible but in any case not later than 1 August 1948.

The armed forces of the mandatory Power shall be progressively withdrawn from Palestine, the withdrawal to be completed as soon as possible but in any case not later than 1 August 1948.

The mandatory Power shall advise the Commission, as far in advance as possible, of its intention to terminate the Mandate and to evacuate each area.

The mandatory Power shall use its best endeavors to ensure that an area situated in the territory of the Jewish State, including a seaport and hinterland adequate to provide facilities for a substantial immigration, shall be evacuated at the earliest possible date and in any event not later than 1 February 1948.

Independent Arab and Jewish States and the Special International Regime for the City of Jerusalem . . . shall come into existence in Palestine two months after the evacuation of the armed forces of the mandatory Power has been completed but in any case not later than 1 October 1948. . . .

Jerusalem

The City of Jerusalem shall be established as a *corpus separatum* [separate body] under a special international regime and shall be administered by the United Nations. The Trusteeship Council shall be designated to discharge the responsibilities of the Administering Authority. . . . The City of Jerusalem shall include the present municipality of Jerusalem plus the surrounding villages and towns, the most eastern of which shall be Abu Dis; the most southern, Bethlehem. . . .

---

*From United Nations General Assembly Resolution #181 (II) (November 29, 1947), *Official Records of the General Assembly,* Second Session, September/November, 1947. American spellings adopted.

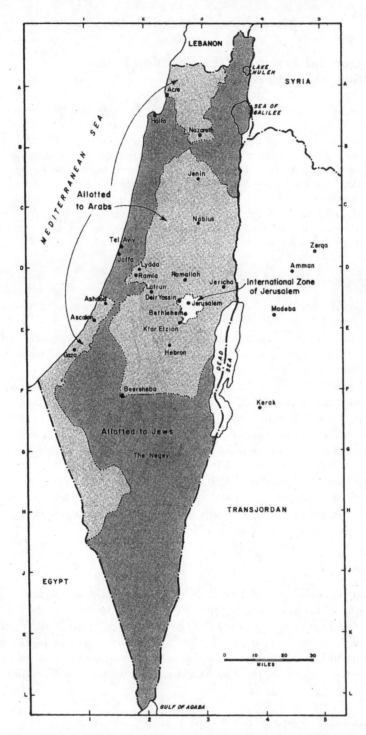

United Nations Partition Plan for Palestine, 1947

The Trusteeship Council shall, within five months of the approval of the present plan, elaborate and approve a detailed Statute of the City which shall contain *inter alia* the substance of the following provisions: *Government machinery; special objectives.* The Administering Authority in discharging its administrative obligations shall pursue the following special objectives:

(a) To protect and to preserve the unique spiritual and religious interests located in the city of the three great monotheistic faiths throughout the world, Christian, Jewish and Muslim; to this end to ensure that order and peace, and especially religious peace, reign in Jerusalem;

(b) To foster cooperation among all the inhabitants of the city in their own interests as well as in order to encourage and support the peaceful development of the mutual relations between the two Palestinian peoples throughout the Holy Land; to promote the security, well-being and any constructive measures of development of the residents, having regard to the special circumstances [of the two] peoples and communities.

B. UN General Assembly, Palestinian Right of Return: Resolution #194 (1948)*

This reading presents portions of UN Resolution #194 that concern the Right of Return for Palestinians displaced from their residences after 1947, and omits sections dealing with Jerusalem and holy sites in Palestine. The portion retained here, along with a later UN Resolution on compensation for and resettlement of Palestinian refugees, has shaped all subsequent negotiations on the issue—as inconclusive as they have been.

Arabs and Israelis take sharply divergent positions on these matters. Palestinians wish to press these claims for compensation and resettlement, while every Israeli government until recently has rejected them on the grounds that the Jewish character of Israel would be undermined if they were to be granted. See part c of this Reading for the very different 1950 Jewish Law of Return.

The General Assembly, having considered . . . the situation in Palestine . . .

Resolves that the refugees wishing to return to their homes and live at peace with the neighbors should be permitted to do so at the earliest practicable date, and that compensation should be paid for the property of those choosing not to return and for loss of or damage to property which, under principles of international law or in equity, should be made good by the Governments or authorities responsible;

---

*From United Nations General Assembly Resolution #194 (III) (December 11, 1948), *Palestine: Progress Report of the United Nations Mediator,* UN Doc. A/810 (1948), pp. 21–25. American spellings adopted.

Instructs the Conciliation Commission to facilitate the repatriation, resettlement and economic and social rehabilitation of the refugees and the payment
of compensation, and to maintain close relations with the Director of the United
Nations Relief for Palestine Refugees and, through him, with the appropriate
organs and agencies of the United Nations.

C. The Israeli *Knesset,* The Law of Return
(1950, 1954, and 1970)*

Passed unanimously by the *Knesset* on July 5, 1950, and anticipated in the passage
in the 1948 Proclamation of Independence stating that the "State of Israel will
be open to the immigration of Jews from all countries of their dispersion," the
Law of Return reflects the establishment of Israel as a sanctuary for Jews worldwide. The *Knesset* amended its original text in 1954 and again in 1970. We reproduce the latest version of the law.

Article 4B of this law has raised contention in Israel and in the Jewish Diaspora,
for under the political arrangements of the new Jewish state responsibility for
interpreting that portion of the law (who is a Jew?) has devolved upon the Orthodox rabbinate, who do not consider any conversions to Judaism as religiously
valid unless done by them. This offended Jews of the Conservative and Reform
persuasion in Israel and in the wider Diaspora, and especially in the United States.
Israel's Supreme Court resolved part of the problem in February 2002 by ruling
that the Israeli state must recognize conversions (and therefore accept immigrant
converts under the Law of Return) supervised by Reform, Conservative, as well
as Orthodox rabbis. Within Israel, however, the Orthodox establishment retains
exclusive control over marriages, divorces, and burials, and still discriminates against
non-Orthodox converts.

1. Every Jew has the right to immigrate to this country.
2. (a) Immigration shall be by immigrant's visa.
   (b) An immigrant's visa shall be given to every Jew who has expressed his
       desire to settle in Israel, unless the Minister of Immigration is satis-
       fied that the applicant:
       (1) is engaged in an activity directed against the Jewish people; or
       (2) is liable to endanger public health or the security of the State; or
       (3) is a person with a criminal past liable to endanger public welfare.
3. (a) A Jew who comes to Israel and subsequently expresses his desire to
       settle may, whilst still in Israel, receive an immigrant's certificate. . . .

---

*From John Norton Moore, ed., *The Arab-Israeli Conflict: Readings and Documents,* abridged and
revised ed. (Princeton, NJ: Princeton University Press, 1977), pp. 991–92, an unofficial translation. By permission.

4.   Every Jew who migrated to this country before the commencement of this Law and every Jew born in the country, whether before or after the commencement of this Law, is in the same position as one who immigrated under this law.

4A. (a) The rights of a Jew under this Law, the rights of an immigrant under the Nationality Law, 1952 and the rights of an immigrant under any other legislation are also granted to the child and grandchild of a Jew and to the spouse of the child and grandchild of a Jew—with the exception of a person who was a Jew and willingly changed his religion.

(b) It makes no difference whether or not the Jew through whom a right is claimed under sub-section (a) is still alive or whether or not he has immigrated to this country. . . .

4B. For the purpose of this Law, "a Jew" means a person born to a Jewish mother or converted to Judaism and who is not a member of another religion.

5.   The Minister of Interior is charged with the implementation of this Law and may make regulations as to any matter relating to its implementation and as to the grant of immigrant's visas and certificates to minors up to the age of 18.

22. Arab Assertions: Out of Despair Revived Nationalism

The Arabs' catastrophic military defeat in 1967 sent shock waves through the Middle East. The following decade, filled with political upheavals, also opened a period of unprecedented self-criticism and the call for radical change in the Arab world. Nizar Qabbani (1923–98) from Damascus, one of the most revered Arab poets, led the way, holding nothing back in scathing condemnation of past Arab errors in part a of this Reading. Three years prior to the 1967 war, the Palestine National Council (PNC), which for decades has served as the Palestinian parliament in exile, first adopted the document in part b of this Reading, the Palestine National Charter. As a body the PNC incorporated representatives from various sectors of Palestinian society, armed groups, and the political and civic organizations, which constitute the Palestine Liberation Organization (PLO). The PNC amended this charter once in 1968 before its 1996 special meeting in which more than five hundred delegates by more than a two-thirds vote opted to change the charter at a future date to include a two-state solution to the Arab-Israeli conflict.

A. Nizar Qabbani, The Catastrophe of Arab Defeat (1967)*

Combining the life of a diplomat with that of a writer, Qabbani took on taboo subjects, which he described in rebellious, well-crafted, popular language, forever changing the nature of Arabic poetry from a formalized medium into a popular one. Like the other great modern poets of the Muslim world—the Turk Nizam Hikmet, the Urdu poet Faiz Ahmad Faiz, the Syrian Adonis (Ali Ahmad Said, a naturalized Lebanese citizen), and the Palestinian Mahmoud Darwish—people brought their poems (Qabbani's among them) into the streets, singing them there and in the markets. Such poets became popular idols.

In 1967 Qabbani retired as a Syrian diplomat. His reputation had grown because of the popular appeal of his love poetry and as a result of a publishing firm that he established in London, where he then lived. He eventually produced more than two dozen volumes of his own work.

To you my friends, I mourn
the ancient books and our mother tongue
like battered shoes
our speech is full of holes
smut and scorn and whorish words
To you, I mourn
the end of thought
that brings defeat.
In our mouths, poems turn to salt
women's braids, nights, curtains and the resting place
before our eyes all immersed into salt.
Heavy-hearted country of my birth
without warning you transformed me
from a poet singing for love
to one writing with a knife.
What we sense is beyond words
poems we had written
now make us blush for shame.
Losing the war after all is not so strange
in the East, we flame into battle
armed to the teeth
with words.

---

*Nizar Qabbani, "*Hawamish 'Ala Daftar al-Naksa*" (Annotations to the Notebook of the Disaster). This poem first appeared in an independent chapbook following the 1967 war. It was later included in Qabbani's collection, *Al-A'mal al-Siyasiya* (The Political Works), published by *Manshurat Nizar Qabbani*, Beirut, 1973. Translated from the Arabic by Kamal Boullata. By permission of the translator.

We swagger
horsemen's thundering orations
that never killed a fly.
With fiddle and tambourine
we enter war.
Enigma of our tragedy:
our howl is deeper than our voices
our swords are taller than our bodies.
In short:
we cloaked ourselves with the skin of civilization
but our souls belong to the stone age.
With reed and flute
no war was won.
Our rashness cost us
fifty thousand new tents.
Don't curse heaven
if it abandons you
don't curse your stars
God bestows victory to whom He pleases
He is not your blacksmith to beat your swords.
It pains me to hear the news in the morning
it pains me to hear dogs barking.
Enemies never crossed our borders
like ants they surged
from our infamy.
For five thousand years
we lived in a cellar
our beards are drooping
our currency is unknown
our eyes are haven for flies.
My friends,
try breaking a door
or washing clothes and washing your thoughts
try reading a book
try writing a book
try growing words with grapes and pomegranates.
Try sailing to lands of fog and snow
where people do not know you exist
outside your holes
they take you for a breed of wolves.
Thick-skinned we are
harrowed hollow souls
our days whirl around
play, sleep and sorcery.

Are we truly,
"a nation chosen by God"?
The flow of our oil in the deserts
could have turned into
a dagger of fire and flame
instead
disgrace dishonors the most virtuous
among the Prophet's tribe:
our oil is spilled under whores' feet.
We run through a street
with ropes under arms
dragging men tied by their feet
smashing glass, blowing up locks
like frogs
we praise, like frogs
we swear, we make
heroes of midgets
knaves of nobles
we improvise our feats.
We settle down in mosques
idle and benumbed
measuring line endings
reciting sayings
begging
God from His high heavens
to grant us victory
over our enemy.
If only someone were to grant me safety
and I were able to meet the Sultan
I would tell him:
Your Majesty, your wild dogs
have torn my clothes
your spies hound me
their eyes follow me
their noses follow me
their feet follow me
like fixed fate
like legal codes
they question my wife
and take down names of my friends.
Your Majesty
just for having been in the vicinity of your deaf walls
and for attempting to uncover my grief
your soldiers kicked me with their boots
forced me to eat

dirt, Your Majesty
twice you lost in war
because half of our nation lost its tongue.
What is a people's worth
without speech?
Half the nation is trapped
like bugs and rats within walls.
If only someone were to grant me safety
from the Sultan's troops
I would tell him:
twice you have lost a war
because you've turned your back on humankind.
If only we had not buried our unity in dirt
If only we had not pierced its tender body with spears
If it had dwelled within sight of our eyes
dogs would not have devoured our flesh.
We call for an angry generation
to uproot history
to plough horizons
to seed the bedrock of new thought.
We call for a generation rising
with new faces
forgiving no mistakes
forfeiting and stooping never more
not knowing a broken word.
A generation of staunch pioneers.
Children
you are the ears of corn
from the shores of the Mediterranean
to the sands of the Arabian Sea
you are the generation that shall break the siege
healing us of our addictions
ridding us of our illusions.
Children pure as dew as snow
do not read of our generation courting defeat
a hopeless case we are
worthless
watermelon rinds.
soles riddled with holes.
Do not read our chronicles
do not trace our footsteps
nor even dwell upon a thought we cherished.
Ours is a generation of vomit
consumed by festering sores
a generation of crooks and evil clowns

and you children
you are spring's rains
hope's sheaths of wheat
fruitful seeds in our barren lives.
You are the generation
that shall vanquish
defeat.

B. Palestinian National Council, The National Charter (1964, 1968)*

The Palestinian National Charter embodied the early ideology of the Palestine Liberation Organization, which called for the establishment of a Palestinian state over all of mandate Palestine. Over the years, the Palestinian National Council has supplanted the original text with other historic PLO documents. The 1988 Palestinian Declaration of Independence advocated creating a Palestinian state on the West Bank and the Gaza Strip alongside Israel. Its capital would be in Arab East Jerusalem. In that same year Yasir Arafat affirmed in Washington that the PLO recognized Israel's right to exist (see Reading 24a). Those 1988 steps did not satisfy Israeli leaders who viewed two clauses of the charter (specifically articles 2 and 3, which affirm the indivisibility of historic Palestine and the right to liberate the country) as evidence of the PLO's desire to eliminate Israel. In 1996 the Palestinian National Council promised to amend their charter. This led Israel to recognize the legitimacy of a future Palestinian state next to Israel, a principle that hangs in balance, as we write these words, under the second *Intifada* and with Ariel Sharon in power in Israel.

Article 1—Palestine is the homeland of the Palestinian people. It is an inseparable part of the bigger Arab nation, and its people are an integral part of the Arab people.

Article 2—Palestine, with the borders that existed during the British Mandate, is an indivisible geographical unit.

Article 3—The Palestinian people have a legitimate right to their homeland. They are the ones to determine their destiny after the liberation of their lands as they will and choose.

Article 4—The Palestinian identity is a permanent and enduring trait that passes from father to son. The Israeli occupation, and the dispersion of the Palestinian people, resulting from the ill fortunes that befell them, cannot deprive the Palestinian people of its Palestinian personality and identity.

---

*Official English translation of the Palestinian National Council text of the National Charter, Palestine Liberation Organization, 1968. Bracketed material added by the editors.

Article 5—The Palestinians are those Arab citizens who under normal conditions used to live in Palestine until 1947; they include those who remained there as well as those who were evicted. The offspring of an Arab Palestinian parent, since that date, whether born in Palestine or outside, are regarded as Palestinians.

Article 6—The Jews who used to live under normal conditions in Palestine until the Zionist invasion of the country are to be considered Palestinians.

Article 7—Identification with, and spiritual, material, and historic attachment to, Palestine are irrefutable truths. It is a national duty to bring up the Palestinian individual as a revolutionary Arab, and to employ all the means of enlightenment and education to acquaint him with his native land—spiritually and materially—and to prepare him for the armed struggle in order to recover his homeland.

Article 8—The Palestinians now live in a stage of national struggle for the liberation of Palestine. . . . The Palestinians, whether inside or outside it, form one national front whose task is the liberation of Palestine through armed struggle.

Article 9—The armed struggle is the only way to liberate Palestine; it is, therefore, a strategy and not a tactic. The Palestinian people confirm their absolute determination and undeniable will to continue the armed struggle and march toward the armed popular revolution for the liberation, and the return to, their homeland, as well as for their right to a normal life and in determining their destiny with sovereignty over their land.

Article 10—The commando action is the nucleus of the Palestinian popular liberation war, and this requires escalation, protection, and mobilization of all the Palestinian massive and scientific resources which should be organized and deployed in the Palestinian revolution. What is also required is to achieve the merger of the national struggle by all classes of the Palestinian people. . . .

Article 11—The Palestinians shall have three slogans: National Unity, National Mobilization and Liberation.

Article 12—The Arab Palestinian people believe in Arab unity, and in order to participate in its fulfillment, they must preserve their Palestinian personality, seek to assert its presence and resist all plans that may seek to obliterate or weaken it.

Article 13—Arab unity and the liberation of Palestine are two complementary objectives in the sense that one prepares the ground for the fulfillment of the other. Arab unity leads to the liberation of Palestine, and the liberation of Palestine leads to Arab unity. . . .

Article 14—The fate of the Arab nation, or even Arab existence itself, is dependent on the fate of the Palestine cause. From this attachment between the two spring the effort and pursuit of the Arab nation to liberate Palestine; the Palestinian people shall play the leading role in the fulfillment of this nationalist and sacred aim.

Article 15—The liberation of Palestine from the pan-Arab point of view is a nationalist duty to repel the Zionist-imperialist invasion of the bigger Arab nation and to liquidate the Zionist presence in Palestine. The full responsibility of this rests on the Arab nation, peoples and governments, and in particular on the Palestinian people. For that, the Arab nation must mobilize all its military, material, spiritual, and human potentials for effectively participating with the Palestinian people in the liberation of Palestine. The Arab nation, especially at this stage of the Palestinian revolution, must fully support and assist the people of Palestine, materially and morally, and to provide them with all the means that would enable them to continue with their leading role in the armed revolution until the liberation of their homeland.

Article 16—The liberation of Palestine, from the spiritual point of view, provides the holy land with an atmosphere of security and peace whereby all the religious sanctities will be protected and religious freedom guaranteed. All people will be allowed to visit their holy places with no discrimination as to color, language, creed, or race. For this reason, the people of Palestine look forward to the support of all the spiritual forces in the world.

Article 17—The liberation of Palestine . . . would bring back to the Palestinian his freedom, integrity, and pride. Therefore, the Arab Palestinian people aspire for the support of all those who believe in the dignity and freedom of man. . . .

Article 18—The liberation of Palestine from the international point of view is . . . made imperative by the necessity of self-defense. . . .

Article 19—The partition of Palestine in 1947 and the creation of Israel are both null and void . . . because they were against the will of the Palestinian people and in contradiction with their natural right to their country as well as with the principle of self-determination.

Article 20—Balfour's Declaration, the mandate pact and all their consequences are also null and void. The claim of historic and spiritual connection between the Jews and Palestine contradict with the facts of history as well as with the conditions that would normally make up a State. Since Judaism is a heavenly religion with no independent national entity, the Jews cannot consider themselves as one nation with an independent national personality, but rather citizens in the countries in which they live.

Article 21—The Arab Palestinian people, who express themselves by the armed Palestinian revolution, reject all solutions that may stand as alternatives to the full liberation of Palestine; they also reject all proposals that seek to liquidate the Palestinian cause. . . .

Article 22—Zionism is a political movement, a part of world imperialism, and is against all liberation movements in the world. It is a fanatic racialist movement in its nature, antagonistic and expansionist in its aims, and fascist and Nazi in its means. Israel is a tool for the Zionist movement and a human and geographic base for world imperialism, and a center inside the Arab world for imperialism to counter the Arab nation and prevent it from progress, unity and liberation. Israel is a constant threat to peace in the Middle East as well as in the whole world. Since the liberation of Palestine obliterates Zionism and imperialism in Palestine, and leads to peace in the Middle East, the Palestinian people, therefore, look forward to the support of all liberals in the world, as well as the support of those who love peace, progress and goodness. They beseech all these elements, regardless of their tendencies and inclinations to assist and support the Palestinians in their just strife for the liberation of their homeland.

Article 23—Peace, security, and justice require of all nations . . . [to] consider the Zionist movement as illegal and to ban it.

Article 24—The Arab Palestinian people believe in the principles of freedom, justice, sovereignty, self-determination, human integrity, and the right of all nations to practice each of them.

Article 25—For the purpose of fulfilling the aims and principles of the Charter, the Palestine Liberation Organization shall undertake its complete role in the liberation of Palestine. . . .

[We omit several articles of the charter expanding on the "complete role in the liberation of Palestine" assigned to the PLO—eds.]

Article 33—This Charter is not to be modified except with a majority of two-thirds of the National Council of the Palestine Liberation Organization in a special session to be convened for that purpose.

23. Reaching for Peace: United Nations Security Council Resolutions (1967, 1973)

A fter the 1967 and 1973 Arab-Israeli wars, the most important UN body, the Security Council, passed resolutions on territories captured in war and how to create "a just and durable peace in the Middle East" (parts a and b, this Reading). Although politicians of many concerned nations refer frequently to these texts, they remain unimplemented.

A. UN Resolution #242: Withdrawal from Occupied Territory (1967)*

Diplomatic language, an argot all its own, specializes in formalistic ambiguous statements. UN resolutions exemplify this genre, as the texts here reveal. Section 1a of Resolution #242 speaks of "Withdrawal of Israel armed forces from territo-

---

*The United Nations Security Council adopted Resolution #242 on November 22, 1967, from *Official Records of the Security Council,* twenty-second year.

ries" without the definite article "the" before "territories." The Israelis interpret this to mean "some" but not "all" territories and have claimed they have completely fulfilled their obligations under #242 by returning the Sinai to Egypt. Arabs interpret the same clause as requiring the return of the Golan Heights to Syria and *all* of the West Bank and Gaza to Palestinian control. The 1992 acknowledgment by Israeli Prime Minister Rabin that the "land for peace" formula applied to the Golan Heights, and the Israeli recognition the next year of Palestinian self-government in the West Bank and Gaza (see Reading 25a), indicated the lines of a possible settlement.

Section 2b, no less ambiguous than Section 1a, calls for "a just settlement of the refugee problem," a thorny problem, which the Israelis and Palestinians addressed seriously in 2002 before negotiations broke down and ushered in another period of violence. Eventually the antagonists have no alternative but to return to the benchmark principles of #242 and #338 if they ever hope to avoid the unspeakable outcome of perpetual war.

The Security Council,
Expressing its continuing concern with the grave situation in the Middle East,
Emphasizing the inadmissibility of the acquisition of territory by war and the need to work for a just and lasting peace in which every State in the area can live in security,
Emphasizing further that all Member States in their acceptance of the Charter of the United Nations have undertaken a commitment to act in accordance with Article 2 of the Charter,
1. Affirms that the fulfillment of Charter principles requires the establishment of a just and lasting peace in the Middle East which should include the application of both the following principles:
    a. Withdrawal of Israel armed forces from territories occupied in the recent conflict;
    b. Termination of all claims or states of belligerency and respect for and acknowledgement of the sovereignty, territorial integrity and political independence of every State in the area and their right to live in peace within secure and recognized boundaries free from threats or acts of force;
2. Affirms further the necessity
    a. For guaranteeing freedom of navigation through international waterways in the area;
    b. For achieving a just settlement of the refugee problem;
    c. For guaranteeing the territorial inviolability and political independence of every State in the area, through measures including the establishment of demilitarized zones;
3. Requests the Secretary-General to designate a Special Representative to proceed to the Middle East to establish and maintain contacts with the States concerned in order to promote agreement and assist efforts to achieve a

peaceful and accepted settlement in accordance with the provisions and principles in this resolution;

4. Requests the Secretary-General to report to the Security Council on the progress of the efforts of the Special Representative as soon as possible.

B. UN Resolution #338: End the Fighting (1973)*

The Security Council,

1. Calls upon all parties to the present fighting to cease all firing and termi-nate all military activity immediately, no later than 12 hours after the mo-ment of the adoption of this decision, in the positions they now occupy;
2. Calls upon the parties concerned to start immediately after the cease-fire the implementation of Security Council Resolution 242 (1967) in all of its parts;
3. Decides that, immediately and concurrently with the cease-fire, negotiations start between the parties concerned under appropriate auspices aimed at establishing a just and durable peace in the Middle East.

24. Transformation of Palestinian Politics

The documents in this Reading represent the culmination of a process long at work within the Palestine Liberation Organization (PLO). Starting in the mid-1970s and continuing in the 1980s, the PLO (and the Palestinian National Council) adopted a new pragmatism, which enabled them to move from a policy of advocating warfare against Israel to one of negotiation and accommodation with the Jewish state. This change became evident in the 1988 Palestinian Decla-ration of Independence, calling for a two-state solution to the Arab-Israeli con-flict, which Arafat publicly supported that same year. Some minority components of the PLO, such as the Popular Front for the Liberation of Palestine, rejected the 1988 consensus. Others outside the PLO, including the Islamic radical group *Hamas* (zeal), also rejected a two-state solution. We present the *Hamas* Charter in part c of this reading. Part b presents the position of those Palestinians who,

---

*The United Nations Security Council Resolution #338, October 21, 1973, from *Official Records of the Security Council,* twenty-eighth year.

like its author, Hanan Mikhail-Ashrawi, organized and supported the *intifada* (uprising) of 1987–1993.

A. Yasir Arafat, We Recognize Israel (1988)*

    At a special session of the United Nations General Assembly convoked at the end of 1988 in Geneva, Switzerland, Arafat recognized Israel's right to exist alongside a Palestinian state. The day after the special session took place he clarified the Palestinian position in a press conference, extracts from which we present in this reading. Soon after Arafat's appearance in Geneva, President Ronald Reagan (1911–) reversed the United States policy of boycotting the PLO and announced that the United States would hold talks with representatives from that organization.

Let me highlight my views before you. Our desire for peace is a strategy and not an interim tactic. We are bent on peace come what may. . . . Our statehood provides salvation to the Palestinians and peace to both Palestinians and Israelis.

    Self-determination means survival for the Palestinians and our survival does not destroy the survival of the Israelis, as their rulers claim. Yesterday in my speech I made reference to the United Nations Resolution 181 [on the partition of Palestine, see Reading 21a] as the basis for Palestinian independence. I also made reference to our acceptance of resolutions 242 and 338 [see Reading 23] as the basis for negotiations with Israel within the framework of the international conference. These three resolutions were endorsed by our Palestinian National Council session in Algiers.

    In my speech also yesterday, it was clear that we mean our people's rights to freedom and national independence, according to Resolution 181 and the right of all parties concerned in the Middle East conflict to exist in peace and security.

    As for terrorism, I announced it yesterday in no uncertain terms, and yet, I repeat for the record . . . that we totally and absolutely renounce all forms of terrorism, including individual, group, and state terrorism.

    Between Geneva and Algiers, we have made our position crystal clear. Any more talk such as "The Palestinians should give more"—you remember this slogan? or "It is not enough" or "The Palestinians are engaging in propaganda games and public relations exercises" will be damaging and counterproductive.

    Enough is enough. . . . All remaining matters should be discussed around the table and within the international conference.

    Let it be absolutely clear that neither Arafat, nor any [one else] for that matter,

---

*From Yasir Arafat's Press Conference statement, Geneva, December 14, 1988. Arabic words italicized. Bracketed material added by the editors.

can stop the *intifada,* the uprising. The *intifada* will come to an end only when practical and tangible steps have been taken toward the achievement of our national aims and establishment of our independent Palestinian state.

In this context, I expect the EEC [European Economic Community] to play a more effective role in promoting peace in our region. They have a political responsibility, they have a moral responsibility, and they can deal with it.

Finally, I declare before you and I ask you to kindly quote me on that: We want peace. . . . We are committed to peace. We want to live in our Palestinian state, and let live. Thank you.

B. Hanan Mikhail-Ashrawi,
The Meaning of the *Intifada* (1989)*

The first *intifada,* a dramatic uprising of Palestinians in the West Bank and Gaza, began in 1987. It marked a major turning point in the region. By its end in the early 1990s, most of the world community accepted the inevitability and the desirability of an independent Palestinian state.

Marginalized by the earlier Egyptian-Israeli Camp David peace treaty and the conflicts in Lebanon, the PLO, its leadership exiled to Tunisia, could not respond directly or openly to the new crisis. Thus, the initiative passed to grassroots Palestinian organizations in the occupied territories, where spontaneous forms of resistance appeared. Ashrawi (1946–), a prominent leader of the *intifada,* describes in this Reading the way in which Palestinian civil society mobilized the personnel for this new struggle and the range of activities it encompassed. She also sets forth Palestinian aims—to seek full independence rather than mere improvement in the conditions of Israeli occupation. We have omitted some of Ashrawi's discussions of Palestinian demands, but the failure to achieve them in the 1987–1993 period explains much of the ferocity of the second *intifada* (see Reading 26c), begun in 2000.

At the time she published this report, Ashrawi had served as Dean of Arts and Sciences and taught English at Bir Zeit University on the West Bank. A Christian Arab, she had attended the American University of Beirut before moving to the United States where she received her Ph.D. in medieval and comparative literature from the University of Virginia. She served as the official spokesperson for Palestinian delegations attending peace negotiations from 1991 to 1993, headed a Palestinian human rights organization, and won a seat on the Legislative Council for Jerusalem before joining the Palestinian Authority as minister of higher education and research (1996–98). In 2001 she became spokesperson for the Arab League, with special responsibility for Palestinians. Her autobiography, *This Side*

---

*From Hanan Mikhail-Ashrawi, *From Intifada to Independence,* the Palestine Information Office in the Netherlands (1989), pp. 15–20.

of Peace: A Personal Account (1995), provides a vivid picture of Palestinian aspirations. She is a signatory of the 2002 appeal by Palestinians to stop suicide bombings (see Reading 26e).

As Palestinians under occupation, it is not only our right but our duty to resist occupation and oppression. We must dispel all illusions of improving the "quality of life" of Palestinians under occupation as inherently unrealistic and in direct contradiction to the aspirations of the Palestinians and the objectives of the *intifada*. There can be no "quality" to life under occupation beyond the quality of resistance to occupation and rejection of all its manifestations, including the unnatural reality of its premises of subjugation and its system of exploitation and inequity. The "quality" argument is just another attempt to "sugar-coat" the occupation for both world consumption . . . and for local consumption as the means of making an abhorrent situation of oppression palatable to the oppressed.

Both rationalizations suffer from political and moral blindness and must be exposed as subversive.

The *intifada* nullifies and exposes all proposals for "autonomy" as insufficient. The Palestinians under occupation have already taken major steps towards creating their own autonomy. The *intifada,* through a conscious effort of will, has created alternative and indigenous structures to replace those imposed by the Israeli military occupation. The newly created infrastructure is statehood at its seminal stages, established in direct defiance to the occupation and as a clear response to the patronizing tactical smokescreen called "autonomy."

The third illusion exposed by the *intifada* is the arrogance and deception implicit in the "Jordanian option" argument. The consistent historical assertion of Palestinians everywhere and the underlying premise of the *intifada* remains the recognition of Palestinian nationhood. As a precondition of statehood, the Jordanian connection is implicitly condescending and premature. The Palestinians are neither an appendage to another state, nor are they so deficient as to require artificial adoption by more responsible and mature parties. It boggles the mind that an infantile state must, even before its establishment, work out the minute details of future alliances and dependencies. Independence is the essence of statehood and cannot be compromised.

What is the *intifada* and what are its unique characteristics? The *intifada* is a simultaneously active statement of rejection and affirmation, an unequivocal rejection of the Israeli occupation . . . and the affirmation of the inalienable rights of the Palestinian people including our right of freedom, self-determination, and statehood. The *intifada* is the coming of age of the Palestinians in the Occupied Territories, a culmination of a gradual process of organization and resistance which has taken the form of a spontaneous eruption, an upheaval that has shaken the very foundations of the occupation and brought into question all the compliant assumptions which underlie its short-sighted policies and expansionist dreams.

The uprising's truly democratic and revolutionary nature has been clearly demonstrated. . . . Comprehensive and deep-rooted, the *intifada* emanates from the grass roots and cuts across all lines such as region, sex, religion, and political/factional affiliation. The uprising unifies all classes and sectors of society in an active pursuit of clear objectives and goals. Its popular mass-struggle character succeeds in creating a two-way system of communication, whereby the Unified National Leadership [UNL] role is not solely to lead, but to articulate the demands and different modes of struggle which the masses seek and sustain. The effectiveness of the leadership lies in its truly popular support, its openness to the needs of the population, and its underground character.

The core of the message of the *intifada* is the Palestinian right to self-determination, including the right to choose their own representatives . . . [in] an independent Palestinian state; and the protection of diaspora Palestinians' right of return. Neither new nor outrageous, Palestinians continue to express these ideas in various forms and at different times, but to deaf ears. By adding another dimension to that of verbal discussion, the *intifada* seeks to make our demands visible and tangible.

C. Charter of the Islamic Resistance Movement of Palestine (*Hamas*) (1988)*

By the late 1980s weakened secular nationalist movements in the Middle East shared the political spotlight with such militant Islamic movements as *Hamas* (zeal), whose 1988 Charter appears here. Such new movements modeled themselves on the Egyptian Muslim Brotherhood, of which *Hamas* considers itself the Palestinian branch. Only their respective leaders know whether organic links exist between these groups, or if *Hamas* merely claims ancestry from one of the oldest militant movements in the region to give it greater legitimacy. Originally established with Israel's acquiescence in order to sow divisions among the Palestinian population, *Hamas* only later became recognized for its intractable opposition to the very existence of Israel, whose government then turned against it.

In the Charter we see several contrasts between *Hamas* and the Palestine Liberation Organization (PLO). First, the PLO adheres to a secular program and welcomes both Christian and Muslim Palestinians in its organization, whereas *Hamas* has an explicitly Muslim religious orientation. *Hamas* also advocates total rejection of Israel and of all peace negotiations with it. The PLO accepts in principle the formula of "land for peace" to resolve the conflict, while *Hamas* wants to defeat the Israeli state by means of suicide bombings and other terrorist actions. Its Charter

---

*From Charter of the Islamic Resistance Movement of Palestine (1988), translated from the Arabic by Muhammad Maqdsi for the Islamic Association for Palestine, Dallas, Texas. Published in *Journal of Palestine Studies*, vol. 22, no. 4 (Summer, 1993), pp. 122–34. Abridged and rearranged. American spelling adopted. Notes removed and bracketed material added by the editors. By permission.

approvingly cites *The Protocols of the Elders of Zion* (forged by the Czarist Russian secret police and first released in 1905), which purported to report the proceedings of a conference of Jews in nineteenth-century Europe to plan the overthrow of other religions and take over the world. The longer the impasse between Israel and the Palestinians continues and violence intensifies, the greater becomes the appeal of extremism on both sides of the Muslim/Jewish divide.

Goals and Structure

The Islamic Resistance Movement [*Hamas*] is a branch of the Muslim Brotherhood chapter in Palestine. . . . It gives its loyalty to Allah, adopts Islam as a system of life, and works toward raising the banner of Allah on every inch of Palestine. Therefore, in the shadow of Islam, it is possible for all followers of different religions to live in peace and with security over their person, property, and rights. In the absence of Islam, discord takes form, oppression and destruction are rampant, and wars and battles take place. . . .

The Islamic Resistance Movement evolved in a time wh[en] . . . [v]alues have deteriorated, the plague of the evil folk and oppression and darkness have become rampant, cowards have become ferocious. . . . The goal of the Islamic Resistance Movement therefore is to conquer evil, break its will, and annihilate it so that truth may prevail, so that the country may return to its rightful place, and . . . proclaim . . . the Islamic state. And aid is sought from Allah. . . .

Jihad *and Nationalism*

Nationalism, from the point of view of the Islamic Resistance Movement, is part and parcel of religious ideology. There is not a higher peak in nationalism or depth in devotion than *Jihad* when an enemy lands on the Muslim territories. Fighting the enemy becomes the individual obligation of every Muslim man and woman. . . .

As far as the ideology of the Islamic Resistance Movement is concerned, giving up any part of Palestine is like giving up part of its religion. . . . [Peace] conferences are nothing but a form of enforcing the rule of the unbelievers in the land of Muslims. . . .

There is no solution to the Palestinian Problem except by *Jihad*. The initiatives, options, and international conferences are a waste of time and a kind of child's play. . . . When an enemy occupies some of the Muslim lands, *Jihad* becomes obligatory for every Muslim. In the struggle against the Jewish occupation of Palestine, the banner of *Jihad* must be raised. That requires that Islamic education be passed to the masses . . . in the Arab . . . and . . . Islamic [world], and that the spirit of *Jihad* must be broadcast among the *Umma*. . . . Fundamental changes must be brought about in the education system to liberate it from the effects of the Ideological Invasion brought about at the hands of the Orientalists and Missionaries. . . .

Jihad is not only carrying weapons and confronting the enemy. The good word, excellent article, beneficial book, aid, and support, if intentions are pure, so that the banner of Allah is the most-high, is a *Jihad* for the sake of Allah. . . .

Tasks of Muslim Women

The Muslim woman has a role in the battle for the liberation which is no less than the role of the man, for she is the factory of men. Her role in directing generations and training them is a big role. The enemies have realized her role: they think that if they are able to direct her and raise her the way they want, far from Islam, then they have won the battle. You'll find that they use continuous spending through mass media and the motion picture industry.

The women in the house of the *Mujahid* [a person who embarks on *jihad*], (and the striving family), be she a mother or sister, has the most important role in taking care of the home and raising children of ethical character and understanding that comes from Islam, and of training her children to perform the religious obligations to prepare them for the *Jihadic* role that awaits them. From this perspective it is necessary to take care of schools and the curricula that educate the Muslim girl to become a righteous mother aware of her role in the battle of liberation. . . .

The Zionist Enemy

Our enemy [Zionism] uses the method of collective punishment, robbing people of their land and property, and chasing them in their migration and places of gathering. They purposely break (bodily) bones, fire (live ammunition directly) at women, children, elders (sometimes) with a reason or without a reason, create concentration camps to place thousands (of people) in inhuman conditions, not to mention the demolition of homes, orphaning of children, and issuance of tyrannical laws on thousands of youth so they spent their best years in the obscurity of prisons. . . .

The enemy planned long ago and perfected their plan so that they can achieve what they want to achieve. . . . [T]hey worked on gathering huge and effective amounts of wealth to achieve their goal. With wealth they controlled the international mass media—news services, newspapers, printing presses, broadcast stations, and more. With money they ignited revolutions in all parts of the world to realize their benefits and reap the fruits of them. They are behind the French Revolution, the Communist Revolution, and most of the revolutions . . . which we have heard of. . . . With wealth they formed secret organizations throughout the world to destroy societies and promote the Zionist cause; these organizations include the freemasons, the Rotary and Lions clubs, and others. These are all destructive intelligence-gathering organizations. With wealth they controlled imperialistic nations and pushed them to occupy many nations to ex-

haust their (natural) resources and spread mischief in them. . . . They are behind the First World War in which they destroyed the Islamic *Caliphate* and gained
material profit, monopolized raw wealth, and got the Balfour Declaration [see
Reading 19a]. They created the League of Nations so they could control the
world through that organization. They are behind the Second World War where
they grossed huge profits from their trade of war materials, and set down the
foundations to establish their nation by forming the United Nations.

There is not a war that goes on here or there in which their fingers are not
playing behind it. . . . Today it's Palestine and tomorrow it will be another country,
and then another; the Zionist plan has no bounds, and after Palestine they wish
to expand from the Nile River to the Euphrates. When they totally occupy it
they will look towards another, and such is their plan in the Protocols of the
Learned Elders of Zion. . . .

So the imperialist powers in the Capitalist West and Communist East support the enemy with all their might—material and human—and they change
roles. When Islam is manifest, the unbelievers' powers unite against it because
the Nation of the unbelievers is one.

Other Islamic Movements

The Islamic Resistance Movement regards the other Islamic Movements with
respect and honor even if it disagrees with them on an issue or viewpoint. . . .
All nationalist elements working in the arena for the sake of liberating Palestine should be assured that it is a helper and supporter and will never be anything but that. . . .

The Palestine Liberation Organization is closest of the close to the Islamic
Resistance Movement, in that it is the father, the brother, the relative, or friend;
and does the Muslim offend his father, brother, relative, or friend? Our nation
is one, [our] plight is one, [our] destiny, and our enemy is the same. . . . {We
must coordinate] . . . work and action, past and present, by uniting, not dividing, repairing, not destroying, valuing benign advice, pure effort, and powerful
actions, closing the door in the face of petty disputes, not listening to rumors
and defamations while realizing the right of self-defense. Everything that contradicts these guidelines is fabricated from the enemy, or those who tread in their
footsteps, to achieve chaos, cleavage of ranks, and entanglement in side issues. . . .

[C]haotic ideologies . . . overwhelm the Arab world due to the ideological invasion
that befell the Arab world since the defeat of the Crusades and the ongoing consolidation of orientalism, missionary work, and imperialism. The organization (PLO)
adopted the idea of a secular state, and as such we considered it.

Secularist ideology is in total contradiction to religious ideologies, and it is
upon ideology that positions, actions, and decisions are made. From here, with
our respect for the Palestine Liberation Organization and what it might become,
and not underestimating its role in the Arab-Israeli struggle, we cannot exchange
the current and future of Islam in Palestine to adopt the secular ideology be-

cause the Islamic nature of the Palestinian issue is part and parcel of our *din* [religion] and whosoever neglects part of his *din* is surely lost.

When the Palestine Liberation Organization adopts Islam as its system of life, we will be its soldiers and the firewood of its fire which will burn the enemies. . . .

Jihad *Against the Zionist Enemy*

The Zionist invasion is a vicious attack that does not have piety . . . [and uses] all methods low and despicable to fulfill its obligations. . . . Zionists are behind the drug and alcohol trade because of their ability to facilitate the ease of control and expansion. The Arab countries surrounding Israel are requested to open their borders for the *Mujahidin* [Islamic fighters] of the Arab and Islamic countries so they can take their role and join their efforts with their Muslim brothers of Palestine. As for the other Arabic and Islamic countries, they are asked to ease the movement of *Mujahidin* from it and to it—that is the least they could do.

World Zionism and Imperialist powers try with audacious maneuvers and well-formulated plans to extract the Arab nations one by one from the struggle with Zionism, so in the end it can deal singularly with the Palestinian people. It already has removed Egypt far away from the circle of struggle with the treason of "Camp David," and it is trying to extract other countries by using similar treaties in order to remove them from the circle of struggle. The Islamic Resistance Movement calls upon the Arab and Islamic people to work seriously and constructively in order to not allow that horrible plan to be carried out . . . and to educate the masses of the dangers of withdrawal from the struggle with Zionism.

25. The Peace Process

One of the intractable problems in the Middle East has centered on who would control the territory of old mandate Palestine. Various attempts to resolve this conflict have met with only partial success during the post-1991 peace process, and a final resolution still remains elusive. As the Cold War came to an end, and following the Gulf War in 1991, the protagonists, with prodding from the United States and at first the Soviet Union, then the Russian Federation, began the negotiating process that led to the signing of the Oslo Accords presented in part a of this reading. Soon thereafter Yitzhak Rabin delivered the speech in part b to the Israeli *Knesset*, which spelled out why he sought peace with the Palestinians. After Rabin's assassination in 1995 and an interlude of a *Likud* government, Labor Prime Minister Ehud Barak and Chairman Arafat accepted a call to meet to iron out differences from lame-duck President Bill Clinton at Camp David. When those negotiations failed, they followed them with a Palestinian/Israeli meeting in 2001 at Taba on the Egyptian border, a partial summary of which appears in part c.

A. Principles of a Peace Agreement—Oslo, Norway (1993)*

Calling for negotiations on the basis of earlier UN Resolutions #242 and #338 (see Reading 23), the United States and the U.S.S.R. issued an invitation in 1991 to the parties in the Arab-Israeli conflict to attend a peace conference in Madrid, which produced few tangible results. But the conference did pave the way for a series of secret meetings in Norway held between high-level representatives from the PLO and Israel, which resulted in this agreement, signed at the White House.

The Oslo Accords, while welcomed by many Israelis and Palestinians, have produced vociferous criticism. Prominent critics include Palestinian professor Edward W. Said, University Professor at Columbia University in New York City, who has rejected the accords because, he argues, they have produced nothing more than "Bantustans," apartheid-type communities similar to those once existing in South Africa (see his contribution to this book, Reading 36b). The Palestinian group *Hamas* (see Reading 24c) rejects any negotiated settlement with Israel, and Jewish settlers living on the West Bank and some members of the ruling *Likud* bloc have voiced unwillingness to give back any territories that once belonged to the biblical Kingdom of Israel. Procrastination in implementing these accords contributed to the second Palestinian *intifada,* and the increased violence between Palestinians and Israelis since September 2000 has called into question the entire Oslo peace process.

The aim of the Israeli-Palestinian negotiations within the current Middle East peace process is, among other things, to establish a Palestinian Interim Self-Government Authority, the elected [Legislative] Council (the "Council"), for the Palestinian people in the West Bank and the Gaza Strip, for a transitional period not exceeding five years, leading to a permanent settlement based on Security Council Resolutions 242 and 338 [see Reading 23]. It is understood that the interim arrangements are an integral part of the whole peace process and that the negotiations on the permanent status will lead to the implementation of Security Council Resolutions 242 and 338.

Elections

1. In order that the Palestinian people in the West Bank and Gaza Strip may govern themselves according to democratic principles, direct, free and general political elections will be held for the Council under agreed supervision and

---

*From the Oslo Accords, September 13, 1993, at www.mideast.org.

international observation, while the Palestinian police will ensure public order. . . . These elections will constitute a significant interim preparatory step toward the realization of the legitimate rights of the Palestinian people. . . .

Jurisdiction of the Council will cover West Bank and Gaza Strip territory, except for issues that will be negotiated in the permanent status negotiations. The two sides view the West Bank and the Gaza Strip as a single territorial unit, whose integrity will be preserved during the interim period.

Transitional Period and Permanent Status Negotiations

1. The five-year transitional period will begin upon the withdrawal from the Gaza Strip and Jericho area.
2. Permanent status negotiations will commence as soon as possible, but not later than the beginning of the third year of the interim period, between the Government of Israel and the Palestinian people representatives.
3. It is understood that these negotiations shall cover remaining issues, including: Jerusalem, refugees, settlements, security arrangements, borders, relations and cooperation with other neighbors, and other issues of common interest. . . .

Preparatory Transfer of Powers and Responsibilities

1. Upon the entry into force of this Declaration of Principles and the withdrawal from the Gaza Strip and the Jericho area, a transfer of authority from the Israeli military government and its Civil Administration to the authorized Palestinians . . . will commence. This transfer of authority will be of a preparatory nature until the inauguration of the Council.
2. Immediately after the entry into force of this Declaration of Principles and the withdrawal from the Gaza Strip and Jericho area, with the view to promoting economic development in the West Bank and Gaza Strip, authority will be transferred to the Palestinians on the following spheres: education and culture, health, social welfare, direct taxation, and tourism. The Palestinian side will commence in building the Palestinian police force, as agreed upon. . . .

Public Order and Security

In order to guarantee public order and internal security . . . the Council will establish a strong police force, while Israel will continue to carry the responsibility for defending against external threats, as well as the responsibility for overall security of Israelis for the purpose of safeguarding their internal security and public order. . . .

Redeployment of Israeli Forces

1. After the entry into force of this Declaration of Principles, and not later than the eve of elections for the Council, a redeployment of Israeli military forces in the West Bank and the Gaza Strip will take place, in addition to withdrawal of Israeli forces. . . .

3. Further redeployments to specified locations will be gradually implemented commensurate with the assumption of responsibility for public order and internal security by the Palestinian police force. . . .

Annex

It is understood that, subsequent to the Israeli withdrawal, Israel will continue to be responsible for external security, and for internal security and public order of settlements and Israelis. Israeli military forces and civilians may continue to use roads freely within the Gaza Strip and the Jericho area.

B. Yitzhak Rabin, The Price of Occupation (1994)*

A soldier all of his adult life, and a war hero as well, Yitzhak Rabin reveals in this reading the complexities of Israeli politics and the contradictions within a military man who sought peace. In this blunt speech to the Israeli *Knesset* he laid out reasons why he thought the time had come to end the conflict between Jews and Palestinians.

Rabin joined the elite *Palmach* brigade of the *Haganah* Jewish military during World War II and participated in the British invasion of Syria and Lebanon. Fifteen years after commanding one of the important brigades of the Israeli Army in 1948, he became military chief of staff. In that role he commanded the IDF (Israel Defense Forces) victory over Arab states in 1967, after which he became Israeli ambassador to Washington. From 1974 through 1977 he served as prime minister, gaining a reputation as a hard-liner. Later he again served as prime minister, bringing his government into the Oslo peace process.

For achieving this agreement (this Reading, part a), Rabin, along with Yasir Arafat and Israel's foreign minister Shimon Peres, received the Nobel Peace Prize. After making peace with Jordan, he reached a further agreement with the Palestinians in October 1995, which projected Israeli withdrawal from seven additional Palestinian towns on the West Bank. He also called for holding elections for a Palestinian Legislative Council, which took place on January 20, 1996, when Arafat was elected president of the Palestinian Authority. Rabin's assassination by an Israeli fanatic occurred just after a November 1995 peace rally in Tel Aviv.

---

*From Prime Minister Yitzhak Rabin's speech to Israel's *Knesset*, April 18, 1994. On Israeli Minister of Foreign Affairs website: www.mfa.il/mfa/home.asp. Hebrew and Arabic words italicized.

* * *

I want to tell the truth. For 27 years, we have controlled another people that does not want our rule. . . . [T]he Palestinians who now number 1,800,000 have risen every morning with a burning hatred for us as Israelis and as Jews. Every morning, they awaken to a hard life and it is partly our fault but not completely. It cannot be denied: the continued rule over a foreign people who does not want us has a price. There is first of all a painful price, the price of constant confrontation between us and them.

For six and a half years, we have witnessed a popular Palestinian uprising against our rule the *intifada.* They are trying, through violence and terrorism, to harm us, to cause us casualties and to break our spirit. . . . Since the beginning of the uprising, 219 Israelis have been killed. . . . A heavy price. . . . [T]he Israelis wounded amounted to 7,872.

1,045 Palestinians have been killed by IDF and security forces. 69 have been killed by Israeli civilians. 922 Palestinians have been killed by their own people. 99 have been killed in unknown circumstances. 21 have blown themselves up . . . handling explosives. A total of 2,156. . . . [The IDF estimate] that at least 25,000 [Palestinians] have been wounded. Between 120,000 and 140,000 have been detained and imprisoned. These are the figures of the confrontation of the past six and a half years.

What are the options which face us after 27 years of ruling . . . an entity which is different from ourselves religiously, politically, nationally; another people? The first is to leave the situation as it is, to make proposals that do not have and never had a partner and there can be no agreement without a partner. To try and perpetuate the rule over another people, to continue on a course of never-ending violence and terrorism, which will bring about a political impasse. All the Governments of Israel certainly since the [October 1973] Yom Kippur War have understood the danger inherent in such an impasse. Accordingly, all the governments have sought the second option. The second option is to try and find a political solution initially through agreements on the separation of forces.

C. The Taba Negotiations (2001)*

Six years after Yitzhak Rabin called for "a political solution" of the Palestinian/Israeli conflict, hasty discussions took place in the context of escalating violence. These negotiations, held at a town on the Israeli-Egyptian border, never resulted in an agreement, much less a revival of the peace process. Nor does a complete, authoritative text of the negotiations exist. Since Israeli and Palestinian negotiators came close to an agreement at Taba, we have tried to assemble

---

*From www.mideast.org website of the Middle East Web. Bracketed material added by the editors. By permission.

as accurate an account as we could of the Taba negotiations. We present first the official joint statement from the Israeli and Palestinian delegations, which lays out the agenda and indicates the mood of the negotiators. Second, we offer the maximalist Palestinian position on the refugee question; thirdly, we present the Israeli responses.

The positions at Taba were probably closer than the unofficial texts suggest. The Israeli side seemed willing to acknowledge some responsibility for the refugee problem, and reportedly agreed to allow some 100,000 refugees into Israel to reunite divided families. The rest would receive compensation from a fund to be established with the help of the international community. Arafat appeared willing to go along with this compromise. Discussions also proceeded on the status of East Jerusalem. These texts come from the Middle East Web website, established in Israel by Jewish and Palestinian peace advocates, who have reproduced the extracts from articles that appeared in the *Jerusalem Post* on January 28, 2001, and from the Paris daily newspaper *Le Monde* at the end of the summer of the same year.

I. Israeli-Palestinian Joint Statement (January 27, 2001)

The Israeli and Palestinian delegations [could not] . . . reach understandings on all issues, despite the substantial progress that was achieved in each of the issues discussed. The sides declare that they have never been closer to reaching an agreement and it is thus our shared belief that the remaining gaps could be bridged with the resumption of negotiations following the Israeli elections.

The two sides take upon themselves to return to normalcy and to establish [a] security situation on the ground. . . .

The negotiation teams discussed four main themes: refugees, security, borders and Jerusalem, with a goal to reach a permanent agreement that will bring an end to the conflict between them and provide peace to both people. [In] light of the significant progress in narrowing differences the two sides are convinced that in a short period of time and given an intensive effort and the acknowledgment of the essential and urgent nature of reaching an agreement, it will be possible to bridge the differences remaining and attain a permanent settlement of peace between them. . . .

II. The Palestinian Proposals on Refugees Presented at Taba . . . (January 22, 2001)

1. The Parties recognize that a just resolution of the refugee problem is necessary for achieving a just, comprehensive and lasting peace. . . .

2. Israel recognizes its moral and legal responsibility for the forced displacement and dispossession of the Palestinian civilian population during the 1948 war and for preventing the refugees from returning to their homes in accordance with United Nations General Assembly Resolution 194 [see Reading 21b].

3. Israel shall bear responsibility for the resolution of the refugee problem. . . .

4. A just settlement of the refugee problem, in accordance with United Nations Security Council Resolution 242 [see Reading 23a], must lead to the implementation of United Nations General Assembly Resolution 194. . . .

5. a. In accordance with United Nations General Assembly Resolution 194, all refugees who wish to return to their homes in Israel and live at peace with their neighbors have the right to do so. . . .

6. a. A Palestinian refugee is any Palestinian who was prevented from returning to his or her home after November 29, 1947.

b. Without limiting the generality of the term "refugee," a "refugee" in this Agreement shall include a refugee's descendants and spouse.

c. [A]ll registered persons with UNRWA [United Nations Relief and Works Agency for Palestine Refugees] shall be considered refugees in accordance with this Article. . . .

[We omit procedural details of the operation of the projected Repatriation Commission—eds.]

9. The Commission shall be composed of representatives from the United Nations, the United States, the Parties, UNRWA, the Arab host countries, the EU, and Canada. The Commission shall consult the governments of the Arab host countries as it may deem it necessary. . . .

14. Refugees shall have the right to appeal decisions rendered by the Commission. . . .

[We omit the projected appeals procedure—eds.]

15. All refugees who currently reside in Lebanon and choose to exercise the right of return in accordance with this Article shall be enabled to return to Israel within two years of the signing of this Agreement.

16. Without prejudice to the right of every refugee to return to Israel, and in addition to refugees returning pursuant to Paragraph 15 above, a minimum of [number left blank] refugees will be allowed to return to Israel annually. . . .

19. Repatriation should be based on an individual voluntary decision, and should be carried out in a way that maintains the family unit.

20. The refugees should be provided with information necessary for them to make an informed decision with regard to all aspects of repatriation.

21. The refugees should not be compelled to remain in or move to situations of danger or insecurity, or to areas lacking in the basic infrastructure necessary to resume a normal life.

22. The refugees shall be permitted to return in safety, without risk of harassment, intimidation, persecution, or discrimination, particularly on account of their national origin, religious belief, or political opinion. . . .

Legal Status of Returning Refugees

25. Returning refugees should enjoy full civil and social rights and should be protected against discrimination, particularly in employment, education and the right to own property.

26. The returning refugees shall assume Israeli citizenship. This shall end his or her status as a refugee.

27. Real property [land and homes] owned by a returning refugee at the time of his or her displacement shall be restored to the refugee or his or her lawful successors.

28. In case where, according to criteria determined by the Repatriation Commission, it is impossible, impracticable or inequitable to restore the property to its refugee owner, the refugee shall be restituted in-kind with property within Israel, equal in size and/or value to the land and other property that they lost. . . .

30. The State of Israel shall compensate refugees for the property from which they were deprived as a result of their displacement, including, but not limited to, destroyed property and property placed under the custodianship of the Custodian for Absentees' Property. Compensation should cover loss of property and loss of use and profit from the date of dispossession to the current day expressed in today's value.

31. The State of Israel shall also compensate refugees for suffering and losses incurred as a result of the refugee's physical displacement.

32. Refugees shall, as the case may be, receive repatriation assistance, in order to help them resettle in their places of origin, or rehabilitation assistance, in order to be rehabilitated in the place of their future residence.

Funds for Repatriation Assistance and Rehabilitation Assistance should come from the International Fund described below.

33. The rights of return and compensation are independent and cumulative. A refugee's exercise of his or her right of return to Israel shall not prejudice his or her right to receive compensation pursuant to Paragraph 30, nor shall a refugee's receipt of compensation prejudice his or her right of return in accordance with this Article.

34. Unless property is collectively owned, material (and non-material) compensation should be awarded on an individual basis. . . .

37. Additional funds from the International Fund referenced below may be used to supplement Israeli funds for compensation purposes.

38. The State of Israel shall pay compensation to the state of Palestine for the Palestinian communal property existing within the internationally recognized borders of the State of Israel.

39. The communal property referenced in Paragraph 36 of this Article shall include real property as well as financial and other movable property. . . .

[We omit clauses dealing with compensation to countries who hosted the refugees—eds.]

54. The World Bank and the United Nations shall be Joint-Secretariat for the [compensation] Fund. The Secretariat shall be based at the World Bank.

55. The Steering Committee shall ask the World Bank to establish multilateral funding instruments to ensure that each aspect of this Agreement on refugees requiring financial assistance has corresponding instruments available to donors wishing to make use of multilateral mechanisms.

56. The World Bank shall have overall responsibility for ensuring that these funds are managed according to international standards of accounting and transparency. . . .

60. The full implementation of this Article shall constitute a complete resolution of the refugee problem and shall end all claims emanating from that problem.

61. The right of each refugee in accordance with United Nations General Assembly Resolution 194 shall not be prejudiced until the refugee has exercised his right of return and received compensation under this Article or until the refugee has, based on his voluntary choice, received compensation and settled somewhere else.

III. The Israeli Response on Palestinian Refugees (January 23, 2001) . . .

1. The issue of the Palestinian refugees is central to Israeli-Palestinian relations. Its comprehensive and just resolution is essential to creating a lasting and morally scrupulous peace. . . .

2. The State of Israel solemnly expresses its sorrow for the tragedy of the Palestinian refugees, their suffering and losses, and will be an active partner in ending this terrible chapter that was opened 53 years ago, contributing its part to the attainment of a comprehensive and fair solution to the Palestinian refugee problem.

3. For all those parties directly or indirectly responsible for the creation of the status of Palestinian refugeeism, as well as those for whom a just and stable peace in the region is an imperative, it is incumbent to take upon themselves responsibility to assist in resolving the Palestinian refugee problem of 1948.

4. Despite accepting the UNGAR [United Nations General Assembly Resolution] 181 of November 1947 [see Reading 21a], the emergent State of Israel became embroiled in the war and bloodshed of 1948–49, that led to victims and suffering on both sides, including the displacement and dispossession of the Palestinian civilian population who became refugees. These refugees spent decades without dignity, citizenship and property ever since.

5. Consequently, the solution to the refugee issue must address the needs and aspirations of the refugees, while accounting for the realities since the 1948–49 war. Thus, the wish to return shall be implemented in a manner consistent with the existence of the State of Israel as the homeland for Jewish people, and the establishment of the State of Palestine as the homeland of the Palestinian people. . . .

7. Since 1948, the Palestinian yearning has been enshrined in the twin principles of the "Right of Return" and the establishment of an independent Palestinian State. . . . The realization of the aspirations of the Palestinian people, as recognized in this agreement, includes the exercise of their right to self-determination and a comprehensive and just solution for the Palestinian refugees, based on UNGAR 194 [see Reading 21b], providing for their return and guaranteeing the future welfare and well-being of the refugees. . . .

8. Regarding return, repatriation and relocation, each refugee may apply to one of the following programs, thus fulfilling the relevant clause of UNGAR 194:

a. To Israel—capped to an agreed limit of [number left blank] refugees, and with priority being accorded to those Palestinian refugees currently resident in Lebanon. The State of Israel notes its moral commitment to the swift resolution of the plight of the refugee population of the Sabra and Shatila camps.

b. To Israeli swapped territory. For this purpose, the infrastructure shall be prepared for the absorption of refugees in the sovereign areas of the State of Israel that shall be turned over to Palestinian sovereignty in the context of an overall development program.

c. To the State of Palestine: the Palestinian refugees may exercise their return in an unrestricted manner to the State of Palestine, as the homeland of the Palestinian people, in accordance with its sovereign laws and legislation. . . .

d. Rehabilitation within existing Host Countries. Where this option is exercised the rehabilitation shall be immediate and extensive.

e. Relocation to third countries: voluntary relocation to third countries expressing the willingness and capacity to absorb Palestinian refugees.

Definition of a Refugee . . .

[We again omit details on compensation of refugees and host countries—eds.]
Former Jewish refugees

15. Although the issue of compensation to former Jewish refugees from Arab countries is not part of the bilateral Israeli-Palestinian agreement, in recognition of their suffering and losses, the Parties pledge to cooperate in pursuing an equitable and just resolution to the issue.

End of claims

16. The Parties agree that the above constitutes a complete and final implementation of Article 11 of UNGAR 194 of 11th December 1948, and consider the implementation of the agreed programs and measures as detailed above constitute a full, final and irrevocable settlement of the Palestinian refugee issue in all its dimensions. No additional claims or demands arising from this issue shall be made by either Party. With the implementation of these articles there shall be no [additional] individuals qualified for the status of a Palestinian Refugee.

26. Impasse and New *Intifada*

From the momentum of the peace process (see Reading 25) we pass to the grim mood of impasse, expressed here in two texts we have chosen from a vast literature on the many impediments to peace. Elsewhere in this part of the book (Reading 24c) we presented the position of the Islamic radical movement *Hamas*, which not only called for all-out war against the Zionists and their supporters but began suicide bombings in Israel, something other Palestinian groups have apparently imitated. On the Israeli side, right-wing settlers have carried out deadly attacks on Palestnians, and even on a peace-seeking Jewish prime minister (see this reading, part a). Part b consists of an article by Israeli hard-liner Ariel Sharon written just before his election as prime minister. In it Sharon bluntly restates his, and the *Likud* Party's, determination to retain effective Israeli sovereignty over the occupied territories, probably a formula for perpetual war.

Other sections of this reading give a range of Palestinian and Arab conviction: a PLO leader explains why violent struggle is necessary (part c); a group of Palestinian intellectuals publicly oppose suicide bombings of Israeli civilians (part e), and in part d the Arab League backs a new Saudi peace initiative. This reading ends with President Bush's call for the ouster of Yasir Arafat as PLO leader (part f).

A. King Husayn I of Jordan, Eulogy of Yitzhak Rabin: (1995)*

In this eulogy, King Husayn (1935–1999), speaking before his slain friend's widow, refers to the blow against peace struck by Yitzhak Rabin's assassin. Husayn and Rabin had collaborated in the last years of their lives in efforts to end the stalemate that blocked a peace settlement of the Arab-Israeli conflict. In that process the two leaders became friends, as this eulogy reveals.

My sister, Mrs. Leah Rabin, my friends, I had never thought that the moment would come like this when I would grieve the loss of a brother, a colleague and a friend—a man, a soldier who met us on the opposite side of a divide whom we respected as he respected us. A man I came to know because I realized, as he did, that we have to cross over the divide, establish a dialogue, get to know each other and strive to leave for those who follow us a legacy that is worthy of them. And so we did. And so we became brethren and friends.

---

*From Jordan's King Husayn I November 6, 1995, Eulogy of Yitzhak Rabin, "A Soldier for Peace Falls," Mount Herzl, Jerusalem. Text from the Israel Ministry of Foreign Affairs.

I've never been used to standing, except with you next to me, speaking of peace, speaking about dreams and hopes for generations to come that must live in peace, enjoy human dignity, come together, work together, to build a better future which is their right. Never in all my thoughts would it have occurred to me that my first visit to Jerusalem and response to your invitation, the invitation of the Speaker of the *Knesset,* the invitation of the president of Israel, would be on such an occasion.

You lived as a soldier, you died as a soldier for peace and I believe it is time for all of us to come out, openly, and to speak our piece, but here today, but for all the times to come. We belong to the camp of peace. We believe in peace. We believe that our one God wishes us to live in peace and wishes peace upon us, for these are His teachings to all the followers of the three great monotheistic religions, the children of Abraham.

Let's not keep silent. Let our voices rise high to speak of our commitment to peace for all times to come, and let us tell those who live in darkness who are the enemies of life, and through faith and religion and the teachings of our one God, this is where we stand. This is our camp. . . . He was a man of courage, a man of vision and he was endowed with one of the greatest virtues that any man can have. He was endowed with humility. He felt with those around him and in a position of responsibility, he placed himself, as I do and have done, often, in the place of the other partner to achieve a worthy goal. And we achieved peace, an honorable peace and a lasting peace. He had courage, he had vision, and he had a commitment to peace, and standing here, I commit before you, before my people in Jordan, before the world, myself to continue with our utmost, to ensure that we leave a similar legacy.

B. Ariel Sharon, Program for Dealing with the Palestinians (2000)*

Running as *Likud* candidate for prime minister Sharon issued this statement following his famous visit to the Muslim shrine in Jerusalem, the Dome of the Rock. Accompanied by hundreds of armed Israeli soldiers, the visit sparked a Palestinian protest movement that, in conjunction with long-standing Palestinian grievances, lead to the second *intifada* (see Reading 26c). The Israeli electorate favored Sharon over the incumbent Ehud Barak. Apparently a majority of Israelis hoped that Sharon would stop the uprising that he had played an important role in starting. Instead, on taking office, he turned his back on the Oslo accords and the Taba negotiations (see Readings 25a and c), and insisted on following a program he outlined that downplayed concessions, insisted on

---

*From Ariel Sharon, "Six Red Lines for Peace," *Jerusalem Post* (July 21, 2000). Bracketed material added by the editors. By permission.

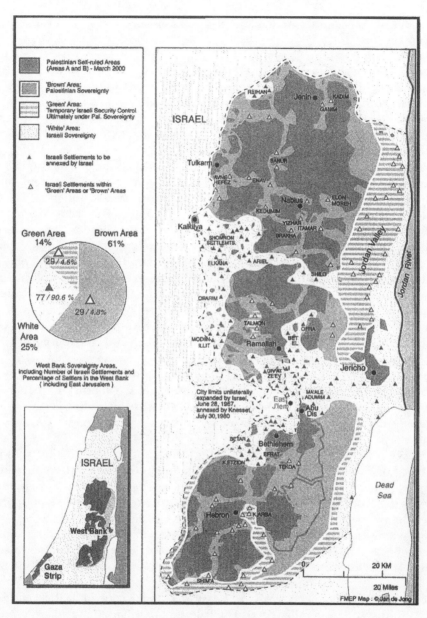

Palestinian Self-ruled Areas
(Areas A and B) - March 2000

'Brown' Area:
Palestinian Sovereignty

'Green' Area:
Temporary Israeli Security Control
Ultimately under Pal. Sovereignty

'White' Area:
Israeli Sovereignty

▲ Israeli Settlements to be
annexed by Israel

△ Israeli Settlements within
'Green' Areas or 'Brown' Areas

Green Area
14%

Brown Area
61%

29 / 4.6%

77 / 90.6 %

29 / 4.8%

White
Area
25%

West Bank Sovereignty Areas,
including Number of Israeli Settlements and
Percentage of Settlers in the West Bank
(including East Jerusalem)

City limits unilaterally
expanded by Israel,
June 28, 1967,
annexed by Knesset,
July 30, 1980

ISRAEL

West Bank

Gaza
Strip

ISRAEL

REIHAN

Jenin   KADIM

GANIM

Tulkarm   SANUR

AVNE
HEFEZ   ENAV

Nablus   ELON
MOREH

KEDUMIM

Kalkilya   YIZHAR   ITAMAR

SHOMRON   BRAKHA
SETTLEMTS.

ELKANA   ARIEL

SHILO

ORARIM

TALMON

MODI'IN   OFRA
ILLIT   BET
Ramallah   EL

GIV'AT   Jericho
ZE'EV

MA'ALE
East   ADUMIM
J'lem   Abu
Dis

BETAR
Bethlehem
EFRAT
K.ETZION   TEKOA

Hebron   KARSA

SHIMA

Jordan Valley

Jordan River

Dead
Sea

0   20 KM

20 Miles

FMEP Map : © Jan de Jong

West Bank Proposed Final Status Presented by Israel, 2000

holding occupied territory, and favored Israel's military responses to Palestinian militancy.

I believe it is possible to reach an agreement with a united and undivided Jerusalem, but in a different way. In my view, we must concentrate all our efforts to arrive at a broad national consensus based on clear unequivocal "red lines." I propose six red lines which can serve as a basis for broad national consensus, strengthen Israel's position, and enable us to reach a better and more secure agreement:

1. Greater Jerusalem, united and undivided, must be the eternal capital of Israel and under full Israeli sovereignty. The question of Jerusalem should not remain open, as it may become the time bomb for the next conflict.

2. Israel will retain under its full control sufficiently wide security zones—in both the East and the West. The Jordan Valley, in its broadest sense, as defined by the Allon Plan [Labor Minister Yigael Allon drafted a plan in July 1967 providing for an Israeli security belt along the Jordan River valley], will be the eastern security zone of Israel. This includes the steep eastern slopes of the hill ridge of Judea and Samaria (west of the Allon Road) overlooking the valley. Israel will maintain contiguous presence and control of the entire valley up to the Jordan River, including the border passes. The western security zone will include the line of hills commanding the coastal plain and controlling Israel's vital underground water sources.

Strategic routes will be retained under Israel's control.

3. Jewish towns, villages and communities in Judea, Samaria [both encompassing the West Bank] and Gaza, as well as access roads leading to them, including sufficient security margins along them, will remain under full Israeli control.

4. The solution to the problem of Palestinian refugees from 1948–1967 will be based on their resettlement and rehabilitation in the places where they live today (Jordan, Syria, Lebanon, etc.). Israel does not accept under any circumstances the Palestinian demand for the right of return. Israel bears no moral or economic responsibility for the refugees' predicament.

5. As a vital existential need, Israel must continue to control the underground fresh water aquifers in western Samaria, which provide a major portion of Israel's water. The Palestinians are obligated to prevent contamination of Israel's water resources.

6. Security arrangements: All the territories under control of the Palestinian Authority will be demilitarized. The Palestinians will not have an army; only a police force. Israel will maintain complete control of the whole air space over Judea, Samaria and Gaza.

I believe that any government in Israel that will adopt and implement these principles will strengthen Israel's deterrence and could reach a better, more secure peace, one that will ensure Israel's long-term national strategic interests.

C. Marwan Barghouti, Grassroots Leadership and the Second *Intifada**

In this interview with a reporter from the Israeli Hebrew-language newspaper *Ma©ariv*, Marwan Barghouti (1960–) gives the perspective of those younger PLO figures who, while critical of Yasir Arafat, are not prepared to repudiate their organization's long-term leader. Arrested six months after publication of this interview, Barghouti, a member of the PLO and the Palestinian Legislative Council in the West Bank, also heads the *Tanzim* militia, accused by the Israelis of carrying out suicide bombings and other terrorist acts. A former student at Bir Zeit University on the West Bank, he helped organize the first *intifada* of 1987–93 and also the second *intifada* in September 2000.

Barghouti gained popularity among Palestinians because he spoke out fearlessly about corruption in the ranks of the Palestinian Authority but also doubted that Israel ever intended voluntarily to withdraw from the occupied territories. In this interview he discusses the Palestinian Right of Return (see Readings 21b and 25c) and indicates how the parties to the conflict could resolve the issue, once the Israelis guarantee their withdrawal from occupied territories. Barghouti has sought to turn his trial before a civilian court into an indictment of Israel's occupation. In prosecuting Barghouti for murder, the Israeli government has taken on a popular grassroots leader whom the *New York Times* observes "might have become—and might yet become—a promising partner in peace negotiations," if they ever recommence.

Q: Do you take into account that you will be ultimately assassinated?

A: Yes. It disappoints me that no one on your side [in Israel] is coming out against this policy of assassinations [of Palestinian leaders by Israeli security forces]. I know that the struggle will continue. This coming year will be very difficult. You will increase the pressure on us. [Prime Minister Ariel] Sharon has no plan. He just pulled out his last card: he entered and recaptured the Palestinian cities. And what happened? Did the tanks in Bethlehem stop the attacks . . . [?] Did the tanks in Nablus stop the attackers . . . [?] Our challenge is to prove to you that there will be no security without peace. Only an agreement, and nothing else. You elected a prime minister who represents, more than anything else, killing, war, and murder, and he has no solution. So we will continue our struggle until you understand. We have much more willpower. Go ahead and keep assassinating. You've assassinated so many people already and you haven't prevented anything.

---

*From Ben Caspit, Interview with Marwan Barghouti, in *Ma'ariv* (Tel Aviv), November 9, 2001, p. B2. English translation from the Hebrew on the Fontenelles Palestine Archive website, http://home.mindspring.com/~fontenelles/barghouti.htm. Bracketed material added by the editors. By permission.

Q: And one of those assassinated could be you.

A: Maybe me as well. But I am committed to continuing . . . carrying out the will of the people. . . . I go to all of the funerals, to all of the demonstrations. I listen to people. My problem is that I'm not a politician. I speak to the point, I tell the truth to your face. On our side as well as on yours. In all those years you spoke with all kinds of Palestinian representatives who misled you, who let you believe that it was possible to reach a solution without ending the occupation.

Q: What is your solution for ending the current situation?

A: It's simple: You must understand, once and for all, that you must end the occupation. You must announce that the occupation is over and that Israel is leaving the territories. Present a timetable of a month, six months, a year. The important thing is that you present a timetable for withdrawal from all of the territories and the dismantling of the settlements, and announce that you recognize an independent Palestinian state with its capital in East Jerusalem. Believe me, such an announcement on the part of Israel will change the situation from top to bottom. Everything will work out. Everything. I have no doubt of that.

Q: And the refugees? What about the refugees? You lost the support of the peace camp when you went back to the right of return.

A: A solution must be found for the refugee problem. I believe that such a solution will be found. The moment you announce the end of the occupation and recognize a sovereign, genuine Palestinian state, not a vassal state, at that very moment everything will change. It will be possible to solve the refugee problem as well, believe me. I mean it. . . .

Q: . . . Your friends on the Israeli Left [who had supported negotiations on the basis of land for peace] are asking, "What happened to Marwan?" How do you answer them?

A: Nothing happened to me. . . . I was one of the bravest peace pioneers. I fought in the streets for Oslo [see Reading 25a for the Oslo Accords]. The problem is that since Rabin's assassination there hasn't been a peace process. I don't know what would have happened had [Prime Minister] Rabin not been murdered [in 1995, see Reading 26a] but I know what happened after the murder. The whole of Israel society changed direction. The process stopped. You didn't leave us any choice.

Q: If Rabin had known in 1993 that you would come in 1999 and demand the right of return, he would have thrown you down the stairs.

A: You're back to that again? Put an end to this mentality of occupation mixed with panic. What are you so afraid of? Between 1967 and 1993 you built 25,000 apartments in the [occupied] territories. Between 1993, after Oslo, and 2000, you built another 23,000 apartments in the territories. Had we known that this is what was going to happen, we also wouldn't have started this process.

Q: You have a degree in history. Did they teach you at Bir Zeit about the Holocaust, for example?

A: Of course. I know all of your history. But the Holocaust of the Jewish people does not justify our disaster. There is a refugee problem and it must be solved. Ways can be found. This is the most important point for Palestinians. The truth must be told. We reached a historic decision to recognize Israel, its security, its legitimacy. You still haven't reached your own decision to recognize us and our rights.

Q: You recognize Israel, but the right of return will destroy it, and it won't be a Jewish state.

A: We recognize Israel as a Jewish state. On the other hand, there is UN Resolution 194 [see Reading 21b] and on the basis of that resolution [which calls for the right of return of Palestinian refugees and compensation for those who choose not to return] it is possible to reach a solution that will satisfy everyone. I tell you again: if tomorrow a government arises in Israel and declares the end of the occupation, announces a timetable for withdrawal from the territories, and supports the establishment of a Palestinian state with its capital in East Jerusalem, everything will be solved. The situation on the ground will also change overnight.

Q: There was a government like that, not long ago. Barak agreed to give you the vast majority of the land and a large part of Jerusalem, and you responded with blood and fire.

A: Once again, you are both mistaken and misleading. We agreed to make do with 22 percent of historic Palestine. At Camp David [II] you tried to take from this small portion an enclave here, a bloc there, the Jordan Valley, border crossings, Jerusalem. This is a state? This is a solution? This is justice? I'm telling you the truth. You have to count on people like me, not on the hypocrites. I belong to the people, to the masses. We go around among the people, we are real, we are not corrupt.

Q: Still Barak's proposal could have been the basis for discussions, not for war. Oslo is based on the idea that your rifles are meant to keep order and fight terror, not shoot at us.

A: But Oslo died with Rabin. How would you feel if on every hill in territory that belongs to you a new settlement would spring up? If your best friends, with whom you fought shoulder to shoulder, continue to rot in jail? I reached a simple conclusion. You [Israel] don't want to end the occupation and you don't want to stop the settlements, so the only way to convince you is by force. This is the *Intifada* of peace. I'm serious. This *Intifada* will lead to peace in the end. We need to escalate the conflict. It will be hard. Many of us will be killed, but there is no choice. Every one of us is willing to sacrifice himself. We have decided that Sharon will not bring you security, and we have succeeded. It's been 274 days since he was elected, and what has happened? Is there security? No. Nothing will help. Only a just agreement, the 1967 borders, a sovereign state, Jerusalem and a solution to the refugee problem. This is the formula and there is no other, and no one has the right to give up on it. The Palestinian people have red lines, and only the people will decide. [The reference to "red lines" probably refers to the hard-line speech of Sharon in Reading 26b.]

Q: What do you think about Arafat's status?

A: Nothing. Arafat is the leader, the symbol, he decides everything. I was five years old when he began the struggle, and today I am fighting beside him and I am proud of that. Everyone supports him. . . .

Q: You speak a lot about corruption in the Palestinian Authority.

A: It's true, we do have corruption, but you do too. You, as usual, exaggerate in order to attack us. The only way for us to deal with the situation is to have elections for the Palestinian parliament and the presidency.

Q: Are you planning to run for the presidency against Arafat?

A: Me? Are you crazy? If Arafat runs, then no one from *Fatah* will run against him. And stop talking about getting rid of Arafat. He is our only leader. Only with him will you be able to make a deal. He is brave, he has already made a historic decision, he recognized Israel and its security. Now it's your turn.

D. The Arab League, Ratification of the Peace Plan Proposed by Crown Prince Abdullah ibn Abd al-Aziz of Saudi Arabia (2002)*

Since the bilateral peace made between the Egyptians and Israelis in 1978 and with Jordan in 1994, other Arab states have shown little inclination to normalize their relations with Israel. But the current impasse between Israel and the Palestinians—the dramatic terrorist acts by Islamic radicals and other Palestinian militants and suicide bombers, the destructive military attacks by the IDF against Palestinian towns and villages, and the inability or disinclination of the United States to effect a breakthrough—has created an opportunity for other initiatives. The most prominent of these came from Saudi Arabia. In early 2002 the de facto leader of the Saudi state, Crown Prince Abdullah, proposed that all Arab states diplomatically recognize and form normal relations with Israel in exchange for full Israeli withdrawal from the occupied territories. Since the UN Security Council passed Resolution #242 calling for the exchange of land for peace (see Reading 23a),

---

*From the Arab League statement of April 25, 2002, in the *New York Times* (April 26, 2002). By permission.

Israel and the Arab states have disagreed on the meaning of the resolution. The Arabs have interpreted #242 to mean Israeli withdrawal from *all* occupied territories, while Israel sees the resolution as meaning its withdrawal from *some* of the West Bank and Gaza. The crown prince merely repeated long-standing Arab policy, but did it in such a way that his remarks captured great media attention. Later, the Arab League meeting at Cairo ratified his proposal, and issued the document here presented.

The Council of the League of Arab States at the summit level, at its 14th ordinary session:

REAFFIRMING the resolution taken in June 1996 at the Cairo extraordinary Arab summit that a just and comprehensive peace in the Middle East is the strategic option of the Arab countries, to be achieved in accordance with international legality, and which would require a comparable commitment on the part of the Israeli government.

HAVING LISTENED to the statement made by His Royal Highness Prince Abdullah bin Abdul Aziz, the crown prince of the Kingdom of Saudi Arabia, in which his highness presented his initiative, calling for full Israeli withdrawal from all the Arab territories occupied since June 1967, in implementation of Security Council Resolutions 242 and 338, reaffirmed by the Madrid Conference of 1991 and the land-for-peace principle, and Israel's acceptance of an independent Palestinian state, with East Jerusalem as its capital, in return for the establishment of normal relations in the context of a comprehensive peace with Israel.

EMANATING FROM the conviction of the Arab countries that a military solution to the conflict will not achieve peace or provide security for the parties, the council:

1. Requests Israel to reconsider its policies and declare that a just peace is its strategic option as well.
2. Further calls upon Israel to affirm:
   a. Full Israeli withdrawal from all the territories occupied since 1967, including the Syrian Golan Heights to the lines of June 4, 1967, as well as the remaining occupied Lebanese territories in the south of Lebanon.
   b. Achievement of a just solution to the Palestinian refugee problem to be agreed upon in accordance with United Nations General Assembly Resolution 194.
   c. The acceptance of the establishment of a sovereign, independent Palestinian state on the Palestinian territories occupied since the 4th of June, 1967, in the West Bank and Gaza Strip, with East Jerusalem as its capital.
3. Consequently, the Arab countries affirm the following:
   a. Consider the Arab-Israeli conflict ended, and enter into a peace agreement with Israel, and provide security for all the states of the region.

  b. Establish normal relations with Israel in the context of this comprehensive peace.
4. Assures the rejection of all forms of Palestinian partition which conflict with the special circumstances of the Arab host countries.
5. Calls upon the government of Israel and all Israelis to accept this initiative in order to safeguard the prospects for peace and stop the further shedding of blood, enabling the Arab countries and Israel to live in peace and good neighborliness and provide future generations with security, stability and prosperity.
6. Invites the international community and all countries and organizations to support this initiative.
7. Requests the chairman of the summit to form a special committee composed of some of its concerned member states and the secretary general of the League of Arab States to pursue the necessary contacts to gain support for this initiative at all levels, particularly from the United Nations, the Security Council, the United States of America, the Russian Federation, the Muslim states and the European Union.

E. Palestinian Intellectuals' Urgent Appeal to Stop Suicide Bombings (June 19, 2002)*

This appeal, initiated by a few of its most prominent signatories, took shape when Palestinian suicide bombings of Israeli civilians had reached a crescendo. After the appeal's initial publication, hundreds more Palestinians signed. Many of these people had been working for years to build contacts with Israelis and create a variety of peace projects. The new upsurge of violence threatened the fragile structure of peace, especially since retaliation by the armed forces of the Ariel Sharon government served to deepen Palestinian determination to resist. Nuseiba, PLO delegate in Jerusalem and president of *Al-Quds* (Jerusalem) University, had long advocated a two-state solution to the Arab-Israeli conflict. While he was out of the country meeting with Israeli peace activists, the Sharon administration raided his university, carted off files, and locked him out. International protests over this action resulted in the government relenting and allowing the office to reopen. The Israelis again later raided his offices while he visited Jordan.

Ashrawi had served as Palestinian spokesperson during the first *intifada* (see Reading 24b). She then and later had set forth the cause of her people with clarity and determination to an international audience. A well-known Jerusalem journalist, Sineora, like the others, had also long practiced and advocated dialogue and negotiations with the Israelis. These are the people who, along with their Israeli counterparts, constitute a constituency for peace. The Israeli government would do well to recognize their contribution.

---

*From the letter of fifty-five Palestinians, in *Al-Quds* (London), June 19, 2002.

* * * * *

We the undersigned feel that it is our national responsibility to issue this appeal in light of the dangerous situation engulfing the Palestinian people. We call upon the parties behind military operations targeting civilians in Israel to reconsider their policies and stop driving our young men to carry out these operations. Suicide bombings deepen the hatred and widen the gap between the Palestinian and Israeli people. Also, they destroy the possibilities of peaceful co-existence between them in two neighboring states.

We see that these bombings do not contribute towards achieving our national project that calls for freedom and independence. On the contrary, they strengthen the enemies of peace on the Israeli side and give Israel's aggressive government under Sharon the excuse to continue its harsh war against our people. This war targets our children, elderly, villages, cities, and our national hopes and achievements.

Military actions are not assessed as positive or negative exclusively out of the general context and situation. They are assessed based on whether they fulfill political ends. Therefore, there is a need to re-evaluate these acts considering that pushing the area towards an existential war between the two people living on the holy land will lead to destruction for the whole region. We do not find any logical, humane, or political justification for this end result.

Dr. Sari Nuseiba
Saleh Ra'fat
Dr. Mohammad Ishtiya
Dr. Moussa El-Budeiri
Saman Khoury
Dr. Jad Is'haq
Shaher Sa'ad
Fadel Tahboub
Dr. Ahmad Majdalani
Zahi Khouri
Dr. Isam Nassar
Dr. Adam Abu Sh'rar
Dr. Munther El-Dajani
Jeana Abu El-Zuluf
Dr. Saleh Abdel Jawwad
Dr. Arafat El-Hadmi
Amna Badran
Dr. Raja'I El-Dajani
Dr. Jumana Odeh
Zahra El-Khaldi

Dr. Hanan Ashrawi
Salah Zuheika
Ibrahim Kandalaft
Huda El-Imam
Dr. Said Zidani
Dr. Manuel Hassasian
Dr. Mohammad Dajani
Majed Kaswani
Dr. Taleb Awad
Majed Abu Qubo'
Dr. Salim Tamari
Dr. Riema Hamami
Osama Daher
Yousef Daher
Dr. Nathmi El-Ju'ba
Dr. Leila Faydi
Dr. Ali Q'leibo
Issa Q'seisiya
Lucy Nuseiba

Hanna Sineora
Mamdouh Nofal
Dr. Eyad El-Sarraj
Dr. Marwan Abu El Zuluf
Dr. Omayya Khammash
Salah Abdel Shafi
Imad Awad
Taysir El-Zibri
Khader Sh'kirat
Ehab Boulous
Dr. Suad El-Ameri
Subhi El-Z'beidi
Simone Cupa
Jamal Zaqout
Dr. Jamil Hilal
Dr. Zakaria El-Qaq
Marwan Tarazi
Hani El-Masri
Abdel Qader El-Husseini

F. George W. Bush, A New and Different Palestinian Leadership (June 24, 2002)*

By summer 2002, the Israelis and Palestinians found themselves locked in unequal battle: one side commanded tanks, helicopters, U.S. F-16 attack aircraft, and armored personnel carriers; the other relied on small arms fire and suicide bombers, which many influential Palestinians questioned (see part e, this reading). Both sides awaited some indication of what the sole superpower intended to do about this bitter, century-long conflict. Would the Saudi proposal of trading general Arab diplomatic recognition for Israeli withdrawal from the West Bank and Gaza (part d, this reading) receive decisive support from Washington? Would the United States convoke an international conference to restart the faltering peace process? Would favorable American statements about a Palestinian state crystallize into actual proposals and a timetable?

The American president had until late June vacillated on key questions. Surrounded by advisers, Bush began to tire of the complexities of the issues, and longed for a simple solution, comparable to his post–September 11th policy: get Osama bin Laden. Finally he came up with an equally simple solution by June 24: get rid of Arafat. But such a formulation contained a major fault: it echoed Ariel Sharon's position exactly. So the president's speechwriters had to rhetorically refashion Bush's words so that Yasir Arafat's name did not appear, although many sympathetic references to Palestinian sufferings did. The speech also included the stark phrase that stunned the Palestinians by reversing Bush's earlier demands for an end to Israeli occupation: ". . . and so Israel will continue to defend herself." Thus, Bush's speech endorses many of Israel's policies.

Too Much Death and Fear

For too long, the citizens of the Middle East have lived in the midst of death and fear. The hatred of a few holds the hopes of many hostage. The forces of extremism and terror are attempting to kill progress and peace by killing the innocent. And this casts a dark shadow over an entire region. For the sake of all humanity, things must change in the Middle East.

It is untenable for Israeli citizens to live in terror. It is equally untenable for Palestinians to live in squalor and under occupation. And the current situation offers no prospect that life will improve. Israeli citizens will continue to be victimized by terrorists, and so Israel will continue to defend herself.

In the situation the Palestinian people will grow more and more miserable. My vision is two states, living side by side in peace and security. There is simply

---

*From George W. Bush's Rose Garden speech calling for "New Palestinian Leadership" (June 24, 2002) at the website www.whitehouse.gov/news/release/2002/06.

no way to achieve that peace until all parties fight terror. Yet, at this critical moment, if all parties will break with the past and set out on a new path, we can overcome the darkness with the light of hope. Peace requires a new and different Palestinian leadership, so that a Palestinian state can be born.

A Practicing Democracy

I call on the Palestinian people to elect new leaders, leaders not compromised by terror. I call upon them to build a practicing democracy, based on tolerance and liberty. If the Palestinian people actively pursue these goals, America and the world will actively support their efforts. If the Palestinian people meet these goals, they will be able to reach agreement with Israel and Egypt and Jordan on security and other arrangements for independence.

And when the Palestinian people have new leaders, new institutions and new security arrangements with their neighbors, the United States of America will support the creation of a Palestinian state whose borders and certain aspects of its sovereignty will be provisional until resolved as part of a final settlement in the Middle East. True reform will require entirely new political and economic institutions, based on democracy, market economics and action against terrorism.

The United States, along with the European Union and Arab states, will work with Palestinian leaders to create a new constitutional framework, and a working democracy for the Palestinian people. And the United States, along with others in the international community will help the Palestinians organize and monitor fair, multiparty local elections by the end of the year, with national elections to follow.

Today, the Palestinian people live in economic stagnation, made worse by official corruption. A Palestinian state will require a vibrant economy, where honest enterprise is encouraged by honest government. The United States, the international donor community and the World Bank stand ready to work with Palestinians on a major project of economic reform and development. The United States, the E[uropean] U[nion], the World Bank, the International Monetary Fund are willing to oversee reforms in Palestinian finances, encouraging transparency and independent auditing.

A Provisional State

And the United States, along with our partners in the developed world, will increase our humanitarian assistance to relieve Palestinian suffering. Today, the Palestinian people lack effective courts of law and have no means to defend and vindicate their rights. A Palestinian state will require a system of reliable justice to punish those who prey on the innocent. The United States and members of the international community stand ready to work with Palestinian leaders to establish finance and monitor a truly independent judiciary.

Today, Palestinian authorities are encouraging, not opposing, terrorism. This is unacceptable. And the United States will not support the establishment of a Palestinian state until its leaders engage in a sustained fight against the terrorists and dismantle their infrastructure. I've said in the past that nations are either with us or against us in the war on terror. To be counted on the side of peace, nations must act. Every leader actually committed to peace will end incitement to violence in official media, and publicly denounce homicide bombings. This will require an externally supervised effort to rebuild and reform the Palestinian security services. The security system must have clear lines of authority and accountability and a unified chain of command.

Israel's Stake

Israel also has a large stake in the success of a democratic Palestine. Permanent occupation threatens Israel's identity and democracy. A stable, peaceful Palestinian state is necessary to achieve the security that Israel longs for. So I challenge Israel to take concrete steps to support the emergence of a viable, credible Palestinian state.

As we make progress towards security, Israel forces need to withdraw fully to positions they held prior to September 28, 2000 [the date of Ariel Sharon's visit to the *Haram al-Sharif* shrine]. And Israeli settlement activity in the occupied territories must stop.

Ultimately, Israelis and Palestinians must address the core issues that divide them if there is to be a real peace, resolving all claims and ending the conflict between them. This means that the Israeli occupation that began in 1967 will be ended through a settlement negotiated between the parties, based on UN Resolutions 242 and 338 [see Reading 23] with Israeli withdrawal to secure and recognized borders. We must also resolve questions concerning Jerusalem, the plight and future of Palestinian refugees.

Three More Years

As new Palestinian institutions and new leaders emerge, demonstrating real performance on security and reform, I expect Israel to respond and work toward a final status agreement. With intensive effort by all, this agreement could be reached within three years from now. And I and my country will actively lead towards that goal.

Chapter VI

Geopolitics of Oil and the Cold War Conflict

Introduction

A n enormous chain of historical interconnections shaped the twentieth-century Middle East, especially its Persan/Arabian Gulf region. The interaction of oil, industrialism, imperialism, and nationalism had immense consequences inside and outside of the oil-producing states. In the early part of the twentieth century, just as the industrial countries reaped the full benefits of their rapid transformations, they also extended their control to the one large remaining unconquered area of the globe—former Ottoman territories in the Middle East and neighboring Qajar Iran. Even those states in the region without oil deposits found themselves incorporated into global energy and economic networks. The opening of new investment opportunities brought major U.S. petroleum companies into the Middle East. For the industrial nations, consolidating Western domination over this region became a prime goal, while the oil-producing nations wanted an increased share of their own countries' wealth. This chapter explores the dynamics of these interconnections and how they affected—and still affect—diplomacy, war, and society.

At the beginning of the twentieth century governments and businesses switched from coal (which had sustained early British industrialization) to oil for their industry, transportation, and military operations. Britain, unaware as yet of North Sea deposits, had no local petroleum resources. The United States did, but its rapid industrial development made it imperative to follow the British model and search for supplementary oil supplies in the Middle East and elsewhere. Thus the United States and Great Britain became powerful allies and competitors in pursuing what Winston Churchill (1874–1965) called "the lure of oil."

The Red Line: Early Search for Middle Eastern Oil

Great Britain had a head start. Having taken control of territory along the sea-lanes to its main colonial possession, India, the British also inadvertently gained access to the world's richest oil deposits—in Iraq, Persia, Bahrain, and Kuwait. The rulers of these areas lacked capital and technology for energy exploration and therefore granted concessions to Western petroleum companies eager to develop oil fields there. Great wealth came to the ruling families of the Gulf states and sometimes even to their subjects, but most profits went to European entrepreneurs. Discontent over profit sharing of Middle Eastern oil merged with other grievances. Eventually, the oil-producing states took action to rectify the monetary imbalances (see Reading 29), but most of their other resentments went unaddressed.

Britain and other Western oil-consuming nations exhibited remarkable concern for their collective stake in Middle East petroleum. Rather than risk competition among themselves, the major energy companies, which had often sponsored joint geological explorations, formed an informal but effective cartel, the Seven Sisters, comprising Royal Dutch Shell, British Petroleum (BP), and five U.S. corporations—Esso (Exxon), Mobil, Standard Oil of California (Socal), Texaco, and Gulf Oil. In conjunction with the French Petroleum Company and independent Armenian businessman Calouste Gulbenkian (1869–1955), all signed the 1928 Red Line Agreement (see Map p. 239), promising to consult and cooperate in seeking concessions and agreeing to pay Gulbenkian (who had legal rights from Ottoman times) 5 percent of the profits. Governments backed these agreements, and since the cartel operated informally its American members avoided antitrust violations. The Seven Sisters came to control most of the world's markets in international oil.

Wealthy Archaic States

Few of the *shaikhs,* tribal princes, and kings who ruled Gulf states saw any need for modern institutions or democratic practices. Their resources and dynasties secured by Western backing, they clung to traditional social practices. Saudi Arabia is the prime example. As we have indicated, the Saudi family embraced Wahhabism, eventually defeated their rivals in Arabia, and in 1932 created the kingdom of Saudi Arabia. Soon afterward U.S. geologists discovered vast reserves of oil there, making the desert kingdom essential to Western economic well-being and national security. To manage their oil wealth the Saudis had to introduce elements of a formal government but one that depended on a strict patriarchal order. With oil flowing, and a friendly regime in Riyadh, there seemed no reason for the United States to prod the Saudis into embracing democratic practices or women's rights.

Despite their great wealth and vast quantity of imported American weapons, the Gulf states still could not defend themselves. Fearful of an organized opposition or of their own armed forces, who might revolt—as happened in Iraq, Egypt, and the Sudan—these states needed foreign troops nearby, at first on offshore aircraft carriers and later on local military bases to deter revolt or external invasion. Much of this mercenary service came from the United States and it had a serious downside: lessened urgency within such dependent societies to root out corruption and create viable, independent states.

Oil and Its Challenges

After 1945, the United States shouldered the responsibility for rebuilding western Europe and Japan. This demanded cheap and plentiful energy that far

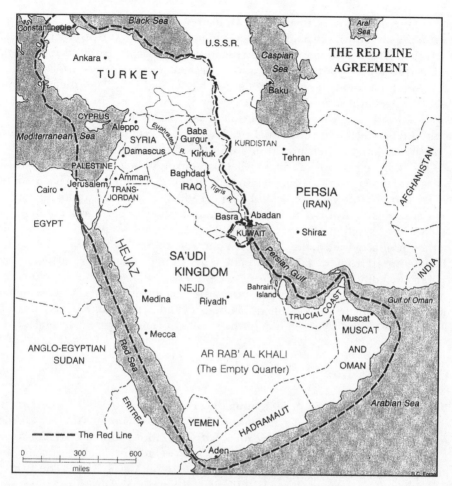

The Red Line Agreement

exceeded U.S. export capacities, so the continuing availability of Middle Eastern oil became a central concern, all the more so since European aid programs required that countries receiving U.S. assistance convert from coal to oil. Geopolitical considerations explain the West's intensified interest in Gulf oil during the Cold War. The Soviet Union too diverted some of its own oil supplies from domestic consumption to support Soviet-dominated states in eastern Europe, which received subsidized oil and gas for their industrialization.

The extremely low extraction costs of Gulf oil—initially less than twenty-five cents a barrel—reinforced American determination to control and protect Middle Eastern producers. Enormous investments by U.S. companies went hand in hand with Washington's military aid to the region. Esso, Mobil, Texaco, and Socal, four of the Seven Sisters, formed the Arabian American Oil Company (Aramco) to run the oil industry in Saudi Arabia. No matter how low the production costs in Arabia, Western petroleum brokers set international prices for oil at the level of U.S. production costs in Texas and Louisiana (just under two dollars a barrel). Adding a twenty-five-cent premium, they brought the sale price of a barrel of oil everywhere in the world to under $2.25 a barrel, no matter where it was produced or at what cost, well into the early 1970s. Run this way, the petroleum industry brought substantial profits to Aramco and other firms working with the backing of their governments in the Middle East.

Oil-producing countries sought what Daniel Yergin in *The Prize* (1991) calls a "New Deal in Oil"—more equitable sharing of energy wealth. Mexico had nationalized its oil industry in 1938, and half a decade later Venezuela gained 50 percent of profits. "Fifty-fifty" and nationalization became popular twin goals in the Middle East as well. Bending to the pressure, American companies granted half of their profits to Iraq, Saudi Arabia, Kuwait, and Bahrain, which the consortium then deducted from the taxes they paid in the United States. More stringent tax laws made it difficult for British firms to pay higher royalties, and they refused to make concessions to Iran, where a group of ardent nationalists went beyond haggling over royalties with the Anglo-Iranian Oil Company and instead wanted direct control. This disagreement triggered one of the twentieth century's great struggles.

Upheavals in Iran

When Iran's ruler, Shah Mohammad Reza Pahlavi (1919–80), shrank from confronting the British on nationalization, Iran's parliament (the *majlis*) did so. When the *majlis'* leading advocate of nationalization, Muhammad Mossadeq (1882–1967), became prime minister, the shah reluctantly had to sign the decree putting the oil industry under state control on May 1, 1951. The British then initiated a worldwide boycott of Iranian oil exports, and pressured the Seven Sisters to support them.

The U.S. government at first opposed the boycott, fearful of driving the Iranians into dependence on the U.S.S.R. But President Harry Truman (1884–1972) saw an opportunity to repay political debts to smaller American petroleum companies (not members of the Seven Sisters network), which had contributed money to his party, the Democrats. Truman agreed to send technical advisers from these corporations to help Iran run its petroleum industry. As soon as Republican Dwight D. Eisenhower (1890–1969) became president in 1953, he reversed Truman's policies and not only threw the weight of the United States behind the Seven Sisters (major contributors to Republican campaign coffers) and the British boycott, but also collaborated with the British in a covert subversion campaign to bring down Mossadeq's government.

The United States Central Intelligence Agency (CIA) and MI6 (British intelligence) engineered a coup d'état against Iran's government, ousted Mossadeq, restored the shah's political power, and placed the country's oil back in the hands of Anglo-Iranian. As payoff for aiding Great Britain, the four U.S. Aramco partners received access to Iranian oil. The 1953 coup stirred deep resentments in Iran and set the stage for a more violent upsurge of Iranian nationalism that ousted the shah, terminated the Pahlavi dynasty, and brought the Islamic Republic to power a quarter-century later (see Reading 28c).

Oil Shocks and New Adjustments

A few years after the U.S.–British coup in Iran, a new organization appeared in the roster of Middle Eastern oil protagonists—the Organization of Petroleum Exporting Countries (OPEC), a cartel formed in 1960 to stabilize the petroleum markets and get a better deal for the oil-producing countries (see Reading 29a). This happened after several cycles of falling oil prices, glut, and fresh waves of petroleum-fueled industralization that increased consumer use, which brought shortages. At first, OPEC found itself unable to effect significant change in global oil policy until the heating up of the Arab-Israeli conflict. Arab members of OPEC, incensed at the failure to reach a settlement of the Palestinian question, attempted to use oil as a weapon. The first campaign in 1967 aimed at cutting off oil to the United States, Britain, and Germany after the Six-Day War. It petered out quickly as Western redistribution of plentiful oil stocks undercut OPEC's action. A more effective attempt to strangle the West's oil supplies took place in 1973 when, in the midst of fighting between Israel and the Egyptian-led coalition, OPEC decided to reduce production progressively by 5 to 10 percent or more monthly and apply more severe cuts to such selected countries as the United States and the Netherlands. By late October the posted price for Arabian Light oil shot up to $5.12 a barrel and rose by December to $11.65. By withholding stocks at a moment of tight supplies, OPEC had for the first time determined oil prices. Low availability of oil in the United States and elsewhere led to major shortages worldwide, long lines at the gasoline pumps, and panic in western Europe, Japan, and North America.

This 1973 oil shock also resulted in major changes in relations between the West and oil providers. Aramco and Saudi Arabia negotiated a new agreement over ownership of the consortium's assets in the kingdom, and soon afterward Saudi Arabia nationalized the company, with the proviso that the international oil firms already in the country could stay there, run the fields, market the oil, and provide services in return for a fee of twenty-one cents per barrel.

The Iranian Revolution of 1979 and the Iran-Iraq war that broke out a year later (see Readings 28c and 30a) delivered another set of jolts to global oil supplies and prices. This eight-year-long war kept some four million barrels of oil off the market daily, raising prices considerably. The Gulf region in general experienced boom times in the 1970s and early 1980s, while the rest of the world got a foretaste of what might happen when fossil fuels run out.

Some of the new Middle East's fabulous oil wealth eventually returned to the Western economies as recycled surplus revenues, used to purchase U.S. Treasury bonds, manufactured goods, and especially expensive armaments. Money also inundated the sparsely populated traditional Middle Eastern oil-rich states, which now had financial resources to ensure material satisfaction for most of their population. They could also purchase political support from internal opposition forces and neighboring states, as well as establish security apparatuses to suppress dissent. In this way the oil-rich Gulf states increasingly developed into authoritarian and undemocratic *rentier* countries, which leased out their petroleum resources to foreigners in exchange for protection.

Policy Alternative: Whom to Support?

As these developments reshaped the Middle East, the United States constructed a system that allowed U.S. oil corporations freer access to Middle Eastern energy resources. This required loosening the hold of the former colonial powers on these territories and preventing the Soviet Union from gaining significant influence in the region. Washington encouraged movements of national independence from colonialism in such selected countries as Lebanon and Syria and in the old British empire. Yet the United States still counted on the British to help maintain the region's postwar security, since significant profits for BP and Shell (of which Britain owned 40 percent) derived from their shares in the Middle East oil industry, and from the marketing of their production worldwide. Britain still held a major stake in maintaining Western influence in the area.

Decolonization shifted the balance of power in former colonized regions: at first collaborationist elites gave way to secular nationalists, often army officers. Modern Islamic radicalism, which, as Chapter VII shows, had burst onto the scene spectacularly with the Iranian Revolution of 1979. Islamic movements among vocal social and political minorities spread. Caught between secular nationalists and Islamic radicals, small leftist political movements suffered severe repression, leaving secular and Islamic groups warily circling one another in complex political maneuvers.

The United States, whose power in the Middle East supplanted French and British colonialism, faced many alternatives. Should they back secular nationalists such as Egypt's Jamal Abd al-Nasser? That entailed risks since such allies might turn radical or (during Cold War years) lean toward the Soviet Union. Or should Washington support traditional regimes, despite their antidemocratic practices? Since many of these countries produced oil, the United States could not abandon them. Islamic radicals shared with Americans a common abhorrence of "Godless Communism," and they could and did serve as allies against the U.S.S.R. in places like Afghanistan. For domestic and global strategic reasons U.S. policy makers continued to lavish support on Israel, which risked alienating all other groups in the region. Washington's shifting policies reflected the many cross-pressures at work.

Afghanistan and Iraq: Centers of Conflict

Shifting U.S. policies toward Iraq and Afghanistan illustrate these cross-pressures. Iraq invaded Iran in 1980, the same year the Soviet Union entered Afghanistan to rescue a Soviet-backed regime unable to retain power on its own. Soviet armed forces fought there for a decade, and went down to defeat at the hands of religiously inspired tribal and ethnic-based *mujahidin* forces. Heavily supported by Pakistan, Saudi Arabia, and the United States, these Islamic militants attracted volunteers from many countries, among them Osama bin Laden (1957–?) from Saudi Arabia. But without the unifying force of a secular Communist enemy, the victorious *mujahidin* forces, after trouncing the Russians, soon lapsed back to their accustomed feuds, which prevented formation of a stable government. This gave the *Taliban,* Islamic student radicals who welcomed wide international support, their chance to seize Afghanistan and rule it on the basis of a narrow, extreme, and brutalizing version of Islamic doctrine (see Reading 33b). The former *mujahidin* made little headway in overturning *Taliban* rule until after September 11, 2001, when the Americans entered the struggle. Unable to stand up to massive U.S. bombing raids and battlefield ordnance, the *Taliban* lost power.

Iraq too experienced almost uninterrupted conflicts since 1980, when its leader, Saddam Husayn (1937–), initiated war against Iran. Iraqi claims of championing *Sunni* Islam against Iranian *Shiite* radicalism cloaked its intent of controlling Gulf oil and attaining regional hegemony after the collapse of the Western-backed Pahlavi dynasty. Postrevolutionary disarray in the Iranian armed forces raised expectations that Iraq could count on a quick victory. But Iran's larger population, the coherence of the purged, but intact, military, which remained in place after the revolution, and the regime's ability to mobilize irregular militias stalled Baghdad's invasion forces. As Joe Stork shows in Reading 30a, the eight-year war settled into an inconclusive stalemate, with the Soviet Union and wealthy Gulf states—especially Saudi Arabia and Kuwait—assisting Iraq, and the United States supplying both sides with armaments, assuring that neither won a decisive victory.

Two years after a cease-fire ended hostilities between Iraq and Iran, Saddam Husayn provoked a second Gulf war by invading Kuwait, which had refused to forgive Iraq's debts from the previous war and would not adjust its oil policies in Iraq's favor. As soon as Iraq invaded, most of Kuwait's ruling al-Sabah dynasty fled the country, along with top military officers. But Saddam Husayn failed to anticipate that the United States, now the world's sole superpower, would take retaliatory action. Winning UN backing and the support of both European and Middle Eastern states, the United States turned the full fury of its military against Iraq and in six weeks of high-tech assault drove Iraqi forces out of Kuwait.

The military strategy chosen resulted in combat deaths of seventy-nine U.S. soldiers, a tiny fraction of the more than a hundred thousand Iraqi soldiers who died in battle. In compensation for war-related expenses, the United States received millions of dollars from wealthy Arab states and Japan (which depends on Middle Eastern oil for a great deal of its energy imports). President George H. W. Bush (1924–   ) claimed a more subtle compensation: the dispelling of the "Vietnam syndrome"—the aura of defeat that had clung to the U.S. military following the United States' loss of the war in Vietnam (see Reading 30c).

The American victory, however, remained incomplete. Saddam Husayn remained in charge of his country at the war's end. The UN Security Council placed Iraq under sanctions and restrictions that severely limited its sovereignty—banning air flights over northern and southern zones of the country where the regime had brutally suppressed opposition movements, and requiring destruction of biological, chemical, and nuclear weapons. (The most important of these resolutions—#687—appears in Reading 30b.) Bush's son George W. Bush became president in 2001, before the September 11 disaster, and in agreement with former Cold Warriors among his advisers he has called for preemptive U.S. attacks against Iraq as part of the American-led "war on terrorism" and, without mentioning it, to retain Washington's control of Middle Eastern oil. This latter theme has dominated U.S. and Western policy toward the region for nearly a century.

27. U.S. Presidential Policies, 1947–2002

G oing back at least to the 1823 Monroe Doctrine (which warned European countries not to intervene in or recolonize the Americas), U.S. presidents have taken certain occasions to issue statements that define their administrations' foreign policies. This reading brings together selected presidential statements on U.S. Middle Eastern policy, from the presidency of Harry S. Truman to that of George W. Bush. Several themes emerge: the replacement of European (especially British) imperial power by American influence and control; the attempts to secure alliances with states in the region that share U.S. policy aims; anti-Communism; curtailment of local radical nationalism; and, above all, protection of American and Western access to Middle East oil and natural gas resources.

Although we have omitted several presidential texts from this reading, they deserve some attention. Richard Nixon's 1969 pronouncement of the need to reduce U.S. military commitments abroad by designating certain states (Iran under the Pahlavi dynasty and Israel) regional surrogates, thereby granting them massive U.S. military aid, came as a result of the U.S. overextending itself in Vietnam and had a great impact on the Middle East. President Jimmy Carter veered in a different direction when he set up in 1980 the U.S. Rapid Deployment Force, renamed the Central Command, to intervene should any "outside force" attempt to gain control of oil-producing countries in the Persian Gulf region.

More recent policy pronouncements by President Clinton and both Presidents Bush (see their texts in this reading, parts c, d, and e) project global policies to counter terrorist movements and restructure international relations after the end of the Cold War.

A. The Truman Doctrine (1947)*

Developments in the Middle East and the weakened condition of America's main ally, Great Britain, prompted this major Cold War statement. Although on the winning side in World War II, Britain soon afterward acknowledged that it could no longer maintain its worldwide empire. It gave up Palestine (see the introduction to Chaper V) and India (see Reading 16) and had to stop propping up Greece, which the British prized mainly because of the peninsula's strategic location in the eastern Mediterranean. During the war British troops in cooperation with leftist Greek anti-Fascists had defeated the Germans in Greece. But when this popular resistance movement positioned itself to take political power after the war, the British established a puppet government and opposed the left. By 1947, however, facing financial crisis, Britain informed the United States that it would soon have to withdraw from Greece.

The United States, deeply engaged in the Cold War, saw the Greek insurgency as Communist-run and backed by the Soviet Union. In actuality, Soviet leader Joseph Stalin (1879–1953) recognized that Greece belonged within a Western sphere of influence and refused to give the Greek revolutionaries any support. Yugoslavia, a Communist state bordering Greece, stepped in and supplied small arms to the Greek leftist opposition, despite Stalin's objections. In those days, the United States viewed Communism as a monolithic force and made no distinctions between Greek, Yugoslavian, and Soviet Communists. Wherever the red flag loomed, Stalin pulled the strings, according to this simplistic version of a complex reality.

Farther to the east, the Soviet Union attempted to secure passage of its shipping from the Black Sea through the Turkish-controlled Dardanelles Strait. Of-

---

*From President Harry S. Truman's message to a joint session of the U.S. Congress, March 12, 1947, in *Public Papers of the Presidents of the United States: Harry S. Truman, 1947* (Washington, DC: U.S. Government Printing Office, 1963), pp. 177–80.

ficial Washington, aiming to draw Turkey into the Western alliance, viewed this Soviet demand as an attack on Turkish sovereignty. President Harry S. Truman wove the very different Greek and Turkish situations into a dual threat to the Free World. Describing the situation in terms of a scenario of imminent totalitarian menace to these countries and to the rest of the world, Truman decided to "scare the hell out of the American people," and got a stingy Congress to fund the early years of Cold War expenditures. Scholars now generally agree that Truman and his advisers also wanted to signal that the United States had assumed the task that Britain could no longer perform: assuring that a cheap and abundant supply of petroleum flowed from the oil fields of the Middle East to the Western countries.

The foreign policy and the national security of this country are involved [in] . . . the present situation . . . [of] Greece and Turkey.

The United States has received from the Greek Government an urgent appeal for financial and economic assistance. . . . [R]eports from the American Economic Mission . . . [and] from the American Ambassador in Greece corroborate the statement of the Greek Government that assistance is imperative if Greece is to survive as a free nation.

The British Government has informed us that, owing to its own difficulties, it can no longer extend financial or economic aid to Turkey.

As in the case of Greece, if Turkey is to have the assistance it needs, the United States must supply it. We are the only country able to provide that help.

One of the primary objectives of the foreign policy of the United States is the creation of conditions in which we and other nations will be able to work out a way of life free from coercion. . . .

We shall not realize . . . [these] objectives . . . unless we are willing to help free peoples to maintain their free institutions and their national integrity against aggressive movements that seek to impose upon them totalitarian regimes. This is no more than a frank recognition that totalitarian regimes imposed upon free peoples, by direct or indirect aggression, undermine the foundations of international peace and hence the security of the United States.

At the present moment in world history nearly every nation must choose between alternative ways of life. The choice is too often not a free one.

One way of life is based upon the will of the majority, and is distinguished by free institutions, representative government, free elections, guarantees of individual liberty, freedom of speech and religion, and freedom from political oppression.

The second way of life is based upon the will of a minority forcibly imposed upon the majority. It relies upon terror and oppression, a controlled press and radio, fixed elections, and the suppression of personal freedoms.

I believe that it must be the policy of the United States to support free peoples who are resisting attempted subjugation by armed minorities or by outside pressures. . . .

It is necessary only to glance at a map to realize that the survival and integrity of the Greek nation are of grave importance in a much wider situation. If Greece should fall under the control of an armed minority, the effect upon its neighbor, Turkey, would be immediate and serious. Confusion and disorder might well spread throughout the entire Middle East.

It would be an unspeakable tragedy if these countries, which have struggled so long against overwhelming odds, should lose that victory for which they sacrificed so much. Collapse of free institutions and loss of independence would be disastrous not only for them but for the world. Discouragement and possible failure would quickly be the lot of neighboring peoples striving to maintain their freedom and independence.

Should we fail to aid Greece and Turkey in this fateful hour, the effect will be far reaching to the West as well as to the East.

We must take immediate and resolute action.

The seeds of totalitarian regimes are nurtured by misery and want. They spread and grow in the evil soil of poverty and strife. They reach their full growth when the hope of a people for a better life has died.

We must keep that hope alive.

If we falter in our leadership, we may endanger the peace of the world, and we shall surely endanger the welfare of this Nation.

Great responsibilities have been placed upon us by the swift movement of events.

I am confident that the Congress will face these responsibilities squarely.

B. The Eisenhower Doctrine (1957)*

This 1957 announcement by U.S. President Dwight D. Eisenhower (1890–1969) indicated his willingness to dispatch troops to the Middle East ostensibly because of Washington's fear of radical nationalism in the region, especially its potential for linking up with "International Communism."

Although Eisenhower did not specifically mention Lebanon in this message, that Middle Eastern country became the place where the Eisenhower Doctrine was first explicitly applied in the following year. (Earlier Eisenhower interventions in Iran and Guatemala operated covertly and received no doctrinal justification.) But the 1958 intervention originated with the appeal of a conservative Lebanese politician, Camille Chamoun (1900–87), threatened not by Communism but by his own political rivals. Somehow that intervention became linked with the near simultaneous overthrow by military officers of the Hashemite

---

*From President Dwight D. Eisenhower's message to a joint session of Congress, January 5, 1957, in *Public Papers of the Presidents of the United States: Dwight D. Eisenhower, 1957* (Washington, DC: U.S. Government Printing Office, 1958), pp. 12–13.

monarchy in Iraq, which also had no discernible relation to Communism. Irene L. Gendzier, in her *Notes from the Minefield: United States Intervention in Lebanon and the Middle East, 1945–1958* (1997), explains the outcome by pointing out that with the Eisenhower Doctrine the United States emerged "as the uncontested Western power . . . in the Middle East."

It is nothing new for the President and the Congress to join to recognize that the national integrity of other free nations is directly related to our own security.

We have joined to create and support the security system of the United Nations. . . . We have joined to take decisive action in relation to Greece and Turkey [see part a, this reading] and in relation to Taiwan.

Thus, the United States through the joint action of the President and the Congress, or, in the case of treaties, the Senate, has manifested in many endangered areas its purpose to support free and independent governments—and peace—against external menace, notably the menace of International Communism. Thereby we have helped to maintain peace and security during a period of great danger. It is now essential that the United States should manifest through joint action of the President and the Congress our determination to assist those nations of the Mid-East area, which desire that assistance.

The action which I propose would have the following features.

It would, first of all, authorize the United States to cooperate with and assist any nation or group of nations in the general area of the Middle East in the development of economic strength dedicated to the maintenance of national independence.

It would, in the second place, authorize the Executive to undertake in the same region programs of military assistance and cooperation with any nation or group of nations which desires such aid.

It would, in the third place, authorize such assistance and cooperation to include the employment of the armed forces of the United States to secure and protect the territorial integrity and political independence of such nations, requesting such aid, against overt armed aggression from any nation controlled by International Communism.

C. George H. W. Bush, The New World Order (1991)*

In this speech delivered to a joint session of the U.S. Congress at the conclusion of the Gulf War of 1991, President Bush (1924–   ) offered his vision of a new world order that he hoped to initiate. Many of the goals he lists for the United States to achieve in the Middle East remain elusive more than a decade later.

---

*From President George Bush's address to a joint session of Congress, March 6, 1991, in *Public Papers of the Presidents of the United States: George Bush, 1991*, 2 vols. (Washington, DC: U.S. Government Printing Office, 1992), vol. 1, pp. 219–22.

Moreover, the United States in its Arabian policy did the exact opposite of what the president said it would do in this speech: to secure Middle East peace, he said, "does not mean stationing U.S. ground forces in the Arabian Peninsula." However, when U.S. troops arrived in Saudi Arabia in 1991, they discovered to their consternation that despite the billions of dollars that the Saudis had spent on sophisticated armaments purchased from the United States, the country's military could not use them effectively in battle. The U.S. General Staff then decided to leave U.S. troops permanently in Arabia to assure the proper functioning of that country's arsenal. That decision galvanized a powerful opposition movement within Saudi Arabia, and the Islamic world generally, because of the presence there of Muslims' holiest sites.

After serving as Republican congressman from Texas, George Bush held the offices of ambassador to the United Nations and director of the Central Intelligence Agency before becoming vice president (1981–89) and president (1989–93) of the United States. His son George W. Bush was elected president in 2000.

Tonight, I come to this House to speak about the world—the world after war. The recent challenge could not have been clearer. Saddam Hussein was the villain; Kuwait, the victim. To the aid of this small country came nations from North America and Europe, from Asia and South America, from Africa and the Arab world, all united against aggression. Our uncommon coalition must now work in common purpose: to forge a future that should never again be held hostage to the darker side of human nature.

Tonight in Iraq, Saddam walks amidst ruin. His war machine is crushed. His ability to threaten mass destruction is itself destroyed. His people have been lied to, denied the truth. And when his defeated legions come home, all Iraqis will see and feel the havoc he has wrought. And this I promise you: For all that Saddam has done to his own people, to the Kuwaitis, and to the entire world, Saddam and those around him are accountable. . . .

America's Challenges

First, we must work together to create shared security arrangements in the region. Our friends and allies in the Middle East recognize that they will bear the bulk of the responsibility for regional security. But we want them to know that just as we stood with them to repel aggression, so now America stands ready to work with them to secure the peace. This does not mean stationing U.S. ground forces in the Arabian Peninsula, but it does mean American participation in joint exercises involving both air and ground forces. It means maintaining a capable U.S. naval presence in the region, just as we have for over 40 years. Let it be clear: Our vital national interests depend on a stable and secure Gulf.

Second, we must act to control the proliferation of weapons of mass destruction and the missiles used to deliver them. It would be tragic if the nations of the Middle East and Persian Gulf were now, in the wake of war, to embark on a new arms race. Iraq requires special vigilance. . . .

[Third], we must foster economic development for the sake of peace and progress. The Persian Gulf and Middle East form a region rich in natural resources with a wealth of untapped human potential. Resources once squandered on military might must be redirected to more peaceful ends. . . .

A New World Order

Now we can see a new world coming into view. . . . In the words of Winston Churchill, a world order in which "the principles of justice and fair play protect the weak against the strong. . . ." A world where the United Nations, freed from cold war stalemate, is poised to fulfill the historic vision of its founders. A world in which freedom and respect for human rights find a home among all nations. The Gulf war put this new world to its first test. And my fellow Americans, we passed that test.

For the sake of our principles, for the sake of the Kuwaiti people, we stood our ground. Because the world would not look the other way . . . tonight Kuwait is free. And we're very happy about that.

Tonight, as our troops begin to come home, let us recognize that the hard work of freedom still calls us forward. We've learned the hard lessons of history. The victory over Iraq was not waged as "a war to end all wars." Even the new world order cannot guarantee an era of perpetual peace. But enduring peace must be our mission. Our success in the Gulf will shape not only the new world order we seek but our mission here at home. . . .

We went halfway around the world to do what is moral and just and right. We fought hard and, with others, we won the war. We lifted the yoke of aggression and tyranny from a small country that many Americans had never even heard of, and we ask nothing in return.

D. William J. Clinton, The Battle Against Terrorism (1998)*

In this radio broadcast during the summer of 1998 President Bill Clinton (1946–) accused Osama bin Laden of masterminding the near-simultaneous August 7 bombings of U.S. embassies in the East African countries of Kenya and Tanzania. U.S. intelligence officials thereafter set up a special situation room in order to track bin Laden and his *Al Qaeda* organization. The president ordered surveillance of money transfers with links to bin Laden's international network. But working through informal Islamic lending institutions and money changers, *Al Qaeda* operatives continued to conduct their business unimpeded. *Al Qaeda* cells, spread throughout western Europe, the United States, and Asia, constituted an informal network that proved impenetrable by normal espionage methods.

---

*From President William J. Clinton's radio broadcast to the nation, August 22, 1998, in *Public Papers of the Presidents of the United States: William J. Clinton, 1998*, 2 vols. (Washington DC: U.S. Government Printing Office, 2000), vol. I, pp. 1464–65.

Lacking sufficiently trained linguists, Middle Eastern and South Asian policy analysts, and credible informants, U.S. intelligence agencies, each jealous of its turf and insufficiently prepared to seize on astute reports from local field agents and messages and signals from scattered terrorist cells of Islamic radical groups, could not assess correctly many of *Al Qaeda*'s plans before they hatched.

Two weeks after he delivered this speech, President Clinton responded to the embassy bombings by sending cruise missiles on an errant mission to destroy bin Laden's alleged hideout in Afghanistan, and by bombing a Somali pharmaceutical factory, which the U.S. falsely claimed housed an *Al Qaeda* weapons facility. These attacks highlighted further failures of U.S. intelligence, for they did not achieve their objectives of stopping bin Laden and his operatives. Bin Laden remained at large, heading the list of the most wanted fugitives on the globe. Despite the $34 billion yearly budget for U.S. intelligence, Americans began questioning—especially after September 11, 2001—whether these significant expenditures actually brought the hoped-for security.

Two weeks ago, a savage attack was carried out against our Embassies in Kenya and Tanzania. Almost 300 innocent people were killed; thousands were injured. The bombs were aimed at us, but they claimed anyone who happened to be near the Embassies that morning. They killed both Africans and Americans indiscriminately, cruelty beyond comprehension.

From the moment we learned of the bombings, our mission was clear: Identify those responsible; bring them to justice; protect our citizens from future attacks. . . .

We also had compelling evidence that the [Osama] bin Laden network was poised to strike at us again, and soon. We know he has said all Americans—not just those in uniform—all Americans are targets. And we know he wants to acquire chemical weapons. . . .

Finally, as we close ranks against international threats, we must remember this: America will never give up the openness, the freedom, and the tolerance that defines us. For the ultimate target of these terrorist attacks is our ideals, and they must be defended at any cost.

E. George W. Bush, Beyond Containment and Deterrence to Preemptive Action (2002)*

> In this post–September 11th commencement address at the U.S. Military Academy at West Point, President Bush referred to the American Cold War policy of containment—the U.S. attempt to limit Soviet expansion beyond eastern Eu-

---

*From George W. Bush's remarks at the 2002 graduation exercises of the United States Military Academy, West Point, New York (June 1, 2002), on the website www.whitehouse.gov/news/releases/2002/06/20020601-3.html.

rope. This policy reluctantly granted the Soviets retention of regions under Moscow's control, but declared further expansion impermissible. Deterrence similarly recognized Soviet gains in military technology (nuclear warheads, missiles, etc.), but committed the United States to build a credible deterrent power while tacitly admitting that the Cold War enemy could develop similar power. Mutually assured destruction (MAD) would prevent either side from risking a first strike.

The policy announced in June 2002 by George W. Bush departs from the element of reciprocity in earlier U.S. foreign policy: after the events of September 11, 2001, the sole superpower has claimed the right to take "preemptive action" on its own initiative and without waiting for threats "to fully materialize." This statement was presumably directed against Iraq and other nations labeled by Washington as members of the "axis of evil" (see Reading 35a), a group that appears high on the list of White House enemies in the post–Cold War era.

In defending the peace, we face a threat with no precedent. Enemies in the past needed great armies and great industrial capabilities to endanger the American people and our nation. The attacks of September the 11th required a few hundred thousand dollars in the hands of a few dozen evil and deluded men. All of the chaos and suffering they caused came at much less than the cost of a single tank. The dangers have not passed. . . .

The gravest danger to freedom lies at the perilous crossroads of radicalism and technology. When the spread of chemical and biological and nuclear weapons, along with ballistic missile technology—when that occurs, even weak states and small groups could attain a catastrophic power to strike great nations. Our enemies have declared this very intention, and have been caught seeking these terrible weapons. They want the capability to blackmail us, or to harm us, or to harm our friends—and we will oppose them with all our power.

Preemptive Action

For much of the last century, America's defense relied on the Cold War doctrines of deterrence and containment. In some cases, those strategies still apply. But new threats also require new thinking. Deterrence—the promise of massive retaliation against nations—means nothing against shadowy terrorist networks with no nation or citizens to defend. Containment is not possible when unbalanced dictators with weapons of mass destruction can deliver those weapons on missiles or secretly provide them to terrorist allies. . . .

Homeland defense and missile defense are part of stronger security, and they're essential priorities for America. Yet the war on terror will not be won on the defensive. We must take the battle to the enemy, disrupt his plans, and confront the worst threats before they emerge. In the world we have entered, the only path to safety is the path of action. And this nation will act.

Our security will require the best intelligence, to reveal threats hidden in caves and growing in laboratories. Our security will require modernizing domestic agencies such as the FBI, so they're prepared to act, and act quickly, against danger. Our security will require transforming the military you will lead— a military that must be ready to strike at a moment's notice in any dark corner of the world. And our security will require all Americans to be forward-looking and resolute, to be ready for preemptive action when necessary to defend our liberty and to defend our lives.

The work ahead is difficult. The choices we will face are complex. We must uncover terror cells in 60 or more countries, using every tool of finance, intelligence and law enforcement. . . . Some nations need military training to fight terror, and we'll provide it. Other nations oppose terror, but tolerate the hatred that leads to terror—and that must change. We will send diplomats where they are needed, and we will send you, our soldiers, where you're needed.

All nations that decide for aggression and terror will pay a price. . . . We are in a conflict between good and evil, and America will call evil by its name. By confronting evil and lawless regimes, we do not create a problem, we reveal a problem. And we will lead the world in opposing it.

28. Intervention and Revolution in Iran

In the early 1950s, the Iranian government had unsuccessfully tried to negotiate a fifty-fifty profit-sharing deal with the British Anglo-Iranian Oil Company (AIOC), which had developed and controlled Iran's oil fields. The British government owned more than half of the company. The head of the Iranian parliament's Oil Committee, Muhammad Mossadeq (1882–1967), opposed profit-sharing schemes and favored outright nationalization of AIOC. Toward this end, his political movement, the National Front, organized strikes and mass demonstrations in favor of his position. When negotiations with AIOC broke down in 1951, Mossadeq's government nationalized the company. The following year Mossadeq stated his case for the nationalization (part a of this reading). But the British, seeing the Iranian government's action as the beginning of the end of the United Kingdom's dominance over the Middle Eastern oil industry, responded with a boycott of Iranian oil. Joining AIOC, the other members of the Seven Sisters oil cartel upheld the boycott, hoping to choke off funds to Mossadeq's government and cause financial havoc in Iran.

This boycott weakened Mossadeq politically and made his regime vulnerable to a 1953 coup d'état engineered jointly by the CIA and its British counterpart. The Shah Muhammad Reza Pahlavi (1919–80), who had fled into exile after an

earlier coup against Mossadeq had failed, approved the overthrow of his opponents and returned. He ruled over a resentful country where Islamic clerics and
liberals slowly united in an opposition that finally ousted the shah and ended
the Pahlavi dynasty in 1979. But far from bringing peace to Iran, the revolution
stirred internal disagreement among the diverse revolutionaries and the creation
of an Islamic Republic (this reading, part c). It also tempted neighboring Iraq
to attack (see Reading 30a).

A. Muhammad Mossadeq, Nationalizing Iranian Oil (1952)*

Mossadeq wrote this letter to a British diplomat, but intended it for the British
public. In it he sets forth Iran's complaint against the Anglo-Iranian Oil Company (renamed after nationalization the Iranian National Oil Company, INOC).
But soon after the Iranian prime minister wrote this letter, the United States
and Britian organized a military coup to overthrow Mossadeq and reinstall
the exiled shah. The U.S. government at first questioned the British boycott of
Iranian oil, but when Dwight D. Eisenhower became president in 1953, the United
States not only backed the boycott but also actively participated in Mossadeq's
overthrow.

[To] our great regret, the diplomatic relations between the two States [Great
Britain and Iran] have reached the present stage, [yet] the Government and
the people of Iran can easily demonstrate to the world that from the very
beginning they have been desiring with utmost goodwill to come to a settlement of the oil dispute, and that they have spared no effort in the fulfillment
of this object. While, on the contrary, the covetous Company, who was conscious
of the fact that it enjoyed full protection of the British Government as far as its
illegitimate expectations and desires were concerned, took resort in threats and
. . . rumors, even in the remotest parts of the world, that the Government and
people of Iran are not prepared to arrive at a settlement of the oil dispute.

[The] British Government established a dictatorial regime in Iran for the
sole purpose of safeguarding its illegitimate interests . . . [while] endanger[ing]
our political integrity and independence by allowing the former Company to
unduly interfere in our social and political affairs.

Taking . . . world developments . . . as regards the self determination of nations, the Iranians could no longer tolerate the behavior of the former Company; and the best interests of the nation demanded . . . the nationalization of
the oil industry. . . . In other words, the Iranians availed themselves of the birth
right of any free and independent nation. Many other countries and particu-

---

*From *Message of Dr. Muhammad Mossadeq, Prime Minister of Iran, to the British Nation* (Tehran: Bank
Melli Iran Press, November 1952). American spellings adopted. Bracketed material added by the
authors.

larly the United Kingdom have availed themselves of the right to nationalize their industries.

Notwithstanding the fact that the Iranian Government were within their established rights to nationalize the oil industry, yet the United Kingdom Government from the outset took measures, inside and outside of Iran, meant for the protection of the unlawful interests of the former Company, which were contrary to the spirit of friendship between the two Governments.

In order to settle the differences, the Iranian Government showed its readiness to pay compensation to the former Company in accordance with nationalization laws enacted in Great Britain or according to laws of any country which the former Company may prefer to choose. . . . [T]his proposal . . . was also rejected.

[T]he British Government . . . did not refrain from supporting the unlawful interests of the former Oil Company by bringing financial and economic pressure on the people of Iran, through prevention of the sale of Iranian oil in world markets and even by refusing to release Iranian sterling holdings in British Banks.

It was made clear that the British Secretary for Foreign Affairs [Anthony Eden, 1897–1977] demanded compensation for profits that would have accrued to the former Company, had the Company continued its activities of plundering the wealth of this country.

Industries are nationalized, evidently, to remove private profiteering, and to pass on the proceeds of nationalization, exclusively, to the public treasury. The British Government . . . demanded such payment of compensation as would cover all unlawful profits supposed to ensure from that Agreement.

These steps compelled the Government of Iran to sever diplomatic relations with the British Government, and to leave the resumption of relations to such time as the British Government may care to revise their policy, with regard to world developments and the awakening of the people of Iran and with due consideration for the principles of justice and equity.

B. Ayatollah Ruholla Khomeini, Iran in Imperialism's Clutches (1964)*

A decade and a half before a coalition of religious revolutionaries and leftist radicals ousted the Pahlavi dynasty, the exiled *Shiite* leader Ayatollah Khomeini sent this speech on audiotape back home to Iran. In it he referred to one of the Middle East's main historical grievances: the capitulations, which we have described in the introduction to Chapter III. Originally agreements by which Western merchants

---

*From a 1964 speech by Ayatollah Ruholla Khomeini, in *Khomeni Va Jonsheb* (Khomeini and the Movement) (Moharram Press, 1973), pp. 30–31. Translated from the Farsi by Ervand Abrahamian. By permission of the translator.

gained extraterritorial rights, the capitulations conferred on foreigners the privilege of being judged in another country by laws of their own countries. Without explicitly mentioning these hated capitulations of an earlier imperial era, Khomeini associated the willingness of the shah's government to extend extraterritoriality to American military advisers in Iran to the earlier oppression practiced by British imperialists.

Strongly criticizing the subservient *majlis* (Iran's parliament) and the country's "ruling circles" for humiliating Iran with the implication that "barbarous" local laws should not apply to foreigners, Khomeini refrained from explicit disapproval of Shah Muhammad Reza or of the monarchy itself. But soon both would come under his scathing attack. Khomeini became the dominant clerical leader after the 1979 revolution succeeded in overthrowing the Pahlavi dynasty.

Do you—the nation of Iran—know what is going on these days in your *majles*? Do you know . . . what is being transacted in the dark—all in your name? Do you know that the *majles,* pressured by the government, has quietly signed a treaty with America enslaving Iran, colonizing Iran, and even asserting that our Muslim nation is barbarous? With one stroke of the pen, the *majles* has signed away our Islamic and Iranian heritage. It has reduced us into the most backward country in the whole world. It has shown utter contempt for Iran—especially for its law courts. What is more, it has done all this after a brief discussion lasting no more than a few hours. Iran is now under American control. American advisers, military and non-military, together with their families, can with impunity disregard our institutions, our laws, and our judicial courts. Why, you may ask, has the government done this? The answer is simple: America is the country of the dollar, and the Iranian government worships the almighty dollar.

With this shameful deed, American military advisers—nay, even servants of American military advisers—have immunity from our laws. They can take liberties with our highest religious and state authorities without having to worry about our police and law courts.

In an age when one colonized country after another is throwing off the shackles of imperialism, the Iranian government is reducing Iran into the most backward country in the world—even while boasting about the 2,500-year-old civilization. I have heard that America tried to impose similar treaties on Pakistan, Turkey, Indonesia, and West Germany, but they—unlike Iran—refused to submit to such humiliation.

It is precisely to avoid such humiliation that the *ulama* oppose the rule of the bayonet and favor national independence with a free press, a representative *majles,* and a patriotic government. The deputies—with a few notable exceptions—sit quietly while this shameful crime is committed because they don't represent the country, because they are spineless weaklings, and because they know they will be carted off to prison if they dare raise any objections.

I proclaim this disgraceful vote to be against the Holy Koran, against Islam, against the Muslim community, and thus to be null and void. The deputies represent bayonets, not the people. Their vote has absolutely no value in the eyes of the nation, of Islam, and of the Holy Koran. The people will know their duty if foreigners try to take advantage of this shameful vote. Everyone should realize that Iran's and the Muslim World's problems are all derived from America. In the past, Britain oppressed us, exploited our natural resources, occupied our lands, and interfered in our internal affairs. Now it is America that tramples over Islam and the Holy Koran, arms Israel against the Arabs, imposes these deputies on us, pressures our government and *majles,* and wants the *ulama* to be incarcerated in prison—for it knows that the *ulama* are the real opponents of imperialism. It is America that wants the *ulama* to be apolitical, the seminaries and the universities to be passive, the various classes in society to be ignorant of what is going on in the *majles. . . .*

Does the Muslim World know that clerics and theology students in Iran have been dragged off to prison without trial? Does it know that no senior cleric is able to put an end to this type of medieval and reactionary behavior? Iran's ruling circle is busy creating chaos when it should be directing attention on the dismal economic situation, protecting respected merchants from bankruptcy, providing the needy with bread, water and housing, creating work for high school graduates. . . .The bazaar is no longer in Iranian and Muslim hands. Increasing numbers of merchants and farmers are falling into bankruptcy, poverty and oblivion. All this because the Iranian economy is now in the clutches of America and Israel.

C. Ervand Abrahamian, Democracy or Theocracy: Iran's Islamic Republic (1995)*

The Iranian revolution of 1979 represents one of the watersheds of twentieth-century history. For the first time in the century an urban revolution against a regime backed up by the greatest power on earth—the United States—had succeeded. Even the Shah Muhammad Reza knew the revolutionaries had won when army units went over to their side. The American-backed shah then left the country for good. A few weeks later Iranians welcomed Ayatollah Ruholla Khomeini back from exile to usher in the newly formed Islamic Republic. One of his earliest acts consisted of inciting students to take diplomats at the U.S. embassy in Tehran hostage, whom they held captive for 444 days. This episode contributed to the reelection defeat of President Jimmy Carter in 1980. In this essay Abrahamian, Distinguished Professor of History at Baruch College of the City University of

---

*From Ervand Abrahamian, "The Making of the Modern Iranian State," in Mark Kesselman, Joel Krieger, and William A. Joseph, eds., *Comparative Politics at the Crossroads* (Lexington, MA: D. C. Heath & Company, 1995), pp. 693–95, 716–19. Notes deleted and foreign words italicized. By permission.

New York, carefully analyzes the elements of theocracy and democracy in post-1979 Iran. He has also written *Khomeinism: Essays on the Islamic Republic* (1993) and several other books on modern Iran. His essay "The 1953 Coup in Iran," in *Science & Society* (Summer 2001), provides an up-to-date, well-documented narrative of that event.

[Khomeini] . . . triumphantly returned home from exile to claim his Islamic Revolution. He promptly replaced the Pahlavi monarchy with an Islamic Republic dominated thoroughly by the clergy. For this reason alone, the Islamic Republic can be described a true theocracy—one of the few in world history. The new regime hailed Khomeini as the Great Leader of the Islamic Revolution, the Founder of the Islamic Republic, the Guide for the Oppressed Masses, and, most potent of all, the *Imam* (Infallible Leader)—a title Iranians had never before bestowed on a living person. . . .

The Islamic Revolution is a landmark in contemporary politics for a number of reasons. First, it is comparable to the other classic revolutions—notably, the French, Russian, and Chinese. It exploded like a volcanic eruption, suddenly and dramatically, utterly destroying the age-old monarchy. Although the last dynasty was only a half-century old, the Iranian monarchy as a whole boasted 2,500 years of history, leading some to claim that it had become part and parcel of the "Iranian mentality." The revolution blew away the society's upper levels, drastically changing the social landscape, scattering debris into the neighboring regions, and affecting the political climate even on the other side of the globe. By the early 1990s, Western governments feared similar Islamic Revolutions would erupt not only in neighboring Turkey, Iraq, Afghanistan, Saudi Arabia, and Central Asia, but also in such faraway areas as Gaza, Egypt, Algeria, Nigeria, and even Indonesia. In fact, this event introduced into our contemporary language the term "Islamic fundamentalism."

Second, it occurred in one of the most important states in the Middle East. On the eve of the revolution, Iran had nearly 36 million people, making it one of the most populous nations in the region. It had one of the area's largest and fastest-growing economies. It was one of the most developed and industrialized societies in the region, with nearly 50 percent of its total population living in urban centers. It was the world's fourth-largest oil producer and second-largest oil exporter, thus making it highly important to such oil-importing countries as Japan, France, Germany, Italy, and the United States. It possessed the world's fifth-largest army, one of the most up-to-date air forces, and by far the largest navy in the Persian Gulf. The United States had appointed the Shah to be its main policeman in the Persian Gulf. Thus, the revolution had drastic repercussions on America's strategic position in the Persian Gulf.

Third, the Islamic Revolution raised theoretical questions about modernization in general and revolutions in particular. Social scientists have often argued that modernization, especially urbanization and industrialization, inevitably produces secularization—the marginalization of religion in public life. Some have even argued that modernization inevitably relegates the clergy to the dustbin of history. Yet in Iran, fifty years of substantial modernization had enhanced the role of the clergy to the point where they could establish a full-fledged theocracy. Furthermore, political scientists have often pointed out that revolutions usually follow defeats in war or peasant rebellions and bring to power the intelligentsia at the head of disciplined political parties. Yet in Iran, the revolution occurred with no foreign wars, no peasant revolts, no triumphant intelligentsia, and no highly organized political parties.

Few observers in 1979–1980 expected the Islamic Republic to last long. They considered a clerical state in the twentieth century to be an anachronism. After all, theocracy appeared incompatible with democracy and the modern demand for popular representation and mass political participation. The clergy, steeped in theology and history, were dismissed as inherently incapable of dealing with the challenges of the contemporary world—that is, with rival states, ultrasophisticated weaponry, the information superhighway, modern mass media, and complex international organizations. Despite predictions of imminent demise, the Islamic Republic of Iran survived to emerge in the 1990s as one of the major threats to U.S. interests in the Middle East—at least in the eyes of U.S. policymakers.

The Islamic Revolution was carried out under the banners of anti-imperialism, republicanism, and Islam—especially *Shi'i* Islam. . . .

The constitution was drafted shortly after the revolution by an Assembly of Religious Experts. It was ratified in December 1979 by a nationwide referendum held in the midst of the American hostage crisis. In fact, the occupation of the U.S. Embassy was, for the most part, motivated by Khomeini's desire to undermine the provisional premier, Mehdi Bazargan [1907–96], who had criticized the proposed constitution for giving too much power to the clergy. During the referendum, anyone faulting the constitution was denounced by Khomeini as favoring the Shah and America. The 1979 constitution was amended in April–June 1989 during the very lasts months of Khomeini's life by a Council for the Revision of the Constitution hand-picked by Khomeini himself. These amendments, in turn, were ratified by a nationwide referendum in July 1989, immediately after Khomeini's death. The final document, totaling 175 clauses and some 40 amendments, is a potpourri of theocracy and democracy with a dash of populist autocracy.

The constitution institutionalized clerical power, creating a full-blown theocracy. It affirmed faith in God, Divine Justice, the *Qur'an*, the Resurrection, Muhammad, the Twelve *Imams,* the eventual return of the Hidden *Imam* (the *Mahdi*), and, of course, Khomeini's doctrine of the jurist's guardianship. All laws, institutions, and state organizations were to be based on these "divine principles."

It named Khomeini to be the Supreme Jurist for life on the grounds that the public overwhelmingly respected him as the "most just, pious, informed, brave, and enterprising" of the very senior clerics. It further described him as the Leader of the Revolution, the Founder of the Islamic Republic, and most potent of all, the *Imam* (Infallible Leader) of the whole community. It furthermore stipulated that if no single Supreme Jurist emerged after Khomeini's death then all his authority would be passed on to a Leadership Council of two or three senior jurists. After Khomeini's death, however, his disciples so distrusted the surviving senior jurists that they did not set up such a council. Instead, they elected one of their own, *Hojjat al-Islam* [Ali] Khamenei (1939–   ), a medium-ranking cleric, to be the new Supreme Leader. All of Khomeini's titles, with the exception of *Imam*, were bestowed on Khamenei. The Islamic Republic has often been described as the regime of the *ayatollahs* (high-ranking clerics). It would be more aptly described as the regime of the *hojjat al-Islams* (medium-ranking clerics).

The constitution gave wide-ranging authority to the Supreme Leader. Described as the "link" between the branches of government, he could mediate between the legislative, the executive, and the judiciary. He could "determine the interests of Islam," "supervise the implementation of general policy," and "set political guidelines for the Islamic Republic." He could eliminate presidential candidates as well as dismiss the duly elected president. He could grant amnesty. As commander-in-chief, he could mobilize the armed forces, declare war and peace, and convene the Supreme Military Council. He could appoint and dismiss the chief of joint staffs as well as the commanders of the army, navy, air force, and revolutionary guards. . . .

The later constitutional amendments transformed the Assembly of Religious Experts, which had originally been convened as a constituent assembly to draft the constitution, into a permanent body. Packed by clerics, the assembly not only elected Khamenei as Khomeini's successor, but also reserved the right to dismiss him if it found him "mentally incapable of fulfilling his arduous duties." In effect, the Assembly of Religious Experts became the second-chamber equivalent of a clerical upper house above the Islamic *Majles*. . . .

Since the whole constitution was based on Khomeini's theory of the jurist's guardianship, it gave wide-ranging judicial powers to the Supreme Jurist in particular and to the clerical strata in general. Laws were supposed to conform to the *shari'a*, and the clergy, particularly the senior jurists, were regarded as the ultimate interpreters of the *shari'a*. In fact, the constitution made the judicial system the central pillar of the state, overshadowing the executive and the legislature. Bills passed by the Islamic *Majles* were to be vetted by the Guardian Council to ensure that they conformed to the *shari'a*. All twelve members of this Guardian Council were to be clerics, with six appointed by the Supreme Leader and six appointed jointly by the Supreme Judge and Islamic *Majles*. . . . The judicial system itself was Islamized all the way down to the district courts with seminary-trained jurists replacing university-educated judges. . . .

To further Islamize the judiciary, the regime enacted a penal law [that] . . . permitted injured families to demand blood money. It mandated the death penalty for a list of "moral transgressions," including adultery, homosexuality, apostasy, drug trafficking, and habitual drinking. It sanctioned stoning, live burials, hand amputations, and physical gouging, citing the *Qur'anic* principle "an eye for an eye, a tooth for a tooth." It divided the population into male and female, Muslim and non-Muslim, and treated them unequally. For example, in court, the testimony of one male Muslim was equal to that of two female Muslims.

[T]he law was Islamized, but the modern centralized judicial system was not dismantled. For years, Khomeini argued that in a truly Islamic society the local *shari'a* judges would pronounce final verdicts without the intervention of the central authorities. Their verdicts would be swift and decisive. This, he insisted, was the true spirit of the *shari'a*. After the revolution, however, he discovered that the central state needed to retain ultimate control over the justice system, especially over life and death. Thus, the new regime retained the appeal system, the hierarchy of state courts, and the power to appoint and dismiss all judges. State interests took priority over the spirit of the *shari'a*.

Although the Islamic Republic is a full-fledged theocracy, some supporters of the regime have argued that it is nevertheless compatible with democracy. According to the constitution, the government represents the "general" electorate. The Supreme Leader is chosen by the Assembly of Religious Experts, who, in turn, are elected by the general population. This is viewed as a two-stage popular election. . . . [T]he legislature also has a considerable constitutional role. According to [Ali Akbar Hashemi] Rafsanjani [1934–   ], previously the legislature's speaker, "the Islamic *Majles* is the centerpiece of the Islamic Constitution. It has many prerogatives, including that of enacting or changing ordinary laws (with the approval of the Guardian Council), investigating and supervising all affairs of state, as well as approving and ousting the cabinet ministers." Finally, some also argue that the public . . . by carrying out an Islamic Revolution, had determined for the future generations that democracy in Iran should be placed within the rubric of the jurist's guardianship. . . . On the eve of the initial referendum for the constitution, Khomeini himself insisted that democracy and the jurist's guardianship in no way contradicted each other:

This constitution, which the people will ratify, is in no way a contradiction with democracy. Since the people love the clergy, have faith in the clergy, want to be guided by the clergy, it is right that the supreme religious authority oversee the work of the Prime Minister or of the President, to make sure that they don't make mistakes or go against the law: that is the Koran.

29. OPEC and the World Economy

From the beginning of the twentieth century until the early 1970s the cost of petroleum remained low and stable, primarily because Western companies set inexpensive energy prices on world markets in order to assure industrialized countries plentiful and cheap supplies. They conrolled the oil wells in places such as Saudi Arabia where oil cost very little to produce and local rulers received meager royalties. As Reading 28a demonstrates, attempts by Iran to nationalize its hydrocarbon industries and place them under state ownership met significant opposition from international oil companies and from the Western countries to which those companies belonged. The founding of the Organization of Petroleum Exporting Countries (OPEC) in 1960 as a consortium of exporting oil states ultimately enabled its members to increase their share of oil revenues and led to large-scale nationalization of the industry beginning in the 1970s. This reading explains the functions of OPEC and the effects of the dramatic petroleum price increases of the 1970s.

A. Organization of Petroleum Exporting Countries: Getting Our Share (1961)*

Five oil-producing countries (Iran, Iraq, Kuwait, Saudi Arabia, and Venezuela), then representing over 80 percent of the world's petroleum exports, founded OPEC in Baghdad at the beginning of the 1960s to coordinate production quotas and stabilize petroleum prices. The members unanimously approved the original text of the organization's statute in January 1961 in Caracas, Venezuela. By 1975 the countries belonging to OPEC had expanded to fifteen, including Libya and Abu Dhabi, which also had large oil reserves. Outside OPEC, at the opening of the twenty-first century, the Russian Federation's revamping of its oil industry allowed it to influence global pricing by pumping additional oil when needed to stabilize prices, thereby weakening the organization.

British and American domination of the oil industry meant that OPEC had to adopt English as its official language and the dollar as the monetary standard for all petroleum sales. The organization expressed its basic conservatism in Article 2c of this document where it acknowledges the importance of maintaining continual and plentiful supplies of oil to consumers and also allowing oil companies to earn fair profits from their businesses. This mild-mannered statement merely asserted that the OPEC countries felt they should finally have what they thought the oil companies owed them.

---

*From OPEC, *The Statute of the Organization of the Petroleum Exporting Countries* (Vienna: Information Department OPEC, 1978), pp. 3–6.

* * *

I. The Organization of the Petroleum Exporting Countries (OPEC), hereinafter referred to as "the Organization," created as a permanent intergovernmental organization in conformity with the Resolutions of the conference of the Representatives of the Governments of Iran, Iraq, Kuwait, Saudi Arabia and Venezuela, held in Baghdad from September 10 to 14, 1960, shall carry out its functions in accordance with the provisions set forth hereunder.

II. A. The principal aim of the Organization shall be the coordination and unification of the petroleum policies of Member Countries and the determination of the best means for safeguarding their interests, individually and collectively.

B. The Organization shall devise ways and means of ensuring the stabilization of prices in international oil markets with a view to eliminating harmful and unnecessary fluctuations.

C. Due regard shall be given at all times to the interests of the producing nations and to the necessity of securing a steady income to the producing countries; an efficient, economic and regular supply of petroleum to consuming nations; and a fair return on their capital to those investing in the Petroleum industry.

III. The organization shall be guided by the principle of the sovereign equality of its Member Countries. Member Countries shall fulfill, in good faith, the obligations assumed by them in accordance with this Statute.

IV. If, as a result of the application of any decision of the Organization, sanctions are employed, directly or indirectly, by any interested company or companies against one or more Member Countries, no other Member shall accept any offer of a beneficial treatment, whether in the form of an increase in oil exports or in an improvement in prices, which may be made to it by such interested company or companies with the intention of discouraging the application of the decision of the Organization. . . .

VI. English shall be the official language of the Organization. . . .

VII. . . . Any other country with a substantial net export of crude petroleum, which has fundamentally similar interests to those of Member Countries, may become a full Member of the Organization, if accepted by a majority of three-fourths of Full Members, including the concurrent vote of all Founder Members.

B. Crown Prince Fahd ibn Abd al-Aziz, Oil and the World Economy (1975)*

This interview with Saudi Arabian Crown Prince Fahd (1932–) took place a week after another Saudi prince had assassinated Fahd's brother, King Faysal, creating turmoil in the kingdom. Prince Khalid (1913–82) became king and prime

---

*From Prince Fahd's interview with *Al-Anwar* (Beirut), April 1, 1975, translated from the Arabic in Foreign Broadcast Information Service (FBIS), *Daily Report*, Arabian Peninsula, April 2, 1975. Bracketed material added by the editors.

minister, but due to his inexperience Crown Prince Fahd, as deputy prime minister and minister of interior, ran domestic and foreign policy until he himself became king in 1982 after Khalid's death. The journalist, from a Beirut Arab-language newspaper, interviewed the crown prince a year after the Arab states belonging to OPEC ended an oil embargo against the United States and the Netherlands. They had also reduced exports by 5 to 10 percent monthly to "unfriendly" states, including Japan, who they accused of supporting Israel in the 1973 Middle Eastern war.

All the industrialized nations felt the shortages caused by the Arab states, since available supplies could not fulfill demand. The embargo led to higher prices for consumers and larger shares in profits for producing countries, but it became clear that OPEC could not long sustain cutbacks and embargos. The well-being of their economies depended on the continual importation of their oil by the very countries they had sought to punish. Fahd shows in this interview that this realization had sunk in, and that Saudi Arabia would seek a stable post-embargo environment in which it would pump and export sufficient oil to satisfy international demand. Once the embargo ended, Saudi Arabia and other Middle Eastern states resumed regular oil sales, but at considerably higher prices than those set before the embargo. The Saudis came to realize that they could not oppose indefinitely the United States, which provided the desert kingdom with its security.

Question: What is your opinion of [U.S. Secretary of State Henry] Kissinger's proposal to impose a minimum price on oil and the effect this will have on the free movement of prices and the consumption of Arab oil?

Answer: We welcome the fixing of oil prices to realize the economic stability for which we are as anxious as the industrialized countries because we are making long-term development plans that require the stability and prosperity of the industrialized world. The fixing of a stable price for oil would mean stabilizing our revenue. This would help us to plan.

But the oil-producing countries are not only exporters. They are also importers. The stability of our economy depends on balancing revenue and expenditures. I therefore believe that the price of oil should be linked with stabilization of the prices of essential goods, i.e., through indexation. This will contribute to international stability, reduce the burden of the developing countries, and provide the developed countries with the stability they want in the cost of energy.

Question: What about U.S. threats?

Answer: I believe the statements by U.S. officials—one was the U.S. ambassador and then Kissinger himself in the kingdom—who assured me that there was no intention of occupying the oil wells.

I believe that this puts an end to the issue which was not in the interest of those who instigated it. Inasmuch as we regret the declaration of such statements or threats, we laud the voices that were raised inside the United States denouncing the return to the . . . diplomacy [of threats].

Question: Does this mean that the danger of these threats has gone?

Answer: I believe that the major aim behind the information media campaign regarding these threats is to frighten the Arabs and influence their stand in the Arab-Israeli confrontation and at the negotiations. It can be said that this aim will not be achieved because the Arabs will not be frightened. Indeed, they asserted that if peace is not achieved in the Middle East then anything is possible. So long as Israeli rejection of the decisions of the international community and of the rights of the Palestinian people continues, threats and eventualities cannot be controlled.

Question: What is the best formula for cooperation between OPEC countries, developing countries, and developed industrialized countries?

Answer: Do not forget that we, too, are a developing country. We believe in international cooperation and we believe that . . . oil-rich Arab countries should promote international cooperation, not the reverse. This requires a deeper look into the required relationship. This should not be based simply on the desire to acquire the surplus money, merely the desire to purchase machinery, or to give loans and aid. . . .

Question: Do you believe that [the recent rise in] oil prices is to maintain the revenues being received by the oil-rich countries?

Answer: I believe that oil represents only a small portion of U.S. imports. Therefore, the devaluation of the dollar would not have consequences and effects on the oil-producing countries only. This devaluation undoubtedly perturbs industrialized oil-consuming countries as much as it does, to a greater extent, the oil-exporting countries. There are $80 billion invested in Europe. It is an American-European war more than an American-oil war. The devaluation of the dollar is, I believe, an expression of the world monetary system and the need for this system to be reorganized in light of the changes which have occurred since the end of World War II. It is also attributable to the economic conflict between the big industrialized countries and the desire of each to increase their exports.

This does not mean, however, that we are not affected by inflation or that we do not require the industrialized countries to work to put an end to it. Inflation reduces the purchasing power of the exports of developing countries and is a means of swallowing up the revenues of developing countries.

30. Wars at the End of the Twentieth Century and the Beginning of the Twenty-First

W ar is a voracious simplifier, and neither Gulf war (not the eight-year struggle between Iraq and Iran—for which, see part a, this reading—nor the six-month conflict of 1990–91) proved exceptions. Saddam Husayn's claim in the first Gulf war to have protected *Sunni* Islam from Iran's threat of *Shiite* revolution provided cover for his desire for greater control over the waterways leading to the Persian/Arabian Gulf and his drive for hegemony in the Gulf region. The even more threadbare rationale for Iraq's 1990 invasion of its southern neighbor Kuwait—that it had once been Iraq's "nineteenth province"—did not even pretend to conceal the petroleum-based rivalry between the two counties. Scarcely more credible are President George H. W. Bush's claims (part c, this reading) that the Americans fought against Iraq in that war to preserve Kuwait's hardly discernable democracy and to create a "new world order" in a world that has become far more disorderly.

The 2002 war in Afghanistan originated in the intersection of two sets of developments: (a) the attempt by leaders of the declining Soviet Union to buttress a friendly regime on its southern borders and (b) the growth of Islamic radicalism. They came together in the 1980s when the Soviets moved military forces into Afghanistan in the futile attempt to maintain the power of the left-wing People's Democratic Party (PDPA), which faced intense attack from Afghans opposed to its rule. Opposition to the Soviet presence in Afghanistan increased through the rest of the decade as the conflict attracted Islamic radicals from outside the country (such as Osama bin Laden), and mobilized them within. The United States, Saudi Arabia, and Pakistan assisted them in mounting a holy war against Communism. But the warriors who fought that war proved unable to govern Afghanistan afterward, and what Ahmed Rashid calls a "second generation" of Afghan religious radicals created the *Taliban* movement, which took over the country and harbored bin Laden. After the September 11 attacks the United States threatened the *Taliban* regime, and invaded and defeated it. So this war spanned two eras—the Cold War conflict to prevent Soviet expansion and the post–Cold War era of the global struggle against terrorism.

A. Joe Stork, The First Gulf War: Iran vs. Iraq, 1980–88 (2001)*

One of the most violent Middle Eastern conflicts in modern times, this war pitted two major Gulf oil states against each other in a struggle for regional domination. Iraq began the war a year after the Islamic Revolution in Iran. The Iraqi ruler, Saddam Husayn, calculated that postrevolutionary turmoil in Iran's military left that country vulnerable to attack and that his army could easily force the new rulers in Tehran to accede to Baghdad's demands for control of the key waterway, the Shatt al-Arab. As Joe Stork shows in this essay, Iran's armed forces managed to hold Iraq's army to modest gains in the border region, and in 1982 began to carry the war to Iraqi territory. Exhausted and battered, both countries agreed to a United Nations cease-fire resolution. The United States first backed Iraq out of hostility to Iran's Islamic revolution and the taking of American hostages. But after 1983, not wanting either side to win the war, the Americans began covertly to support Iran through a tangle of international connections involving Israel and far-off Nicaragua. For that complicated story, see Stuart Schaar's essay on "Irangate" in *The United States and the Middle East,* edited by Hooshang Amirahmadi (1993). Stork formerly served as editor of *Middle East Report* and now directs Human Rights Watch's Middle East and North African Division.

In September 1980, Iraq launched full scale air and ground attacks across the 730-mile . . . border it shares with Iran, initiating a war that raged intermittently until a cease-fire was declared in August 1988. This protracted contest—the longest conventional interstate war of the twentieth century—recalled the infantry trench warfare of World War I, while its later phases incorporated modern ballistic missile technology to attack cities and economic targets. Some 367,000 Iraqis and Iranians were killed and more than 700,000 wounded, by conservative Western estimates, and the war devastated both economies.

The ostensible causes of the Iran-Iraq War . . . included disputed borders and rights to a vital waterway, the Shatt al-Arab. Fundamentally at issue was the question of regional hegemony. On one level this was the latest episode in a history of contention for regional power between Iran and Iraq. At another level, it pitted the revolutionary Islamism of the new regime in Tehran against the Arab nationalist dictatorship in Baghdad, now backed by most of the major powers.

The outbreak of full-scale armed conflict between the two states was preceded by a series of border clashes, and by Tehran's appeals to Iraq's *Shi'i* Muslims (about 55 percent of the population) to follow Iran's revolutionary example and overthrow the secular tyranny of President Saddam Hussein. This campaign included sabotage bombings in Baghdad and at least one attempt to assassinate a major Iraqi government official. Baghdad, for its part, escalated hostilities in order to take advantage of the postrevolutionary disarray in Iranian society, especially in the armed forces, and Iran's international isolation, particularly

---

*From Joe Stork, "The Iran-Iraq War," in Joel Krieger, editor in chief, *The Oxford Companion to Politics of the World,* 2d ed. (New York: Oxford University Press, 2001), pp. 432–33. Arabic and Persian words italicized. By permission.

its estrangement from the United States. Its immediate pretext and goal was to overturn the 1975 Algiers agreement, signed by Saddam Hussein and the shah of Iran, which ratified Iranian demands for sharing sovereignty over the Shatt al-Arab in return for ending Iranian support of Kurdish insurgents in northern Iraq.

Iraq's initial incursion captured some 6,000–8,000 square miles . . . of Iran's oil-rich and Arab-populated Khuzestan province, destroying several cities and numerous towns, but failed to inflict any decisive defeat on Iran's forces. The contest was mainly waged by ground forces, though the opening weeks of the war saw both countries' air forces engaged as well.

After the first six months, by March 1981, Iranian forces had rallied to prevent further Iraqi advances. A second phase of the war began in mid-1982, when Iran took the offensive to push Iraq out of most of Iranian territory it had occupied and, a year later, carried the ground war into Iraqi territory. The war settled into a pattern of stalemate, as year after year Iran launched seasonal "final offensives" which never successfully broke through Iraqi defenses. This second phase coincided with the emergence of a new regional dimension, as the Iran-Iraq war became an Iranian-Arab war. Iraq secured the financial and political support of Saudi Arabia, Kuwait, and other oil-rich Arab states of the gulf, as well as political and limited military support from Jordan and Egypt. The goal of preventing an Iraqi defeat was also shared by the major powers. The Soviet Union, which had cut off arms shipments to Iraq at the beginning of the war, resumed its role as Iraq's major military supplier; France supplied sophisticated warplanes and missile systems; the United States provided important agricultural shipments and credits.

From the outset, both combatants targeted one another's oil export facilities. Iraqi facilities were closer to the war zone, and thus effectively closed early in the conflict. Iraq's vulnerability was compounded when Syria, in 1982, supported Iran by closing off Iraq's pipeline outlet across Syria to the Mediterranean. This left a pipeline through Turkey as Iraq's only oil export outlet until late in the war, when new pipelines through Saudi Arabia were opened. A third phase, the "tanker war," began in early 1984, when Iraq used French-supplied jets and missiles to interdict Iranian oil exports. Baghdad's aim was to employ technological superiority to break the Iranian siege on the ground. Because Iraqi oil exports by tanker were already closed down, Iran could retaliate only by attacking the shipping of Iraq's allies, Kuwait and Saudi Arabia, risking Western intervention to impose a cease-fire that would appear to favor Iraq.

Something like this scenario finally occurred by early 1987, when the United States responded to Kuwaiti requests for protection of its tankers by dispatching a naval force that grew to some fifty warships. This corresponded with the fourth and final phase of the war. Iran's last, unsuccessful "final offensive" of January–February 1987 was followed by a series of successful Iraqi campaigns to recover lost territory. The combination of Iraqi ground victories and a series of naval clashes with U.S. forces in the gulf, culminating in the destruction of an Iranian airliner that killed 291 civilians, persuaded Iran to accept UN Security Council Resolution 598 which established a cease-fire more or less on Iraqi terms. Negotiations toward a final settlement proceeded in a desultory fashion until the fall of 1990. Then Iraq, in the context of confrontation with the United States following Baghdad's invasion of Kuwait, accepted Iran's terms for settlement based on the status quo ante—namely, the 1975 Algiers accord.

Several dimensions to this conflict deserve mention. The first is the extent to which this was an "oil war." Without access to oil revenues—their own and in the case of Iraq those of its Arab allies—neither country could have sustained a war of this scope, intensity, and duration. The conflict, moreover, grew out of the Iranian Revolution, itself profoundly shaped by Iran's oil-based political economy, and both countries had experienced oil-motivated overt and covert interventions by the United States and other powers, interventions that also directly influenced the outcome of this conflict.

A second notable aspect is the durability of the postcolonial nation-state. Iranian appeals to *Shi'i* coreligionists had no more impact on Iraqi morale or loyalty than did Iraq's efforts to enlist the ethnically Arab population of southern Iran. National rather than sectarian or ethnic solidarities prevailed.

Finally, in many ways the Iran-Iraq War linked the Iranian Revolution of 1978–1979 to the 1991 Gulf War, the regional confrontation that followed Iraq's invasion of Kuwait in August 1990. Iraq emerged with its economy exhausted and its political ambitions frustrated, but its military much stronger and more cohesive. Kuwait provided both the provocations and the pretexts for Baghdad to make a new bid for regional hegemony. The war had also facilitated the extension of U.S. military forces in the region, both the important naval combat experience of 1987–1988 and, more significantly, the construction of sophisticated bases and ports in Saudi Arabia, without which the deployment of half of U.S. combat forces worldwide to the Gulf in the fall of 1990 would have been impossible.

B. The United Nations and the Second Gulf War: Security Council Resolution #687 (1991)*

Although the United States dominated the strategic planning and the actual fighting of the second Gulf war, an international coalition including such Arab states as Saudi Arabia, Egypt, and Syria took shape to back the American effort. The United Nations Security Council (the policy-making body of the UN) was also active during the conflict, monitoring it closely by issuing resolutions demanding that Iraq withdraw from Kuwait, imposing sanctions on the Baghdad government, and criticizing its mistreatment of Kuwaiti nationals. In late Febru-

---

*From United Nations Department of Public Information, DPI/110/Rev.3–41183, December 1991.

ary the Iraqi government accepted most of the UN resolutions and withdrew from Kuwait, deploying its forces to crush two rebellions in Iraq: the *Shiites* in the south and the Kurds in the north. Of the nineteen UN resolutions relating to the war, we print only one, #687, setting the conditions for the withdrawal of sanctions: Iraqi destruction of its nonconventional (chemical and nuclear) weapons. In the decade that followed a complicated interaction between Iraq, the UN, and the United States ensued over Resolution #687, as Saddam Husayn clearly wished to rebuild Iraq's military power and assert his country's sovereignty. The ability of UN inspectors to ensure that Iraq had ceased to produce chemical, biological, and atomic weapons provided one of the main issues. As we write these words the United States has threatened to invade Iraq (see Reading 27e) and Saddam Husayn has offered to readmit inspectors in order to head off such an invasion. Meanwhile the United States showed its intent to march to war, preferably backed by the United Nations, but alone if it seemed necessary.

Resolution 687   3 April 1991

The Security Council,

Welcoming the restoration to Kuwait of its sovereignty, independence, and territorial integrity and the return of its legitimate government,

Affirming the commitment of all Member States to the sovereignty, territorial integrity and political independence of Kuwait and Iraq, and noting the intention expressed by the member States cooperating with Kuwait . . . to bring their military presence in Iraq to an end as soon as possible. . . .

Reaffirming the need to be assured of Iraq's peaceful intentions in light of its unlawful invasion and occupation of Kuwait. . . .

Demands that Iraq and Kuwait respect the inviolability of the international boundary and the allocation of islands set out in the "Agreed Minutes Between the State of Kuwait and the Republic of Iraq Regarding the Restoration of Friendly Relations, Recognition and Related Matters. . . ."

Decides that Iraq shall unconditionally accept the destruction, removal, or rendering harmless, under international supervision, of:

all chemical and biological weapons and all stocks of agents and all related subsystems and components and all research, development, support and manufacturing facilities;

all ballistic missiles with a range greater than 150 kilometers and related major parts, and repair and production facilities. . . .

Decides . . .

Iraq shall submit to the Secretary-General, within fifteen days of the adoption of this resolution, a declaration of the locations, amounts and types of all items specified in paragraph[s 6 and 7] and agree to urgent, on-site inspection as specified below . . .

the forming of a Special Commission, which shall carry out immediate on-site inspection of Iraq's biological, chemical and missile capabilities, based on

Iraq's declarations and the designation of any additional locations by the Special Commission itself;

the yielding by Iraq of weapons in its possession to the Special Commission for destruction, removal or rendering harmless, taking into account the requirements of public safety . . .

the Secretary-General, in consultation with the appropriate Governments and, where appropriate, with the Director-General of the World Health Organization (WHO), within 45 days of the passage of this resolution, shall develop, and submit to the Council for approval, a plan calling for the completion of the following acts within 45 days of such approval:

[R]equests the Secretary-General, in consultation with the Special Commission, to develop a plan for the future ongoing monitoring and verification of Iraq's compliance with this paragraph, to be submitted to the Council for approval within 120 days of the passage of this resolution. . . .

Invites Iraq to reaffirm unconditionally its obligations under the Treaty on the Non-Proliferation of Nuclear Weapons, of 1 July 1968. . . .

Decides that Iraq shall unconditionally agree not to acquire or develop nuclear weapons or nuclear-weapons-usable material or any subsystems or components or any research, development, support or manufacturing facilities related to the above; to submit to the Secretary-General and the Director-General of the International Atomic Energy Agency (IAEA) within 15 days of the adoption of this resolution a declaration of the locations, amounts, and types of all items specified above; to place all of its nuclear-weapons-usable materials under the exclusive control, for custody and removal, of the IAEA.

Requires Iraq to inform the Council that it will not commit or support any act of international terrorism or allow any organization directed towards commission of such acts to operate within its territory and to condemn unequivocally and renounce all acts, methods, and practices of terrorism.

C. George H. W. Bush, The Second Gulf War and Kicking the Vietnam Syndrome (1991)*

The *Public Papers* of George Bush make it clear that during and after the second Gulf war, the campaign called Desert Storm, the U.S. president's mind, or the minds of his speechwriters, often turned to the Vietnam War of three decades or more earlier. He repeatedly assured his audiences that the war against Saddam Husayn was "not another Vietnam." By saying this Bush implied that the

---

*From various 1991 speeches of President George H. W. Bush, all found in *Public Papers of the Presidents of the United States: George Bush, 1991,* 2 vols. (Washington, DC: U.S. Government Printing Office, 1992), vol. I, pp. 44, 61, 78–79, 208.

United States would not lose its struggle in the Gulf region. The U.S. defeat in Vietnam obviously still rankled. In a radio broadcast to U.S. troops in the Gulf region, Bush proclaimed in triumph that the Americans had finally "kicked the Vietnam syndrome"—the unwillingness of the American public to see a war through to victory. But wars in the Middle East pose in a particularly acute way the problem of what "victory" means. Clearly in 1991 the United States and its allies won a military victory against Saddam Husayn, who had to withdraw his armies from Kuwait. But a decade later the designated enemy still ruled his country and at present the son of President George H. W. Bush has laid out his plans for another war against Iraq if U.N. inspections break down, or if Iraq impedes their operation.

Most Americans know instinctively why we are in the Gulf. They know we had to stop Saddam now, not later. They know that this brutal dictator will do anything, will use any weapon, will commit any outrage, no matter how many innocents suffer.

They know we must make sure that control of the world's oil resources does not fall into his hands, only to finance further aggression. They know that we need to build a new, enduring peace, based not on arms races and confrontation but on shared principles and the rule of law.

Democracy brings the undeniable value of thoughtful dissent, and we've heard some dissenting voices here at home—some, a handful, reckless; most responsible. But the fact that all voices have the right to speak out is one of the reasons we've been united in purpose and principle for 200 years.

Not Another Vietnam

Prior to ordering our forces into battle, I instructed our military commanders to take every necessary step to prevail as quickly as possible, and with the greatest degree of protection possible for American and allied service men and women. I've told the American people before that this will not be another Vietnam, and I repeat this here tonight. Our troops will have the best possible support in the entire world, and they will not be asked to fight with one hand tied behind their back. . . .They will continue to have the support they need to get the job done, get it done quickly, and with as little loss of life as possible. And that support is not just military, but moral—measured in the support our servicemen and women receive from every one of us here at home. When the brave men and women of Desert Storm return home, they will return to the love and respect of a grateful nation.

Kicking the Vietnam Syndrome

I made a comment . . . the other day about shedding the divisions that incurred from the Vietnam war. And I want to repeat and say especially to the Vietnam veterans that are here—and I just had the pleasure of meeting some in the hall—it's long overdue. It is long overdue that we kicked the Vietnam syndrome, because many veterans from that conflict came back and did not receive the proper acclaim that they deserve—that this nation was divided and we weren't as grateful as we should be. So somehow, when these troops come home, I hope that message goes out to those that served this country in the Vietnam War that we appreciate their service as well.

D. Zbigniew Brzezinski, "Some Stirred-up Muslims": Reflections on Soviet Intervention in Afghanistan (1998)*

This reading shows former national security adviser Zbigniew Brzezinski (1928–) reflecting on the advice he gave President Jimmy Carter in 1979 when the Soviet Union was contemplating its invasion of Afghanistan. An adherent of realpolitik, Brzezinski suggested that the United States discreetly encourage the Soviets to intervene, in order to accelerate the drain on Moscow's dwindling economic resources and hasten the Communist regime's collapse.

A decade after the Soviet Union had collapsed, in part because of its Afghan intervention, a French newspaper journalist gave Brzezinski a chance to reflect on his 1979 advice. He had no regrets, nor did he acknowledge the impact on U.S. global politics of having organized an international *jihad* against the Soviet Union and having armed and trained radical Muslims (some of whom would later turn against the United States and its allies) to act as U.S. surrogates. The sometimes devastating fallout created by "some stirred-up Muslims" counted little in Brzezinski's calculations when advancing American geopolitical aims.

Q: The former director of the CIA, Robert Gates, stated in his memoirs, *From the Shadows,* that American intelligence services began to aid the *Mujahadeen* in Afghanistan 6 months before the Soviet intervention. In this period you were the national security adviser to President Carter. You therefore played a role in this affair. Is that correct?

Brzezinski: Yes. According to the official version of history, CIA aid to the *Mujahadeen* began during 1980, that is to say, after the Soviet army invaded Afghanistan, 24 Dec 1979. But the reality, secretly guarded until now, is completely otherwise: Indeed, it was July 3, 1979, that President Carter signed the first directive for secret aid to the opponents of the pro-Soviet regime in Kabul. And that very day, I wrote a note to the president in which I explained to him that in my opinion this aid was going to induce a Soviet military intervention.

Q: Despite this risk, you were an advocate of this covert action. But perhaps you yourself desired this Soviet entry into war and looked to provoke it?

---

*From Zbigniew Brzezinski's interview in *Le Nouvel Observateur* (Paris), January 15–21, 1998, translated by Bill Blum and posted on www.emperors-clothes.com/interview/brz.html. By permission.

B: It isn't quite that. We didn't push the Russians to intervene, but we knowingly increased the probability that they would.

Q: When the Soviets justified their intervention by asserting that they . . . [intended] to fight against a secret . . . [intervention] of the United States in Afghanistan, people didn't believe them. However, there was a basic truth. You don't regret anything today?

B: Regret what? That secret operation was an excellent idea. It had the effect of drawing the Russians into the Afghan trap and you want me to regret it? The day that the Soviets officially crossed the border, I wrote to President Carter: We now have the opportunity of giving to the USSR its Vietnam war. Indeed, for almost 10 years, Moscow had to carry on a war unsupportable by the government, a conflict that brought about the demoralization and finally the breakup of the Soviet empire.

Q: And neither do you regret having supported the Islamic [radicalism)] . . . and advice to future terrorists.

B: What is most important to the history of the world? The Taliban or the collapse of the Soviet empire? Some stirred-up Muslims or the liberation of Central Europe and the end of the cold war?

Q: Some stirred-up Muslims? But it has been said and repeated: Islamic fundamentalism represents a world menace today.

B. Nonsense! It is said that the West had a global policy in regard to Islam. That is stupid. There isn't a global Islam. Look at Islam in a rational manner and without demagoguery or emotion. It is the leading religion of the world with 1.5 billion followers. But what is there in common among Saudi Arabian fundamentalism, moderate Morocco, Pakistan militarism, Egyptian pro-Western or Central Asian secularism? Nothing more than what unites the Christian countries.

Chapter VII

Ideologies, Movements, and Social Trends

Introduction

We use the term "ideologies" to denote theoretical visions of current reality that emerge from daily life, define paths to the future, and motivate people to collective action for change. They may be secular or religious, oppositional or supportive of existing conditions, and their efforts to initiate change may have positive or negative results. Leaders mobilize mass constituencies by offering ideologies in accessible forms. Inclusive, humane, and consistent ideologies may lead to beneficial changes, while narrowing, hateful ones tend to end in war and destruction. Often many ideologies exist, interact, and compete for followers at the same time. In this section we seek to show how the creators of twentieth-century ideologies in the modern Middle East and the larger Muslim world drew selectively on their predecessors, and sought to articulate and spread their diverse visions.

Young Ottomans

We start with one of the major breeding grounds for new ideas in the recent Middle East—the Ottoman empire. As we indicate in Chapter III, many of its inhabitants attempted to change in response to contemporary demands while accommodating imperial rule to the needs of different ethnic and religious communities. A new, highly articulate group of intellectuals, the Young Ottomans, appeared during the *Tanzimat* reform period of the nineteenth century (see Reading 10) and devised new ways to achieve state cohesiveness. By breaking down the old building blocks of the empire—the internally autonomous religious communities, the *millets*—they sought to substitute a society that brought all individuals directly under state control.

These reformers favored expansion of individual rights and civil liberties as well as the establishment of a constitution and a parliament. They also believed that Islam and modernity could coexist and opposed autocracy. Their persistence produced the short-lived 1876 Constitution, which Sultan Abd al-Hamid II (1842–1918) suspended when the 1878 Russo-Turkish War broke out. The Young Ottomans found themselves outmaneuvered by the sultan and his retinue of military officers who used this war, which the Ottomans lost, to silence domestic opposition.

Young Turks and Emerging Feminism

In 1909 Young Turks in the Ottoman army ousted the autocratic ruler and, as we discussed in Chapter III, took control of the state, reducing the sultans to figureheads. One of the active members of this group, a young military officer, Mustafa Kemal (1881–1938), would soon become the founder of modern Turkey (see Reading 15b).

Another prominent Young Turk activist, the feminist Halidé Edib (Adivar) (1884–1964), achieved fame and notoriety as a novelist and champion of women's emancipation. Her newspaper articles criticized polygamy and women's subordination and she joined the pan-Turkish Hearth movement to which the influential Ziya Gökalp (1876–1924) belonged. Outspoken, courageous, and democratic, she opposed as unrealistic Gökalp's notion of uniting all Turks across national boundaries including those living outside Turkey. She found Mustafa Kemal's reform program far more practical. But when Kemal became president, Edib criticized his dictatorial methods (see Reading 15c) and went into exile.

Earlier, during Abd al-Hamid II's reign, many Turkish intellectuals, male and female, fled to Cairo where British officials welcomed reformers who opposed the conservative *ulema* and advocated changes in the legal and educational systems. Several women's magazines at the turn of the century contributed to Egyptian intellectual ferment and its robust debates on such social issues as women's education and feminism. The idea of educating girls in primary and secondary schools took hold. The prominent Egyptian judge Qasim Amin (1863–1908) wrote *Liberation of Women* (1899), arguing in favor of marriage and divorce law reforms and the abolition of veiling.

The twentieth century brought major changes to the lives of Muslim women generally. Feminists called for suffrage extension, access to education, and changes in marriage and family laws. Huda Sharawi (1879–1947), an upperclass woman, founded with Mai Ziyada (1886–1941) the Intellectual Association of Egyptian Women, the forerunner of several other women's organizations. Upper-class women sponsored and helped run medical clinics and hospitals. Others from all classes participated actively in the mass movement to gain Egypt's independence.

Egyptian feminism developed in tandem with nationalism. Nationalist movements, though they rejected many feminist issues, provided an arena in which women could participate. By 1919 Sharawi, active in the *Wafd* Party, the leading Egyptian political movement, became president of its Women's Central Committee and four years later she founded the Egyptian Feminist Union. Her dynamism and organizational abilities, learned in the *harem*, helped propel women significantly forward. The movement spawned numerous organizations and journals for feminist assertion, and spurred awareness of women's issues throughout Egyptian urban society. Feminists won a major victory when Egypt raised the marriageable age to sixteen. By the end of the First World War Middle Easterners enjoyed access to some thirty women's publications and soon thereafter women could attend feminist meetings in urban settings, join with other women in political demonstrations, attend secondary schools, and work in new fields now opening up to them.

Young Turks in the Late Ottoman Empire

The ferment of the times affected the Ottoman empire and inspired activists to organize for rapid change. The Young Turks, organized in the Committee of Union and Progress (CUP), wanted a secular constitution that did not privilege Islam. After European territories, along with their populations, had seceded from the empire during the 1912 Balkan War, debate among these Young Turks centered on the two remaining groups remaining within the empire—Arabs and the Turks themselves—and whether they should share power, as the liberal faction believed, or exercise Turish domination as adherents of a centralized state maintained.

As defeat in the Balkan War marginalized the liberals and focused attention on holding together what remained of the Ottoman empire. Centralizers took charge of the state and adopted a program of Turkification, including harsh policies toward Arabs and Armenians (see Reading 14). In reaction, some Arabs within the empire began plotting ways to shake free of Turkish domination. As we showed in Chapter IV, Arab nationalism gained strength from Arab opposition to the new Turkish exclusionary policies.

Universalism, Conflict, and the Quest for Unity

The most compelling vision for unifying Muslim peoples came much earlier from the pan-Islamic advocate Jamal al-Din al-Afghani (1839–97), whose ideas and activism inspired many later movements. In his "Plan for Islamic Union" (see Reading 12), Afghani urged Muslims to embrace modern science and rationality and reject blind following of Islamic traditions. He incorporated religion into his broad universalistic pan-Islamic vision, which resonated across national boundaries. Believing that imperialism prevented achieving political unity, Afghani advocated the enhancement of the already considerable cultural unity among Muslims to facilitate resistance to European intervention. His unquestioned reputation as an anti-imperialist allowed his followers to adopt Western ideas and modern concepts without feeling that they had lost their identities as Muslims.

Other pan-nationalists such as Ziya Gökalp, mentioned above, and, even more ambitiously, the pan-Turanists who advocated unity of the varied people living in Central Asia, could not overcome the fact that Europeans controlled the vast regions that the pan-nationalists hoped to unite.

Muslims had lived for centuries in societies where Islam provided integrating concepts, while tribes, lineages, and villages gave people's lives local meanings consistent with Islam's universalizing beliefs. The balance between these two, the particular and the universal, allowed Muslim states to thrive. By creating artificial political units, as we showed in Chapters IV and V, European imperialism shattered this delicate balance that had evolved in the preceding Islamic centuries and produced the competing modern movements and ideologies this chapter explores.

Equilibrium did not imply frictionless harmony. The Muslim world experienced (and still experiences) war, conflict among states and social classes, and major intellectual disputes. Four schools of Islamic law, and divisions between *Sunnis* and *Shiites*, allowed diverse peoples to define codes of behavior and social practices in regional terms. While consensus existed on core religious beliefs, local laws and values varied sufficiently to allow for differences to develop and flourish. *Sufism*, or mysticism (see the introduction to Part I and Reading 4), continued to enrich and diversify Muslim experience.

The *Salafiyya* Reformist Movement

Variety of religious experience did not prevent Muslims from attempting to bring their societies into line with changing times. The *Salafiyya* movement, the name of which means return to the examples of the pious ancestors, tried to do that. Although the movement hearkened back to the traditions of the Prophet's time, it also embraced later scientific and technological advancements and attracted al-Afghani as one of its progenitors (see Reading 12). It also engaged many other Muslim intellectuals, such as Muhammad Abduh (1849–1905), a former collaborator of al-Afghani. Abduh gained great distinction in his time and accepted British appointment as *mufti* (chief Islamic religious judge) of Egypt, a position from which he could counter some of the influence of the conservative *ulema*. Although Abduh rejected al-Afghani's s anti-imperialism, the *mufti* accepted the *salafi* belief that Muslims need not follow Islamic teachings blindly, but should take advantage of their abilities to reason and choose among available alternatives. Abduh favored a popularly chosen representative government in which legislation would be guided by Islamic law and therefore saw no need to create an Islamic state. *Salafi* doctrines supporting rational choice provoked strong opposition from the more conservative *ulema* who, because they viewed the *Quran* and *hadith* as God's final word, followed these religious texts closely and discouraged most innovations.

The Syrian *salafi* intellectual Rashid Rida (1865–1935), whose opinions on Zionism we presented in Reading 18b, edited an influential Cairo newspaper, *al-Manar* (The Beacon). He differed from Abduh in his conviction that Muslims should one day live under an Islamic state.

By the 1930s and 1940s many *salafi* reformers made their peace with the colonial regimes. The old dynamism of the *salafiyya* movement evaporated in many parts of the Muslim world. Pan-Islam too had ebbed after Mustafa Kemal won power and abolished the Ottoman monarchy (see Chapter IV), thereby depriving Muslims of a *caliph* as a symbolic unifying figure. Abd al-Rahman Kawakabi (1849–1902), a Kurd living in Cairo, argued in favor of returning the caliphate to Arabia and a movement arose among Muslims in India to revive the institution. Although debates raged on this subject, nothing ever came of it. As *salifiyya* faded, other doctrines appeared, enabling colonized populations to confront their European overlords more effectively. These ideologies took both secular and religious form.

Arab Nationalist Ideology

In the immediate post–World War II era Arab nationalism emerged as the most potent Middle Eastern ideology and reshaped the politics and society of several states, including Egypt. While Jamal Abd al-Nasser (1918–70) defined the contents of Arab nationalism, it also had several lesser-known theoretical progenitors. One such figure, the educator Sati al-Husri (1882–1968), profoundly influenced the new generation of Arabs—especially military officers—who came of age after World War I. Influenced by European Romanticism and by al-Afghani, al-Husri viewed the Árab nation as a unit whose common language, history, and Islamic culture (shared also by Christians and Jews living in predominantly Muslim states) provided the cement for the cultural unity that would lead to the creation of the longed-for Arab state. Once Arabs had experienced their full national awakening, they could, al-Husri believed, establish that unified state. Until that time, he urged Arabs to keep alive the ideals of eventual unity.

Al-Husri's ideas influenced the *Baath* or Renaissance Party, founded by another Syrian, Michel Aflaq (1910–89), whose views on Arab unity we presented in Reading 15d. Aflaq viewed European imperialism as the main obstacle to social justice in the Arab world, so that the Baathist revolutionary movement had to unify Arabs, for the struggle against imperialism could not succeed in any single state. Aflaq believed that intellectuals had a special responsibility to create just societies throughout the Middle East—including the liberation of Palestine from Zionism. An ardent anti-Communist, Aflaq promoted a conception of socialism that had nothing in common with Marxism. Despite its belief in Arab unity, the internally contentious *Baath* movement split into two main factions—one Syrian, the other Iraqi—bitterly opposed to each other.

Nationalism had a great impact on Egypt, where military academies trained native soldiers to keep order and protect European influence. These schools became hotbeds of clandestine nationalist sentiment and discontent with Egypt's political and social system. Soldiers had a special set of grievances, having fought in the 1948 war that led to the creation of the state of Israel, and experienced the humiliation of defeat, which they blamed on the ineptitude of the corrupt, flamboyant King Farouk I (1920–65). The poorer ones knew Egypt's grinding poverty. Nearly everyone resented the persistence of British military occupation and recognized the inability of the *Wafd* or other political parties to achieve independence. A nearly bloodless uprising in 1952 by a secret group called the "Free Officers" included the young Colonel Jamal Abd al-Nasser, who abolished the monarchy and took power.

Nasser's Arab nationalism developed simultaneously with the growth of American global power. They both detested old European colonialism and Communism, but they projected very different postcolonial futures. The nationalists wanted self-government, control over their own resources, and a fairer distribution of wealth. The United States wanted an informal empire based on the "open door" concept: formally independent countries ruled by leaders who protected U.S. and allied states' investments and interests, opposed Communism, maintained stability, and received lavish compensation for these services. Although promoted in the vocabulary of "freedom," this U.S. agenda, advanced in the Cold War years, collided with the Arab nationalist agenda.

The Vulnerability of the Left

At first the Egyptian military coup d'état of 1952 gave new hope to the small leftist movements that had managed to emerge in several Middle Eastern countries. Compared to other ideological trends, Marxism had attracted relatively few adherents in this region: mainly in Afghanistan, on the Indian subcontinent, and among Jewish settlers in Palestine and the Labor Party in Israel. In Iraq the Communists had succeeded in extending party influence into rural areas, while the Iranian *Tudeh* (Communist) Party had made inroads among some urban intellectuals. With Soviet support a leftist People's Democratic Party of Afghanistan (PDPA) even succeeded in temporarily winning state power, as we point out in Chapter VIII. A small Egyptian Communist party developed, but found itself alternatively hounded and tolerated by Nasser's government. Fiercely anti-Communist *Baath* parties dominated Syria and Iraq and permitted no left opposition to exist openly. Other Socialist and Communist parties that emerged in the region made no secret of their secular and antireligious outlooks, which, coupled with their class-based universalism ("workers of the world unite!"), marginalized them, or set them in opposition to local nationalist and religious movements.

Independent movements, unions, organizations, and parties could not easily survive in one-party regimes. They challenged the very concept of unity within the national state. The efforts to build institutions of civil society and create strong nongovernmental organizations, trade unions, professional associations, and feminist groups in the authoritarian states of the Muslim world ran into major hurdles. Most nationalist regimes did not tolerate any internal opposition.

Nasser from Triumph to Defeat

When Nasser nationalized the Suez Canal in 1956 he ended Great Britain's three-quarter-century civilian and military presence in Egypt and won enormous popularity. The idea of Arab unity suddenly appeared as a genuine possibility.

Two years later Iraqi military officers overthrew the British-dominated monarchy. Under Nasser's guidance the moribund Arab League, founded in 1945, took on new life. In 1958 Syria and Egypt joined together in a single state, the United Arab Republic, which lasted a scant three years. Nasser's Syrian partners repudiated the merger when it became clear that he had subordinated Syrian interests to those of Egypt.

At home, Nasser's government advocated Arab socialism. At first they instituted a sweeping agrarian reform law, which took aim at the main cause of the country's poverty—the concentration of land ownership in the hands of a few. The new law limited the amount of land that individuals could own, and even though landlords found ways to circumvent it, many poor peasants and tenants received their own acreage. In addition, the regime enacted health and welfare measures, introduced minimum wages, and made provision for the improvement of the condition of women (see Reading 31a). Ambitious plans to increase food resources for Egypt's growing population envisioned construction of the Aswan dam on the Nile. At first Nasser's government gained acclaim throughout the Middle East for its developmental policies and its commitment to social justice, but when the regime outlawed all political parties except the official one (the socialist union), and cracked down on political dissent and radical movements, the cause of social justice in Egypt suffered.

Nasser's dramatic foreign policy steps gained him fame, as well as the wrath of Western countries and Israel. As a committed Arab nationalist, he advocated taking over foreign property. His popular ideas stirred much discussion in other Muslim countries where many favored nationalization of foreign industries and oil fields. Although his ideas potentially ran counter to Western interests, his European and American opponents misunderstood Nasser as a supporter of Communism.

Nasser also challenged the West by joining the leaders of Yugoslavia and India in refusing to align themselves either with the Soviet- or American-led power blocs. U.S. Secretary of State John Foster Dulles (1888–1959) viewed this neutralism as heresy and canceled promised U.S. assistance for the Aswan dam. Thereupon Nasser turned to the Soviet Union for aid and built the dam anyway. The British and French resented Nasser's anti-imperialism and his dealings with the Soviet Union, while Israel feared any assertive Arab state that might be able to forge durable Arab unity.

War followed war. Nasser's nationalization of the Suez Canal prompted an invasion of Egypt by Great Britain, France, and Israel. This blatant example of old-fashioned imperialism moved President Eisenhower to intervene diplomatically to force withdrawal. A decade later, in 1967, disputes between Israel and its Arab neighbors provoked another major war, which the Arabs decisively lost. With this loss the entire secular radical nationalist program that Nasser represented came crashing down, opening the way for the abandonment of Arab socialism.

Changing Course: Egypt Under Sadat and Mubarak

Nasser died three years after the 1967 defeat. His successor and former army officer Anwar Sadat (1918–1981) shifted course dramatically and stressed Egyptian rather than Arab nationalism. Sadat abandoned Nasser's nonalignment and sought American approval for his domestic policies, particularly the *infitah,* or opening of the Egyptian economy to the West (see Reading 31b).

Eventually, Sadat offered to make peace with Israel, but not before Egypt and Syria in 1973 jointly launched a surprise military assault on Israeli positions in former Egyptian territory. These attacks caught the Israeli armed forces in Sinai off guard and surprised the general Israeli population, which had a contemptuous opinion of the Arabs' military abilities. The initial victories of Arab armies, despite their eventual defeat, gave a great boost to Arab prestige and self-esteem.

After the 1973 war Sadat visited Jerusalem and by the end of the decade negotiated a peace agreement with Israel, under the auspices of U.S. President Jimmy Carter, at Camp David, Maryland. Done without support from neighboring Arab states, this act weakened regional unity. The Arab League expelled Egypt, and relocated its headquarters from Cairo to Tunis. Another, more dramatic sign of the furious hostility to Sadat came in 1981 when Egyptian Islamic radical soldiers—belonging to an offshoot organization of the Muslim Brotherhood—assassinated him during a military parade. Egypt's isolation from the Arab world continued under Sadat's successor, Hosni Mubarak (1928–   ), but eased in 1987 when the Arab League readmitted Egypt, and ended altogether in 1990–91 when, along with other Arab states, Egypt joined the U.S.–led anti-Iraq coalition. But Egypt never afterward regained the stature and authority it had enjoyed under Nasser.

Mubarak continued Sadat's Western-oriented economic policies and gained billions of dollars in annual aid from the United States for retaining peaceful relations with Israel. Disturbing trends developed, however, as Egypt cracked down on all oppositional activity.

Lebanon: The Path to Civil War

The United States demonstrated in 1956 its power to discipline its own allies when it forced Britain, France, and Israel to withdraw their troops from Egypt—sent to punish Nasser in 1956 for nationalizing the Suez Canal. A year later, faced with Nasser's growing popularity and the growth of radical nationalism throughout the region, and suspecting Soviet meddling, President Dwight D. Eisenhower (1890–1969) issued a pledge to send armed forces to any Middle Eastern country under assault from "International Communism" (Reading 27b). Months later he dispatched 15,000 U.S. marines to Lebanon on the request of rightist politicians who felt threatened not by Communists but by the unraveling of that country's archaic "confessional system." Eisenhower intended to bolster conservative regimes such as the one in Lebanon in order to thwart the spread of radical Arab nationalism in the oil-rich Middle East.

It did not work. Soon after U.S. troops arrived in Lebanon, a nationalist revolt in Iraq overthrew the monarchy, and hastened the collapse of the anti-Communist Baghdad Pact, once the keystone of a U.S.–designed alliance system along the southern perimeter of the Soviet Union. The subsequent U.S. intervention froze Lebanon's politics and the unresolved tensions between opposing Lebanese parties and sects led in 1975 to a ferocious civil war that soon brought first the Israelis as invaders into Lebanon, then the Syrians as new political arbiters (see Reading 31c).

Sadat's decision to make peace with Israel in 1977 had ripple effects throughout the region and abroad. It formed part of his *infitah* policy of opening his country to Western investment and privatizing the economy, which aligned Egypt with the United States (see Reading 31b). This also had serious consequences for Lebanon, where Palestinians, expelled in 1970–71 from Jordan because they posed a threat to the Hashemite ruling dynasty, had settled. Prime Minister Menachem Begin (1913–92) of Israel took the Camp David agreements as assurance that the Egyptians would not retaliate from the south when Israeli forces attacked Palestine Liberation Organization (PLO) bases across the northern border in Lebanon. The U.S. approved such an attack on the PLO because its ally, Israel, wished it, and also because of Washington's long-standing desire to weaken Arab radical nationalism,

The Israelis followed an initial foray into Lebanon in 1978 by a 1982 assault deep into Lebanese territory led by Defense Minister (and future prime minister) Ariel Sharon. The Palestinians set themselves up, alongside Lebanese warlords, as rivals for power in the increasingly bitter civil war between Lebanese sectarian factions.

The Israeli invasions did not end this war, nor were they intended to do so; they aimed at driving the Palestinian commandos away from Israel's borders, and that was the result. The PLO and its leader, Yasir Arafat, had taken refuge in distant Tunisia, leaving Palestinian civilians in the undefended Sabra and Shatila refugee camps in Beirut, where they were massacred by Lebanese Maronite soldiers allied with the Israelis. Both Sharon and Begin soon after left office in shame.

By 1991, with all sides exhausted, the Arab League had agreed to allow Syrian troops to enter Lebanon and end the civil war (see Reading 31c). Syrians remained in the country as the dominant force, except in a southern zone held by Israel. In response this Israeli occupation, a new Iranian-supported Islamic radical movement, *Hezbollah* (Party of God), arose among Lebanon's *Shiite* population. *Hezbollah* carried out a guerrilla war that eventually wore down the occupying Israelis, who withdrew from most of the occupied zone in 2000. *Hezbollah's* success in ridding Lebanon of the Israelis, and of Israel's collaborationist Lebanese militia, gave a great boost to Islamic radicals throughout the Middle East and the Islamic world, and contributed to their growing militancy.

Islamic Radicalism in Egypt

After the assassination of the Muslim Brotherhood's founder, Hasan al-Banna (1906–49), the head of the Brotherhood's women's division, Zainab al-Ghazzali (1917–   ) encouraged the Egyptian writer Sayyid Qutb (1906–66) to take over as the principal ideologue and leader of this important Islamic radical movement. As we see in Reading 32c, Qutb advocated the temporary withdrawal of Muslims from the corruption of Egyptian life, similar to the *hijra*, the migration of early Muslims from Mecca to Medina fourteen centuries before. Away from compromised rulers and regimes, people would learn proper Quranic principles. Later, when they returned to their communities, some of them, Qutb preached, should prepare to infiltrate the military and seize power. The Nasser regime executed Qutb in 1966.

Qutb's Islamic radical followers, and those active in later offshoots of the Muslim Brotherhood, came mainly from two recent rural migrant groups populating the slums that surrounded most Egyptian towns: young professional engineers and technicians and also jobless and underemployed youth, casualties of the inability of both the government and private businesses to create jobs for the growing population. These conclusions are suggested by Saad Ibrahim's study of the social origins of imprisoned Egyptian Islamic radicals in Reading 33a. To such recruits, Iran's 1979 Islamic revolution proved that determined militants could overturn a corrupt, powerful modern secular state, even one backed by the United States.

The secret Islamic radical organizations that grew up in the shadow of the secular states that dominated the Middle East and the Islamic world since the 1950s represent an entirely modern phenomenon. Although their leaders often embrace ideologies rooted in the distant Islamic past, they employ up-to-date technology for communications, transportation, and, when deemed necessary, initiating violence.

Rhetorically and increasingly in practice many radical Muslims oppose the Western countries and particularly the United States, which support Israel, viewed by them as an alien state inserted into the Muslim world. They argue that Muslim countries such as Egypt should never have diplomatically recognized the Jewish state, and look toward its eventual destruction. They reject on principle the 1978–79 Camp David accords, and all following attempts to make peace, and not only because these diplomatic efforts failed to solve the Zionist-Palestinian conflict. They believe that secular groups that fight against Israel and its external allies lack the dedication and fervor that Islamic conviction alone can bring to the struggle. The Muslim radicals call for armed *jihad,* and they also believe that the willingness of suicide bombers to die in attacks on Israeli soldiers and civilians and to launch guerrilla attacks on Jewish settlements in the West Bank and Gaza territories works to counter Israel's overwhelming military strength— fed as it is by U.S. military aid and diplomatic backing. Such groups as Lebanon's

Islamic *Jihad* and *Hezbollah,* and the Islamic Resistance Movement of Palestine (*Hamas,* Reading 24c), share these views. Aside from their military and terrorist activities, some Islamic organizations follow the lead of the Muslim Brotherhood in carrying out extensive social welfare, health, and educational activities, which the regimes that they oppose often neglect.

Until recently, both Israel and the United States found it in their interests to encourage and even support selectively the growth of some of these Islamic radical movements. Israeli leaders initially perceived such groups as useful since they deepened divisions in Palestinian society and weakened the PLO. Starting in 1987, as the first *intifada* developed, Israel allowed *Hamas* to organize, hold demonstrations, and collect funds, while attempting to restrict similar activities within the ranks of the PLO.

Out of overriding concern that secular Arab nationalists in the Middle East would attack foreign interests and challenge Western control of the region's oil, the United States too began to look more favorably on Islamic radical regimes and movements. This became particularly evident for a short time under President Reagan's administration when U.S. relations temporarily thawed with the Islamic Republic of Iran. Washington came to realize that despite their frequent denunciation of Israel and of "the Great Satan" (the Iranian nickname for the United States), the Iranian ayatollahs, believing in private property, might pose little long-term threat to U.S. interests in the region. After the revolution, when socialists in the Iranian parliament attempted to nationalize factories and farms in that country, the Council of Experts, made up of clergy, vetoed the legislation. The scandal known as Irangate then followed, that ill-conceived policy whereby Israel secretly supplied Iran with U.S. weapons with Washington's approval. A confused U.S. public could not fathom how their government had embraced the same regime that held more than fifty U.S. hostages for fifteen months during Jimmy Carter's presidency.

U.S. policy in Afghanistan provides the most significant recent example of the primacy of Washington's Cold War–based policies. When local Communists, and later the Soviets themselves, tried to maintain a Marxist regime, the Americans backed the anti-Communist *mujahidin,* whom they then called "Islamic freedom fighters." But when these *mujahidin* proved incapable of maintaining a society stable enough to support investment in pipelines to carry oil and natural gas through Afghanistan from Central Asia, or to protect the population from harm, Washington turned to the most extreme of Islamic radical movements, Afghanistan's *Taliban.*

Changing U.S. Priorities

The 1993 bombing of the World Trade Center towers prompted the American government to begin reconsideration of its policy of pragmatic support of

Islamic radicals over secular nationalists. Later, when Osama bin Laden's *Al Qaeda* organization initiated its systematic attacks on U.S. installations and military targets, Washington switched priorities to what President Bill Clinton called the global battle against terrorism (see Reading 27d), which intensified under George W. Bush's administration following September 11, 2001.

As this antiterror campaign developed, its momentum reshaped American policy toward the Israeli-Palestinian conflict. American denunciations of global terrorism facilitated a more sympathetic attitude in Washington toward the renewed Israeli offensive against the PLO in response to intensified suicide bombings by Palestinians. While occasionally criticizing Prime Minister Sharon's excesses, President Bush essentially gave a green light to the government in Israel to reoccupy Palestinian West Bank territory as part of the new global war on terrorism and to undermine and weaken the PLO (see Reading 26f).

31. Egypt and Lebanon:
Secularism and Confessionalism

This reading shows the very different ways in which two Middle Eastern states, Egypt and Lebanon, organized their societies and politics. These differences have historical roots, which we explore in the earlier sections. The Egyptians chose primarily secular options, while the Lebanese built their constitution around religious confessionalism, with each of the important religious groupings in the country sharing political power. Part a of this reading presents Nasser's views on nationalism and Arab Socialism; part b gives Sadat's very different pro-Western, capitalist visions for Egypt. Under both Nasser and Sadat, and their successor, Hosni Mubarak, Egypt remained a secular one-party state that tolerated little dissent. As the government tried to deal with Islamic radicals by co-opting and placating some of them, however, the situation in Egypt became grim for most dissenters of varying political tendencies, who often underwent harassment, imprisonment, torture, exile, and death.

Part c shows how even the Syrians—Baathists and secularists—had to recognize the confessional nature of Lebanese politics in order to help bring peace to that country after years of civil war. With Arab League backing, in 1989 Syria forced Lebanon's battling sects (some of whom long opposed the confessional system) into endorsing at Taif a new constitution for Lebanon that called for the abolition of confessionalism, while actually reinforcing it. The presidency and other high posts of the government would still be allocated to each of the important religious groupings, or confessions, but the Syrians made sure that Lebanon's Muslims got a greater share of power.

A. Jamal Abd al-Nasser, Arab Socialism (1964)*

Grandson of peasants, Nasser had a natural sympathy for the poor that supplied much of the impetus for his reforms. His program of Arab Socialism embodied the search for a middle way between what he called the "exploitative" system of unbridled capitalism on the one hand and the rigidities of centrally directed socialist states on the Soviet model on the other. Nasser's Egypt rhetorically embraced "unrestricted social and political democracy" and the achievement of social justice, but in practice it remained an authoritarian state that fell far short of attaining either democracy or justice. The Socialist Union, a government-dominated political party, was the only party allowed to exist. Egypt under Nasser did, however, manage to throw off imperial domination, as well as carry out land reform.

The elected popular Assembly is a serious and decisive event in the life of the Arab nation. The revolutionary popular will has opened the road and prepared for it this major role. The will of the popular revolution has paved the way for what it was able to achieve with God's help, namely, the defeat of imperialism, the overthrow of reaction and exploitative capitalism [which are] partners [in an] unholy alliance against the people, [and which] wish to terrorize and subjugate the people so that they may be able to proceed in the spoliation of their wealth and labor and ensure their own luxury and wealth at the expense of the blood and sweat which flow unlimited from millions of workers.

This Assembly which stems from the will of the masses must always stay with them. It cannot afford to raise itself pompously above their demands; nor can it forgetfully drop behind their aspirations. It must always keep abreast of the masses and must never forget to light up their life. This Assembly has . . . grown out of a revolution and it must march along the path toward the revolution to the end. It has grown out of hope and it must carry this hope all the way [to] fruition. It has grown out of the will for drastic change and it must attain the broad objectives of change, the objectives of unbounded sufficiency and justice, of unrestricted social and political democracy, of a society with equal opportunities for all and no class differences, and of new vistas in which the Arab individual can do honor to life and life can do honor to the Arab individual.

[Certain . . .] principles [guided Egypt's political life in 1952–64]: . . . the elimination of imperialism and its traitorous Egyptian agents; the eradication of feudalism; the destruction of monopoly and of the domination of capital over the government; [and] the establishment of social justice.

What happened to each of these . . . principles? How did each one of them turn into a weapon bringing victory and sovereignty to the Egyptians over the few years which have elapsed since then?

---

*From Jamal Abd al-Nasser's "Address . . . at the Meeting of the National Assembly's Ordinary Session," March 26, 1964 (Cairo: Egyptian State Information Department, 1964), pp. 3–7. Bracketed material added by the editors.

[T] *he elimination of imperialism.* I do not think we need much effort to prove that this nation today is foremost among the independent countries of the world after having been a foreign-occupied base firmly gripped for more than 70 years and terrorized by 80,000 armed British soldiers on the banks of the Suez Canal.

[The] *eradication of feudalism.* The ownership of the greater and more fertile part of the agricultural land was in the hands of a small number of big landlords, besides other vast areas held by agricultural companies that were owned by foreigners, though they tried to conceal their real identity behind Egyptian facades. In accordance with the socialist laws, including the Agrarian Reform law, the area of lands that has been expropriated for distribution to farmers amounted to 944,457 *feddans* [980,346 acres].

Through [regulation] of the rental of agricultural land, which was a part of the Agrarian Reform [Law]; through the consolidation of cooperation and availability of interest-free financing as well as [reorganization] of agricultural land on the largest scale, there came about a transformation in the conditions governing the productivity of the agricultural land, besides the transformation which took place in connection with its ownership.

[T] *he abolition of monopoly and the domination of capital over the government.* . . . [T]he public sector . . . consolidated itself through the complete domination of capital . . . in banks, insurance companies, foreign and internal trade companies which were nationalized and which became public property. It [i.e., the consolidation of the public sector] was followed by the socialist decrees of July, 1961, which ensured the public ownership of the larger part of the means of production, particularly in the industrial field. Clear limits for public ownership were then drawn so as to include the main skeleton of production, such as railways, roads, ports, airports, motor power, the means for land, sea, and air transport, then the heavy, medium, mining and [the] building materials industries, the effective part of the consumer industries, in a manner which would leave no room for exploitation. This was connected with the realization of complete popular supervision over foreign trade, the breaking of any monopoly in internal trade which was thrown open to private activity.

[T] *he establishment of social justice.* Experience has proven that social justice cannot be attained except upon the two bases of sufficiency and justice. . . . Sufficiency—that is, increased production—without justice means a further monopolization of wealth. Justice—that is, the distribution of national income without increasing its potentiality—ends only in the distribution of poverty and misery. But both together—that is, sufficiency and justice—hand in hand [they] reach their objective.

In the field of international action: The final step lay in the liquidation of the ruling alliance between reaction and imperialism as well as the liquidation of their inherited privileges. There was no enmity toward any individual or family. . . . We were opposed to class distinction. It was our right to eliminate its effect but it was not our right to destroy the dignity and humanity of individuals. Therefore, a new page should be opened in front of all without distinction.

We should not at any cost, permit the emergence of a new class which would believe that it is entitled to inherit privileges from the old class.

We moved from the domination of one class which monopolized all privileges, to . . . social democracy.

The old picture of a state of princes, pashas, and foreigners has disappeared and [has been] replaced by a state of farmers, workers, intellectuals, soldiers, and national capital.

[T]here are three major objectives which we have unlimited capacity to achieve.

First: There is the objective of continuous development, a comprehensive plan preparing for another comprehensive plan, a doubling of the national income followed by another doubling based on the result of the first doubling.

Second: There comes after development the objective of democracy and the continuous expansion of its framework and deepening of its concept.

We have to complete the structure of the political organization of the Socialist Union. Though the general structure of this Union is now perceptible before us, [it] . . . should be full of effective and creative life.

The Socialist Union, in short, is the political organization of the working popular powers through which they work to ensure that authority shall, at all times, remain in their hands and shall not move into other hands.

This is the aim of all political organizations, including parties. But whereas a party represents a certain interest in any country or class, the Socialist Union does not represent a group or a class but expresses the political will of the active popular powers allied within its framework.

Third: There follows the stage . . . of realizing over-all Arab unity. Although we cannot as yet, give this inevitable unity its final shape, the success in realizing the aim of development and the aim of democracy in this country, which we consider to be the base and vanguard of the Arab nation, will bring nearer the day of unity defined its final form, and mold it in accordance with the will and requirements of national conscience.

B. Anwar Sadat, *Infitah:* Opening to the West (1975)*

In the *infitah*, or opening to the West, Sadat offered a domestic policy that anticipated what others would later call "neoliberalism." It involved privatization of government-owned enterprises, cutting back on subsidies to the poor, and aimed at pleasing the United States in order to attract foreign investment. These policies deepened inequality and triggered riots in many parts of the country. Sadat quelled the discontent by rescinding some of the International Monetary Fund's

---

*From Anwar Sadat's speech to the New York Economic Club (October 30, 1975), in *Speeches and Interviews of President Anwar Al Sadat During His Official Visit to the United States* (Cairo: Egyptian State Information Service, n.d.), pp. 47–53. American spellings adopted.

prescriptions for cutbacks in welfare and other unpopular measures. The ease
with which Nasser's successor reversed Egypt's leftist experiment reveals the
shallowness of the government-directed program of Arab Socialism.

Sadat delivered this speech in New York City, to an audience largely made up
of approving American businessmen. Near the end, Sadat referred to "the process
of peace," apparently in anticipation of his 1979 overture to Israel. It took several years before U.S. business leaders and the U.S. government responded to
the Egyptian president's sharp shift in policy and when he and Israeli Prime Minister
Menachem Begin signed the peace treaty at the White House in 1979, Sadat got
his reward for joining the Western camp. Other Arabs took a dimmer view.

Egypt, which was traditionally thought of and classified as an agricultural society, was among the first states to introduce industry to our region. By the nineteen thirties we were able to lay the foundation of a modern industrial base
capable of propelling us later into the contemporary industrial revolution. Thus,
when we embarked on a vigorous drive in the sixties to revitalize our system of
production and widen the scope of our manufactured commodities, the transformation was a natural and smooth one. As we went along, we discovered the
need for making adjustments here and there and I believe we have been quite
flexible. Those among you who are acquainted with us know that we are open-
minded and willing to do everything we can for the success of our people.

We continued to develop our agriculture and the past few years have witnessed a vigorous drive on our part with the aim of increasing production and
rejuvenating the system. We are accelerating the rate of mechanization, intro-
ducing higher yield varieties of grain, and doubling our production of ferti-
lizers. We are spreading light industry and handicrafts in the countryside. Together
with that we have been focusing on the need for social development in over
4,000 Egyptian villages. Schools are being built every day, medical centers
established, family planning units set, running water is replacing canal water
for human use and last, but not least, electricity is changing the quality of life
altogether in the country.

Today, agriculture remains the largest sector of the Egyptian economy,
accounting for 30 percent of the gross national product and providing for almost one half of the labor force. Industry contributes 20 percent of the gross
national product and employs 13 percent of the labor force. We are developing our economy in both sectors simultaneously and along parallel lines.

One of the main fruits of our industrialization drive has been the training
of a skilled labor force capable of absorbing and assimilating new . . . techniques
and processes. In fact, this skilled labor force is one of the pillars of development in the entire region, not only in Egypt.

Without getting into the details of our development plans, suffice it to mention a few words about our open-door economic policy which is a corner-stone
in our endeavor to rejuvenate the Egyptian economy. This policy is designed
to encourage and stimulate more capital investment, be it local, regional or foreign
capital. To reach this end, we are liberalizing our laws . . . combating bureau-

cracy and rewarding initiative. The objectives of that policy have not been fully attained yet and some remnants of the past still persist. But we are working very hard on it with determination, for we know that reforming an established structure could be much more difficult than creating a new one.

We realize as well the need to reassure foreign investors and convince them that they are not taking any risk while investing in Egypt in this era. At a time when runaway inflation is rampant and recession is overshadowing many parts of the world, capital could be scarce and hard to get. But we are doing everything we can to make Egypt an attractive spot for investors. So long as their objective is mutual benefit and not exploitation, they will find us most responsive and attentive to their needs. Any economic activity has to fit in our overall plans for economic development which sets the priorities of our national endeavor. We are not forfeiting our economic independence or mortgaging our economy. But we welcome a profitable and rewarding partnership from which both sides would benefit. We promulgated a law ... for regulating foreign investment and free zones. It granted foreign investment numerous immunities, privileges and exemptions. Foreign investors are now immune to nationalization, sequestration, expropriation and seizure. The law also guarantees the free repatriation of profit and capital. . . . Also we have just concluded a convention for the avoidance of double taxation which aims, among other things, at the elimination of obstacles to international trade and investment. Still, we are prepared to respond to any constructive suggestions and make the necessary adjustment as we proceed ahead in this process.

We are also reviving the stock exchange, which remained defunct for about 15 years.

With the peace structure we are building, the situation will certainly be more promising and conducive. We are doing everything we can to reinforce and accelerate the process of peace, at some cost occasionally. But we are determined to pursue this road for the good of our people and in the interest of other nations. At the time when there were some discouraging signs I took my decision to reopen the Suez Canal. I did that as a unilateral contribution on our part to world trade and prosperity. We firmly believe that all nations have much to gain and nothing to lose by doubling their exchange[s] and intensifying their transaction[s]. To this goal, we are committed and devoted and I am sure that you are too. Thank you.

C. The Taif Agreement: Syrian Influence Over Lebanon (1989)*

The political instability that gradually overwhelmed Lebanon after World War II, and erupted into civil war in the mid-1970s originated in the mandate

---

*From *The Beirut Review*, vol. 1, 1 (Spring 1991), 122–23, 127, 130, 147–48. Bracketed material added by the editors. By permission.

period when the French carved a Lebanese state out of the former Ottoman province of Syria (see Part IV). Created initially both to maximize the political power of the Christian Maronites and to give France a colony in the eastern Mediterranean, Lebanon gained its independence in 1946. But its political system bore marks of its origin. Maronite leadership predominated and resisted the idea of an Arab Lebanon, which would challenge their privileged political position. Muslims, rapidly becoming the majority group, identified with the Arab world and resented Maronite domination of the country.

In addition to Lebanon's considerable internal problems, the Palestinian-Israeli conflict migrated across Lebanon's southern border, reshaping and intensifying the sectarian divisions. Attacking and being attacked by Israeli forces, the Jordanian-based Palestine Liberation Organization (PLO) had become a threat to Jordan's government, which ordered its expulsion in 1970. The PLO, forced to relocate to Lebanon, greatly complicated the Christian-Muslim struggle there. This reading presents a Syrian-inspired solution that emphasized Lebanon's connection to the Arab world but also retained much of its former confessionalism.

The deal was made in an extraordinary way: the entire Lebanese parliament flew into the Saudi Arabian city of Taif at the end of September 1989 where under Syrian pressure they adopted a "Document of National Accord" (the Taif Agreement). Later Lebanese parliamentarians grafted the agreement onto the pre-existing Lebanese Constitution, which, leaving out routine clauses, we present in this reading. After Syrian troops neutralized and disarmed several Lebanese militias, these parliamentary steps effectively ended the Lebanese Civil War, which had lasted for sixteen years.

Changes in the Constitution of Lebanon

PREAMBLE (Introduced in 1990)

Lebanon is a sovereign, free, and independent country. It is a final homeland for all its citizens. It is unified in its territory, people, and institutions within the boundaries defined in this Constitution and recognized internationally.

Lebanon is Arab in its identity and in its association. It is a founding and active member of the League of Arab States and abides by its pacts and covenants. Lebanon is also a founding and active member of the United Nations Organization and abides by its covenants and by the Universal Declaration of Human Rights. The Governments shall embody these principles in all fields and areas without exception.

Lebanon is a parliamentary democratic republic based on respect for public liberties, especially the freedom of opinion and belief, and respect for social justice and equality of rights and duties among all citizens without discrimination.

The people are the source of authority and sovereignty; they shall exercise these powers through the Constitutional institutions.

The political system is established on the principles of separation, balance, and cooperation amongst the various branches of Government.

The economic system is free and ensures private initiative and the right of private property.

The even development among regions on the educational, social, and economic levels shall be a basic pillar of the unity of the state and the stability of the system.

The abolition of political confessionalism shall be a basic national goal and shall be achieved according to a gradual plan.

Lebanese territory is one for all Lebanese. Every Lebanese shall have the right to live in any part of it and to enjoy the sovereignty of law whenever he resides. There shall be no segregation of the people on the basis of any type of belonging, and no fragmentation, partition, or colonization.

There shall be no constitutional legitimacy for any authority which contradicts the "pact of communal coexistence" [the National Pact of 1943].

Article 17. (As amended in 1990) Executive power shall be entrusted to the Council of Ministers, and the Council shall exercise it in accordance with conditions laid down in this Constitution.

Article 24. (As amended in 1990) The Chamber of Deputies shall be composed of elected members; their number and the method of their election shall be determined by the electoral laws in effect. Until such time as the Chamber enacts new electoral laws on a non-confessional basis, the distribution of seats shall be according to the following principles:

a. Equal representation between Christians and Muslims.
b. Proportional representation among the confessional groups within each religious community.
c. Proportional representation among geographic regions.

Exceptionally, and for one time only, the seats that are currently vacant, as well as the new seats that have been established by Law, shall be filled by appointment, all at once, and by a two-thirds majority of the Government of National Unity. This is to establish equality between Christians and Muslims as stipulated in the Document of National Accord [i.e., the Taif Agreement]. . . . The electoral laws will specify the details regarding the implementation of this clause.

Article 65. (As amended in 1990) Executive authority shall be vested in the Council of Ministers. It shall be the authority to which the armed forces are subject. Among the powers that it shall exercise are the following:

1. It shall set the general policy of the Government in all fields, prepare Bills and organizational Decrees and make the decisions necessary for implementing them.
2. It shall watch over the execution of Laws and regulations and supervise the activities of all the Government's branches including the civil, military, and security administrations and institutions without exception.

3. It shall appoint Government employees and dismiss them and accept their resignations according to the Law.

4. It shall dissolve the Chamber of Deputies upon the request of the President of the Republic if the Chamber of Deputies, for no compelling reasons, fails to meet during one of its regular periods and fails to meet throughout two successive extraordinary periods, each longer than one month, or if the Chamber returns an annual budget plan with the aim of paralyzing the Government. This right cannot be exercised a second time if it is for the same reasons which led to the dissolution of the Chamber of the first time.

5. The Council of Ministers shall meet in a locale specifically set aside for it, and the President shall chair its meetings when he attends. The legal quorum for a Council meeting shall be a two-thirds majority of its members. It shall make its decisions by consensus. If that is not possible, it shall make its decisions by vote of the majority of attending members. Basic national issues shall require the approval of two-thirds of the members of the Council named in the Decree forming the Cabinet. Basic national issues are considered the following:

   The amendment of the Constitution, the declaration of a state of emergency and its termination, war and peace, general mobilization, international agreements and treaties, the annual Government budget, comprehensive and long-term development project, the appointment of Grade One government employees and their equivalents, the review of the administrative map, the dissolution of the Chamber of Deputies, electoral Laws, nationality Laws, personal status Laws, and the dismissal of Ministers.

32. Early Ideologues of Islamic Radicalism

This reading presents the ideas of three important Muslim thinkers and activists separated by seven centuries, all influential in shaping the ideas and movements of contemporary Islamic radicalism. We start with Taqi al-Din Ahmad ibn Taimiyya (1263–1328), one of the most important jurists of the Hanbali school of legal interpretation, which we described in the Introduction to Chapter I. His influence extended to the eighteenth century and beyond and helped shape the views of Muhammad ibn Abd al-Wahhab (1703–92), whose alliance with the Saudi dynasty in Arabia made Wahhabism—an uncompromising unitarian view of God—the official doctrine of Saudi Arabia. The two other Muslim radicals we have chosen for this reading flourished in the twentieth century:

the Egyptians Hasan al-Banna (1906–49, in part b) and Sayyid Qutb (1906–66, part c), both of the Muslim Brotherhood.

Westerners often sum up the common features of the ideologies created by these men, and others like them, by the term "fundamentalism." But that term lacks precision, so we prefer Islamic radicalism. Whatever we call these beliefs, in the twentieth century they exuded a disdain for Western materialism and a longing for a substantial Muslim portion of the earth free of corrupt leaders in which an Islamic state (or states) can lead the faithful. We can see in some of these texts the pervasive influence of Jamal al-Din al-Afghani, whose activism, ideas about pan-Islam, and contempt for unworthy leaders we presented in Reading 12.

A. Taqi al-Din Ahmad ibn Taimiyya, Against Heretical Innovation (early fourteenth century)*

Ibn Taimiyya, who used to storm into taverns and smash wine bottles, has greatly influenced present-day Islamic radicalism. His writings, still largely untranslated from the Arabic, consist of scholarly works, demonstrating a wide knowledge of the Islamic corpus, as well as *fatwas* (legal opinions) against those who stray from what he believed to be the clearly demarked path of Islam. This required submission to the will of God as revealed in the *Quran* and in other holy texts, rather than using communal consensus to define new areas of the law. From his position of stern theological certainty, ibn Taimiyya criticized *Sufi* saint worship and the philosophers' quest for knowledge as impermissible heretical innovations. Unlike some of his Islamic radical followers, ibn Taimiyya treated with respect those Muslims who followed the core of the religion and lived righteously, and while he might have criticized their ideas, he did not attempt to dictate to them his conception of proper behavior.

Enjoying a large popular following in his lifetime, ibn Taimiyya often offended the authorities in Cairo and Damascus by his *fatwas* and his unsparing criticism of theological error. He paid for his outspokenness by spending long periods in prison, from where he continued to issue *fatwas*. Legend has it that in his last prison sentence, some five months after his jailers had deprived him of paper, ink, and quill pens, he died in despair.

Consensus (Ijmā)

The Sufis built their doctrine on desire (*al-irāda*) and that is indispensable—but on the condition that it is the desire to serve God alone in what He has commanded. The exponents of *kalām* [theology] have built their doctrine on

---

*From various Arabic-language writings by ibn Taimiyya, in John Alden Williams, ed., *The Word of Islam* (Austin, TX: University of Texas Press, 1994), pp. 164–69. Notes deleted. Bracketed material added by the editors. By permission.

reason, which leads to knowledge, and it is also indispensable—on condition that it is knowledge of those things about which the Messenger has informed us, and reasoning about the sure things which he indicated—Divine Revelation. Both of these conditions are indispensable (to right use of desire and knowledge).

Whoever seeks knowledge without desire, or desire without knowledge is in error, and whoever seeks them both without following the Prophet is also in error.

Desire is only profitable if it is the desire to serve God according to the Law He laid down, not with heretical innovation.

It is similar with those who part with the Prophet and follow a way other than that of the believers. . . . And whoever has followed another way has separated from the Prophet, and exposed himself to the Divine Threat (*wa'īd*). Whoever departs from the consensus of the Muslims has followed another way absolutely, and accordingly exposed himself to the Divine Threat. If it says they are only to blame if they separate from the way of the Prophet, we reply: The two things are bound together, because everything in which Muslims agree must be backed by texts from the Messenger of God, so that whoever opposes them opposes the Messenger, and whoever opposes the Messenger opposes God. It necessarily follows that everything the Muslims agree on was clearly revealed through the Messenger, and that is the truth.

So there is absolutely no question on which they unite which has not been clearly demonstrated by the Messenger, but this has escaped some people, and they know of Consensus and point to it as one would point to a text, without knowing the text. Consensus is a second proof added to the text, like an example. Whatever Consensus indicates is indicated by the Book and the *Sunna* [behavior of the Prophet Muhammad]. All that the *Qur'ān* indicates also came from the Prophet, since the *Qur'ān* and the *Sunna* both came through him, so there can be no question on which Muslims agree not based on a text.

The Companions had an understanding of the *Qur'ān* hidden from the moderns . . . who now seek for precepts in what they believe about Consensus and Logical Analogy (*qiyās*). Whatever modern says that Consensus is the basis of the greater part of the Law has given himself away, for it is lack of knowledge of the Book and the *Sunna* which obliges him to say it. Similarly when they hold that new events require use of logical analogy for interpretation, because there is no indication in the texts—that is only the statement of one who has no knowledge of Book or *Sunna*, with their clear rules for making all judgments.

It is often, or even usually, impossible to know what is Consensus—for who can encompass all the opinions of all religious experts (*mujtahidīn*)? Quite the contrary with the texts; knowledge of these is possible, and easy by comparison. The ancient (*salaf*) judged by the Book first, since the *Sunna* would not contradict the *Qur'ān* . . . if there is anything abrogated in the *Qur'ān*, the abrogation is written there. . . . If an answer is not found in the *Qur'ān*, one should look in the *Sunna*, and . . . there is nothing there which is abrogated, by Consensus or anything else . . . for true Consensus cannot contradict the *Qur'ān* and the *Sunna.*

The Necessity of the Legal Punishments (Hudūd)

It is not permissible when guilt is established by proof or by witness to suspend the legal punishment, either by remitting it or by substituting a fine or any other thing: the hand (of a thief) must be cut off, for the application of the punishments is one of the acts of cult (*'ibādāt*), like the Holy War in the Way of God, and it must be kept in mind that the application of legal sanctions is one of the acts of God's mercy, so that the ruler must be strict by applying it and let no compassion deter or delay him in the observance of God's religion. Let his goal be to have mercy on God's creatures by deterring men from things rejected by God, and not to discharge his wrath or gratify his desire for power.

The Hisba

To bid to good and reject the reprehended is not obligatory on every individual in essence, but is to be carried out as far as is possible, and since the Holy War is its completion, it is exactly like the Holy War. Any man who performs his (other) duties and does not fight the Holy War sins; and every one must act according to his ability, as the Prophet said: "Whoever sees something reprehensible, let him change it with his own hand, and if he is unable, with his tongue, and if he is unable to do that, in his heart."

So if it is thus, it is known that the bidding to good and the rejection of the reprehended, together with its completion, the Holy War, is one of the most important things we are ordered to perform.

Pantheists

Often have I thought that the appearance of such as these [pantheist *Ṣūfīs*] is the chief cause for the appearance of the Mongol Tatars and the disappearance of the Law of Islam, and that they are the vanguard of Antichrist the One-eyed, the Great Liar who shall assert that he is God.

On Philosophy and al-Ghazālī [1058–1111]

According to the so-called philosophers, there are three kinds of happiness; sensual, imaginative, and intellectual which is knowledge. . . . Thus they hold that the happiness of the soul consists in the knowledge of eternal things . . . then they imagine that the heavens . . . (are eternal) and that the soul acquires happiness through knowing them.

Abū Hāmid (al-Ghazālī) in his works . . . also suggests this. His statements are a bridge between the Muslims and the philosophers. . . . This is why in his works like the *Ihyā'* he teaches that the goal of all action is only knowledge, which is also the essence of the philosopher's teaching. He magnifies the renunciation of the world which (preoccupies him more) than *tawhīd*, which is serving God alone. *Tawhīd* alone comprises true love of God.

These so-called philosophers magnify the separation of the soul from the material body, which means renunciation of physical desires and of the world. . . . In pursuance of this, Abū Hāmid has divided the mystic path into three stages . . . . What he has made the goal of human life, *viz.* the knowledge of God, His attributes, His actions, and angels, in his *Al-Madnūn*—which is pure philosophy—is worse than the beliefs of the (old) idolatrous Arabs, let alone of Jews and Christians.

B. Hasan al-Banna, Overcome Western Materialism (late 1930s)*

While a small stratum of Middle Easterners benefited from imperialism, the vast majority experienced daily oppression, misery, and disdain from the haughty imperial officials who swarmed into Muslim lands. With its immensely valuable man-made waterway, the Suez Canal, the British took over Egypt in 1882, as we discussed in Chapter III, and Egyptians bore a heavy burden of outside control. From this colonial historical context arose one of the region's most significant protest movements—the Muslim Brotherhood (*al-Ikhwan al-Muslimin*). Founded in the canal town of Ismailiya by schoolteacher Hasan al-Banna in 1928, the organization grew rapidly inside and outside of Egypt during the 1930s. The Brotherhood had five hundred branches in Egypt alone by the end of that decade. Its membership rapidly grew to hundreds of thousands, its adherents from different social strata: poor urban immigrants from the countryside, university students who faced prospects of low-paid civil service positions, and petty professionals. Al-Banna headed the Brotherhood until his 1949 assassination, most likely carried out by Egyptian security forces.

Al-Banna adapted the Islamic doctrines of *Salafiyya*, which we discussed in the introduction to this section, to a world of uncertainty and insecurity. Initially aimed at ousting the British, the Muslim Brotherhood also aided the Palestinians in the 1930s and established in Egypt social welfare and charitable operations that often responded to social needs more effectively than governmental agencies. After World War II, the Muslim Brotherhood set up underground paramilitary units to murder politicians, which unleashed a wave of terror and counterterror operations in Egypt. After al-Banna's death the organization

*From Hasan al-Banna, "Between Yesterday and Today" (n.d., c. late 1930s), in *Five Tracts of Hasan al-Banna*, edited and translated by Charles Wendell (Berkeley, CA: University of California Press, 1978), pp. 27–28, 31–34. Arabic words italicized. By permission.

reconstituted itself and remained an important institution as its branches spread throughout the Middle East and influenced Islamic radicals elsewhere in the Muslim world.

The Europeans worked assiduously to enable the tide of . . . materialistic life, with its corrupting traits and its murderous germs, to overwhelm all the Islamic lands toward which their hands were outstretched. An ill destiny overtook these under their domination, for they were avid to appropriate for themselves the elements of power and prosperity through science, knowledge, industry, and good organization, while barring these very nations from them. They laid their plans for this social aggression in masterly fashion, invoking the aid of their political acumen and their military predominance until they had accomplished their desire. They deluded the Muslim leaders by granting them loans and entering into financial dealings with them, making all of this easy and effortless for them, and thus they were able to obtain the right to infiltrate the economy and to flood the countries with their capital, their banks, and their companies; to take over the workings of the economic machinery as they wished; and to monopolize, to the exclusion of the inhabitants, enormous profits and immense wealth. After that, they were able to alter the basic principles of government, justice, and education, and to imbue political, juridical, and cultural systems with their own peculiar character in even the most powerful Islamic countries. They imported their half-naked women into these regions, together with their liquors, their theaters, their dance halls, their amusements, their stories, their newspapers, their novels, their whims, their silly games, and their vices. Here they countenanced crimes they did not tolerate in their own countries, and decked out this frivolous, strident world, reeking with sin and redolent with vice, to the eyes of deluded, unsophisticated Muslims of wealth and prestige, and to those of rank and authority. . . . The day must soon come when the castles of this materialistic civilization will be laid low upon the heads of their inhabitants. They will feel the burning of a spiritual hunger in which their hearts and souls will go up in flames, and they will find no sustenance, no healing, no remedy, save in the teachings of this Noble Book.

Our General Aims: What do we want, Brethren? Do we want to hoard up wealth, which is an evanescent shadow? Or do we want dominion over the earth? . . . [A]lways bear in mind that you have two fundamental goals:

(1) That the Islamic fatherland be freed from all foreign domination.

(2) That a free Islamic state may arise in this free fatherland, acting according to the precepts of Islam, applying its social regulations, proclaiming its sound principles, and broadcasting its sage mission to all mankind. For as long as this state does not emerge, the Muslims in their totality are committing sin, and are responsible before God the Lofty, the Great, for their failure to establish it and for their slackness in creating it. In these bewildering circumstances, it is counter to humanity that a state should arise, extolling an ideology of injustice and proclaiming a propaganda of oppression, while there should be no one

among all mankind working for the advent of a state founded on truth, justice, and peace. We want to realize these two goals in the Nile Valley and the Arab domain, and in every land which God has made fortunate through the Islamic creed: a religion, a nationality, and a creed uniting all Muslims.

Our Special Aims: Following these two aims, we have some special aims without the realization of which our society cannot become completely Islamic. Brethren, recall that more than 60 percent of the Egyptians live at a subhuman level, that they get enough to eat only through the most arduous toil, and that Egypt is threatened by murderous famines and exposed to many economic problems of which only God can know the outcome. Recall too that there are more than 320 foreign companies in Egypt, monopolizing all public utilities and all important facilities in every part of the country; that the wheels of commerce, industry, and all economic institutions are in the hands of profiteering foreigners; and that our wealth in land is being transferred with lighting speed from the possession of our compatriots to that of these others. Recall also that Egypt, out of the entire civilized world, is the most subject to diseases, plagues, and illnesses; that over 90 percent of the Egyptian people are threatened by physical infirmity, the loss of some sensory perception, and a variety of sicknesses and ailments; and that Egypt is still backward; . . . more than 100,000 have never gone farther than . . . elementary school. . . . Recall that crime has doubled in Egypt, and that it is increasing at an alarming rate to the point that the prisons are putting out more graduates than the schools; that up to the present time Egypt has been unable to outfit a single army division with its full complement of materiel; and that these symptoms and phenomena may be observed in any Islamic country. Among your aims are to work for the reform of education; to war against poverty, ignorance, disease, and crime; and to create an exemplary society which will deserve to be associated with the Islamic Sacred Law.

Our General Means of Procedure: How will we arrive at these goals? Speeches, pronouncements, letters, lessons, lectures, diagnosis of the ailment and prescription of the medicine—all these by themselves are useless and will never realize a single aim, nor will they advance a single agent of our mission to any one of his goals. Nevertheless, missions do have certain means of procedure which they must adopt and according to which they must operate. The general procedural means used by all missions are invariable and unchanging, and they are limited to the three following matters:

(1) Deep faith.
(2) Precise organization.
(3) Uninterrupted work.

These are your general procedural measures, Brethren, so believe in your ideology, form your ranks about it, work on its behalf and stand unwaveringly by it.

Additional Procedures: Besides these general procedures, there may be additional ones which must be adopted and strictly adhered to. . . . We may be asked to go against entrenched habits and usages, and to rebel against regulations and situations which people take for granted and are familiar with. But then in its deeper essence, our mission is actually a rebellion against accepted usage and a change in habits and situations. Are you then prepared for this, brethren?

Some Discouragement: Many people will say: What do these tracts mean? Of what use can they be for building an *umma* and rebuilding a society burdened with these chronic problems and sunk in such a welter of corruptions? How will you manage the economy on a nonprofit basis? How ill you act on the woman question? How will you obtain your rights without the use of force? Know, Brethren, that Satan slips his whispered suggestions into the aspirations of every reformer, but that God cancels out what Satan whispers; then God decrees His miracles, for God is Knowing, Wise. Remind all of these people that history, in telling us of past and contemporary nations, also gives us admonitions and lessons. And a nation that is determined to live cannot die.

C. Sayyid Qutb, Corruptions of the Modern World (1964)*

An Egyptian writer and teacher, Qutb (1906–66) took over as the Muslim Brotherhood's principal strategist soon after Hasan al-Banna's death (see section b, this reading). At first the Brotherhood welcomed the 1952 military revolt that overthrew Egypt's monarchical regime, which had remained subservient to Great Britain. But when the secular orientation of Egypt's leader, Jamal Abd al-Nasser, became evident, and the new ruler's agenda of Arab Socialism unfurled (see Reading 31a), the Islamic radicals turned against it.

The argument made by Qutb invoked the ancient Islamic notion of *jahiliyya*, an Arabic word that combines the meanings of ignorance and barbarism and describes the condition of the world before the *Quran*'s revelation. Qutb, writing his *Milestones* in prison where he witnessed the torture and killing of his fellow Muslim Brothers, pondered the lack of moral fiber in Egypt's regime and society. Qutb advocated using force to transform the state according to Islamic norms. After an assassination attempt on his own life, Nasser ordered Qutb's execution.

Mankind today is on the brink of a precipice, not because of the danger of complete annihilation . . . but because humanity is devoid of those vital values which are necessary not only for its healthy development but also for its real progress. Even the Western world realizes that Western civilization is unable to present any healthy values for the guidance of mankind.

---

*From Sayyid Qutb, *Milestones* (1964, rev. ed., Cedar Rapids, IA: Unity Publishing Co., n.d.), pp. 7–13. Notes removed. By permission.

Democracy in the West has become infertile to such an extent that it is borrowing from the systems of the Eastern bloc, especially in the economic system, under the name of socialism. It is the same with the Eastern bloc. Its social theories, foremost among which is Marxism, in the beginning attracted not only a large number of people from the East but also from the West, as it was a way of life based on a creed. But now Marxism is defeated on the plane of thought, and if it is stated that not a single nation in the world is truly Marxist, it will not be an exaggeration. On the whole this theory conflicts with man's nature and its needs. This ideology prospers only in a degenerate society or in a society which has become cowed as a result of some form of prolonged dictatorship. But now, even under these circumstances, its materialistic economic system is failing, although this was the only foundation on which its structure was based. Russia, which is the leader of the communist countries, is itself suffering from shortages of food. Although during the times of the Tsars Russia used to produce surplus food, it now has to import food from abroad and has to sell its reserves of gold for this purpose. The main reason for this is the failure of the system of collective farming, or, one can say, the failure of a system which is against human nature.

It is essential for mankind to have new leadership!

The leadership of mankind by Western man is now on the decline, not because Western culture has become poor materially or because its economic and military power has become weak. The period of the Western system has come to an end primarily because it is deprived of those life-giving values which enabled it to be the leader of mankind.

It is necessary for the new leadership to preserve and develop the material fruits of the creative genius of Europe, and also to provide mankind with such high ideals and values as have so far remained undiscovered by mankind, and which will also acquaint humanity with a way of life which is harmonious with human nature.

Islam is the only system which possesses these values and this way of life.

The period of the resurgence of science has also come to an end. This period, which began with the Renaissance in the sixteenth century after Christ and reached its zenith in the eighteenth and nineteenth centuries, does not possess a reviving spirit.

All nationalistic and chauvinistic ideologies which have appeared in modern times, and all the movements and theories derived from them, have also lost their vitality. In short, all man-made individual or collective theories have proved to be failures.

At this crucial and bewildering juncture, the turn of Islam and the Muslim community has arrived—the turn of Islam, which does not prohibit material inventions.

Islam cannot fulfill its role except by taking concrete form in a society, rather, in a nation; for man does not have to listen, especially in this age, to an abstract theory which is not seen materialized in a living society. From this point of view, we can say that the Muslim community has been extinct for a few centuries. . . . The Muslim community with these characteristics vanished at the moment the laws of God became suspended on earth.

If Islam is again to play the role of the leader of mankind, then it is necessary that the Muslim community be restored to its original form.

It is necessary to revive that Muslim community which is buried under the debris of the man-made traditions of several generations, and which is crushed under the weight of those false laws and customs which are not even remotely related to the Islamic teachings, and which, in spite of all this, calls itself the "world of Islam."

I am aware that between the attempt at "revival" and the attainment of "leadership" there is a great distance, as the Muslim community has long ago vanished from existence and from observation, and the leadership of mankind has long since passed to other ideologies and other nations, other concepts and other systems. This was the era during which Europe's genius created its marvelous works in science, culture, law and material production, due to which mankind has progressed to great heights of creativity and material comfort. It is not easy to find fault with the inventors of such marvelous things, especially since what we call the "world of Islam" is completely devoid of all this beauty.

But in spite of all this, it is necessary to revive Islam. The distance between the revival of Islam and the attainment of world leadership may be vast, and there may be great difficulties on the way; but the first step must be taken for the revival of Islam.

The Muslim community today is neither capable of nor required to present before mankind great genius in material inventions, which will make the world bow its head before its supremacy and thus re-establish once more its world leadership. Europe's creative mind is far ahead in this area, and at least for a few centuries to come we cannot expect to compete with Europe and attain supremacy over it in these fields.

Hence we must have some other quality, that quality which modern civilization does not possess.

But this does not mean that we should neglect material progress. . . . [I]t is an essential condition for our very existence; and Islam . . . makes material progress obligatory for us.

To attain the leadership of mankind, we must have something to offer besides material progress, and this other quality can only be a faith and a way of life which on the one hand conserves the benefits of modern science and technology, and on the other fulfills the basic human needs on the same level of excellence as technology has fulfilled them in the sphere of material comfort. And then this faith and way of life must take concrete form in a human society— in other words, in a Muslim society.

If we look at the sources and foundations of modern ways of living, it becomes clear that the whole world is steeped in *Jahiliyyah* and all the marvelous material comfort and high-level inventions do not diminish this ignorance. This

Jahiliyyah is based on rebellion against God's sovereignty on earth. It transfers to man one of the greatest attributes of God, namely sovereignty, and makes some men lords over others. It . . . takes the form of claiming that the right to create values, to legislate rules of collective behavior, and to choose any way of life rests with men, without regard to what God has prescribed. The result of this rebellion against the authority of God is the oppression of His creatures. Thus the humiliation of the common man under the communist systems and the exploitation of individuals and nations due to greed for wealth and impe- rialism under the capitalist systems are but a corollary of rebellion against God's authority and the denial of the dignity of man given to him by God.

[W]e need to initiate the movement of Islamic revival in some Muslim country. Only such a revivalist movement will eventually attain to the status of world leadership, whether the distance is near or far.

How is it possible to start the task of reviving Islam?

It is necessary that there should be a vanguard which sets out with this determination and then keeps walking on the path, marching through the vast ocean of *Jahiliyyah* which has encompassed the entire world. During its course, it should keep itself somewhat aloof from this all-encompassing *Jahiliyyah* and should also keep some ties with it.

It is necessary that this vanguard should know the landmarks and the mile- stones of the road toward this goal so that they may recognize the starting place, the nature, the responsibilities and the ultimate purpose of this long journey. Not only this, but they ought to be aware of their position as opposed to this *Jahiliyyah*, which has struck its stakes throughout the earth: when to co-operate with others and when to separate from them; what characteristics and qualities they should cultivate, and with what characteristics and qualities the *Jahiliyyah* immediately surrounding them is armed; how to address the people of *Jahiliyyah* in the language of Islam, and what topics and problems ought to be discussed; and where and how to obtain guidance in all these matters.

The milestones will necessarily be determined by the light of the first source of this faith—the Holy *Qur'an*—and from its basic teachings, and from the concept which it created in the minds of the first groups of Muslims, those whom God raised to fulfill His will, those who once changed the course of human history in the direction ordained by God.

33. Modern Islamic Radicalism

This reading presents two very different accounts of contemporary Islamic radical movements. Part a is a sociological analysis of Egyptian Islamic radi- cals by Saad Eddin Ibrahim based on his interviews with them in prison. Part b consists of decrees issued by one of the few Islamic movements to hold (temporarily) state power—the *Taliban* in Afghanistan. Neither of these selections are pleasing to read: they uphold humiliation of people, curbing happiness and killing, and deviate significantly from the tenets of mainstream Islamic practice and belief. It would give an inaccurate picture of Islam to look only at the most militant of its radical adherents. Would practitioners of any religion like to be judged by the most extreme of their fellow believers?

A. Saad Eddin Ibrahim, Egypt's Muslim Militants (1985)*

Ibrahim's study is one of the few available examples of empirical research on Islamic radicalism. Some of the 34 imprisoned Islamic radicals he interviewed belonged to al-Fanniya al-Askaria, the Technical Military Academy (MA), the group that assassinated Egyptian President Anwar al-Sadat in 1981.

In the early sections of his essay (not printed here) Ibrahim reported that his sample included no alienated misfits, but devout, technically educated young men of good families most of whose fathers held mid-level government jobs. Deeply affected by the Arab defeat in the 1967 war with Israel, they turned to Islam for answers to their anguish. They read and pondered the writings of Jamal al-Din al-Afghani (see Reading 12), the *Shiite* Iranian intellectual, Ali Shariati (1933–77), Hassan al-Banna and Sayid Qutb (see Reading 32, parts b and c), and considered their own activities continuations of the work of the Muslim Brotherhood. Since they believed that righteous Muslims must devote themselves to building a community of the faithful, these men joined organizations of like-minded militants, rather than following conventional *ulema* whom they called "pulpit parrots" more concerned about rituals rather than the core beliefs of Islam. The radicals embraced assassinations and other forms of violence, according to Ibrahim. They derived "deep joy in defying society," and willingly endured imprisonment and torture for their beliefs.

A sociologist and pro-democracy activist, Ibrahim received his Ph.D. from the University of Washington, and taught at the American University in Cairo. A paperback collection of his essays, *Egypt, Islam and Democracy*, appeared in 2002. Several times he found himself imprisoned for "spreading tendentious rumors" about election fraud and government corruption in Egypt. In 2002 an Egyptian court sentenced Ibrahim to seven years of hard labor, prompting President George W. Bush to threaten to withhold U.S. aid funds unless Egyptian authorities released Ibrahim.

---

*From Saad Eddin Ibrahim, "Egypt's Islamic Militants," in Nicholas S. Hopkins and Saad Eddin Ibrahim, eds., *Arab Society: Social Science Perspectives* (Cairo: American University in Cairo Press, 1985), pp. 497–506. Arabic words italicized. American spellings adopted. Bracketed material added by the editors. By permission.

Social Profile

. . . The social profile of those who join radical leftist groups seems quite similar to that of the Islamic militants [studied here]. The only significant difference, in the case of Egypt, is a preponderance of those with rural backgrounds among Islamic militants, compared with a typically urban background among the leftists. Why have people with roughly the same social profile flocked to militant Islamic movements more than to leftist and Marxist groups?

At least four factors seem . . . to have tilted the balance in favor of the Islamic groups. One is the ability of the ruling elites to discredit leftist and Marxist opponents and atheists and agents of the Soviet Union, bent on destroying the authentic Islamic national heritage. Such charges are drummed in day after day by the state-controlled media, enabling the state to crush the left with impunity. It is much harder to use the same weapons against groups which proclaim Islam as their ideology and are avowedly anti-foreign and anti-communist.

A second factor has to do with the recent historical setbacks of quasi-socialist experiments in Egypt and the Arab world. Nasser's crushing defeat in the 1967 war was attributed to his entire system, including his socialist policies and his relationship with the Soviet Union. Socialism, Marxism and the Soviet Union, so it is claimed, have been "tried" and found wanting.

A third factor has to do with the pervasiveness and deep rootedness of Islam throughout the entire region. In Egypt, particularly, people are said to be quite religious. Even the most avowed liberal or leftist secularist regimes in the area find it necessary and expedient to invoke Islam when they institute any major new policy. For any militant Islamic movement, nearly half of its task with potential recruits is accomplished by virtue of socialization and cultural sanctions since childhood. All that remains is to raise political consciousness and to impose organizational discipline. For a Marxist movement, the task includes the eradication of negative cultural stereotypes of Marxism as well as politicizing, organizing and inculcating its precepts.

A fourth factor is the strong sense of communion which Muslim groups provide for their members. The typical recruit is usually of recent rural background, a newcomer to a huge, impersonal city. In an earlier time, relatives and fellow villagers would offer the newcomer a soft landing in the city. This mode of adjustment still exists for some, but for an increasing number of migrants such mechanisms are not there. The militant Islamic groups, with their emphasis on "brotherhood," and mutual material and spiritual support, become the equivalent of an extended family. This function in particular is not matched by other, rival political movements.

Islamic militancy has assumed the task of repelling external encroachment, enhancing the socioeconomic prospects of the middle and lower classes, and galvanizing the imagination of the educated youth. These classes have tried other, secular alternatives, but all seem to have fallen short of fulfilling their promises. With the mounting troubles of each secular alternative, the appeal of Islamic militancy grows until it becomes a tidal force. The last such cycle was stemmed only by the 1952 revolution, which addressed itself to the national and socioeconomic issues bedeviling the middle and lower classes. When Nasserism seemed to have run out of steam in the late 1960s, Islamic militancy began its present ascendancy.

Two factors will determine the future of Egypt's Islamic militants. The first is the ability of the present regime or another secular alternative to address itself to the issues of independence, social equity, and a credible vision for the future which enlists the commitment of the educated youth. The second is the presence of other regional models. An effective secular alternative may appear in a neighboring country, with great appeal to middle class educated youth in Egypt. But the most imposing regional model today is Iran. The Islamic republic's success in dealing with a host of global, societal and individual issues would enhance Islamic militancy. Its failure, especially from within and in the absence of foreign intervention, would set back Islamic militancy. The vision of establishing an Islamic social order has dazzled the imaginations of Muslim for ages. It usually becomes a passionate craving during social crises or in the aftermath of national humiliation at the hands of an outside power. The Islamic vision will never be reduced to its proper size until it is tried at least once. This why the Iranian revolution is uniquely significant at this time for the future of the region, and Egypt in particular, as well as for Iran itself. . . .

The militants concede that men have neglected women's rights and been excessive in extracting obligations. But this is due to the overall corruption and irreligiosity of the present social order. They are not against women receiving equal education up to the highest level. They insist, however, that woman's rightful place is the home and that her first obligation is to her husband and to the socialization of true Muslim children. Women could work outside the home if they had fulfilled their primary obligation, and if the interests of the community . . . called for it. The Military Academy group was closer to this egalitarian model than [the other Islamic radical group under study], *al-Takfir wal-higra*. But *al-Takfir* had female members while the former did not. Both groups insisted on the imperative of modesty, protecting women from temptation . . . and the separation of sexes in public places. The application of *hudud* (Islamic legal codes) with regard to sexual offenses are both necessary and sufficient to ensure these ends. The family is perceived as the basic unit of Muslim society. Its soundness derives from strict observance of *shari'a* values and regulation. Authority and protection flow from the male head of household down to females and the young; respect and obedience flow in the opposite direction. In short, the Muslim family is built around obedience, complementarity, protection and respect—not around equality, competition, and self-reliance. . . .

B. Taliban Decrees about Women, Men's Beards, Children's Games and Music (1996)*

Ahmed Rashid entitles the chapter on women in his 2000 book *Taliban* "A Vanished Gender," and then he provides the evidence in the texts that make up this reading—documents distributed by *Taliban* officials in Kabul to Western agencies operating in Afghanistan. By 1998 most Western nongovernmental organizations (NGOs), United Nations agencies, and offices of the European Community had left the country because of their unwillingness to implement the *Taliban* strictures on women and because of the dangers of war.

Rashid traces *Taliban* attitudes to the internal dynamic of the movement, its adherents drawn from rootless boys, war orphans, refugees and trained in the "totally male society" of politicized *madrasas,* or religious schools. The *Taliban* have spent little time in the company of women. For them women belong confined within the family, under the authority of father, brother, or husband. The *Taliban* forbade female employment except for medical work (and that carried out only under severe restrictions). Eventually most women's work and education halted under wartime *Taliban* rule.

The Religious Police regulated men's, women's, and children's behavior. Restrictions fell on men with short beards or long uncut hair, on children who flew kites or played soccer, on people who watched television, and on wedding guests who enjoyed music.

Decree announced by the General Presidency of . . . the Religious Police. . . . Kabul, November 1996.

Women you should not step outside your residence. If you go outside the house you should not be like women who used to go [out] with fashionable clothes wearing much cosmetics and appearing in front of every man [as if it was] before the coming of Islam.

Islam as a rescuing religion has determined specific dignity for women, [and] Islam has valuable instructions for women. Women should not create such opportunity to attract the attention of useless people who will not look at them with a good eye. Women have the responsibility as a teacher or coordinator for her family. Husband, brother, father have the responsibility for providing the family with the necessary life requirements (food, clothes, etc). In case women are required to go outside the residence for the purposes of education, social needs or social services they should cover themselves in accordance with Islamic *Sharia* regulation. If women are going outside with fashionable, ornamental,

---

*Taliban decrees relating to cultural issues and women (Kabul, 1996) in Ahmed Rashid, *Taliban: Militant Islam, Oil and Fundamentalism in Central Asia* (New Haven and London: Yale University Press, 2000), pp. 217–19. Bracketed material added by the editors. Arabic words italicized. By permission.

tight and charming clothes to show themselves, they will be cursed by the Islamic *Sharia* and should never expect to go to heaven.

All family elders and every Muslim have responsibility in this respect. We request all family elders to keep tight control over their families and avoid these social problems. Otherwise these women will be threatened, investigated and severely punished as well as the family elders by the forces of the Religious Police.

The Religious Police . . . have the responsibility and duty to struggle against these social problems and will continue their effort until evil is finished.

Rules of work for the State Hospitals and private clinics based on Islamic *Sharia* principles. Ministry of Health, on behalf of *Amir ul Momineen Mullah* Mohammed Omar. Kabul, November 1996.

1. Female patients should go to female physicians. In case a male physician is needed, the female patient should be accompanied by her close relative.
2. During examination, the female patients and male physicians both should be dressed with Islamic *hijab* (veil).
3. Male physicians should not touch or see the other parts of female patients except for the affected part.
4. Waiting room for female patients should be safely covered.
5. The person who regulates turn [the receptionist] for female patients should be a female.
6. During the night duty, in . . . [the] rooms [in] which female patients are hospitalized, the male doctor without the call of the patient is not allowed to enter the room.
7. Sitting and speaking between male and female doctors are not allowed, if there be need for discussion, it should be done with *hijab*.
8. Female doctors should wear simple clothes, they are not allowed to wear stylish clothes or use cosmetics or make-up.
9. Female doctors and nurses are not allowed to enter the rooms where male patients are hospitalized.
10. Hospital staff should pray in mosques on time.
11. The Religious Police are allowed to go for control at any time and nobody can prevent them.

Anybody who violates the order will be punished as per Islamic regulations.

General Presidency . . . of Religious Police, Kabul, December 1996.

1. To prevent sedition and female uncover[ing]. . . . No drivers are allowed to pick up women who are using Iranian *burqa* [*chadors*, or scarves, covering the hair but not the face]. In case of violation the driver will be imprisoned. If such kind of female are observed in the street their house will be found and their husbands punished. If the women . . . [wear] stimu-

lating and attractive cloth[ing] and [there are] . . . no accompany[ing] . . . close male relative[s] with them, the drivers should not pick them up.

2. To prevent music. . . . In shops, hotels, vehicles and rickshaws[,] cassettes and music are prohibited. . . . If any music cassette [is] found in a shop, the shopkeeper should be imprisoned and the shop locked. If five people guarantee [the good character of the shopkeeper,] the shop should be opened [and] the criminal released later. If [a] cassette [is] found in the vehicle, the vehicle [will be impounded] and the driver will be imprisoned. If five people guarantee[,] the vehicle will be released and the criminal released later.

3 To prevent beard shaving and its cutting. After one and a half months if anyone . . . has shaved and/or cut his beard, they should be arrested and imprisoned until their beard gets bushy.

4 To prevent keeping pigeons and playing with birds. Within ten days this habit/hobby should stop. After ten days this should be monitored and the pigeons and any other playing birds should be killed.

5 To prevent kite-flying. The kite shops in the city should be abolished.

6. To prevent idolatry. In vehicles, shops, hotels, rooms and any other place pictures/portraits should be abolished. The monitors should tear up all pictures in the above places.

7. To prevent gambling. In collaboration with the security police the main centers should be found and the gamblers imprisoned for one month.

8. To eradicate the use of addictions. Addicts should be imprisoned and investigation made to find the supplier and the shop. The shop should be locked and the owner and user should be imprisoned and punished.

9. To prevent the British and American hairstyle. People with long hair should be arrested and taken to the Religious Police department to shave their hair. The criminal has to pay the barber.

10. To prevent interest on loans, charge on changing small denomination notes and charge on money orders. All money exchangers should be informed that the above three types of exchanging the money should be prohibited. In case of violation criminals will be imprisoned for a long time.

11. To prevent washing cloth[es] by young ladies along the water streams in the city. Violat[ing] . . . ladies should be picked up with [a] respectful Islamic manner, taken to their houses and their husbands severely punished.

12. To prevent music and dances in wedding parties. In the case of violation the head of the family will be arrested and punished.

13. To prevent the playing of music drum[s]. The prohibition of this should be announced. If anybody does this then the religious elders can decide about it.

14. To prevent sewing ladies cloth[es] and taking female body measures by [a] tailor. If women or fashion magazines are seen in the shop the tailor should be imprisoned.
15. To prevent sorcery. All the related books should be burnt and the magician should be imprisoned until his repentance.
16. To prevent not praying ... at the bazaar. Prayer should be done on their due times in all districts. Transportation should be strictly prohibited [during prayer times] and all people are obliged to go to the mosque. If young people are seen in the shops they will be immediately imprisoned.

Chapter VIII

9/11: Terrorism, War, Global Responsibility

Introduction

Although we end this book with a brief narrative of the September 11, 2001, attacks on the United States, we do not imply that all that has gone on before inevitably led up to the destruction wrought that day. We intended mainly to demonstrate the historical diversity of the Middle East, and to suggest the other histories that might have unfolded as well as explore the one that did come to pass. The proximity of September 11 makes it quite difficult for us to offer an attempt at a grand synthesis or predictions of what a cloudy future may hold in store. We need instead to raise questions.

9/11

On the morning of Tuesday, September 11, 2001, a hijacked American Airlines Boeing 767 aircraft with eighty-one passengers aboard crashed into the North Tower of the World Trade Center in downtown New York City. Eighteen minutes later another commercial aircraft carrying fifty-six passengers hit the South Tower, which collapsed an hour later. The North Tower soon came down too, like its twin, in a crescendo of flames and debris. Riveting photographs and TV footage showed human bodies tumbling from these towers. On that same morning a third hijacked plane slammed into the Pentagon, the headquarters of the United States Department of Defense just outside Washington, DC. Later still a fourth airliner originally heading west from Washington, DC, made an unscheduled course change, and then crashed in rural Pennsylvania after the passengers battled against the plane's hijackers. All on board the four aircraft died, including nineteen hijackers. Official accounts estimate that on September 11 just over three thousand people perished at these four crash sites.

Although no court of inquiry has yet fixed blame, the U.S. government and knowledgeable observers have attributed these attacks to an Islamic terrorist group, *Al Qaeda* (The Source), headed by the wealthy Saudi Arabian businessman Osama bin Laden (born in Yemen in 1957). Bin Laden seems to have masterminded the near-simultaneous 1998 bombings of American embassies in Nairobi, Kenya, and Dar es Salaam, Tanzania, in retribution for which the United States sent cruise missiles against his headquarters in Afghanistan (see Reading 27d). He escaped unscathed. Bin Laden may have had a hand in a 1996 attack on U.S. military facilities in Saudi Arabia, and in the bombing in October 2000 of the U.S. Destroyer *Cole* at anchor off Aden, Yemen. (In the United States, many people initially suspected that Middle Eastern Muslims were behind the still unsolved post–September 11, 2001, anthrax scare, now widely attributed to an unknown, disgruntled U.S. government scientist.)

At the time of the 2001 hijackings in the United States, bin Laden's *Al Qaeda* enjoyed the hospitality of the Afghan *Taliban,* an organization of Islamic radical students who had made their appearance in 1994 and who rapidly managed to dominate much of the country. Ahmed Rashid's 2000 book *Taliban,* from which we have drawn a collection of the regime's decrees (Reading 33b), has explored the origins of this movement that became a government. Rashid and other writers, such as Barnett Rubin, have shown what countries backed the *Taliban,* and the circumstances that had brought bin Laden back to Afghanistan in 1996 after an earlier stint there as a fighter in the U.S.–supported anti-Soviet *jihad.* By 1998, with the disappearance of the Soviet Union and the failure of the post-*jihad* coalition to provide a stable government for Afghanistan, the United States had become the new target of attack for Islamic radicals, especially *Al Qaeda* (see Reading 34a). On September 20, 2001, President George W. Bush ordered the *Taliban* to turn bin Laden over to the Americans (see Reading 34b). They refused unless they could see incontrovertible evidence of *Al Qaeda*'s involvement in the September 11 attacks. The United States presented no such evidence and the U.S. bombing of *Taliban* sites in preparation for ground battles soon began.

The War to Get bin Laden and Mullah Omar

The United States had built-in allies for this conflict: the Northern Alliance in Afghanistan, a later incarnation of the 1980s coalition of *mujahidin* (holy warriors) who, with American backing, had fought against the leftist People's Democratic Party of Afghanistan (PDPA) and their Russian sponsors. The PDPA consisted mostly of Afghan Pashtuns, and the *mujahidin* coalition drew heavily on Tajiks and Uzbeks. Its leader was a Tajik former engineering student, Ahmed Shah Massoud (1953–2001). But once the Russians left Afghanistan not even Massoud could hold the coalition together. As Ahmed Rashid portrays the situation that brought the *Taliban* to power: "The country was divided into warlord fiefdoms and all the warlords . . . fought, switched sides and fought again in a bewildering array of alliances, betrayals and bloodshed." In this context the *Taliban,* led mainly by ethnic Pashtuns from the district of Kandahar, established their control of Afghanistan with financial support from the United States, Pakistan, and Saudi Arabia.

The *Taliban* offered a radical Muslim solution to the country's crumbling society, and the organization's leader, Mullah Muhammad Omar (c. 1959–?), extended hospitality to Osama bin Laden and many other radical Muslims who had battled Communism in Afghanistan. Committed to a society run according to *sharia* (Islamic law), the *Taliban* issued few manifestos, much less a constitution. For them Islamic law as interpreted by radical *mullahs* (teachers at *madrasas,* religious schools) provided all the model needed. They did, however, set forth their highly patriarchal, repressive view of the proper role for women

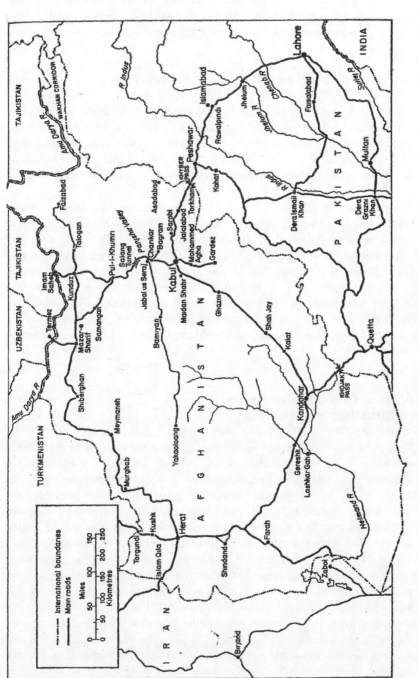

Afghanistan and Its Neighbors

(see decrees in Reading 33b). Although the remnant of the *mujahidin* who clustered around Massoud in northern Afghanistan also devoutly followed Islam, the *Taliban* saw them as competing non-Pashtun enemies whom they had to destroy.

The Northern Alliance and the Decision for War

After the *Taliban* took over most of the country between 1994 and 1995, the *mujahidin* concentrated in the north and awaited the hoped-for outside support that would enable them to defeat these new rulers of Afghanistan. September 11, 2001, brought that support from the United States, but Massoud did not live to see it. A pair of Tunisians posing as journalists assassinated him two days earlier.

Soon after, and more effectively than many thought possible, the American-backed forces defeated the *Taliban* and *Al Qaeda,* although thousands of their fighters seem to have melted into the Afghan population, or took refuge in Pakistan's lawless Northwest Frontier. Did both Mullah Omar and Osama bin Laden survive the war? If so, will they or their followers regroup to fight again? Have they already done so? It seems that in this age of globalism *Al Qaeda* has become a truly international organization, a sort of "Islamic foreign legion," based in no single country. Even Americans joined. It may still strike again, using its "sleeper cells," anonymous groups virtually impossible to discover, scattered throughout the world.

Strategic and Tactical Questions: Support and Dissent after 9/11

Should the gruesome killings of September 11 have led to a generalized "war against terrorism" using mostly conventional military methods? Many scholars and writers have suggested another paradigm—a vigorously pursued international police action. But President George W. Bush and his advisers became determined to wage war. On September 12 the president stated that the "deliberate and deadly attacks which were carried out yesterday against our country were more than acts of terror. They were acts of war" (see Reading 34b).

The debate has a domestic dimension. *The New York Times* struck a cautionary note in its editorial on that same day: that "Americans must rethink how to safeguard the country without bartering away the rights and privileges of the free society we are defending." Since September 11 the Bush administration has initiated several policies—secret detention of Muslim immigrant suspects, repudiation of international laws on rights of captured soldiers, military instead of civilian tribunals, fingerprinting Muslim holders of immigration visas for the United States, interference with lawyer-client contacts—that do exactly what the *Times* warned against.

Yet it may be too late to revise the paradigm under which Americans perceive the terrorist assaults, and to halt the war juggernaut, which now extends
far beyond *Al Qaeda,* Osama bin Laden, and the apparently defeated *Taliban*
of Afghanistan. Former Cold Warriors in the Bush administration have actively
promoted an enlarged war encompassing a group of target countries somehow
associated in what President Bush has called an "axis of evil" that the United
States intends to punish (see Reading 35a). Defeated in the Gulf War a decade
earlier, Iraq has emerged as Washington's new prime target. Its unsavory leader,
Saddam Husayn, remains in charge. Bush also named North Korea and Iran,
whose connections to the original culprits (the *Taliban* and *Al Qaeda*) remain
unsubstantiated. In short, American war aims have broadened and threaten to
go far beyond (or in a different direction from) what many think the September 11 provocations called for.

Fighting terrorism involves arcane and sophisticated skills: careful espionage,
agents with extensive linguistic abilities, and the analytic competence to
interpret large amounts of data, as well as profound knowledge of the diverse
countries and cultures that support terrorist activities. But U.S. intelligence and
counterterrorism agencies exhibited such grave deficiencies before September 11 that congressional investigators have begun inquiring into what went
wrong. Plans to establish effective "homeland security" by high-profile appointments, press releases promising effective bureaucratic coordination, and such
schemes as color-coded public warnings tailored to the level of threat seem
ludicrously ineffective.

The main substantive innovations in counterterror tactics that the Bush
administration has proposed involve application of war measures, especially the
revival of expensive programs of missile defense and wholesale imprisonment
of Muslims living in the United States. Do such tactics work? The roundups have
already generated serious doubts as to their legality, along with fueling the
admittedly exaggerated notion that the United States has declared war on all
Muslims, despite official statements to the contrary. Does the great emphasis
placed on weaponry make sense? How would death by smart bombs deter such
terrorists as the hijackers of September 11, who were willing to die in assaults
on supposed enemies? The Israeli government has certainly found that its attacks on West Bank civilian populations have not reduced the determination
of Palestinian suicide bombers; if anything, intensified attacks increase the supply
of potential martyrs. Action by Palestinians themselves, such as the June 2002
appeal by Palestinian intellectuals to stop suicide bombings (see Reading 26e)
may have more effect. Nevertheless Ariel Sharon's Israeli government continues collective punishment—demolishing sections of Palestinian towns and refugee
camps in the West Bank and Gaza, uprooting populations, and assassinating
suspects and bystanders—despite its long-term lack of deterrent effect.

Another shortcoming of a military strategy to deal with terrorism—whether
by Israel or by the United States—lies in its potential impact on America's allies. The tremendous expenditure on armaments (President Bush wants to

increase the Pentagon's budget in fiscal 2003 to $379 billion—more, the *New York Times* reported on March 16, 2002, than the total budgets of the fourteen next highest arms-spending countries put together!) worries many inside the United States and overseas. Will the sheer availability of weaponry tend to preclude nonmilitary solutions to problems, including diplomatic initiatives and overhauling and upgrading of security and intelligence services? Will military planners in their obsession with new technology, guided missiles, and the like forget preventive efforts to combat the dictatorships that stifle normal dissent in the countries that produce terrorists? Will countries sympathetic to American aims willingly send their soldiers to the battlefields of future wars while U.S. warriors sit among high-tech electronic controls in aircraft and ships beyond the range of ground fire, or in fortified bunkers well behind the lines? Deployment of such military equipment in Afghanistan kept U.S. casualties low and shortened the war. They nevertheless killed as many Afghan civilians as Americans who died in the September 11 attacks in New York City.

For Afghan civilians, subject to errant bombs unleashed by the U.S. air force in attempts to kill remnants of *Al Qaeda* and *Taliban* forces still at large, the war did not quite end with the *Taliban* defeat. Warlord rule, which brought the *Taliban* to power a decade earlier, also seems to have reappeared in Afghanistan. So have murders and attempted murders of key governmental officials. The accidental bombings, high-level assassinations, and resurgent warlordism generate significant hostility toward the United States in Afghanistan and raise questions as to whether the long-term result of the U.S. intervention will produce a better life for their country, especially if American forces are removed to fight in Iraq or elsewhere.

Nor have most Americans recognized that the *Taliban* and Osama bin Laden and Islamic radicalism generally emerged from a world that the United States itself has helped to shape. Although the United States and the Soviet Union never went to war against each other, the militarized strategy of the Cold War helped cause the Soviet collapse; it also contributed to the persistence of post–Cold War militarism—especially in the Middle East. The United States sponsored and helped to finance the war against Communism in Afghanistan, which enlisted, trained, and armed "freedom fighters," and then abandoned them once the Soviets withdrew. And it left behind a clear message: America pursues its own aims and, once achieved, other nations matter little—until the next round of trouble. (For the view of a prominent Carter administration official on fallout from the Afghanistan war see Reading 30d.)

A Balance Sheet

After September 11 the United States first backed the Northern Alliance against the *Taliban*, then decisively intervened itself in Afghanistan and fought a quick, successful war with the help of troops from the Northern Alliance and several other countries. Then the Americans brokered and financed the emergence of a fragile interim government in Afghanistan, officially committed to increasing its legitimacy and transforming itself into a functioning, democratic state in the near future. The *Loya Jirga* (council of tribal representatives) that met in June 2002 in Kabul ratified the continuation of U.S.–backed Hamid Karzai (1957–   ) as head of a new two-year interim government. But that government consists largely of regional warlords who proved their inability to create a viable state a decade earlier. Assassinations of two top officials in Karzai's government, and an attempt to kill Karzai himself, reveal underlying instability. Will Afghan cultivators be aided in regenerating their agriculture or will they continue to focus on that sure crop, the heroin poppy? Will the international community allow Afghanistan to lapse back into what Barnett Rubin defines in his *Fragmentation of Afghanistan* (2002) as a "regional conflict complex," a daunting situation in which "several different conflicts become linked through flows of people, arms, ideology and resources"? One can add to these problems the further questions of whether Afghan women, an especially oppressed group, will be encouraged or even permitted to help shape that country's future, and whether *Al Qaeda* will reemerge.

Surrounding, nearby, and even far distant countries each have their own agendas that impact on Afghanistan. The struggle between the two regional nuclear powers, India and Pakistan, over Kashmir rages menacingly near Afghanistan's eastern border. To the west, Iran, trying to break out of the isolation imposed years earlier because of its radical revolution, finds itself menacingly labeled as part of President Bush's "axis of evil." On the north stands the smoldering powder keg of Uzbekistan, rent by antagonism between a repressive government and an *Al Qaeda*–linked Islamic movement. Then there abound the criminalized groups that conduct the weapons—and drug—smuggling trades through the old Spice Road threading Afghanistan's remote valleys. Finally and of far more than local significance, the issues we discussed in Chapter VI remain pertinent: Central Asian gas and oil reserves, their distribution, and who will profit from them. As with the other questions we raise here, these too have no apparent answers at present.

The Arab-Israeli crisis, as we write these words, has reached new levels of urgency. Despite moderating voices, both Palestinians and Israelis have dangerously escalated their violence—each side claiming they retaliate for the assaults of the other. Palestinian suicide bombers heighten insecurity throughout the Jewish state. Israeli military assaults against Palestinian towns, villages, and individual Palestinian leaders intensify. As long as the issues we have discussed in Chapter V and elsewhere in this book fester unresolved, more young men and women will join the ranks of suicide bombers or their victims. Or will we see new outrages that we can now scarcely imagine?

After September 11 no one can believe any longer in the invulnerability of United States. In that horror we see the full reality of the interconnectedness of our planet: what happens in Kabul, Ramallah, Yemen, or in Uzbekistan's

Fergana valley will reverberate throughout the Middle East and the Islamic world generally, and beyond. We need greater efforts at conflict resolution and fewer smart bombs, more food shipments and less construction of missile shields, more ways to comprehend our differences so as to resolve them if we hope to get through even the early decades of this new, badly begun century with grave portents of unforeseen dangers ahead.

34. The Threat of Osama bin Laden and American Responses

In his indispensable book *Taliban* (2000), Pakistani journalist Ahmed Rashid described the arrival of tens of thousands of Arab radicals to Afghanistan in the 1980s to fight against the Russian "infidels" and their local supporters. Many came from Saudi Arabia, whose ruling dynasty, along with Pakistani and U.S. government agencies, assisted the anti-Communist *mujahidin*. Osama bin Laden, a young Saudi volunteer, arrived to fight in Afghanistan. This tall, thin student came from a fabulously wealthy Yemeni family whose members had earlier migrated to Saudi Arabia and established a multibillion-dollar construction business in that kingdom. After aiding the Afghans to defeat the Soviet forces in Afghanistan, the young bin Laden and his associates gathered in an organization named *Al Qaeda,* now dedicated to the destruction of another "nation of materialists" that they believe have harmed Islam—the United States.

In retaliation for this harm, *Al Qaeda* militants attacked U.S. embassies in East Africa (see Reading 27d) and an American naval vessel (the destroyer U.S.S. *Cole*) docked in Yemen, with great loss of life. But buoyed by the defeat of the Soviet Union, and soon after its collapse, the Islamic radicals perceived that the Americans too, their power and authority spread all over the world, were vulnerable.

Bin Laden and other Islamic radicals attached great importance to the stationing of U.S. troops in Saudi Arabia during the second Gulf war and, especially, the willingness of the Saudi government to allow the Americans to establish permanent military bases in the country that contains the holy cities of Mecca and Madina. The Islamic radicals (drawing on a tradition that goes back to early Arab opposition to Zionism) view the American-backed Israeli regime, and its repressive policies toward Palestinians, as another intolerable set of affronts to Islam. To them the United States, the sole superpower, bears the main responsibility for Islam's present degradation. They routinely call the Americans "crusaders," a term that evokes the late medieval period in which Western European Christians invaded and brought temporary humiliation to the Islamic world. We dealt with the Crusades in Reading 6a and in the introduction to Chapter II.

The 2002 battles in Afghanistan between Osama bin Laden's *Al Qaeda* and U.S. forces underscores Americans' need to understand the variant of Islamic radicalism they represent—one extremist tendency within the broad, variegated spectrum of Islamic thought and conviction—whose adherents attacked New York and Washington, DC, on September 11, 2001. Despite the subsequent U.S. military victory in Afghanistan and the worldwide U.S.–led effort to hunt down those responsible for the killings and destruction perpetrated on that date, we already see that we have not heard the last of *Al Qaeda*.

A. *Jihad* Against Jews and Crusaders: The 1998 *Fatwa**

Since September 11, 2001, a whole library of books of very uneven quality have appeared purporting to reveal the mystery of Osama bin Laden. We believe that the study of original texts provides the best way to understand bin Laden's message. We present a particularly chilling example of these texts—the February 1998 *fatwa* issued by bin Laden and four other Islamic radicals, which calls on "every Muslim" to "kill the Americans and plunder their money whenever and wherever and whenever they find it." A *fatwa* usually comes from a learned Islamic scholar, a *mufti* in *Sunni* Islam, in the form of a legal judgment, which provides an opinion about problems arising in new contexts for which no traditional textual solution exists.

Most Muslims reject the notion that any group of self-proclaimed *ulema* can legitimately pass a death sentence on others, or on an entire national group, as bin Laden and his associates have done. Most Muslims also disavow the position held by the most extreme of Islamic radicals, which reduces the concept of *jihad* (struggle for the faith) to holy war.

Praise be to God, who revealed the Book, controls the clouds, defeats factionalism, and says in His Book "But when the forbidden months are past, then fight and slay the pagans wherever ye find them, seize them, beleaguer them, and lie in wait for them in every stratagem (of war)"; and peace be upon our Prophet, Muhammad Bin-'Abdallah, who said "I have been sent with the sword between my hands to ensure that no one but God is worshipped, God who put my livelihood under the shadow of my spear and who inflicts humiliation and scorn on those who disobey my orders."

The Arabian Peninsula has never—since God made it flat, created its desert, and encircled it with seas—been stormed by any forces like the crusader armies now spreading in it like locusts, consuming its riches and destroying its plantations. All this is happening at a time when nations are attacking Muslims like

---

*From World Islamic Front Statement, February 23, 1998, www.fas.org/irp/world/para/docs/980223-fatwa.htm.

people fighting over a plate of food. In the light of the grave situation and the lack of support, we and you are obliged to discuss current events, and we should all agree to settle the matter.

No one argues today about three facts that are known to everyone; we will list them, in order to remind everyone:

First, for over seven years the United States has been occupying the lands of Islam in the holiest of places, the Arabian Peninsula, plundering its riches, dictating to its rulers, humiliating its people, terrorizing its neighbors, and turning its bases in the Peninsula into a spearhead through which to fight the neighboring Muslim peoples.

If some people have formerly debated the fact of the occupation, all the people of the Peninsula have now acknowledged it. The best proof of this is the Americans' continuing aggression against the Iraqi people using the Peninsula as a staging post, even though all its rulers are against their territories being used to that end, still they are helpless.

Second, despite the great devastation inflicted on the Iraqi people by the crusader-Zionist alliance, and despite the huge number of those killed, in excess of 1 million . . . despite all this, the Americans are once again trying to repeat the horrific massacres, as though they are not content with the protracted blockade imposed after the ferocious war or the fragmentation and devastation.

So here they come to annihilate what is left of this people and to humiliate their Muslim neighbors.

Third, if the Americans' aims behind these wars are religious and economic, the aim is also to serve the Jews' petty state and divert attention from its occupation of Jerusalem and murder of Muslims there. The best proof of this is their eagerness to destroy Iraq, the strongest neighboring Arab state, and their endeavor to fragment all the states of the region such as Iraq, Saudi Arabia, Egypt, and Sudan into paper statelets and through their disunion and weakness to guarantee Israel's survival and the continuation of the brutal crusader occupation of the Peninsula.

All these crimes and sins committed by the Americans are a clear declaration of war on God, his messenger, and Muslims. And *ulema* have throughout Islamic history unanimously agreed that the *jihad* is an individual duty if the enemy destroys the Muslim countries.

On that basis, and in compliance with God's order, we issue the following fatwa *to all Muslims:*

The ruling to kill the Americans and their allies—civilians and military—is an individual duty for every Muslim who can do it in any country in which it is possible to do it, in order to liberate the al-Aqsa Mosque and the holy mosque [in Mecca] from their grip, and in order for their armies to move out of all the lands of Islam, defeated and unable to threaten any Muslim. This is in accordance with the words of Almighty God, "and fight the pagans all together as they fight you all together," and "fight them until there is no more tumult or oppression, and there prevail justice and faith in God."

This is in addition to the words of Almighty God "And why should ye not fight in the cause of God and of those who, being weak, are ill-treated and oppressed—women and children, whose cry is 'Our Lord, rescue us from this town, whose people are oppressors; and raise for us from thee one who will help!'"

We—with God's help—call on every Muslim who believes in God and wishes to be rewarded to comply with God's order to kill the Americans and plunder their money wherever and whenever they find it. We also call on Muslim *ulema*, leaders, youths, and soldiers to launch the raid on Satan's U.S. troops and the devil's supporters allying with them, and to displace those who are behind them so that they may learn a lesson.

Almighty God said "O ye who believe, give your response to God and His Apostle, when He calleth you to that which will give you life. And know that God cometh between a man and his heart, and that it is He to whom ye shall all be gathered."

Almighty God also says "O ye who believe, what is the matter with you, that when ye are asked to go forth in the cause of God, ye cling so heavily to the earth! Do ye prefer the life of this world to the hereafter? But little is the comfort of this life, as compared with the hereafter. Unless ye go forth, He will punish you with a grievous penalty, and put others in your place; but Him ye would not harm in the least. For God hath power over all things."

Almighty God also says "So lose no heart, nor fall into despair. For ye must gain mastery if ye are true in faith."

Shaykh Usamah Bin-Muhammad Bin-Laden
Ayman al-Zawahiri, *Amir* of the *Jihad* Group in Egypt
Abu-Yasir Rifa'i Ahmad Taha, Egyptian Islamic Group
Shaykh Mir Hamzah, secretary of the Jamiat-ul-Ulema-e-Pakistan
Fazlur Rahman, *Amir* of the *Jihad* Movement in Bangladesh

B. George W. Bush, Hand Over Terrorists or Share Their Fate (2001)*

President Bush delivered the speech excerpted here before a televised session of both houses of the U.S. Congress. It directed an explicit warning to the *Taliban* leaders who then ruled much of Afghanistan. The *Taliban* did not comply with Bush's demand to turn over Osama bin Laden, and after intensive air bombardments of Afghanistan the U.S.–led coalition, including Northern Alliance fighters, evicted Mullah Omar and his followers from power. As we write

---

*From President George W. Bush's speech to a joint session of Congress (September 20, 2001). Arabic words italicized. The full text appears at www.whitehouse.gov/news/releases/2001/09/20010920-8.htm. Bracketed material added by the authors.

these words President Bush is sending similar warnings to Iraqi leaders, and when this book is published war with Iraq may have already begun. Historians in the future will ponder these messages, in search of their deeper meanings. Do these threats to go to war—to punish those who dared attack the United States, who befriended the attackers, or those who may carry out future attacks—reveal an insecure president who took office by a flawed electoral process, and who needed to prove his legitimacy? Or did Bush merely follow the advice of former Cold Warriors in his inner circle of advisers who apparently cannot conceive of a world without a prime enemy to battle against? Or did the threats to Afghanistan (and the war that followed) represent an authentic voice of a fearful American population intent on revenge at any cost and for any duration against an enemy who gave bin Laden sanctuary and coordinated its armed forces with his? Or was it the contemporary version of Manifest Destiny—a supposed God-given right claimed by Americans to battle evil, defend freedom and spread democracy—that may have played a role in the president's marshaling of the American public for his policies?

This last point raises the problem of other countries and movements whose adherents also claim divine sanction, among them *Al Qaeda* itself. And whatever other significance September 11 bears, it shows that, while the United States remains the uncontested military superpower, the playing fields of surprise attack and terrorism have become dangerously level.

Americans are asking, why do they [the Islamic radicals and their supporters] hate us? They hate what we see right here in this chamber—a democratically elected government. Their leaders are self-appointed. They hate our freedoms— our freedom of religion, our freedom of speech, our freedom to vote and assemble and disagree with each other.

Tonight we are a country awakened to danger and called to defend freedom. Our grief has turned to anger, and anger to resolution. Whether we bring our enemies to justice, or bring justice to our enemies, justice will be done.

On September the 11th, enemies of freedom committed an act of war against our country. Americans have known wars—but [they have mainly taken place] . . . on foreign soil. . . . Americans have known the casualties of war—but not at the center of a great city on a peaceful morning. Americans have known surprise attacks—but never before on thousands of civilians. All of this was brought upon us in a single day—and night fell on a different world, a world where freedom itself is under attack.

Who Attacked Our Country?

Americans have many questions tonight. Americans are asking: Who attacked our country? The evidence we have gathered all points to a collection of loosely affiliated terrorist organizations known as *Al Qaeda.* They are the same murderers indicted for bombing American embassies in Tanzania and Kenya, and responsible for bombing the U.S.S. *Cole.*

Al Qaeda is to terror what the mafia is to crime. But its goal is not making money; its goal is remaking the world—and imposing its radical beliefs on people everywhere. The terrorists practice a fringe form of Islamic extremism that has been rejected by Muslim scholars and the vast majority of Muslim clerics—a fringe movement that perverts the peaceful teachings of Islam. The terrorists' directive commands them to kill Christians and Jews, to kill all Americans, and make no distinction among military and civilians, including women and children.

This group and its leader—a person named Osama bin Laden—are linked to many other organizations in different countries, including the Egyptian Islamic *Jihad* and the Islamic Movement of Uzbekistan. There are thousands of these terrorists in more than 60 countries. They are recruited from their own nations and neighborhoods and brought to camps in places like Afghanistan, where they are trained in the tactics of terror. They are sent back to their homes or sent to hide in countries around the world to plot evil and destruction.

U.S. Demands on the Taliban

The United States respects the people of Afghanistan—after all, we are currently its largest source of humanitarian aid—but we condemn the *Taliban* regime. It is not only repressing its own people, it is threatening people everywhere by sponsoring and sheltering and supplying terrorists. By aiding and abetting murder, the *Taliban* regime is committing murder.

And tonight, the United States of America makes the following demands on the *Taliban:* Deliver to United States authorities all the leaders of *Al Qaeda* who hide in your land. Release all foreign nationals, including American citizens, you have unjustly imprisoned. Protect foreign journalists, diplomats and aid workers in your country. Close immediately and permanently every terrorist training camp in Afghanistan, and hand over every terrorist, and every person in their support structure, to appropriate authorities. Give the United States full access to terrorist training camps, so we can make sure they are no longer operating.

These demands are not open to negotiation or discussion. The *Taliban* must act, and act immediately. They will hand over the terrorists, or they will share in their fate.

C. Congresswoman Barbara Lee, No Blank Check to President Bush (2001)*

Standard procedural custom in the U.S. House of Representatives requires that when a member of this body rises to speak he or she addresses the Speaker of the

---

*From Congresswoman Barbara Lee's speech of September 14, 2001, in the *Congressional Record*, 107th Congress, First Session, pp. H5642–H5643.

House, chosen from the majority party. In 2001 Dennis Hastert (1942–   ), Republican from Illinois, second in line in the presidential succession after the vice president, held that position. Congresswoman Barbara Lee, Democrat from California, represents the Ninth District in the San Francisco Bay area. Daughter of a U.S. Army lieutenant colonel, Lee graduated from Mills College in Oakland, California, and from the University of California, Berkeley, after which she served as aide to Congressman Ron Dellums (1935–   ), whom she succeeded. On September 14 Lee cast the sole vote against a resolution giving the president the right to use unlimited force against suspected terrorists. Two hundred and forty members of the House of Representatives voted yes, as did ninety-eight senators. In an interview a week later, Lee explained that she favored bringing the terrorists to justice and making "sure that they're never allowed to perpetrate such an evil act as they did." Later she voted for the $40 billion recovery and anti-terrorism bill. She voted no on September 14 for two reasons: because the bill introduced that day empowered the president to go to war without specifying which country the United States proposed to fight against and what "exit strategy," if any, the administration contemplated, and because she felt obliged to activate the checks and balances in the U.S. Constitution. Her lone dissenting vote brought her several death threats.

Mr. Speaker, I rise today with a heavy heart, one that is filled with sorrow for the families and loved ones who were killed and injured in New York, Virginia, and Pennsylvania. Only the most foolish or the most callous would not understand the grief that has gripped the American people and millions around the world.

This unspeakable attack on the United States has forced me to rely on my moral compass, my conscience, and my God for direction.

September 11 changed the world. Our deepest fears now haunt us. Yet I am convinced that military action will not prevent further acts of international terrorism against the United States.

I know that this use-of-force resolution will pass although we all know that the President can wage war even without this resolution. However difficult this vote may be, some of us must urge the use of restraint. There must be some of us who say, let's step back for a moment and think through the implications of our actions today—let us more fully understand their consequences.

We are not dealing with a conventional war. We cannot respond in a conventional manner. I do not want to see this spiral out of control. This crisis involves issues of national security, foreign policy, public safety, intelligence gathering, economics, and murder. Our response must be equally multifaceted.

We must not rush to judgment. Far too many innocent people have already died. Our country is in mourning. If we rush to launch a counterattack, we run too great a risk that women, children, and other non-combatants will be caught in the crossfire.

Nor can we let our justified anger over their outrageous acts by vicious murderers inflame prejudice against all Arab Americans, Muslims, Southeast Asians, and any other people because of their race, religion, or ethnicity.

Finally, we must be careful not to embark on an open-ended war with neither an exit strategy nor a focused target. We cannot repeat past mistakes.

In 1964, Congress gave President Lyndon Johnson the power to "take all necessary measures" to repel attacks and prevent further aggression. In so doing, this House abandoned its own constitutional responsibilities and launched our country into years of undeclared war in Vietnam.

At that time, Senator Wayne Morse, one of two lonely votes against the Tonkin Gulf Resolution, declared, "I believe that history will record that we have made a grave mistake in subverting and circumventing the Constitution of the United States . . . I believe that within the next century, future generations will look with dismay and great disappointment upon a Congress which is now about to make such a historic mistake."

Senator Morse was correct, and I fear we make the same mistake today. And I fear the consequences. I have agonized over this vote. But I came to grips with it in the very painful yet beautiful memorial service today at the National Cathedral. As a member of the clergy so eloquently said, "As we act, let us not become the evil that we deplore."

35. The Policy Debate

L ong a beneficiary of what historian C. Vann Woodward called the "free security" of protection by vast bodies of water on each shore keeping attackers out, the United States never experienced so dramatic and deadly an assault before September 11, 2001. Most Americans initially responded by looking to the national government to investigate the crimes, punish those responsible, and prevent future terrorist actions. But as the administration of George W. Bush vented its anger against the perpetrators, and as its responses to September 11 unfolded, dissenting voices began to register doubts and fears.

Dissent has had a checkered history in the United States. On the one hand leaders cite its existence as evidence of a free society, but the frequent efforts to suppress dissent in American history (most notably in the McCarthy era of the mid-twentieth century) raises doubts about whether American society tolerates dissent during periods of crisis. During the early nineteenth century those dissenters who denounced slavery sometimes paid for such advocacy with ostracism, physical attack, and death. Antislavery militants developed a strategy of dissent: the dissenting agitators attempted to rouse a somnolent public to heightened awareness of governmental faults and called attention to the fallacies of the defenders of injustice. So the post–September 11 dissenters presented in this chapter argue against the self-delusions and errors of dismissing the country's enemies as cowards, of embracing the model of war as the best or only way to fight terrorism, of hastily adopting dubious and simplistic solutions to complex problems and employing unilateralist strategies rather than seeking advice and help from allies. Some of these dissenters are lawmakers in the U.S. national government, others are veteran journalists and scholars. Time will tell whether or not President Bush and his advisers have made wise choices.

A. George W. Bush, Battling the Axis of Evil (2002)*

In 1936 two fascist states in Europe—Germany and Italy—concluded a diplomatic alliance that they strengthened by another pact, which they signed just before World War II began. Called the Rome-Berlin Axis, this alliance enlarged to include Japan and several right-wing countries in eastern Europe. The Axis lost the war to the opposing British–Soviet–U.S. alliance. Its association with the negative images of fascism and World War II aggression supplied the likely reasons for President Bush (or his speechwriter David Frum) to put the word "axis" into this belligerent State of the Union address to Congress. In it he announced future American war plans against a coalition of states that, unlike the Axis of World War II, did not ally among themselves but received their collective status as the "axis of evil" from the president of the United States. Bush offered no evidence for a formal or informal alliance among the three—Iran, Iraq, and North Korea.

We have omitted from this condensed version of the 2002 State of the Union address President Bush's treatment of domestic policy, traditionally a primary subject of a president's annual presentation to Congress. We focus instead on the president's developing strategy and institutional structure to enhance "homeland security," including improving "intelligence capacities and sharing," expanding border controls, tightening airport safety, and using better technology "to track the arrivals and departures of visitors to the United States."

America After 9/11

In four short months [after September 11], our nation has comforted the victims, begun to rebuild New York and the Pentagon, rallied a great coalition, captured, arrested, and rid the world of thousands of terrorists, destroyed Afghanistan's terrorist training camps, saved a people from starvation, and freed a country from brutal oppression.

---

*From George W. Bush's State of the Union address to the U.S. Congress (January 29, 2002). Bracketed material added by the editors. The full text appears at www.whitehouse.gov/news/releases/2002/01/20020120-8.html.

Our cause is just, and it continues. Our discoveries in Afghanistan confirmed our worst fears, and showed us the true scope of the task ahead. We have seen the depth of our enemies' hatred in videos, where they laugh about the loss of innocent life. And the depth of their hatred is equaled by the madness of the destruction they design. We have found diagrams of American nuclear power plants and public water facilities, detailed instructions for making chemical weapons, surveillance maps of American cities, and thorough descriptions of landmarks in America and throughout the world.

Terrorist Underworld

What we have found in Afghanistan confirms that, far from ending there, our war against terror is only beginning. Most of the 19 men who hijacked planes on September the 11th were trained in Afghanistan's camps, and so were tens of thousands of others. Thousands of dangerous killers, schooled in the methods of murder, often supported by outlaw regimes, are now spread throughout the world like ticking time bombs, set to go off without warning.

Our military has put the [terrorist] training camps of Afghanistan out of business, yet [such] camps still exist in at least a dozen countries. A terrorist underworld . . . operates in remote jungles and deserts, and hides in the centers of large cities.

Our nation will continue to be steadfast and patient and persistent in the pursuit of two great objectives. First, we will shut down terrorist camps, disrupt terrorist plans, and bring terrorists to justice. And, second, we must prevent the terrorists and regimes who seek chemical, biological or nuclear weapons from threatening the United States and the world.

Axis of Evil

Our second goal is to prevent regimes that sponsor terror from threatening America or our friends and allies with weapons of mass destruction. Some of these regimes have been pretty quiet since September the 11th. But we know their true nature. North Korea is a regime arming with missiles and weapons of mass destruction, while starving its citizens.

Iran aggressively pursues these weapons and exports terror, while an unelected few repress the Iranian people's hope for freedom.

Iraq continues to flaunt its hostility toward America and to support terror. The Iraqi regime has plotted to develop anthrax, and nerve gas, and nuclear weapons for over a decade. This is a regime that has already used poison gas to murder thousands of its own citizens—leaving the bodies of mothers huddled over their dead children. This is a regime that agreed to international inspections—then kicked out the inspectors. This is a regime that has something to hide from the civilized world.

States like these, and their terrorist allies, constitute an axis of evil, arming to threaten the peace of the world. By seeking weapons of mass destruction, these regimes pose a grave and growing danger. They could provide these arms to terrorists, giving them the means to match their hatred. They could attack our allies or attempt to blackmail the United States. In any of these cases, the price of indifference would be catastrophic.

The U.S. Will Not Wait

We'll be deliberate, yet time is not on our side. I will not wait on events, while dangers gather. I will not stand by, as peril draws closer and closer. The United States of America will not permit the world's most dangerous regimes to threaten us with the world's most destructive weapons

Our war on terror is well begun, but it is only begun. This campaign may not be finished on our watch—yet it must be and it will be waged on our watch.

Steadfast in our purpose, we now press on. We have known freedom's price. We have shown freedom's power. And in this great conflict, my fellow Americans, we will see freedom's victory.

B. Brent Scowcroft, Don't Attack Saddam (2002)*

> Former national security adviser to Presidents Gerald Ford and George H. W. Bush, Scowcroft (1925–) heads the Forum for International Policy. Educated at West Point and Columbia University, he has impeccable credentials as a conservative Republican. His opposition to President George W. Bush's policy is therefore all the more significant. It points up the space between realists like Scowcroft and the group of ideologues around Vice President Richard Cheney (1941–) and Paul Wolfowitz (1944–) who are eager to begin a war in which they personally will never fight.

Our nation is presently engaged in a debate about whether to launch a war against Iraq. Leaks of various strategies for an attack on Iraq appear with regularity. The Bush administration vows regime change, but states that no decision has been made whether, much less when, to launch an invasion.

It is beyond dispute that Saddam Hussein is a menace. He terrorizes and brutalizes his own people. He has launched war on two of his neighbors. He devotes enormous effort to rebuilding his military forces and equipping them with weapons of mass destruction. We will all be better off when he is gone.

That said, we need to think through this issue very carefully. We need to analyze the relationship between Iraq and our other pressing priorities—notably the

---

*Brent Scowcroft, "Don't Attack Saddam," *Wall Street Journal*, August 15, 2002. By permission.

war on terrorism—as well as the best strategy and tactics available were we to move to change the regime in Baghdad.

Saddam's strategic objective appears to be to dominate the Persian Gulf, to control oil from the region, or both.

That clearly poses a real threat to key U.S. interests. But there is scant evidence to tie Saddam to terrorist organizations, and even less to the September 11 attacks. Indeed Saddam's goals have little in common with the terrorists who threaten us, and there is little incentive for him to make common cause with them.

He is unlikely to risk his investment in weapons of mass destruction, much less his country, by handing such weapons to terrorists who would use them for their own purposes and leave Baghdad as the return address. Threatening to use these weapons for blackmail—much less their actual use—would open him and his entire regime to a devastating response by the U.S. While Saddam is thoroughly evil, he is above all a power-hungry survivor.

Saddam is a familiar dictatorial aggressor, with traditional goals for his aggression. There is little evidence to indicate that the United States itself is an object of his aggression. Rather, Saddam's problem with the U.S. appears to be that we stand in the way of his ambitions. He seeks weapons of mass destruction not to arm terrorists, but to deter us from intervening to block his aggressive designs.

Given Saddam's aggressive regional ambitions, as well as his ruthlessness and unpredictability, it may at some point be wise to remove him from power. Whether and when that point should come ought to depend on overall U.S. national security priorities. Our pre-eminent security priority—underscored repeatedly by the president—is the war on terrorism. An attack on Iraq at this time would seriously jeopardize, if not destroy, the global counterterrorist campaign we have undertaken.

The United States could certainly defeat the Iraqi military and destroy Saddam's regime. But it would not be a cakewalk. On the contrary, it undoubtedly would be very expensive—with serious consequences for the U.S. and global economy—and could as well be bloody. In fact, Saddam would be likely to conclude he had nothing left to lose, leading him to unleash whatever weapons of mass destruction he possesses.

Israel would have to expect to be the first casualty, as in 1991 when Saddam sought to bring Israel into the Gulf conflict. This time, using weapons of mass destruction, he might succeed, provoking Israel to respond, perhaps with nuclear weapons, unleashing an Armageddon in the Middle East. Finally, if we are to achieve our strategic objectives in Iraq, a military campaign very likely would have to be followed by a large-scale, long-term military occupation.

But the central point is that any campaign against Iraq, whatever the strategy, cost and risks, is certain to divert us for some indefinite period from our war on terrorism. Worse, there is a virtual consensus in the world against an attack on Iraq at this time. So long as that sentiment persists, it would require the U.S. to pursue a virtual go-it-alone strategy against Iraq, making any military operations correspondingly more difficult and expensive. The most serious cost, however, would be to the war on terrorism. Ignoring that clear sentiment would result in a serious degradation in international cooperation with us against terrorism. And make no mistake, we simply cannot win that war without enthusiastic international cooperation, especially on intelligence.

Possibly the most dire consequences would be the effect in the region. The shared view in the region is that Iraq is principally an obsession of the U.S. The obsession of the region, however, is the Israeli-Palestinian conflict. If we were seen to be turning our back on that bitter conflict—which the region, rightly or wrongly, perceives to be clearly within our power to resolve—in order to go after Iraq, there would be an explosion of outrage against us. We would be seen as ignoring a key interest of the Muslim world in order to satisfy what is seen to be a narrow American interest.

Even without Israeli involvement, the results could well destabilize Arab regimes in the region, ironically facilitating one of Saddam's strategic objectives. At a minimum, it would stifle any cooperation on terrorism, and could even swell the ranks of the terrorists. Conversely, the more progress we make in the war on terrorism, and the more we are seen to be committed to resolving the Israel-Palestinian issue, the greater will be the international support for going after Saddam.

If we are truly serious about the war on terrorism, it must remain our top priority. However, should Saddam Hussein be found to be clearly implicated in the events of September 11, that could make him a key counterterrorist target, rather than a competing priority, and significantly shift world opinion toward support for regime change.

No-Notice Inspections

In any event, we should be pressing the United Nations Security Council to insist on an effective no-notice inspection regime for Iraq—any time, anywhere, no permission required. On this point, senior administration officials have opined that Saddam Hussein would never agree to such an inspection regime. But if he did, inspections would serve to keep him off balance and under close observation, even if all his weapons of mass destruction capabilities were not uncovered. And if he refused, his rejection could provide the persuasive *casus belli* which many claim we do not now have. Compelling evidence that Saddam had acquired nuclear-weapons capability could have a similar effect.

In sum, if we will act in full awareness of the intimate interrelationship of the key issues in the region, keeping counterterrorism as our foremost priority, there is much potential for success across the entire range of our security interests—including Iraq. If we reject a comprehensive perspective, however, we put at risk our campaign against terrorism as well as stability and security in a vital region of the world.

C. Richard A. Falk, Global Patriotism (2002)*

Until his recent retirement, Falk was Albert G. Milbank Professor of International Law and Practice at Princeton University, and he remains a prolific writer on public affairs, having published more than twenty books. His eloquent appeal for Israeli-Palestinian accord ("Ending the Death Dance") appeared in *The Nation* in April 2002. In the essay that follows, Falk suggests that citizens' passive attitude of unquestioned obedience to the U.S. government's handling of the September 11, 2001, crisis does not suit the requirements of a democratic society, especially one facing a threat as great as the present one. Falk invokes the notion of a global, cosmopolitan patriotism, rather than its tribal variant, as an attitude more in tune with the ever more complex post–Cold War world.

I think it is not an exaggeration to say that this period since the attacks of 9/11 poses the greatest threat since at least early in the Cold War to the traditional liberties of the American people, and it may turn out to be worse and more enduring. The United States government now possesses a virtually unchallengeable mandate from Congress and the public to claim virtually unlimited authority in the exercise of its role to restore and protect the internal security authority of the American people.

It really requires, depending on your point of view, either an extraordinary innocence or an unwarranted level of trust to feel that this new kind of authority that is being conferred upon our government will be used in a manner that reconciles the security needs of the citizenry with the values of a free society. Those of us who care about being members of a free society must not allow anxious attitudes of grief, fear, and anger resulting from the grim reality of the 9/11 experience to prevent our realization that there are other threats to our well being that arise from "the security syndrome" that prevails, and provides justifications for the most fearsome claims by government over our freedoms as a people that have ever been made. For the first time America has a homeland security czar with vast resources and the authority to consolidate the overall effort to sustain internal security. What this has already meant in practice is a greatly expanded mandate for unregulated law enforcement, for wide discretion to maintain secrecy, for lengthy detention of suspects without due process, for racial profiling as the basis of police action, and for a frightening suspension of legal protection for those in our midst who are not citizens, especially if they should come from Islamic countries, and particularly those from the Arab world.

An American citizen at this time is doubly challenged: to worry quite naturally about the terrorist threats that continue to be directed against our society

---

*From Richard A. Falk, "Patriotism and Dissent After 9/11," the Frederic Ewen Memorial Lecture, Brooklyn College of the City University of New York, November 7, 2001. Revised and updated for this book in 2002. By permission.

but also to recognize that under the guise of meeting those threats, basic liberties are being sacrificed in ways that are not required to carry on the proper work of government. It is true that the frightening nature of the September 11 attacks leads to what can be accurately described as a popular demand that the government take all necessary steps, regardless of their infringements on rights, to restore as quickly as possible a strong feeling of security in relation to terrorism. The events of September 11, combined with the disturbing failure of thousands of FBI agents to identify the source of the anthrax disseminated by mail, leave an overall sense that America is now a terribly vulnerable society in a manner that can be exploited by vicious enemies within and without. The deeper significance of September 11 is to instruct enemies of America about this vulnerability and to scare Americans into a sudden awareness of how many soft targets there are within the country that could produce mass tragedies more devastating than the attacks on the World Trade Center.

Such a background does create strong public demands that the state restore the confidence of the citizenry, and that these security requirements do alter expectations about what it is reasonable for law enforcement authorities to do under these circumstances of urgency and emergency. Part of this demand is that the government do better than *react* to terrorism but move quick to develop the capacity to *prevent* it. In this atmosphere the question posed is how to balance the threats to liberty with these new imperatives of security. We must ask ourselves whether we have the kind of leadership in the White House and Justice Department that is capable of striking such a balance in an acceptable form?

The Patriotic Moment

It doesn't take a sophisticated sociologist to conclude that there has been a dramatic surge in patriotism since September 11. I have never in my entire life seen so many American flags on display or heard so often "God Bless America." You cannot operate inside the beltway in Washington without the show of a flag in your lapel. This emotional assertion of American pride associated with these manifestations of patriotism needs to be interpreted from several directions. On the one side it is, of course, a healthy emotion to express solidarity with those in your own country who have suffered in the manner that those victimized did suffer, and to show a willingness to stand firm, without fear, and seek retaliation and an effective response. Such a display also expresses a national resolve to do whatever is necessary to restore security. What makes this outpouring of patriotism so ambiguous is that it also acts as a way of celebrating ourselves as we are rather than as we should be.

The encoded meaning of this patriotic message, as it has evolved out of the September 11 experience, is to inhibit dissent and criticism, especially within government circles and by the media where it is most needed. The mainstream media in the United States has voluntarily adopted a relatively rigid form of self-censorship, and more than this, acted mainly to fan the flames of the national disposition toward war and war-making. The main TV channels have given much viewing time to an array of previously obscure retired generals, Special Forces veterans, and pro-war think tank specialists night after night in the period leading up and including the Afghanistan War. Doubting voices that questioned the direction of the internal or international response, either on grounds of law or morality—or for that matter, on the basis of prudence and effectiveness—were nowhere to be heard. At the very moment when the circumstances associated with the threat and with its continuation challenge the political imagination of the country in a way that it has never been challenged before, we have not had the kind of debate and discussion that should occur in a democracy in times of crisis. Such a failure also hampers the prospects for a creative, effective, and legitimate response that depends on a degree of self-criticism that is virtually precluded because of this univocal and self-serving view of what patriotism means. The absence of skeptical voices in the national discussion has seriously eroded the vital distinction between citizen and subject, seemingly making passivity a political virtue instead of a dangerous liability for a society that supposedly values its freedom.

It is my strong belief that a citizen expresses his or her love of country through the expression of conscience, through taking so seriously the well-being of the country and its potentiality for change as to be willing to voice unpopular opinions. Those who are good *citizens* in this sense are always seeking to realize the potentiality implicit in the promise of America. Those who are good *subjects* are content with the posture of obedience, of deference to the governing authorities and believe, particularly in times of crisis and war, that the way in which one is a good American is to wave the flag vigorously and otherwise shut up. I am ambivalent about flying the flag, but unconditionally opposed to shutting up, especially under current conditions of crisis, and with warmongers pressing for an ever wider, ever less justifiable war.

Putting this critical perspective in its strongest form, to meet successfully the September 11 challenge will almost certainly require lively debate and intelligent criticism based on a far wider understanding of what more is at stake than merely dealing with the perpetrators of the attack. If we expand the war without adequate justification, the threats directed at America and Americans are likely to increase, perhaps exponentially. It is this element that distinguishes this war, if we can even agree to call it a war, from all other wars. This is a war without a military solution. It is a war that is essentially between the most powerful state in all of history and a non-territorial network of political extremists whose location and identity cannot be firmly fixed. It seems certainly correct that the Afghan dimensions of this threat needed to be addressed by relying on force, but the post-Afghanistan approach needs to remain sharply focused on the residual *Al Qaeda* capabilities, and to be non-military in character. To expand the war by attacking other states is both unwarranted by September 11, and at odds with international law and morality, as well as with geopolitical prudence.

In past wars just at their origins, what counted above all else was military effectiveness. If military effectiveness was sustained in such a way as to prevail in a just war, the methods used to fight the war were more or less forgotten or forgiven, or the victorious side engaged in denial that insulated the victors from any remorse or responsibility regarding objectionable methods of combat. World War II provides the best example for Americans, a just war that represented a necessary response to the criminality and militarism of fascism and Nazism. For the United States the war commenced with the surprise Japanese attack on Pearl Harbor, and over the course of the next four bloody years, yielded an outcome that did rescue the many surviving victims from further abuse at the hands of these totalitarian rulers, and saved the world as a whole from the degenerate menace of fascism and Nazism. But the conduct of the war involved the indiscriminate area bombing of cities, the deliberate and massive use of military instruments against civilian society in order to weaken the morale of the adversary, and at the end of the war a most questionable attack on two Japanese cities with the first atomic bombs ever exploded as weapons of war. Americans to this day cannot acknowledge the suffering generated by these attacks on Hiroshima and Nagasaki. Several years ago when the Smithsonian Institution in Washington, D.C. tried to arrange an exhibition of the human suffering experienced by the Japanese residents of those cities, a furor occurred, the curator of the exhibition was dismissed, and the show was cancelled and reconstituted in a very anodyne way. It is virtually impossible for most Americans to look back on those aspects of their past that cast any doubts on their claims of innocence and virtue, and associated pretensions of moral exceptionalism (a Lockean nation in a Hobbesian world!).

The Great Terror War

Let us confront the fact that America is now at war, engaged in a struggle against a threat that does not fall within the traditional definitions of international conflict. We do not really know how to describe the enemy or the adversary. We speak in terms, not of the enemy state, but of the *Al Qaeda* network. It is not clear what it is, where it is, or how it operates. President Bush initially seemed preoccupied with the demonic role of Osama bin Laden and his support for a visionary extremism that identified America as a hated enemy of Islam. Later on the White House shifted its emphasis to a supposed "axis of evil" linking Iran, Iraq, and North Korea in an infernal triangle that were solemnly warned in Bush's State of the Union Address [see Reading 35a] that they were potential targets of military intervention in the aftermath of the Afghanistan phase of the Great Terror War. Such an expansion of the scope of the war effort is only linked to September 11 in a tenuous fashion, and receives almost no international support. It ignores the degree to which the persisting *Al Qaeda* threat remains real, but can and should be addressed by primary reliance on cooperative law enforcement, intelligence activities, and occasional recourse to covert operations. The internationalization of the war by defining states as enemies is a policy almost certain to backfire on a variety of levels.

The Great Terror War is much more a political struggle than it is a military struggle. It is a political struggle that can only be successfully waged if the great majority of the peoples living in the Islamic World and the Arab parts of the Islamic World do not end up with the conclusion that their suffering and their grievances are a result of the abusive ways in which America uses its power and wealth in the world. If in the pursuit of the *Al Qaeda* enemy the U.S. Government unleashes its military power in the manner of Afghanistan relying on B-52 bombers to engage in carpet bombing, on cluster bombs, and on huge Daisy Cutter percussion bombs—that is, employing some of the most objectionable tactics of war among those earlier so widely discredited by the Viet Nam experience—we can be fairly certain that such military assaults will produce many converts to *Al Qaeda,* or at least intensify anti-Americanism around the world. We cannot, in other words, hope to conduct this war as the Gulf War was waged, or as the Kosovo War was fought. The dangerous luxury of casualty-free wars where our weaponry is used in a one-sided way and the victims are to some extent those who are opposed to what we represent, but also include completely innocent civilians on a large scale, and in which we do not take any substantial risks, is bound to reinforce the rampant anti-Americanism that already exists in most parts of the Muslim world. The noted British historian, Michael Howard, who is a quite conservative observer of international politics, described these tactics deployed in Afghanistan as equivalent to using a blow torch to remove a small cancer. Such criticism of the Afghanistan War fell away because the *Taliban* so quickly and unexpectedly collapsed, and this outcome seemed to please the great majority of the Afghan people.

Revamping Patriotism

The preceding discussion intended to highlight the significance of patriotism in the present war atmosphere, but also to call attention to some troubling aspects of the kind of patriotic mood that has risen from the ashes of 9/11. It suggests that we should not take the content and outlook of patriotism for granted, but should rethink its relevance in the altered global setting of the early twenty-first century. The form of patriotism that has surfaced in the United States was shaped by the trauma associated with 9/11, giving rise to a tribal patriotism that has strong chauvinistic overtones and, as earlier mentioned, a patriotism that devalues an active citizenry and stresses unity as a cardinal virtue. Such a patriotism refuses as a matter of principle to see the world from the perspective of the other. Now that the period of mourning those lost in the attacks seems over, it is important to resist the facile temptations of tribal patriotism. We need to understand how others perceive and experience the American role in the world, and why this role produces such intense resentment, particularly among Arabs in the Middle East. Tribal patriotism may yet hamper an effective response to the more subtle challenges of September 11.

The outcome in Afghanistan to a large degree vindicated the first stage of the American response, despite the inability to track the leadership of *Al Qaeda,* especially Osama bin Laden. The logic of this response together with the military success of the campaign has brought a new and welcome future to Afghanistan, although the conduct of the war produced an excessive number of Afghan civilian casualties that might have been considerably reduced had the U.S. Government been prepared to put its own personnel on the ground earlier and relied less fully on intensive aerial bombardment. Such a victory given the popularity of the American president and the influence of tribal patriotism makes it very difficult to cast the policy discussion of further stages in the American response in a way that serves the global public good, maintains values here at home associated with constitutionalism, and adheres to the international rule of law.

America badly needs another kind of patriotism, what I will call cosmopolitan or worldly patriotism, a sense of country that blurs the boundaries between the self and others and that is aware that in an era of globalization, all of us have multiple identities based on nationality, race, religion, gender, age, and professional and vocational activities. . . . The physical boundaries of the state never were, and are less and less the source of meaning for our collective selves. To adapt to a world of the Internet and the global market and media, we need to soften the exclusivity of our tribal attachments to a single national narrative. We need to adjust to an increasingly post-sovereignty world that is richly diverse and grossly uneven in wealth and influence, and we need to address the injustices that this unevenness of wealth and power has produced over the centuries, and recognize the dangers of these widening disparities between rich and poor. We cannot dispense with patriotism in such an emergent world, but what is needed are collective attachments that are not tightly tied to an outmoded and myopic nationalist ethos.

If we are serious about becoming cosmopolitan patriots, it is helpful to recognize that there are two challenges, not just one, that was posed on 9/11. The first challenge is preoccupied with security—both international and internal security—and how to use the capabilities of the government to meet that challenge in a way that is responsive to the threat that has been posed without abandoning the values and practices of a free and decent society.

The second challenge is, of course, that of justice, to render justice unto others in a way that acknowledges our power and past mistakes, as well as their suffering. Underneath the political fanaticism and pathology of *Al Qaeda* were widely shared attitudes of anger and distress among Arabs about America's role in the Islamic world and generally. It is important to appreciate about this political challenge that you cannot regard Osama bin Laden and *Al Qaeda* as a strange cult that represents some sort of crazed politics of suicidal fanaticism. Although the attacking mentality is pathological it cannot be reduced to political pathology without losing a sense of its political significance. The extremism needs to be understood in relation to grievances that are deep and often well founded. Some of the anti-Americanism arises from the rage that is associated with the mere existence of a state as powerful and rich and pervasive as is the United States. These attacks on 9/11 had a sympathetic resonance, in other words, that was in evidence even in Europe. Such attitudes were a kind of endorsement of the view that the United States has often misused its power in ways that have dismayed many people, and particularly people in the Islamic World. So long as Americans are captives of tribal patriotism they cannot appraise this dimension of the threat and will be unable to take the action needed to overcome it.

It is also relevant to point out that the only response to American dominance in the Middle East and elsewhere has been mounted by militant Islam. The Arab governments of secular persuasion have either bought entirely into the American game plan of subordination or have been mired in their own corruption. The secular power of the Arab governments has been a consistent source of humiliation for the peoples of the region, turning out to be ineffectual or worse with respect to the highly charged symbolic issues of Palestinian self-determination and the status of Jerusalem. The only Muslim political successes have been associate with Ayatollah Khomeini in Iran, the *Hezbollah* in southern Lebanon, and the early Osama bin Laden in resisting the invasion of Afghanistan by the Soviet Union. We forget, of course, that bin Laden was our hero during the struggle to defend Afghanistan against Soviet domination. The reason why the political challenge of 9/11 is so central is that it touches on these very deep and persisting grievances and the widespread sense that the United States is responsible directly and indirectly for much Arab suffering and injustice. To respond means not only addressing in some fair way the Palestinian-Israeli relationship and creating for the Palestinian people self-determination of the sort that almost every people in the Third World has achieved long ago during the period of decolonization. The Palestinians remain forsaken, excluded from the benefits of decolonization, and enduring a form of occupation far harsher than what was the experience of the region throughout most of the colonial era.

Along these lines it is also essential that the indiscriminate sanctions applied to Iraq for more than a decade come to an end. UNICEF reported some years ago that these sanctions were responsible for the death of over 500,000 children under the age of five. Although formally under UN auspices, the maintenance of sanctions is understood to occur solely because of American insistence. There have been recent Department of Defense documents declassified that indicate that the water system of Iraq was deliberately targeted during the Gulf War so as to disable the civilian society of Iraq.

There are other issues that concern the cosmopolitan patriot. How can the United States mount a credible campaign against the development of chemical and biological weapons and against proliferation of nuclear weapons, while retaining the world's largest and most widely deployed nuclear weapons arsenal of its own? How can the U.S. expect the weaker countries of the world to give up their weapons of mass destruction while [the U.S. persists in] retaining and further developing its own weapons of mass destruction, as well as moving rapidly to control the earth from space.

The cosmopolitan patriot is also working for an equitable form of economic globalization—as contrasted with the current form of globalization that has been continually heightening the disparities between rich and poor throughout the world.

To make this policy agenda more than a pipe dream, cosmopolitan patriotism has to become a civic force in American society. It cannot hope to change the approach in Washington if it is espoused by isolated and disorganized individuals. There are glimmers of hope. Universities have sponsored many events in the past several months. There are signs that some alternative thinking is gaining a following and that an unusual process of legitimizing dissent in the midst of this period of crisis is gaining support. Such developments are indirect challenges to the hold that tribal patriotism exercises over the political and moral imagination of a country, and open space for a future-oriented, hope-centered cosmopolitan patriotism to take shape and take hold.

From the perspective of tribal patriotism, the rise of cosmopolitan patriotism is certain to be regarded as unwelcome, and as a posture that flirts with disloyalty. From the perspective of cosmopolitan patriotism, the citizen of conscience who voices criticism that offers guidance can alone help the country respond to the deeper challenges of 9/11, which have been ignored by tribal patriotism with its fixation on winning the war, which is measured by an almost exclusively military calculus. The German novelist [and Nobel laureate] Günter Grass exemplifies the cosmopolitan patriot, offering (in *Yesterday: Fifty Years Ago* [1999], p. 19) sage advice: ". . . a critical view is the most precise expression of the love of our countries."

36. The Historical Context: The West and Islam

E dward W. Said's enormously influential and controversial book *Orientalism* (1978) advanced the notion that Western ideas of Islam as one huge, hostile entity threatening Europe originated early in Western history. These notions became incorporated into modern scholarship as the expanding West itself found a stubborn, rebellious Islamic culture in the Middle East and elsewhere resisting its imperial domination. Persisting into the modern postcolonial era, the orientalists, according to Said (1935–), continue to argue, as Bernard Lewis (1916–) does, that Muslims collectively remain inveterate opponents of the West's democracy and freedom. He identifies Lewis as a prominent modern practitioner of orientalist modes of distorted conceptualization of the Muslim world. In a series of tart polemical exchanges over the quarter-century since *Orientalism*'s appearance, Lewis has vigorously defended his interpretations, and challenged Said's. The disputes cannot be resolved here, and we present representative arguments from both. Readers will easily recognize areas of agreement as well as disagreement, and see connections to the Zionist-Palestinian conflict and other themes of this book.

A. Bernard Lewis, The Clash of Civilizations (1990)*

Recognizing the tolerance of Islamic societies in the past, Bernard Lewis also believes that now "Muslim rage" has transcended "the level of issues and policies" to become the catalyst for a grand struggle of civilizations. Educated at the University of London, Lewis taught at the School of Oriental and African Studies in London until he came to Princeton University in 1974. Retired in 1986, he holds the position of Cleveland E. Dodge Professor of Near Eastern Studies, emeritus, at Princeton. His many books over more than forty years include *The Arabs in History* (6th ed., 2002), *The Emergence of Modern Turkey* (3rd ed., 2001), and *What Went Wrong? Western Impact and Middle Eastern Response* (2002).

The origins of secularism in the West may be found in two circumstances—in early Christian teachings and, still more, experience, which created two institutions, Church and State; and in later Christian conflicts, which drove the two apart. Muslims, too, had their religious disagreements, but there was nothing remotely approaching the ferocity of the Christian struggles between Protestants and Catholics, which devastated Christian Europe in the sixteenth and seventeenth centuries and finally drove Christians in desperation to evolve a doctrine of separation of religion from the state. Only by depriving religious institutions of coercive power, it seems, could Christendom restrain the murderous intolerance and persecution that Christians had visited upon the followers of other religions and, most of all, on those who professed other forms of their own.

Muslims experience no such need and evolved no such doctrine. There was no need for secularism in Islam, and even its pluralism was very different from that of the pagan Roman Empire, so vividly described by Edward Gibbon when he remarked that "the various modes of worship, which prevailed in the Roman world, were considered by the people, as equally true; by the philosopher, as equally false; and by the magistrate as equally useful." Islam was never prepared, either in theory or in practice, to accord full equality to those who held other beliefs and practiced other forms of worship. It did, however, accord to the holders

---

*From Bernard Lewis, "The Roots of Muslim Rage," *Atlantic Monthly*, vol. 266 (September 1990), 56, 59–60. Subheadings added by the editors. By permission.

of partial truth a degree of practical as well as theoretical tolerance rarely paralleled in the Christian world until the West adopted a measure of secularism in the late seventeenth and eighteenth centuries.

Admiration and then Repugnance

At first the Muslim response to Western civilization was one of admiration and emulation—an immense respect for the achievements of the West, and a desire to imitate and adopt them. This desire arose from a keen and growing awareness of the weakness, poverty, and backwardness of the Islamic world as compared with the advancing West. The disparity first became apparent on the battlefield but soon spread to other areas of human activity. Muslim writers observed and described the wealth and power of the West, its science and technology, its manufactures, and its forms of government. For a time the secret of Western success was seen to lie in two achievements: economic advancement and especially industry; political institutions and especially freedom. Several generations of reformers and modernizers tried to adapt these and introduce them to their own countries, in the hope that they would be able to achieve equality with the West and perhaps restore their lost superiority.

In our own time this mood of admiration and emulation has, among many Muslims, given way to one of hostility and rejection. In part this mood is surely due to a feeling of humiliation—a growing awareness, among the heirs of an old, proud, and long dominant civilization of having been overtaken, overborne, and overwhelmed by those whom they regarded as their inferiors. In part this mood is due to events in the Western world itself. One factor of major importance was certainly the impact of two great suicidal wars, in which Western civilization tore itself apart, bringing untold destruction to its own and other peoples, and in which the belligerents conducted an immense propaganda effort, in the Islamic world and elsewhere, to discredit and undermine each other. The message they brought found many listeners, who were all the more ready to respond in that their own experience of Western ways was not happy. The introduction of Western commercial, financial and industrial methods did indeed bring great wealth, but it accrued to transplanted Westerners and members of Westernized minorities, and to only a few among the mainstream Muslim population. In time these few became more numerous, but they remained isolated from the masses, different from them even in their dress and style of life. Inevitably they were seen as agents of and collaborators with what was once again regarded as a hostile world. Even the political institutions that had come from the West were discredited, being judged not by their Western originals but by their local imitations, installed by enthusiastic Muslim reformers. These, operating in a situation beyond their control, using imported and appropriated methods that they did not fully understand, were unable to cope with the rapidly developing crises and were one by one overthrown. For vast numbers of Middle Easterners, Western-style economic methods brought poverty, Western-style political institutions brought tyranny, even Western-style warfare brought defeat. It is hardly surprising that so many were willing to listen to voices telling them the old Islamic ways were best and that their only salvation was to throw aside the pagan innovations of the reformers and return to the True Path that God had prescribed for his people.

Aimless and Formless Resentment and Anger

Ultimately, the struggle of the fundamentalists is against two enemies, secularism and modernism. The war against secularism is conscious and explicit, and there is by now a whole literature denouncing secularism as an evil neo-pagan force in the modern world and attributing it variously to the Jews, the West, and the United States. The war against modernity is for the most part neither conscious nor explicit, and is directed against the whole process of change that has taken place in the Islamic world in the past century or more and has transformed the political, economic, social, and even cultural structures of Muslim countries. Islamic fundamentalism has given an aim and a form to the otherwise aimless and formless resentment and anger of the Muslim masses at the forces that have devalued their traditional values and loyalties and, in the final analysis, robbed them of their beliefs, their aspirations, their dignity, and to an increasing extent even their livelihood.

There is something in the religious culture of Islam which inspired, in even the humblest peasant or peddler, a dignity and a courtesy toward others never exceeded are rarely equaled in other civilizations, And yet, in moments of upheaval and disruption, when the deeper passions are stirred, this dignity and courtesy toward others can give way to an explosive mixture of rage and hatred which impels even the government of an ancient and civilized country—even the spokesmen of a spiritual and ethical religion—to espouse kidnapping and assassination, and try to find, in the life of their Prophet, approval and indeed precedent for such actions.

The instinct of the masses is not false in locating the ultimate source of these cataclysmic changes in the West and in attributing the disruption of their old way of life to the impact of Western domination, Western influence, or Western precept and example. And since the United States is the legitimate heir of European civilization and unchallenged leader of the West, the United States has inherited the resulting grievances and become the focus for pent-up hate and anger. Two examples may suffice. In November of 1979 an angry mob attacked and burned the U.S. Embassy in Islamabad, Pakistan. The stated cause of the crowd's anger was the seizure of the Grand Mosque in Mecca by a group of Muslim dissidents—an event in which there was no American involvement whatsoever. Almost ten years later, in February of 1989, again in Islamabad, the USIS [United States Information Service] center was attacked by angry crowds, this time to protest the publication of Salman Rushdie's *Satanic Verses*. Rushdie is a British citizen of Indian birth, and his book had been published five months previously in England. But what provoked the mob's anger, and also the Ayatollah Khomeini's subsequent pronouncement of a death sentence on the author, was the publication of the book in the United States.

Clash of Civilizations

It should now be clear that we are facing a mood and a movement far transcending the level of issues and policies and the governments that pursue them. This is no less than a clash of civilizations—the perhaps irrational but surely historic reaction of an ancient rival against our Judeo-Christian heritage, our secular present, and the worldwide expansion of both. It is crucially important that we on our side should not be provoked into an equally irrational reaction against that rival.

Not all the ideas imported from the West by Western intruders or native Westerners have been rejected. Some have been accepted by even the most radical Islamic fundamentalists, usually without acknowledgment of source, and suffering a sea change into something rich but often strange. One such was political freedom, with the associated notions and practices of representation, election, and constitutional Government. Even the Islamic Republic of Iran has a written constitution and an elected assembly, as well as a kind of episcopate, for none of which is there any prescription in Islamic teaching or any precedent in the Islamic past. All these institutions are clearly adapted from Western models. Muslim states have also retained many of the cultural and social customs of the West and the symbols that express them, such as the form of male (and to a much lesser extent female) clothing, notably in the military. The use of Western-invented guns and tanks and planes is a military necessity, but the continued use of fitted tunics and peaked caps is a cultural choice. From constitutions to Coca-Cola, from tanks and television to T-shirts, the symbols and artifacts, and through them, the ideals of the West have retained—even strengthened—their appeal.

The movement nowadays called Islamic fundamentalism is not the only Islamic tradition. There are others, more tolerant, more open, that helped inspire the great achievements of Islamic civilization in the past, and we may hope that these other traditions will in time prevail. But before this issue is decided there will be a hard struggle, in which we in the West can do little or nothing. Even the attempt might do harm, for these are issues that Muslims must decide among themselves. And in the meantime we must take great care on all sides to avoid the danger of a new era of religious wars, arising from the exacerbation of differences and the revival of ancient prejudices.

To this end we must strive to achieve a better appreciation of other religions and political cultures, through the study of their history, their literature, and their achievements. At the same time, we may hope that they will try to achieve a better understanding of ours, and especially that they will understand and respect, even if they do not choose to adopt for themselves, our Western perception of the proper relationship between religion and politics.

B. Edward W. Said, The Clash of Ignorance (2001)*

Beginning with a critique of Harvard political scientist Samuel Huntington's essay "The Clash of Civilizations?," the main ideas of which Huntington traces to Bernard Lewis, Said delivers a powerful argument against orientalists who claim that they can explain "Islam" through simple generalizations. Rather he urges examining a multiplicity of "Islams," with all their many diverse features, if we hope to make sense of Muslims. Himself a Palestinian, Said studied at Harvard and now holds the position of University Professor of English and Comparative Literature at Columbia University. Besides *Orientalism* (1978), Said has published many other books, including *Covering Islam* (1997), *The Question of Palestine* (1992), *Culture and Imperialism* (1993), an autobiographical memoir, *Out of Place* (2000), and *The End of the Peace Process: Oslo and After* (2000). Moustafa Bayoumi and Andrew Rubin have edited *The Edward Said Reader* (2000). A major literary and music critic, Said began his scholarly career writing about the novelist Joseph Conrad. At the end of this essay he cites one of Conrad's novels.

Samuel Huntington's article "The Clash of Civilizations?" appeared in the Summer 1993 issue of *Foreign Affairs,* where it immediately attracted a surprising amount of attention and reaction. Because the article was intended to supply Americans with an original thesis about "a new phase" in world politics after the end of the cold war, Huntington's terms of argument seemed compellingly large, bold, even visionary. He very clearly had his eye on rivals in the policy-making ranks, theorists such as Francis Fukuyama and his "end of history" ideas, as well as the legions who had celebrated the onset of globalism, tribalism and the dissipation of the state. But they, he allowed, had understood only some aspects of this new period. He was about to announce the "crucial, indeed a central, aspect" of what "global politics is likely to be in the coming years." Unhesitatingly he pressed on:

"It is my hypothesis that the fundamental source of conflict in this new world will not be primarily ideological or primarily economic. The great divisions among humankind and the dominating source of conflict will be cultural. Nation states will remain the most powerful actors in world affairs, but the principal conflicts of global politics will occur between nations and groups of different civilizations. The clash of civilizations will dominate global politics. The fault lines between civilizations will be the battle lines of the future."

Most of the argument in the pages that followed relied on a vague notion of something Huntington called "civilization identity" and "the interactions among seven or eight [*sic*] major civilizations," of which the conflict between two of them, Islam and the West, gets the lion's share of his attention. In this bellig-

---

*From Edward Said, "The Clash of Ignorance," *The Nation* (New York), vol. 273, no. 12 (October 22, 2001), pp. 11–14. By permission.

erent kind of thought, he relies heavily on a 1990 article by the veteran Orientalist Bernard Lewis, whose ideological colors are manifest in its title, "The Roots of Muslim Rage" [see part a, this reading]. In both articles, the personification of enormous entities called "the West" and "Islam" is recklessly affirmed, as if hugely complicated matters like identity and culture existed in a cartoonlike world where Popeye and Bluto bash each other mercilessly, with one always more virtuous pugilist getting the upper hand over his adversary. Certainly neither Huntington nor Lewis has much time to spare for the internal dynamics and plurality of every civilization, or for the fact that the major contest in most modern cultures concerns the definition or interpretation of each culture, or for the unattractive possibility that a great deal of demagogy and downright ignorance is involved in presuming to speak for a whole religion or civilization. No, the West is the West, and Islam Islam.

The challenge for Western policy-makers, says Huntington, is to make sure that the West gets stronger and fends off all the others, Islam in particular. More troubling is Huntington's assumption that his perspective, which is to survey the entire world from a perch outside all ordinary attachments and hidden loyalties, is the correct one, as if everyone else were scurrying around looking for the answers that he has already found. In fact, Huntington is an ideologist, someone who wants to make "civilizations" and "identities" into what they are not: shut-down, sealed-off entities that have been purged of the myriad currents and countercurrents that animate human history, and that over centuries have made it possible for that history not only to contain wars of religion and imperial conquest but also to be one of exchange, cross-fertilization and sharing. This far less visible history is ignored in the rush to highlight the ludicrously compressed and constricted warfare that "the clash of civilizations" argues is the reality. When he published his book by the same title in 1996, Huntington tried to give his argument a little more subtlety and many, many more footnotes; all he did, however, was confuse himself and demonstrate what a clumsy writer and inelegant thinker he was.

The basic paradigm of West versus the rest (the cold war opposition reformulated) remained untouched, and this is what has persisted, often insidiously and implicitly, in discussion since the terrible events of September 11. The carefully planned and horrendous, pathologically motivated suicide attack and mass slaughter by a small group of deranged militants has been turned into proof of Huntington's thesis. Instead of seeing it for what it is—the capture of big ideas (I use the word loosely) by a tiny band of crazed fanatics for criminal purposes—international luminaries from former Pakistani Prime Minister Benazir Bhutto to Italian Prime Minister Silvio Berlusconi have pontificated about Islam's troubles, and in the latter's case have used Huntington's ideas to rant on about the West's superiority, how "we" have Mozart and Michelangelo and they don't. (Berlusconi has since made a halfhearted apology for his insult to "Islam.")

But why not instead see parallels, admittedly less spectacular in their destructiveness, for Osama bin Laden and his followers, in cults like the Branch Davidians or the disciples of the Rev. Jim Jones at Guyana or the Japanese Aum Shinrikyo? Even the normally sober British weekly *The Economist,* in its issue of September 22–28 [2001], can't resist reaching for the vast generalization, praising Huntington extravagantly for his "cruel and sweeping, but nonetheless acute" observations about Islam. "Today," the journal says with unseemly solemnity, Huntington writes that "the world's billion or so Muslims are 'convinced of the superiority of their culture, and obsessed with the inferiority of their power.'" Did he canvass 100 Indonesians, 200 Moroccans, 500 Egyptians and 50 Bosnians? Even if he did, what sort of sample is that?

Uncountable are the editorials in every American and European newspaper and magazine of note adding to this vocabulary of gigantism and apocalypse, each use of which is plainly designed not to edify but to inflame the reader's indignant passion as a member of the "West," and what we need to do. Churchillian rhetoric is used inappropriately by self-appointed combatants in the West's, and especially America's, war against its haters, despoilers, destroyers, with scant attention to complex histories that defy such reductiveness and have seeped from one territory into another, in the process overriding the boundaries that are supposed to separate us all into divided armed camps.

This is the problem with unedifying labels like Islam and the West: They mislead and confuse the mind, which is trying to make sense of a disorderly reality that won't be pigeonholed or strapped down as easily as all that. I remember interrupting a man who, after a lecture I had given at a West Bank university in 1994, rose from the audience and started to attack my ideas as "Western," as opposed to the strict Islamic ones he espoused. "Why are you wearing a suit and tie?" was the first retort that came to mind. "They're Western too." He sat down with an embarrassed smile on his face, but I recalled the incident when information on the September 11 terrorists started to come in: how they had mastered all the technical details required to inflict their homicidal evil on the World Trade Center, the Pentagon and the aircraft they had commandeered. Where does one draw the line between "Western" technology and, as Berlusconi declared, "Islam's" inability to be a part of "modernity"?

One cannot easily do so, of course. How finally inadequate are the labels, generalizations and cultural assertions. At some level, for instance, primitive passions and sophisticated know-how converge in ways that give the lie to a fortified boundary not only between "West" and "Islam" but also between past and present, us and them, to say nothing of the very concepts of identity and nationality about which there is unending disagreement and debate. A unilateral decision made to draw lines in the sand, to undertake crusades, to oppose their evil with our good, to extirpate terrorism and, in [U.S. Deputy Secretary of Defense] Paul Wolfowitz's nihilistic vocabulary, to end nations entirely, doesn't make the supposed entities any easier to see; rather, it speaks to how much simpler it is to make bellicose statements for the purpose of mobilizing collective passions than to reflect, examine, sort out what it is we are dealing with in reality, the interconnectedness of innumerable lives, "ours" as well as "theirs."

In a remarkable series of three articles published between January and March 1999 in *Dawn*, Pakistan's most respected weekly, the late Eqbal Ahmad, writing for a Muslim audience, analyzed what he called the roots of the religious right, coming down very harshly on the mutilations of Islam by absolutists and fanatical tyrants whose obsession with regulating personal behavior promotes "an Islamic order reduced to a penal code, stripped of its humanism, aesthetics, intellectual quests, and spiritual devotion." And this "entails an absolute assertion of one, generally de-contextualized, aspect of religion and a total disregard of another. The phenomenon distorts religion, debases tradition, and twists the political process wherever it unfolds." As a timely instance of this debasement, Ahmad proceeds first to present the rich, complex, pluralist meaning of the word *jihad* and then goes on to show that in the word's current confinement to indiscriminate war against presumed enemies, it is impossible "to recognize the Islamic—religion, society, culture, history or politics—as lived and experienced by Muslims through the ages." The modern Islamists, Ahmad concludes, are "concerned with power, not with the soul; with the mobilization of people for political purposes rather than with sharing and alleviating their sufferings and aspirations. Theirs is a very limited and time-bound political agenda." What has made matters worse is that similar distortions and zealotry occur in the "Jewish" and "Christian" universes of discourse.

It was Conrad, more powerfully than any of his readers at the end of the nineteenth century could have imagined, who understood that the distinctions between civilized London and "the heart of darkness" quickly collapsed in extreme situations, and that the heights of European civilization could instantaneously fall into the most barbarous practices without preparation or transition. And it was Conrad also, in *The Secret Agent* (1907), who described terrorism's affinity for abstractions like "pure science" (and by extension for "Islam" or "the West"), as well as the terrorist's ultimate moral degradation.

For there are closer ties between apparently warring civilizations than most of us would like to believe; both Freud and Nietzsche showed how the traffic across is carefully maintained, even policed boundaries moves with often terrifying ease. But then such fluid ideas, full of ambiguity and skepticism about notions that we hold on to, scarcely furnish us with suitable, practical guidelines for situations such as the one we face now. Hence the altogether more reassuring battle orders (a crusade, good versus evil, freedom against fear, etc.) drawn out of Huntington's alleged opposition between Islam and the West, from which official discourse drew its vocabulary in the first days after the September 11 attacks. There's since been a noticeable de-escalation in that discourse, but to judge from the steady amount of hate speech and actions, plus reports of law enforcement efforts directed against Arabs, Muslims and Indians all over the country, the paradigm stays on.

One further reason for its persistence is the increased presence of Muslims all over Europe and the United States. Think of the populations today of France,

Italy, Germany, Spain, Britain, America, even Sweden, and you must concede that Islam is no longer on the fringes of the West but at its center. But what is so threatening about that presence? Buried in the collective culture are memories of the first great Arab-Islamic conquests, which began in the seventh century and which, as the celebrated Belgian historian Henri Pirenne wrote in his landmark book *Mohammed and Charlemagne* (1939), shattered once and for all the ancient unity of the Mediterranean, destroyed the Christian-Roman synthesis and gave rise to a new civilization dominated by northern powers (Germany and Carolingian France) whose mission, he seemed to be saying, is to resume defense of the "West" against its historical-cultural enemies. What Pirenne left out, alas, is that in the creation of this new line of defense the West drew on the humanism, science, philosophy, sociology and historiography of Islam, which had already interposed itself between Charlemagne's world and classical antiquity. Islam is inside from the start, as even Dante, great enemy of Mohammed, had to concede when he placed the Prophet at the very heart of his *Inferno*.

Then there is the persisting legacy of monotheism itself, the Abrahamic religions, as Louis Massignon aptly called them. Beginning with Judaism and Christianity, each is a successor haunted by what came before; for Muslims, Islam fulfills and ends the line of prophecy. There is still no decent history or demystification of the many-sided contest among these three followers—not one of them by any means a monolithic, unified camp—of the most jealous of all gods, even though the bloody modern convergence on Palestine furnishes a rich secular instance of what has been so tragically irreconcilable about them. Not surprisingly, then, Muslims and Christians speak readily of crusades and *jihads*, both of them eliding the Judaic presence with often sublime insouciance. Such an agenda, says Eqbal Ahmad, is "very reassuring to the men and women who are stranded in the middle of the ford, between the deep waters of tradition and modernity."

But we are all swimming in those waters, Westerners and Muslims and others alike. And since the waters are part of the ocean of history, trying to plow or divide them with barriers is futile. These are tense times, but it is better to think in terms of powerful and powerless communities, the secular politics of reason and ignorance, and universal principles of justice and injustice, than to wander off in search of vast abstractions that may give momentary satisfaction but little self-knowledge or informed analysis. "The Clash of Civilizations" thesis is a gimmick like "The War of the Worlds" [the 1938 hoax by the American actor Orson Welles who broadcast a radio version of H. G. Wells' novel that portrayed an invasion of the earth so realistically that it created a national panic— eds.], better for reinforcing defensive self-pride than for critical understanding of the bewildering interdependence of our time.

Glossary

Agha: chief, master (Ottoman); sir or gentleman (Persian); village leader or tribal chieftain.

Allah: God.

Amir/Emir: prince, commander, ruler.

Asabiyya: group or tribal solidarity.

Ashkenazic: Jews of European origin.

Ayan: notables.

Ayatollah: "Sign of God"; title of the highest-ranking *Shiite* cleric.

Baath, renaissance/resurrection: Arab socialist political party, which rules in Iraq and Syria.

Bedouin: Arab pastoral nomads, especially in the Arabian peninsula.

Bida: innovation.

Burqa: a woman's garment covering the head and the entire body.

Caliph/Khalifa: successor of the Prophet Muhammad as leader of the *Sunni* Muslim community. The equivalent in *Shiite* Islam is *Imam*.

Capitulations: treaties between Muslim and European states granting Europeans living under Muslim rule trading and extraterritorial privileges.

Chador: "tent"; Iranian veil for women.

Dar al-Islam: "abode of Islam"; those areas ruled by Islamic law.

Dervish: an adherent of a *Sufi*, or mystical order.

Devshirme/devşirme: Ottoman system of selective conscription of Christian boys for training, conversion, and sometimes placement in high positions in the palace, the military, and the government administration.

Dhimmi (ahl al-dhimmi): a Muslim regime's protected subjects who followed a monotheistic religion.

Diaspora: Jewish communities located outside of Palestine. Today it describes the exile situation of any nationality forced to leave its homeland.

Din: religion.

Dinar: Muslim gold coin.

Dirham: Muslim silver coin.

Druze: mystical, nonorthodox Muslim sect found in Lebanon, Syria, and Israel.

Entente: agreement, alliance.

Fatah, conquest: Palestine Liberation Organization group founded by Yasir Arafat.

Fatimid dynasty: *Shiite* dynasty (909–1171) that originated in *Ifriqiya* (today's Tunisia) and conquered Egypt and Syria.

Fatwa: opinion on a religious question, usually issued by a *mufti*.

Fedayeen: adherents of religious or political organizations who risk their lives to fulfill their goals.

Fellah (fallah, pl. fellaheen or fallahin): peasant, tiller of the soil.

Fiqh: understanding of the law, jurisprudence.

Firman: an official decree.

Ghazi: Muslim frontier warrior fighting against non-Muslims to extend Islamic territories.

Gulhane: Rose Chamber of the Ottoman palace where Ottoman sultans issued official decrees.

Hadith: sayings and actions of the Prophet Muhammad; one of the bases for Islamic law.

Haganah: "defense"; military arm of the Jewish Agency in mandate Palestine, which later became the nucleus of the Israeli army.

Hajj: formal pilgrimage to Mecca and its surrounding area in a designated lunar month.

Hamas: "zeal"; a Palestinian Islamic radical group.

Hanafi: *Sunni* school of legal interpretation founded by Abu Hanifa.

Hanbali: *Sunni* school of legal interpretation founded by Ahmad ibn Hanbal.

Haram al-Sharif: shrine on the Temple Mount in Jerusalem commemorating the site from which the Prophet Muhammad miraculously rose to heaven while still alive.

Harem: sacred, forbidden, taboo; women's private quarters.

Hashemite: The family of the *Quraysh* tribe to which Muhammad belonged. The British established *Hashemites* in power in Arabia, Transjordan, and Iraq following World War I.

Hatt-i Humayan: Ottoman Imperial edict.

Hatt-i Sharif: Ottoman Illustrious decree.

Herut: "freedom"; party formed by the Revisionist Zionist followers of Vladimir Jabotinsky. Led by Menachim Begin after 1948 and became part of the *Likud* bloc in 1973.

Hezbollah: "party of God"; a Lebanese radical Islamic movement.

Hijab: in modern times a head covering that allows a woman to show her face.

Hijra: "emigration," especially of the Prophet Muhammad and his companions in 622 from Mecca to Madina; marks the beginning of the Muslim calendar.

Hisba: duty of a Muslim to fulfill obligations in Islamic law. The function of regulating public businesses and public morality. See *muhtasib.*

Histadrut: the General Federation of Jewish Workers in Palestine both during and after the British mandate period.

IDF: Israel Defense Force.

Ijma: consensus of the community; one of the sources of *Sunni* law.

Ijtihad: interpreting religious texts in the light of new challenges and circumstances.

Al-Ikhwan al-Muslimin: the Egyptian Muslim Brotherhood founded in 1928 by Hasan al-Banna.

Iltizam: an allocation of tax revenues from land by the state from which an official or a military officer could live.

Imamate: a *Shiite* principle that establishes a leader of the community as a successor to Muhammad's prophethood.

Imams: descendants of the Prophet Muhammad's son-in-law and daughter, Ali and Fatima, whom *Shiites* view as the legitimate and divinely guided leaders of the community. Also, the leader of the Muslim public prayers.

Intifada: "shaking off"; two Palestinian uprisings (1987–91 and 2000–) to dislodge Israel from territories it occupied in 1967 on the West Bank and the Gaza Strip.

Infitah: opening of the Egyptian economy to the West under President Anwar Sadat.

Irgun (Irgun Zvai Leumi, or ETZEL, its initials in Hebrew): "National Military Organization." Military branch of the Revisionist Zionist movement, which carried out armed attacks against the British and Arabs during the mandate period. Dissolved after the formation of the state of Israel.

Islam: "submission"; a Muslim is one who submits to the will of God, or *Allah*. The religion is called Islam.

Ismali: member of *Shiite* sect that believes that Imamate should have gone to Ismail, the eldest son of the sixth Imam, and his descendants.

Jahannam: hell.

Jahiliyya: the state of ignorance and barbarism Arabs lived in before the revelation of the *Quran*.

Jamaat-i-Islami: Islamic radical party founded by Abu Ala Mawdudi in British-controlled India in 1941.

Janissary corps: Ottoman infantry corps recruited through the *devshirme*.

Jihad: exertion of effort in the cause of Islam. Religiously sanctioned holy war against non-Muslims.

Kaaba (Ka'ba): "cube"; the principal Islamic sanctuary in Mecca.

Kadi: see *Qadi*.

Kataeb/Kataib: Phalange Party of Maronite Christians in Lebanon.

Khan: chief.

Il-Khanid Dynasty: established by the Mongols during and after their conquest of the Middle East and Central Asia (1256–1353).

Kharajites: a sect of early Islam. Today its members are found scattered living in isolated communities through the Middle East and North Africa.

Khedives: title of Egyptian rulers, 1866–1914; after that, they took the title *sultan*.

Kibbutz: a Jewish collective community in mandate Palestine and in Israel, often combining agricultural production, canning and preserving facilities, and cooperative stores to sell the produce.

Knesset: Israel's parliament.

Lehi (Lohame, Herut Israel): "Fighters for the Freedom of Israel"; also known as the Stern Gang, an underground armed militia of Revisionist Zionists active during the Palestinian mandate.

Likud: "unity"; the bloc of right and centrist parties created in Israel in 1973, which won its first election in 1977. Menachem Begin became *Likud*'s first prime minister.

Loya Jirga: Afghan grand council of tribal representatives.

Lutf: what God does, directly or indirectly, to make it easier for people to obey His divine will.

Madrasa: secondary school that teaches religious subjects.

Maghreb (Maghrib): northwest Africa.

Mahabharate: one of two great Sanskrit poems of Hinduism, which teach that violence is folly.

Majlis: consultative assembly, parliament.

Maliki: *a Sunni* school of legal interpretation founded by Malik ibn Anas.

Mamluks: Circassian "slave" dynasty that ruled Egypt and Syria (1250–1517). Originally purchased as slaves and then freed after being trained and instructed in Islam, the Mamluks served the Ottoman empire from 1517 to 1798 as governors of Egypt.

Mapai: "the Workers Party of the Land of Israel"; a socialist Zionist party formed by David Ben-Gurion. In 1949 it joined other left and left-of-center parties to form the Labor Alignment, which dominated Israel's politics until 1977.

Maronite: A Christian sect close to Roman Catholicism located mainly in Lebanon.

Millet: an internally autonomous religious community in the Ottoman empire.

Minaret: tower next to a mosque from where a *muezzin* calls Muslims to prayer.

Mufti: high-ranking member of the *ulema,* who is trained as a jurist to give nonbinding legal opinions in response to submitted questions.

Mughal dynasty: Founded by Babur, who conquered India in 1526. The British deposed the dynasty's last emperor in 1857.

Muhtasib: market inspector, also in charge of enforcing public morality. See *hisba.*

Mujahidin: warriors fighting holy war.

Mujtahid: religious scholar who strives to interpret religious texts in the light of new challenges and circumstances. *Shiites* have permitted their *ulema* this role, while for some periods it was denied to some *Sunni ulema.*

Mullah: member of the *ulema.* Leader of prayer in local mosques. In Shiite Islam an individual earns the title after completing a certain level of education.

Muslim: an adherent of the religion *Islam.*

OPEC: Organization of Petroleum Exporting Countries.

Ottoman empire: Muslim state (c. 1288–1922) founded in Asia Minor and expanded into the European Balkans, the Middle East, and North Africa.

Pasha: Turkish title for high Ottoman officials, normally in the military.

Phalange: see *Kataeb.*

Pogrom: state-sponsored terror carried out against Eastern European Jews in the late nineteenth and early twentieth centuries.

Qadi/Kadi: a judge in a court administering Muslim law, ranking lower than a *mufti.*

Al Qaeda: "the source"; an Islamic radical organization founded by Osama bin Laden initially to fight *jihad,* or holy war, against the Soviet Union in Afghanistan and, after 1991, against the United States. Responsible for several significant terrorist attacks, presumably including those of September 11, 2001.

Qajar: ruling dynasty in Iran from 1779–1924.

Qaymmaqam: Ottoman subgovernor.

Quran: God's words revealed to the Prophet Muhammad forming the holy book of Islam.

Quraysh: The Prophet Muhammad's tribe.

Raj: in India, dominion, rule.

Rajput: member of a landholding and military caste of the former Rajputana states of north India, now part of Rajasthan. The *Rajputs* dominated much of central India from the seventh century to the eighteenth century.

Ramadan: Ninth month of the Muslim lunar calendar, when Muslims fast from sunrise to sundown.

Revisionist movement: ultranationist, antisocialist form of Zionism founded by Vladimir Jabotinsky in the 1920s that advocated Jewish settlement on both sides of the Jordan River and used force to create the state of Israel. Forerunner of the *Likud* bloc.

Safavid dynasty: established *Shi'ism* as the state religion in Persia/Iran. Ruled from 1501–1732.

Salafiyya: "ancestor"; a reform movement in late-nineteenth-century and early-twentieth-century Islam, which called for the return to the models and examples of original pious ancestors during the lifetime of the Prophet Muhammad.

Seljuks: Turkish dynasty that ruled over five separate states in the Middle East during the eleventh and twelfth centuries.

Sephardic: Jews who lived under Muslim rule in the Middle East, North Africa, and Spain.

Shafii: a *Sunni* school of legal interpretation founded by Muhammad ibn Idris al-Shafii.

Shah: king (Persian).

Sharia: the codified law of Islam based on the *Quran* and the *Hadith* (sayings and actions) of the Prophet Muhammad.

Sharif (Sherif): noble; a descendent of the Prophet Muhammad.

Sheikh (shaykh, shaikh, sheik, sheih): tribal leader; religious scholar, *Sufi* master, tribal chief, pious individual.

Sheikh al-Islam: the supreme jurist; the leading religious figure in the state.

Shiite: Muslims who regard Ali ibn Abi Talib and his children with the Prophet Muhammad's daugher Fatima as the legitimate successors to the Prophet Muhammad. According to *Shiites,* Ali and his acknowledged heirs are divinely guided leaders, or *Imams.* See *Twelvers.*

Simsar: intermediary, broker.

Sipahi: cavalryman in the Ottoman empire, usually possessing a *timar.*

Sira: the life of the Prophet Muhammad.

Stern Gang: see *Lehi.*

Sufism/Sufi: Islamic mysticism and an adherent thereto.

Sultan: holder of power; Turkish ruler, emperor.

Sunna: behavior of the Prophet Muhammad, which established examples for Muslims to emulate.

Sunnis: a majority of Muslims who follow the "way" of Muhammad and accept one of the four schools of interpretation of the law, as opposed to *Shiites* who have a separate Islamic legal system, also based on the *Quran* and the Prophet's *sunna*.

Sura: a chapter of the *Quran*.

Takfir: to judge and pronounce a Muslim an infidel; somewhat similar to "excommunication."

Al-Takfir wal-higra: "Repentence and Holy Flight"; an Egyptian Islamic radical group.

Taliban, Taleban: Afghan students from Pakistani *madrasas* who, after their indoctrination, returned to their country and captured power in 1994–95 with the help of the Pakistani secret service, Saudi Arabia, and the United States. As a result of their giving Osama bin Laden and *Al Qaeda* coalition sanctuary, the United States led a post–September 11, 2001, coalition that attacked and overthrew the *Taliban* regime.

Tanzim: a Palestinian paramilitary force created in 1995 to organize armed resistance to Israeli occupation. Linked to *Fatah* but separate from the Palestinian Authority.

Tanzimat: "reordering/reorganization"; a period of reform in the Ottoman empire from 1839–76.

Tariqas: *Sufi* brotherhoods as well as the path of meditation and action to reach mystical fulfillment.

Tatar: a member of the Mongolian horde that overran Eurasia starting in the thirteenth century. Also Turks who lived in what today is the Ukraine and southern European Russia.

Tawhid: worship and serving *Allah* as the only God.

Timar: state land held in exchange for military or administrative service.

Timurids: dynasty (1370–1506) established by Timur or Tamarlane (1336–1405).

Turk: nomadic, Turkic-speaking people from Central Asia who, during the tenth to the fifteenth centuries, moved into the Middle East and then became its rulers. The Seljuks and the Ottomans were the most well known of the Middle Eastern Turks.

Twelver: a member of a *Shiite* sect that recognizes twelve Imams and awaits the reappearance of the last one, who disappeared in 878, as the *mahdi* ("divinely guided one") who will usher in the Day of Judgment. *Twelver* doctrines have formed the basis of Persia's official religion since 1502.

Ulema, Ulama: Muslim religious scholars.

Umayyad: the first Muslim dynasty, with its capital in Damascus (661–750).

Umma: Muslim community.

Vilayet: Ottoman province.

Vizir (Wazir): government minister; it can also mean prime minister.

Yishuv: the Jewish community in Palestine before 1948.

Young Turks: group of military officers and young professionals who overthrew Ottoman Sultan Abd al-Hamid II (r. 1876–1909) and ruled Turkey until the end of World War I.

Wafd (Wafd Party): "delegation"; formed after the British refused to allow a delegation of Egyptians to attend the Versailles Peace Conference following World War I. The *Wafd* became the major nationalist party in Egypt during the interwar years.

Wahhabism: a strictly *Hanbali* doctrine, veering little from the holy texts of Islam, founded in Arabia in the eighteenth century by Muhammad Abd al-Wahhab. They prefer the term *muwahhidun* (believers in the unity of God) to describe themselves.

Waqf, Awqaf: charitable trust serving pious or social welfare purposes.

Wazir: see *Vizir.*

Wilayah: Ottoman province.

Zakat: obligatory alms giving. One of the five pillars of the Islamic faith.

Zoroastrianism: the religion of pre-Islamic Persia.

Zawiya: *Sufi* lodge.

Select Bibliography

We only present here some of the most important English-language books on the Middle East and the Islamic world. We have not included on this list most books that we have already cited in our introductions and in the footnotes to documents. We have also omitted many excellent monographs dealing with individual states and specific time periods. We suggest that readers who wish comprehensive bibliographic data consult four of the sources listed below, and follow through on the materials mentioned in them: the first, *Islamic History* by R. Stephen Humphreys, offers a comprehensive survey; the second, *Approaching Ottoman History* by Suraiya Faroqhi, introduces a variety of sources and books dealing with that empire; the third, the *International Journal of Middle East Studies*, published quarterly by Cambridge University Press, carries important scholarly articles and reviews of recent books; the fourth, *Middle East Report*, also appearing quarterly, publishes topical articles and lists selected recent books. Finally, for the Arab-Israeli conflict and for background on Zionism and Palestinian nationalism, Ian J. Bickerton and Carla L. Klausner, *A Concise History of the Arab-Israeli Conflict*, and Yazid Sayigh, *Armed Struggle and the Search for State: The Palestinian Nationalist Movement, 1949–1993,* include thorough bibliographies, which readers might wish to consult.

Abou-El-Haj, Rifaʿat ʿAli, *Formation of the State: The Ottoman Empire Sixteenth to Eighteenth Centuries* (Albany, NY: State University of New York Press, 1991).

Abrahamian, Ervand, *Iran Between Two Revolutions* (Princeton, NJ: Princeton University Press, 1982).

———, *Khomeinism: Essays on the Islamic Republic* (Berkeley, CA: University of California Press, 1993).

Adas, Michael, *Islamic and European Expansion: the Forging of a Global Order* (Philadelphia, PA: Temple University Press, 1993).

Ahmed, Leila, *Women and Gender in Islam* (New Haven, CT: Yale University Press, 1992).

Ajami, Fuad, *The Dream Palace of the Arabs: A Generation's Odyssey* (New York: Vintage Books, 1999).

Ali, Ahmed, *Al-Qur'ân: A Contemporary Translation,* bilingual edition (Princeton, NJ: Princeton University Press, 2001).

Allsen, Thomas T., *Culture and Conquest in Mongol Eurasia* (New York: Cambridge University Press, 2001).

Allworth, Edward, ed., *Central Asia, 130 Years of Russian Domination: A Historical Overview,* 3rd ed. (Durham, NC: Duke University Press, 1994).

Amitai-Preiss, Reuvan and D. O. Morgan, eds., *The Mongol Empire and its Legacy* (Boston, MA: Brill Academic Publishers, 2000).

Andersen, Roy R., Robert F. Seibert, and Jon G. Wagner, *Politics and Change in the Middle East: Sources of Conflict and Accommodation,* 6th ed. (Upper Saddle River, NJ: Prentice Hall, 2000).

Arjomand, Said Amir, *The Shadow of God and the Hidden Imam* (Chicago, IL: The University of Chicago Press, 1984).

——, *The Turban for the Crown: The Islamic Revolution in Iran* (New York: Oxford University Press, 1988).

Arkoun, Mohammed, *Rethinking Islam: Common Questions,* translated from the French and edited by Robert D. Lee (Boulder, CO: Westview, 1994).

Asad, Talal, *Genealogies of Religion: Discipline and Reasons of Power in Christianity and Islam* (Baltimore, MD: Johns Hopkins University Press, 1993).

Ayubi, Nazih, *Political Islam: Religion and Politics in the Arab World* (New York: Routledge, 1991).

Bacharach, Jere L., *A Middle East Studies Handbook,* revised ed. (Seattle, WA: University of Washington, Press, 1990).

Barakat, Halim, *The Arab World: Society, Culture, and State* (Berkeley, CA: University of California Press, 1993).

Bates, Daniel G. and Amal Rassam, *Peoples and Cultures of the Middle East,* 2nd ed. (Upper Saddle River, NJ: Prentice Hall, 2001).

Beinin, Joel, *Workers and Peasants in the Modern Middle East* (New York: Cambridge University Press, 2001).

Beinin, Joel and Joe Stork, eds., *Political Islam: Essays from Middle East Report* (Berkeley, CA: University of California Press, 1997).

Bickerton, Ian J. and Carla L. Klausner, *A Concise History of the Arab-Israeli Conflict,* 4th ed. (Upper Saddle River, NJ: Prentice Hall, 2002).

Bodman, Herbert L. and Nayereh Tohidi, eds., *Women in Muslim Societies: Diversity Within Unity* (Boulder, CO: Lynne Rienner, 1998).

Bromley, Simon, *Rethinking Middle East Politics: State Formation and Development* (Austin, TX: University of Texas Press, 1994).

Brown, Leon Carl, ed., *Imperial Legacy: The Ottoman Imprint on the Balkans and the Middle East* (New York: Columbia University Press, 1996).

——, ed., *Diplomacy in the Middle East: the International Relations of Regional and Outside Powers* (New York: I. B. Tauris, 2001).

Bulliet, Richard, *Islam: The View From the Edge* (New York: Columbia University Press, 1994).

Burke, Edmund, III, ed., *Struggle and Survival in the Modern Middle East* (Berkeley, CA: University of California Press, 1993).

Bushnaq, Inea, ed., *Arab Folktales* (New York: Pantheon, 1986).

Chaudhuri, K. N., *Trade and Civilization in the Indian Ocean: An Economic History from the Rise of Islam to 1750* (New York: Cambridge University Press, 1991).

Chittick, William C., *The Sufi Path of Knowledge* (Albany, NY: The State University of New York Press, 1989).

Chomsky, Noam, *Fateful Triangle: The United States, Israel & the Palestinians,* revised ed. (Boston, MA: South End Press, 1999).

Cleveland, William L., *A History of the Modern Middle East,* 2nd ed. (Boulder, CO: Westview, 2000).

Cole, Juan R. I., *Comparing Muslim Societies: Knowledge and the State in a World Civilization* (Ann Arbor, MI: University of Michigan Press, 1992).

———, *Sacred Space and Holy War: The Politics, Culture and History of Shi'ite Islam* (New York: I. B. Tauris, 2002).

Cole, Juan R. I., and Nikki R. Keddie, eds., *Shi'ism and Social Protest* (New Haven, CT: Yale University Press, 1986).

Crone, Patricia, *Meccan Trade and the Rise of Islam* (Princeton, NJ: Princeton University Press, 1986).

Denny, Frederick M., *An Introduction to Islam* (New York: Macmillan, 1993).

Dols, Michael, *The Black Death in the Middle East* (Princeton, NJ: Princeton University Press, 1977).

Dowty, Alan, *The Jewish State* (Berkeley, CA: The University of California Press, 1998).

Eaton, Richard M., *India's Islamic Traditions: 711–1750* (New York: Oxford University Press, 2002).

Eickelman, Dale, *The Modern Middle East and Central Asia: An Anthropological Approach,* 4th ed. (Upper Saddle River, NJ: Prentice Hall, 2001).

Faroqhi, Suraiya, *Approaching Ottoman History: an Introduction to the Sources* (New York: Cambridge University Press, 1999).

Faroqhi, Suraiya, Donald Quartaert, and Sevket Pamuk, *An Economic and Social History of the Ottoman Empire, 1600–1914,* vol. 2 (New York: Cambridge University Press, 1997).

Gendzier, Irene L., *Notes from the Minefield: United States Intervention in Lebanon and the Middle East, 1945–1958* (New York: Columbia University Press, 1997).

Gerber, Haim, *The Social Origins of the Modern Middle East* (Boulder, CO: Lynne Rienner, 1987).

Gerner, Deborah J., ed., *Understanding the Contemporary Middle East* (Boulder, CO: Lynne Rienner, 2000).

Gilsenan, Michael, *Recognizing Islam: An Anthropological Introduction* (New York: I. B. Tauris, 1990).

Goitein, S. D., *A Mediterranean Society: The Jewish Communities of the Arab World as Portrayed in the Documents of the Cairo Geniza,* 4 vols. (Berkeley, CA: University of California Press, 1967–1983).

Gross, Jo-Ann, ed., *Muslims in Central Asia: Expressions of Identity and Change* (Durham, NC: Duke University Press, 1994).

Haddad, Yvonne Yazbeck and John L. Esposito, eds., *Islam, Gender and Social Change* (New York: Oxford University Press, 1998).

Hertzberg, Arthur, ed., *The Zionist Idea: A Historical Analysis and Reader* (New York: Jewish Publications Society, c. 1959, reprint ed. 1997).

Hiro, Dilip, *War Without End* (New York: Routledge, 2002).

Hodgson, Marshall G. S., *The Venture of Islam: Conscience and History in a World Civilization,* 3 vols. (Chicago, IL: The University of Chicago Press, 1974).

Hourani, Albert, *A History of the Arab Peoples* (Cambridge, MA: Belknap Press of Harvard University Press, 1991).

Humphreys, R. Stephen, *Islamic History: A Framework for Inquiry,* revised ed. (Princeton, NJ: Princeton University Press, 1991).

———, *Between Memory and Desire: The Middle East in a Troubled Age* (Berkeley, CA: University of California Press, 1999).

Inalcik, Halil and Donald Quartaert, eds., *An Economic and Social History of the Ottoman Empire, 1300–1914,* vol. 1 (New York: Cambridge University Press, 1994).

International Journal of Middle East Studies (*IJMES*). Published under the auspices of the Middle East Studies Association of North America (1080 S. University Ave., Suite 4659, University of Michigan, Ann Arbor, MI 48109) by Cambridge University Press (New York).

Joseph, Suad and Susan Slyomovics, eds., *Women and Power in the Middle East* (Philadelphia, PA: University of Pennsylvania Press, 2001).

Keddie, Nikki R., ed., *Scholars, Saints, and Sufis: Muslim Religious Institutions Since 1500* (Berkeley, CA: University of California Press, 1972).

Keddie, Nikki R., and Beth Baron, eds., *Women in Middle Eastern History: Shifting Boundries in Sex and Gender* (New Haven, CT: Yale University Press, 1991).

Keddie, Nikki R. and Rudi Mathee, eds., *Iran and the Surrounding World: Interactions in Culture and Cultural Politics* (Seattle, WA: University of Washington Press, 2002).

Kennedy, Hugh, *The Prophet and the Age of the Caliphates: The Islamic Near East from the Sixth to the Eleventh Century* (New York: Longman, 1986).

———, *The Armies of the Caliphs: Military and Society in the Early Islamic State* (New York: Routledge, 2001).

Khalidi, Rashid, *Palestinian Identity: the Construction of Modern National Consciousness* (New York: Columbia University Press, 1998).

Khalidi, Rashid, Lisa Anderson, Muhammad Muslih, and Reeva S. Simon, eds., *The Origins of Arab Nationalism* (New York: Columbia University Press, 1991).

Khoury, Philip S. and Joseph Kostner, eds., *Tribes and State Formation in the Middle East* (Berkeley, CA: University of California Press, 1990).

Lapidus, Ira M., *A History of Islamic Societies,* 2nd ed. (New York: Cambridge University Press, 2002).

Lewis, Bernard, *The Middle East: A Brief History of the Last 2000 Years* (New York: Simon and Schuster, 1997).

Lockman, Zachary, ed., *Workers and Working Class in the Middle East: Struggles, Histories, Historiographies* (New York: State University of New York Press, 1994).

Macfie, Alexander Lyons, ed., *Orientalism: A Reader* (New York: New York University Press, 2001).

Marsot, Afaf Lufti al-Sayyid, *Egypt in the Reign of Muhammad Ali* (Cambridge and New York: Cambridge University Press, 1984).

Meriwether, Margaret L. and Judith E. Tucker, eds., *A Social History of Women & Gender in the Modern Middle East* (Boulder, CO: Westview, 1999).

Metcalf, Barbara D. and Thomas R. Metcalf, *A Concise History of India* (New York: Cambridge University Press, 2002).

Middle East Report. Published by the Middle East Research and Information Project (MERIP) by Blackwell Publishers (Malden, MA).

Mottahedeh, Roy, *The Mantle and the Prophet: Religion and Politics in Iran* (Oxford, UK: Oneworld Publishers, 2002).

Nashat, Guity and Judith Tucker, *Women in the Middle East and North Africa: Restoring Women to History* (Bloomington, IN: Indiana University Press, 1999).

Nasr, Seyyed Hossein, Hamid Dabashi, and Seyyed Vali Reza Nasr, eds., *Expectation of the Millennium: Shi'ism in Hisory* (Albany, NY: State University of New York Press, 1989).

Niblock, Timothy and R. J. A. Wilson, *The Political Economy of the Middle East* (Northampton, MA: Edward Elgar, 1999).

Norris, Harry, *Islam in the Balkans: Religion and Society between Europe and the Arab World* (Columbia, SC: University of South Carolina Press, 1993).

Owen, Roger, *State, Power and Politics in the Making of the Modern Middle East*, 2nd ed. (New York: Routledge, 2000).

———, *The Middle East in the World Economy*, revised ed. (New York: St. Martin's Press, 1993).

Peters, F. E., *Muhammad and the Origins of Islam* (Albany, NY: State University of New York Press, 1994).

Quandt, William B., *Peace Process: American Diplomacy and the Arab-Israeli Conflict Since 1967*, revised ed. (Berkeley, CA: University of California Press, 2001).

Rashid, Ahmed, *Taliban: Militant Islam, Oil and Fundamentalism in Central Asia* (New Haven, CT: Yale University Press, 2000).

Raymond, André, *Arab Cities in the Ottoman Period: Cairo, Syria and the Maghreb* (Burlington, VT: Ashgate/Variorum, 2002).

Richards, Alan and John Waterbury, *A Political Economy of the Middle East: State, Class, and Economic Development*, 2nd ed. (Boulder, CO: Westview, 1996).

Richards, J. F., *The Mughal Empire* (New York: Cambridge University Press, 1993).

Roy, Olivier, *The New Central Asia* (New York: New York University Press, 2000).

Rubin, Barnett R., *The Fragmentation of Afghanistan: State Formation and Collapse in the International System*, 2nd ed. (New Haven, CT: Yale University Press, 2002).

Said, Edward W., *Orientalism* (New York: Vintage Books, 1978).

———, *The Politics of Dispossession: The Struggle for Palestinian Self-Determination 1969–1994* (New York: Random House, 1995).

Saunders, J. J., *The History of the Mongol Conquests* (Philadephia, PA: University of Pennsylvania Press, 2001).

Sayigh, Yazid, *Armed Struggle and the Search for State: The Palestinian Nationalist Movement, 1949–1993* (New York: Oxford University Press, 1999).

Schimmel, Anne Marie, *Islam: An Introduction* (Albany, NY: State University of New York Press, 1992).

Sprinzak, Ehud, *The Ascendance of Israel's Radical Right* (New York: Oxford University Press, 1991).

Stivers, William, *America's Confrontation with Revolutionary Change in the Middle East* (New York: St. Martin's Press, 1986).

Tora, Miura and John Edward Philips, eds., *Slave Elites in the Middle East and Africa: A Comparative Study* (New York: Kegan Paul International, 2000).

Van Schendel, Willem and Erik J. Zürcher, eds., *Identity Politics in Central Asia and the Muslim World: Nationalism, Ethnicity and Labour in the Twentieth Century* (New York: I. B. Tauris, 2001).

Voll, John O., *Islam: Continuity and Change in the Modern World*, 2nd ed. (Syracuse, NY: Syracuse University Press, 1994).

Waardenberg, Jacques J., *Muslim Perceptions of Other Religions Throughout History* (New York: Oxford University Press, 1999).

Walther, Wibke, *Women in Islam from Medieval to Modern Times*, translated from the German by C. S. Salt (Princeton, NJ: Markus Weiner, 1992).

Watt, Montgomery, *Muhammad: Statesman and Prophet* (New York: Oxford University Press, 1990).

Weaver, Mary Anne, *A Portrait of Egypt: A Journy Through the World of Militant Islam* (New York: Farrar, Straus and Giroux, 1999).

———, *Pakistan: In the Shadow of Jihad and Afghanistan* (New York: Farrar, Straus and Giroux, 2002).

Yapp, M. E., *The Near East Since the First World War: A History to 1995*, 2nd ed. (New York: Longman, 1996).

Yergin, Daniel, *The Prize: The Epic Quest for Oil, Money & Power* (New York: Simon and Schuster, 1991).

Zilfi, Madeline, *Women in the Ottoman Empire: Middle Eastern Women in the Early Modern Era* (New York: Brill Academic Publishers, 1997).

Zubaida, Sami, *Islam, the People and the State: Essays on Political Ideas and Movements in the Middle East* (New York: Routledge, 1989).

Index

Copyright Acknowledgments